CADOGAN GUIDES

"Cadogan Guides are mini-encyclopaedic ... they give the explorer, the intellectual or culture buff—indeed, any visitor—all they need to know to get the best from their visit ... a good read too by the many inveterate armchair travellers.'
—The Book Journal

"The quality of writing in this British series is exceptional ... From practical facts to history, customs, sightseeing, food and lodging, the Cadogan Series can be counted on for interesting detail and informed recommendations."
—Going Places (US)

"Standouts these days are the Cadogan Guides ... sophisticated, beautifully written books."
—American Bookseller Magazine

"Entertaining companions, with sharp insights, local gossip and far more of a feeling of a living author ... The series has received plaudits worldwide for intelligence, originality and a slightly irreverent sense of fun."
—The Daily Telegraph

CADOGAN GUIDES

ECUADOR, THE GALÁPAGOS AND COLOMBIA

JOHN PAUL RATHBONE

CADOGAN BOOKS
London

THE GLOBE PEQUOT PRESS
Chester, Connecticut

Cadogan Books Ltd
Mercury House, 195 Knightsbridge, London SW7 IRE

The Globe Pequot Press
138 West Main Street, Chester, Connecticut 06412, USA

Copyright © John Paul Rathbone 1991
Illustrations © Antonia Phillips 1991
Maps © Cadogan Books Ltd 1991

Cover design by Keith Pointing
Cover illustration by Povl Webb
Maps by Thames Cartographic Services Limited
Index by Dorothy Frame

Editor: Chris Schüler
Series Editors: Rachel Fielding and Paula Levey

First published 1991

British Library Cataloguing in Publication Data

Rathbone, John Paul
    Ecuador, the Galapagos and Colombia.—(Cadogan guides).
    1. Ecuador. Colombia. Galapagos Islands.
    I. Title
    918.604

ISBN 0–947754 19–9

Library of Congress Cataloging-in-Publication Data

Rathbone, John Paul.
    Ecuador, the Galapagos and Colombia. / John Paul Rathbone: illustrations by Antonia
Phillips.
        p.   cm.—(Cadogan guides)
    Includes index.
    ISBN 0–87106–248–8
        1. Ecuador—Description and travel—1991-   —Guide-books.
    2. Galapagos Islands—Description and travel—1991-   —Guide-books.
    3. Colombia—Description and travel—1991-   —Guide-books.
    I. Title. II. Series.
    F3716.R38 1991   91–21692
    918.604—dc20   CIP

Photoset in Ehrhardt on a Linotron 202
Printed and bound in Great Britain by
Redwood Press Limited, Melksham, Wiltshire

The sanctuary of Las Lajas, Ipiales—'A miracle of faith over gravity.'

ABOUT THE AUTHOR

For the past 2½ years, John Paul Rathbone has journeyed through the varied terrains of Colombia and Ecuador, and the libraries of London and New York. Half Cuban, half English, he was born in New York in 1964. He read Human Science and Anthropology at Oxford University, and now lives in London, where he works in publishing.

ACKNOWLEDGEMENTS

In Colombia: thanks to Poly and Ignacio; to Cusi, Gonzalo and their family, for so patiently putting up with me during a difficult time; to Mr and Mrs Robert Nielson, and Fritz, for an extraordinary time on the plains; to Benedetta and Louis—should they ever read this in their far-flung western capitals—for introducing me to Bogotá the first time round; to Robert and Tania Arab; and, of course, to all the Colombians I chanced to meet on the road—it was their generosity, brio and occasional malice that made my time there such a heady mix of delights, marvels and, sometimes, despair. In Ecuador: thanks to Xavier Moscoso for his hospitality and wonderful conversation, and to Alegria for her consistent help. In England, I would like to thank my mother; my father and Sue, for lending me such a wonderfully quiet place to work; Malcolm Deas who, apart from the historical gems that he occasionally drops, also, unwittingly, only ever confirms that my affection for Latin America, and Colombia in particular, is not misplaced; and everyone at Cadogan Books—Paula, Vicki, Jackie, and Chris Schüler.

It is perhaps a commonplace to say that 'this book could not have been written without'. So to Gustavo—the infamous Barranquilla painter, *despechista* and backporch raconteur—one thousand thanks for the good directions, and the fun that was had during even the most bitter of 'Off Nights'.

CONTENTS

COLOMBIA

Introduction *Pages 143–7*

Part I: General Information *Pages 148–54*

Part II: Colombian Topics *Pages 155–65*

Part III: History and Chronology *Pages 166–82*

Part IV: The Caribbean *Pages 183–227*

Part V: The Sierra *Pages 228–84*

Part VI: The Pacific *Pages 285–95*

Part VII: Los Llanos *Pages 296–302*

Part VIII: The Amazon *Pages 303–309*

Language *Pages 310–16*

Selected Bibliography *Pages 317–19*

Index (Ecuador) *Pages 320–24*

Index (Colombia) *Pages 325–31*

LIST OF MAPS

INTRODUCTION

There are many wrongly pitched clichés about Latin America, as there are about everything, and the continent's dangers have been consistently exaggerated.

Life there can be every bit as brutal as the headlines about the region: politically, the continent is hyperspacing through one thousand years of European history, and the ride is bumpy, often unstable. But there is another life in Latin America; an everyday life of everyday pleasures and satisfactions. Paradoxically, this quality stems from a feature rarely associated with the region: security. The predominant note in Latin American life is still tradition and, stemming from that, a certainty about family and relationships. So if Latin Americans have a 'romantic' reputation it is perhaps because theirs is a culture where one can securely devote oneself to the cultivation of relationships, to loving and being loved.

There is no one Latin America—perhaps there never was. Consequently there are two quite different books here. Colombia and Ecuador might share the world's longest mountain chain (the Andes), largest rainforest (the Amazon), and greatest river. They might both be places where objects and events tend towards a particularly local strain of surrealism—an amazing leakage of some concealed and mysterious inner life. They might even share a common language and a similar cultural heritage. But they are not the same. Colombia and Ecuador are as different as Italy and Switzerland: Ecuador is well-visited, small, quiet, predominantly rural, even Tintin-esque; Colombia, on the other hand, is a country ventilated by a vast and corrupt energy that seems to magnify characteristic Latin American traits—and these can be what you are looking to find. (See page 155). Latin Americans love their countries and recognise their differences. Cross their borders and everything changes. In Colombia, for instance, you can, on occasion, seen even more flags than in a yellow ribbon-festooned USA...

If you are thinking about making a trip to Latin America, but cannot decide when, if ever, to go, the best time to set off, of course, is now. It's worth remembering that our greatest disappointments are nearly always for what we have not done, rather than for what we have. These last words are John Hatt's, another tropical traveller, not mine.

Guide To The Guide

Part I provides 'General Information' for all travellers, with the rest of the book subsequently divided up between the two countries.

Each country section includes an 'Introduction' followed by local 'Practical Information'; then 'Topics'—a series of short excursions into certain (curious, useful, or just entertaining) features of Latin American culture and history; then the country's 'History'; and finally a country-wide gazetteer.

Within the gazetteer the regions and cities are laid out in a similar manner to the above, much like Russian dolls; first an 'Introduction', then 'How to Get There', next 'History' and some suggestions as to 'What to See' and 'Where to Stay', next 'Eating Out', and finally some brief descriptions of a few short excursions.

At the back of the guide you will find a Glossary, a Bibliography, and separate Indexes to both countries.

PLEASE NOTE

Every effort has been made to ensure the accuracy of the information in this book at the time of going to press. However, practical details such as opening hours, travel information, standards in hotels and restaurants and, in particular, prices are liable to change.

We will be delighted to receive any corrections and suggestions for improvement which can be incorporated into the next edition, but cannot accept any responsibility for consequences arising from the use of this guide.

GENERAL INFORMATION

Before You Go

What To Take

Anything to avoid being a snail with a house on your back, so take as little as possible. Even the lightest and loosest of suitcases has the habit of swelling, and you will only need to pack half of what you have laid out.

Both Ecuador and Colombia's climates vary greatly, so even though you are going to the tropics, you will need a warm sweater and/or jacket for those chilly mountain nights. Tee-shirts pack up small and are light, but short-sleeved cotton shirts with breast pockets are cooler and more useful in the coastal heat. You will need a waterproof for the jungle.

Soft bags are better than rucksacks, if only for the greater freedom of movement that they provide. A half-bottle of duty-free whisky goes down well during first nights away; it can be used as a gift, or to alleviate the boredom of long airport waits. A small combination padlock is always useful, as is a medical kit (see below), and an alarm clock for those early morning aeroplane flights. You will regret not having at least one smart change of clothes on that stray night when you are invited for dinner by the Ambassador. And if you take valuable equipment abroad—such as a Walkman or camera—you should reckon that in all likelihood it will be stolen, or damaged, or lost, or dropped, or rained on at least once while you are away.

Climate and When to Visit

In terms of weather, there is no best time to visit; climate in both Colombia and Ecuador is a function of altitude. Escaping the close heat of the tropics, for instance, requires only the execution of a simple manoeuvre—ascent; while warming yourself after the chill nights of the mountains requires only a descent.

As with all tropical countries, however, there are two roughly demarcated seasons: the rainy and the dry. The rainy season does not mean that it rains all the time, only that when it rains, it rains *hard*; most often it is vehemently sunny. On Colombia's Caribbean coast the dry season lasts from around December through to late May, while on Ecuador's Pacific coast the converse is true. Here, from January to April, temperatures can rise upto 90°C, but always cool after rain.

The dry and wet seasons in the mountains are less distinctly marked, and usually it rains once a day—normally in the early evening but clearing by nightfall—throughout the year. Daytime temperatures in Quito can reach a midday high of 22°C, dropping at night to as low as 7°C. Bogotá is not as high so the temperature is less variable.

The Amazon is always hot and rainy, and although June through August are meant to be the wettest months (and September through December the driest) there is no typical pattern. Temperatures are consistently high however, around 88°C, and humidity rarely drops below 90%.

Finally, although the Galápagos lie smack on the Equator, the islands' climate is cooled by the Humboldt current, and although the weather is hot (between 28°C and 32°C) all the year round, you will never experience the dog-day heat of high summer.

In terms of festivals, however, there is a best time to visit Colombia; late February to late April marks a period that encompasses the Barranquilla carnival, the Caribbean music festival in Cartagena, the Festival de Leyenda Vallenata in Valledupar and, depending on the positioning of Easter, Holy Week in either Mompós or Popayán. These are all well worth seeing.

Budgeting and Expenses

Colombia is not dirt cheap, nor is it suprisingly expensive. Budget for about US$25 a day if you wanted to slum it in style, slaloming in between three-star hotels and grass huts, with unlimited freedom of movement and as much to eat and drink as you care for. If travelling on a shoestring you could probably swing it, albeit uncomfortably, on as little as US$10 a day.

Ecuador is notably cheaper, however, and you could travel comfortably here for as little as US$15 a day. Your largest expenses will be trips to the Galápagos and the Amazon: the former will cost at least US$1000, the latter anything from US$250.

Health and Insurance

Although you do not need an International Immunization Certificate for either Colombia or Ecuador, you should have all the shots for cholera, typhoid, tetanus, yellow fever and hepatitis before you leave.

Malaria is harder to judge; in the highlands malaria is non-existent, but in the Amazon and on some parts of the Pacific coast it can be rife. Although some people prefer using mosquito nets and insect repellents to taking prophylactic malaria pills—claiming that taking the pills over a long period can damage the eyes and the liver—pills are the only way to guarantee yourself against malaria, a debilitating disease that could trouble you for life.

A small medical kit should include: Immodium/Lomotil (for diarrhoea); Triludan (anti-histamine); Amoxil (general antibiotic); Septrin (for bloody diarrhoea); Temazepan 10 mg (sleeping pills); and betadine paint (an antiseptic for scratches).

You should certainly consider insuring yourself and your property before you leave. Choose an insurance company with a 24-hour emergency number and one that will speak your own language if your Spanish isn't up to a crisis. Many credit card companies, such as Access/Mastercard, automatically issue a form of travel insurance, and American Express offers Centurion Assistance, a very good policy for card holders. Endsleigh Insurance (tel 071 436 4451 in UK; 213 937 5714 or 212 986 9470 in USA; 416 977 3703 in Canada) are also recommended.

Passports and Visas

When travelling within either Ecuador or Colombia it is important always to carry your passport with you, and within easy reach. If you are checkpointed, failure to produce any ID can result in arrest. Rest assured, however, this is not a dramatic problem, just a bore.

Ecuador

Travellers visiting Ecuador as tourists do not require visas, only a valid passport. On arrival you will be given a tourist stamp, valid for up to 60 days. If you are given a stamp for fewer days, such as 30 (the given length of time depends solely on the whim of the immigration official) your visa can be extended at the immigration office in Quito, at Avenida 2639.

Colombia

Only Canadian and US citizens visiting Colombia require visas, which are easily obtainable from local consulates. Visas are restricted to 90 days, and are issued on arrival. To obtain one for longer requires a mountain of paperwork and notaried certificates; this process has to be initiated at home and is not for the impatient or weak-hearted.

Getting There

Ecuador

By Air

KLM, Avianca, Ecuatoriana, Eastern, Air France and **Iberia** all have flights to Ecuador, and they all land at Quito. If you are on business, however, and Guayaquil is your destination, the fast, frequent and easy air-shuttle between the capital and the coast only takes 1 hour (US$15). On leaving Ecuador, a departure tax of US$25 is payable by all visitors.

From Europe

All cheap flights leave from London, and at time of writing cost about £550 for an open return, or £300 one way.

From the USA

Check the listings in the Los Angeles or New York *Times*, or phone **Council Travel Services**, which has offices on both east and west coasts. Typical round-trip fares from the USA currently stand at about: US$680 from New York; US$580 from Miami; and US$800 from Los Angeles.

From Australia

See below, under 'Colombia'.

3

By Sea
Finding a berth on a steamer bound for Guayaquil is just as expensive as flying.

By Land
Formalities at the the Colombian and Peruvian borders are very straightforward.

Colombia

By Air
Colombia has six international airports: Bogotá, Cali, Medellín, Barranquilla, San Andrés and Cartagena. International fares out of Colombia are very expensive, so it is always better to travel with a return ticket. A departure tax of US$15 is payable on all international flights.

From Europe
Avianca, the national airline, flies from Frankfurt via Madrid, and Air France, Viasa, Iberia and Lufthanasa all fly from their respective capitals. London, however, is the cheapest point of departure and there is a direct weekly flight to Bogotá with British Airways. Although you might be able to get student, standby or Apex discounts, expect to pay about £450 for a return ticket, and £250 for one-way. Cheap tickets can sometimes be found by flicking through the back pages of *Time Out* magazine. Otherwise get in touch with the long-time experts in the field, Journey Latin America, 14–16 Devonshire Road, Chiswick, London W4 2HD, tel (081) 747 3108, telex 925068.

From the USA
Flying direct to Colombia from the USA can work out quite expensive. The cheapest option, if you have the time, is to fly to either Panama and change planes there, or to Caracas, continuing your journey by land to the Colombian border at Cúcuta or Maicao.

Avianca and Eastern Airlines have frequent direct flights from New York, Miami and Los Angeles to Cartagena, Barranquilla and Bogotá. Round-trip fares from New York work out at about US$650, from Miami about US$550, and from Los Angeles around US$750. For cheaper flights, check the listings in the Los Angeles or New York *Times*.

A final option is to travel via the Colombian Caribbean island of San Andrés. This can sometimes work out the cheapest way of getting to Colombia from the USA. San Andrés also has frequent connections to Central America and Mexico.

From Canada
There are no direct scheduled flights to Colombia from Canada; all routes go via Miami. During the winter months, however, package tour companies occasionally organize charter flights from Toronto and Montreal, and booking a return ticket with them can work out as cheap as C$300.

4

From Australia

There are no direct routes, and all flights must go via either Los Angeles on **Continental Airlines,** or via Chile on **Aerolineas Argentina** or **Lan Chile Air.** This is expensive, about AUS$2000. For cheaper possibilities, check the back pages of the *Sydney Morning Herald* or contact the *Andes Pacific Travel Service,* Suite 1010, the American Express Tower, 388 George Street, Sydney, NSW 2000, tel 235 1785/1858. It claims to be Australia's best Latin American travel agent.

By Sea

Arriving by sea is uncertain and finding a berth on a steamer bound for Cartagena, Buenaventura, Barranquilla, Santa Marta or San Andrés is just as expensive as flying. From Panama you might be able to find passage on a smugglers' boat to Turbo; take care.

By Land

Colombia is linked by highways with Venezuela and Ecuador. The border with Ecuador is at Ipiales. Venezuela has two two border crossings; the little town of Maicao on the dusty Guajira Peninsula in the north, and the city of Cúcuta in the mountains. From Brazil it is possible to take the river as far as Leticia and continue by air (see p. 307).

On Arrival

Orientation and Town Plans

Both Ecuador and Colombia's cities and towns are mostly built to a grid plan, with Carreras running north-south and Calles running east-west. At first the system of addresses can be confusing. But once you learn that Carrera 16 5–28 means the house 28 metres from Calle 5 on Carrera 16, you will have no problem.

Health

Only Bogotá has drinkable tap water. Otherwise either boil the water, use sterilizing tablets, or buy bottled waters.

Electricity

A standard 110 volts, 60 cycles AC.

Film and Photography

Camera film is readily available. Developing snaps is also quick and easy at any of the 24-hour places dotted around Ecuador and Colombia's larger towns. High-quality developing is best left until you return home.

Money Matters

Yo no soy dollar, pero subo y bajo.
'I'm not a dollar, but I go up and down'.

—Street grafitti

The US dollar is the most widely used and accepted foreign currency in South America, and Visa travellers' cheques are the easiest to change. Credit cards, especially Diners and Visa, are very commonly used; if you pay the bill in pesos you will also eventually win on the devaluation. When travelling outside large towns and cities, take enough local currency to meet requirements, as it is often very difficult to change money in outlying towns. There is a no significant currency black market in either country as the differential between official and unofficial rates is negligible.

Receiving money from abroad is a relatively simple operation. If you carry a Visa or American Express card, cash advances are immediate. Bank transfers by telex from your home branch take around three days.

Ecuador's currency is the sucre. As Ecuador has very lax currency regulations, foreign money is easy to change in any Casa de Cambio or bank. Banks are open from 9–1 Mon–Fri, and Casas de Cambio from 9–6 Mon–Fri, and occasionally on Saturday mornings.

Colombia's currency is the peso, divided into 100 centavos. Exchange regulations are very strict and foreign currency can only be changed with documented proof of identity, such as your passport, at branches of the national bank, **El Banco de la República**. All branches are open Mon–Thur, 8–11.30 and 2–4, Fri 8–11.30 and 2–4.30.

Flora, Fauna and National Parks

Because South America never experienced an ice-age it has some of the world's most remarkable flora and fauna. And both Ecuador and Colombia, because of their positions on the equator and their changes in altitude—which give rise to numerous micro-climates and ecosystems, ranging from desert to rainforest, and lowland to mountain-ous—can in turn boast some of South America's most remarkable natural systems. These include the Amazon, the high altitude Paramo, and the Galápagos, amongst many others. For the natural history of these regions, please see under the relevant Amazonian and Galápageñan sections, and under the topic 'A Brief South American *Natural History*'.

Both Ecuador and Colombia have established national parks throughout their countries, and to feel the full presence of South American nature you really should try to spend time in at least one.

Ecuador: apart from the Galápagos (see p. 115), Mt Cotopaxi National Park (see p. 72) and the Amazonian reserve at Cuyabeno, the country boasts a wonderful bird-watching sanctuary. Over 2000 species of birds have been identified in Ecuador alone, and so if you are looking for bird-life you should go to the remarkable Hotel Tinalandia, just outside Santo Domingo de los Colorados. Here you will find perfect bird-watching conditions for at least 150 species of birds. The definitive and illustrated *Guide to the Birds of Ecuador* by R. Ridgely and P. Greenfield, and *Guide to the Birds of*

6

Colombia by Brown and Hilty (both Princeton University Press) will be your best sources of reference.

In Colombia the most remarkable national parks are: the integrated beach and mountain ecosystems of Tayrona National Park (see p. 208); the completely unspoilt island ecology of La Isla Gorgona National Park (see p. 291); the marine life at Las Islas del Rosario (see p. 193); the high altitude ecological systems at Puracé National Park (see p. 280); the Amazonian Amacayacu National Park (see p. 307); and the ancient geological formations and ecosystems at the Serranía de la Macarena which, unfortunately, is also a very dangerous place to visit (see p. 300).

Accommodation

It is odd how few people do, but wherever you stay, and however much you are willing to pay, always ask to see the room first. This costs nothing and incurs no bad feeling. If you don't like what you are shown, you can always excuse yourself by saying that you wanted a room with windows, or if the room already has windows, with a certain view. Could you please be shown another one please, this one no thank you...

Ecuador

There are two broad types of hotel in Ecuador; luxurious, big-city five-star hotels that charge western prices; and the rest.

However, the rest (which is also incidentally the norm) can be every bit as comfortable as the luxurious. And for as little as between US$4 and US$8 a night, you can expect to find yourself a large, comfortable room, with good views, en suite bathroom and constant hot water. Standards drop qualitatively for anything under US$3 a night, and for this kind of price you can expect to find a bare but nonetheless comfortable room with a shared exterior bathroom. If you are paying less than US$1.50 a night, and it has not already become apparent, you are probably staying in a whorehouse.

As you shy away into more inaccessible areas, rest assured that in every village, no matter how remote, there will be a hotel (of sorts), or if not a hotel, a village shop floor, or if not a village shop, someone's house. Accommodation, if you are not fussy, can always be found.

Camping

Camping sites with running water and other facilities, although more common than in Colombia, are only ever laid on in areas popularly frequented by backpackers. Often, however, the price for using them is as much as if you were staying in town in a comfortable but cheap hotel. If camping in remote areas, it is best to cover your bets by asking at the nearest house for permission before pitching your tent; it is rare that anyone refuses.

In Colombia

The problem is not finding a hotel, but choosing one that suits; the standard varies a great deal. As a general rule however, in Colombia you pay for privacy and security and the less that you pay, the more you must be prepared for strange incidents, intrusions and unexpected scenarios. (All hotels have safety deposit boxes and it is a good idea to use them.)

In the big cities and beach resorts, hotels are up-to-date and expensive; Hiltons around the world charge the same rates. On the other hand, for US$10–15 a night you will find comfortable accommodation in a pension or residencia, with private bathroom and hot water. You may or may not get air-conditioning, but make sure that you do at least have a fan, and at high altitudes enough blankets.

For US$4–8, you will get simpler accommodation that may or may not have a private bathroom. Hotels in this category, although plain, can provide as much comfort as you would expect in a three-star hotel at ten times the rate. In far-off places, this will often be all that you will be able to find. Below US$4 you are entering the shadowy world of budget accommodation, often clustered around bus terminals. Hotels in this category sometimes double up as brothels. Colombia also specializes in love-hotels, which are rented out by the hour to couples.

Camping
Campsites are few and far between, but those that exist are listed in the text.

Eating Out

Ecuadorean Food
With the exception of seafood—which is almost unparalleled—national Ecuadorean food is at best plain, largely based around potatoes, eggs and grains. But it is not a health risk for the unaccustomed stomach and you are unlikely to fall ill in the same way that you might in India or Mexico.

Your best eats will be found in the restaurants of big hotels where you can expect to eat a large dinner or lunch from a recognizable 'International' menu and pay only US$10 a head. In many small towns the hotel restaurant is the only restaurant in town. If you are a vegetarian, *Chifas* (Chinese restaurants, which can be found in nearly all towns) usually have large vegetarian menus. If you are not, *Parilladas* are wholesome steak house grills that serve huge portions of meat, usually accompanied with a fried banana on the side; for carnivores only.

Cevicherias—an Ecuadorean speciality—serve delicious marinated seafood, with pop-corn and small salads on the side. This is a recognized hangover cure. *Ceviche* can be made with fish (*de pescado*), shrimp (*de camarones*), shellfish (*de concha*), or all three (*mixto*). On the coast, the seafood gets even better, and here you can find lobster meals (*langosta*) for only US$6, and huge plates of King Shrimp (of the tasteful Eastern Pacific brown variety, as opposed to the blander white meat of Japan or Taiwan) for much less.

Failing restaurants, and in every bus station, there are always the roadside stalls where, apart from ice-creams kept cool over smoking dry ice, you will usually be able to find:

Cuy: whole roasted guinea pig, which tastes rather like chicken
Tostadas de maíz: fried corn pancakes
Llapingachos: delicious mashed potato and cheese pancakes
Caldos, sopas and *locros*: soups.

Breakfast
Huevos fritos are fried eggs; *revueltos* are scrambled eggs often mixed with chopped peppers and onions. *Tostada* is toast, and *pane* is bread, to be had with *mantequilla* (butter) and *mermelada* (jam).

8

Lunches and Dinners

In cheap restaurants set meals are the norm, and these are quick and filling. For under US$2, a set lunch (*almuerzo*) or dinner (*merienda*) typically consists of a soup for the first course followed by a *seco* (a dry stew) with rice and a small salad on the side for the second. Occasionally a *postre* (dessert, usually ice-cream) comes included, and a *jugo* (fruit juice).

Chicken is an infallible Third World menu item and, if you order off the menu, it is mostly all that you will find. *Arroz con pollo* is a variably delicious mound of chicken risotto; *pollo frito* is fried chicken; and *gallina* is a thick chicken soup made from a boiled-up old egg layer.

Colombian Food

One thing is certain—you will never go hungry; food in Colombia is simply prepared but amply served. In the big cites you will always be able to count on a recognizable international menu (at close to international prices; a pizza will cost US$3), and sophisticated restaurants. But in outlying areas and small towns, despite the proliferation of small restaurants, only cowboy fare is usually available and if you are a vegetarian you may have problems.

Colombian cooking is also very regional and it is not always possible to find on the coast the meal that you had enjoyed so much in the mountains. The delicious *ajiaco* for example (an avocado soup, with chicken, corn on the cob and capers) can only be found in Bogotá. And finding *locros de choclos* (a thick and nourishing maize and potato soup) is hard to find north of Popayán. Generally, grilled fish predominates in the coastal regions, meat in the highlands and potato-based meals in the south, towards Ecuador.

The basic meal that fuels the nation however, is the *comida corriente*, and it never varies. It costs about US$2 and consists of two courses: a soup, followed by a meat- or fish-based dish, with plantains (*platanos*), rice (*arroz*) or fried yucca on the side. Appended to the *comida corriente* is an immortal list that you will find everywhere. Typically chalked-up on a small board pinned to the wall, you will soon come to recognize: *carne asada* (grilled meat), *sobrebarriaga* (grilled belly of beef) and *arroz con pollo* (chicken risotto). On the coast, *mojarra* means nothing more than the fish which has been caught that day.

Below follows a list of some of the rarer regional dishes you might come across:

Arroz con chipichipi: rice and shellfish
Arroz con coco: delicious rice and coconut combo
Cabrito: grilled goat, usually served with fried yucca
Cazuela de mariscos: a very fine casserole of mixed Caribbean seafoods
Chocolate santafereño: a Bogotá tea-time speciality—a cup of hot chocolate served with cheese (which you put into the chocolate) and a bread roll
Hormiga culona: a Santander speciality of fried ants, usually only available from March to May
Lechona: suckling pig stuffed with rice and spit-roasted
Mondongo: soup with beef (or tripe), beans, carrots and potatoes
Rondón: a San Andrés soup made with fish, shellfish, coconut milk, yucca and plantains
Sancocho: a common stew found everywhere although the ingredients vary; a *sancocho* basically includes whatever was at hand.

9

Snacks

They are everywhere and you can live off them. Vended on street corners, by old men pushing barrows, in walled niches, outside shops, by young boys through your bus window, and in town plazas, there are so many types that what follows below is only a partial list:

Arepas: a Caribbean speciality; toasted or fried maize pancakes
Empanadas: a meat, chicken or vegetable pasty
Arequipe: a white milk fudge, usually served sandwiched between over-sized communion-style wafers
Buñuelos: fried dough-and-cheese balls
Bocadillos: a *dulce*, or sweet, of guava paste often sold wrapped around cheese.
Jugos: fruit juices, see 'Topic' on p. 161
Mazamorra: a suprisingly refreshing drink of maize boiled in milk
Perros: hot dogs, of course
Quesillo: runny cheese wrapped in banana leaves
Tamales: chopped pork or chicken with rice and vegetables folded in a maize dough and wrapped in a plantain leaf.

Drinks

Coffee

Colombian coffee has a very fine taste and like all of the best things in life doesn't so much push as lift you into the day. *Tinto* is black coffee; *perico* is a milky coffee; and *café con leche* is a large cup of frothed milk coloured by coffee. Café means instant coffee (or, alternatively, *No-es-café*).

Ecuadorean coffee, however, is quite a different ball-game. See that dark oily liquid in the small glass jar lying in the middle of your restaurant table? It's a boiled-down, flavourless essence *pretending* to be coffee. Pour a little into your cup and fill the rest with boiling water. There! A pale dye that somewhat resembles your favourite early-morning caffeine crank. But can you ever remember coffee ever tasting so, so, so ... bad?

For a coffee-producing country, Ecuador offers suprisingly distasteful coffee. There is a 100-year tradition of travel writers noting it with displeasure. Ludwig Bemelmans wrote, 'if you love coffee, you must bring your own.' Taking his advice to heart most Ecuadoreans now use coffee smuggled in from Colombia. Ecuadorean tea is just as bad.

Soft Drinks

Coca-cola is consumed in vast quantities and is available everywhere, as are a variety of other fizzy drinks.

Alcohol

Wine is expensive and often of poor quality. Beer on the other hand is good, the Barranquilla beer *Aguilla* being the best. Unless you buy beer in a can (*lata*), a deposit is payable on all bottles.

Whisky is the preferred poison, especially imported single malts; *Tres Esquinas* white rum (*ron blanco*) is drunk in large quantities on the coast; the aniseed-flavoured liqueur *aguardiente*, everywhere.

Jugos

Jugos, or fruit juices, are wonderful. The most common kinds are:

Maracuya: passion fruit
Naranjilla: equivilant to the Colombian *lulo*, a bitter orange-tasting drink
Mora: blackberry
Naranja: orange
Toronja: grapefruit
Papaya

Security

In September 1989 Joey Arroyo, Colombia's leading salsa singer and supposedly most street-cred man, had a bundle of money stolen while staying in London during his European tour. He remarked to the police and the Colombian journalists who later interviewed him, 'Now who would have imagined that this could ever have happened in England?'.

Courtesy breeds courtesy—Joey Arroyo shows us that tourists everywhere make mistakes, and that the dangers of South America have been exaggerated. Nothing maladroit will happen to you if you use just the common sense and open eye that you would normally use in any big world city. Keep your money close to you, in a money belt for example, and it is unlikely that you will be mugged. Look to see how other people carry their handbags. Looking respectable saves harrassment and will always lend you credibility in front of officials, but if you over-dress and hang yourself with jewels and watches, you are inviting temptation. If you go walking through rough downtown barrios or red light districts, you are asking for trouble. (See also the 'Topic' on p. 164.)

Police

If anything is stolen, but especially your passport, report the theft to the police immediately. It is unlikely that you will ever see it again, but the police will issue you with temporary identification papers (very important) and a receipt that you can later use to claim against insurance.

Routine road checks and baggage searches are frequent all over South America but exactly that—routine. They take a dull half an hour and you will need to show your passport; that's all (but make sure that you have your passport). The police, like police all over the world, like to cause trouble; looking respectable and remaining patient will save you time and trouble in the long run should you fall into their hands.

Bribes

How corrupt is Latin America? An important question. More or less corrupt than Japan, Italy, Oklahoma, Austria, or what used to be known as the GDR? The South American Handbook offers some sage advice concerning bribes and corruption—'Do not assume

11

that an official who accepts a bribe is prepared to do anything else illegal. You bribe him to persuade him to do his job, or not to do it, or to do it more quickly, or more slowly. You do not persuade him to do something which is against the law—the mere suggestion would just make him upset.' Clearly, this is just plain good manners.

However, if caught by the police doing something that you shouldn't, one way of approaching the situation is by suggesting that, 'at home we pay an on the spot fine (*una multa*), is that the case here?' The hint is usually taken as bribees are exceptionally good sports. If you end up in jail, however, everything gets much harder (more paperwork). And if you end up in jail for drug use, everything gets much much harder—fines are large, sentences can be long and your consul will be of little help to you—he can only recommend a lawyer, no more.

Drugs—Here's the Dope
In his sock, the fisherman carries a small twist of grass that he will smoke out at sea. So too labourers, as they clamber about construction sites. Big city down-towners turn their brains to rubble by smoking *basuko*, a local varient of crack. And people in the media are not averse to the odd toot. But South America is not Nepal, and South Americans, on the whole, abhor drugs. It is very unlikely that you will be offered drugs on the streets of any—especially Colombia's—cities, and if you do, take care; it might be a set-up. If you must buy drugs, do it through a trusted friend, but be aware that if you are caught, penalities are steep.

Colombia—a Special Note
It is very difficult to explain why Colombia is, and yet is not, a dangerous place. Contrary to popular expectation, you do not have to dodge bandits and bullets on immediate arrival. Most of the country's violence is directed against and within itself, rather than against foreigners; in the main part Colombians will have no beef against you, a tourist. They're not interested, and why should they be? In this relatively prosperous country, with a low rate of inflation and a well-managed economy, you are also less likely to be taken for a walking dollar than you are, say, in Peru or Brazil.

However, if you do go adventuring in remote areas away from the main tourist sites, you will find that lawfulness is at best a vaguely entertained notion. In the main, this is either because of Mafia activity or guerrillas. As is to be expected tourists have little, if any, automatic credence in such situations. But dangerous areas generally remain dangerous because they are remote and inaccessible, and it is very difficult to stumble into one—you have to work at it. The main dangerous areas include:

- the strictly Indian areas of the Guajira Peninsula
- the Medio Magdalena, around Barrancabermeja; a crucible of Colombian politics
- the Boyacá Emerald Mines
- the countryside around Monteria and Sincelejo, where there is guerrilla activity
- the Sierra Macarena, where there are guerrillas and coca-cultivators
- the Amazon basin, especially around Puerto Asís and in the Putumayo, where there is guerrilla and narco activity.

ECUADOR

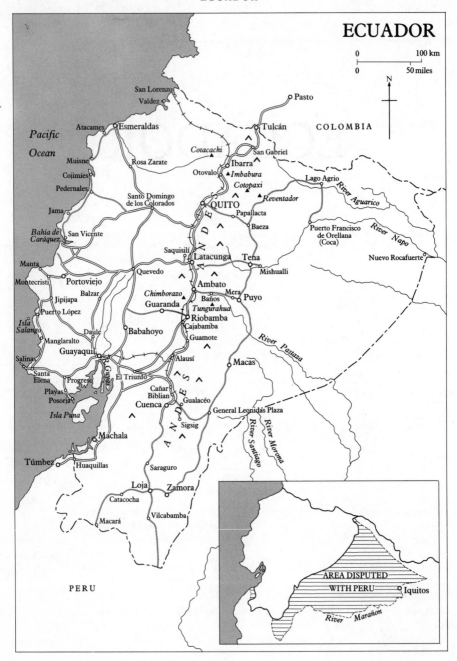

ECUADOR

0   100 km

0   50 miles

N

Pacific
Ocean

COLOMBIA

San Lorenzo
Valdez

Pasto

Atacames   Esmeraldas

Tulcán

Cotacachi

San Gabriel

Muisne

Rosa Zarate

Cojimíes

Otovalo   Ibarra

Pedernales

Imbabura

Cotopaxi

Lago Agrio

Santo Domingo
de los Colorados

River Aguarico

Jama

QUITO

Reventador

*Bahía de
Caráquez*   San Vicente

Papallacta

River Napo

Baeza

Puerto Francisco
de Orellana
(Coca)

Manta

Saquisilí

Latacunga   Tena

Nuevo Rocafuerte

Montecristi

Portoviejo

Quevedo

Mishualli

Jipijapa   Balzar

Ambato

Mera

Chimborazo   Baños   Puyo

Puerto López   Guaranda

Tungurahua

*Isla
Salango*

Daule

Babahoyo

Riobamba
Cajabamba

Manglaralto

Guamote

River Pastaza

Salinas   Guayaquil

Santa   Alausí
Elena   Progreso   El Triunfo

Macas

Playas
Posorja

Cañar
Biblian

Gualacéo

Cuenca

General Leonidás Plaza

Isla Puna

Sigsig

Machala

River Santiago

River Morona

Túmbez   Huaquillas

Saraguro

Loja   Zamora

Catacocha

Vilcabamba

Macará

PERU

AREA DISPUTED

WITH PERU   Iquitos

River Marañon

14

INTRODUCTION

Sangay Volcano

'As a region Ecuador is set apart both by its altitude, which ranges from 0–19,000 feet at its centre, and by its place on the globe, which its name already indicates.'

—Henri Michaux

Ecuador—as the Spanish name tells us—straddles the Equator and is a continent in miniature; everything is within easy reach. Quito, the capital, lies in the Andes at 2850 m above sea-level, and is one of the most beautifully preserved colonial cities in the Americas. Three hours by bus to the east of Quito lies the steam heat of the Amazon; five hours to the west, warm Pacific beaches; and only two hours by plane out over the Pacific lies the Galápagos Archipelago, one of the most remarkable wildlife reserves in the world.

Ecuador provides a perfect introduction to Latin America; it is also one of the securest of Latin America's tropical republics, lacking the intense guerrilla and narcotics activity to which its better known neighbours, Colombia and Peru, are prone. In fact, so well buried is any sense of discord that Ecuador feels like a place where nothing really happens: a feeling that Ecuadoreans, with mixed emotions but always a smile, will tell you is true.

In the mountains you can visit bright Indian markets; in the Amazon travel through areas only partially explored; and on the Pacific coast's long surf- and palm-rimmed beaches, slurp up king prawns the size of billboard commas. Whether slumming or travelling in style, Ecuador is also very cheap; you can travel and live well here for as little as US$10 a day. So if you dream of Quechuan cosmogonies and tropic isles, hidden

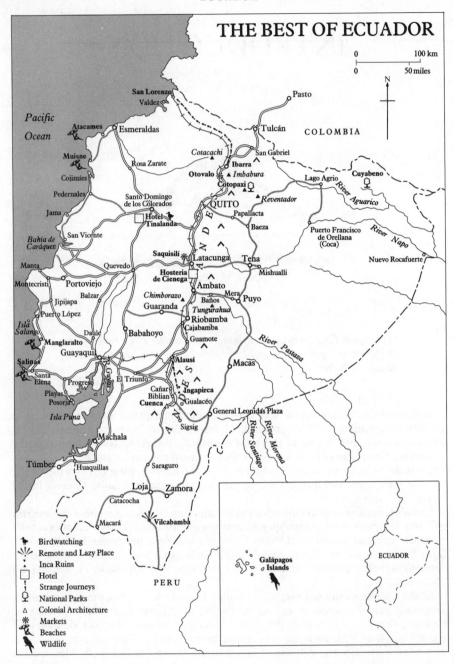

THE BEST OF ECUADOR

0   100 km

0   50 miles

N

Pacific Ocean

COLOMBIA

San Lorenzo
Valdez

Pasto

Atacames   Esmeraldas

Muisne

Cojimíes

Pedernales

Jama

Bahía de Caráquez

San Vicente

Manta

Montecristi

Isla Salango

Manglaralto

Salinas

Santa Elena

Playas

Posorja

Isla Puna

Túmbez

Huaquillas

Cotacachi

Rosa Zarate

Santo Domingo
de los Colorados

Hotel Tinalanda

Quevedo

Portoviejo

Balzar

Jipijapa

Puerto López

Daule

Babahoyo

Guayaquil

Progreso

El Triunfo

Machala

Saraguro

Loja   Zamora

Catacocha

Macará

San Gabriel

Ibarra

Otovalo ▲ *Imbabura*

Cotopaxi

Lago Agrio

Cuyabeno

River Aguarico

QUITO

Papallacta

Baeza

Puerto Francisco
de Orellana
(Coca)

River Napo

Nuevo Rocafuerte

▲ *Reventador*

Saquisilí

Latacunga

Tena

Mishualli

Hostería de Cienega

Chimborazo ▲

Ambato

Mera

Baños

Puyo

Guaranda

Tungurahua

Riobamba

Cajabamba

Guamote

Alausí

Macas

Cañar
Biblian

Ingapirca

Cuenca   Gualacéo

General Leonidás Plaza

Sigsig

River Pastaza

River Morona

River Santiago

Vilcabamba

PERU

Legend

🐦 Birdwatching
☀ Remote and Lazy Place
⋮ Inca Ruins
▢ Hotel
⋮ Strange Journeys
⚘ National Parks
△ Colonial Architecture
✳ Markets
🏖 Beaches
🐦 Wildlife

Galápagos Islands

ECUADOR

16

volcanoes and mountain lakes, Amazonian rainforests and lonely Pacific beaches, this tranquil tropical republic is for you.

A Little Geography: the Lie of the Land and its People

As in all Andean republics, Ecuador's dominant feature is the mountains. Running the entire length of the country, they divide it and separate its people.

The Andes are predominently Indian, and their central valley, the 'Avenue of the Volcanoes', holds the bulk of the country's population. In many respects, with its mountain lakes and pine forests, it resembles a Latin American Switzerland. Move west from the mountains however, down to Ecuador's 600 km of Pacific coast, and you are in another world. The climate is tropical, the *costeños* looser than the *sierranos*, and there is a greater blood-mixing; the coast is predominantly creole. In fact, in the coast's mangrove swamps to the north against the Colombian border, most of the population is black, and northern towns such as Esmeraldas can sometimes closer resemble Africa than Latin America. In the southern areas of the coast on the other hand, the land is arid, and agriculture is only possible with intensive irrigation.

East of the mountains lies the steamy heat of the Amazon; the world's largest rain forest. And although it is perhaps a nonsense to talk of countries and states when the forest so blithely disregards all international boundaries, the Amazon is perhaps no more easily reached in South America than from within Ecuador. The Amazon accounts for more than one half of Ecuador's land area, but only 5 per cent of the country's population live there; some Indian, a few white, but mostly mestizos, in small towns and villages.

The Best of Ecuador

Beaches: Deserted beaches—Muisne in the north, Manglaralto in the south. Holiday beaches—Salinas in the south, Atacames in the north.

Bird watching: Hotel Tinalandia, just outside Santo Domingo.

Climbing: Chimborazo, a difficult peak; Cotopaxi, for gentler lower slopes.

Colonial architecture: Quito and its churches; Cuenca.

Festivals: the December Festival de Quito—bullfights, street parties and Caribbean music.

Hotel: Hosteria de Cienega, a converted colonial hacienda.

Inca ruins: Ingapirca.

Markets: Otovalo, for *artesania*; Saquisilí, for local trading.

National Parks: Cuyabeno, for Amazonian rain forest; Cotopaxi, for Andean flora.

Rain forest: a river trip through the Amazon jungle from the small port of Mishualli.

Remote and lazy places: Vilcabamba.

Strange journeys: the old Inca trail from Alausí to Ingapirca; the train journey from Ibarra to San Lorenzo.

Wildlife: the Galápagos Islands.

Part I

ECUADOR:
GENERAL INFORMATION

Otovaleño

Itineraries

Because Ecuador is so small and so easily explored by plane or bus from Quito, most Ecuadorean itineraries consist of a series of exploratory loops out into the country from a base in the capital. Thus, from Quito, you could visit the Amazon via Baños and then loop back; make exploratory day trips to Otovalo and Ibarra in the northern Sierra, or make a longer week-trip to Cuenca and Vilcabamba in the south. The Galápagos can also be reached from either Quito or Guayaquil.

Finally, for a long and unforgettable Pacific trip, vagabond north from Guayaquil along the beaches of the coast up to San Lorenzo, catching the train back up to Ibarra in the Sierra from there.

Getting Around Ecuador

Ecuador is a small country with a well-developed transport system and everywhere is readily accessible, whether by canoe, *burro*, bus or plane. (Stay a couple of months and you are likely to use all four.) Journeys in the mountains or along the coast are by bus; journeys within the Amazon are nearly all by dug-out canoe; and trans-Ecuadorean journeys, such as from Quito to the coast, are most easily done on a cheap plane hop with

18

TAME or SAN. (For a full list and pricing of Ecuador's internal air services, see p. 49, under 'Quito'.)

By Bus

Buses go everywhere and the system is well-developed and well-used. But—as you will soon discover—long bus journeys can be very uncomfortable; their romance and the seats of your trousers both soon wear out and the prospect of spending 10 cramped hours on a long-distance inter-city bus journey can make even the hardiest traveller choose a plane, if there is a choice. For shorter journeys however—especially through the Sierra—the bus is indispensible.

All towns have long- distance bus terminals, and seats on the buses are booked before the journey. If you are in a hurry, however, just turn up and listen out for your destination amongst the hawking cries of the drivers and their conductors; it is likely that you will be away within a few minutes. To dismount from a local bus, tell the driver *Por acá, por favor* (over here, please). To climb up onto a local bus, just flag it down and jump aboard.

By Train

The train never really achieved a glorious hour in Ecuador, which makes Ecuadorean train journeys picturesque and an end in themselves, but not for those in a hurry. Sadly the glorious Guayaquil–Quito railway link is now defunct and the only train that still travels between the mountains and the coast is the San Lorenzo–Ibarra link. There are also two other small train lines which run through the mountains; from Quito to Riobamba, and from Otovalo to Ibarra.

Car Hire

As an oil-producing country, Ecuador enjoys very cheap petrol but car-hire is expensive, at European rates. **Hertz** and **Avis** both have representatives in Quito and Guayaquil, but if you do hire a car check that it has a jack and a spare wheel before setting off.

By Taxi

Taxis provide a reasonable alternative to car rental. They can be hired for the day, for as little as US$25–30, which makes them cheaper, and you gain the benefit of a driver who knows the way.

Tourist Information

The Government-run tourist agencies are called **DITURIS**, and offices can be found in every major town. Although the staff are friendly, the offices are rarely useful, unless you have specific questions, such as 'How do I get to . . .?' Occasionally they stock local maps, and have English-speaking staff. In remote areas, the village shop is everyone's nexus of local information.

Embassies and Consulates

UK: Ave González Suárez 111, Quito, tel 560 309.
USA: Ave Patria y 12 de Octubre, Quito tel 562 890.
Germany: Ave Patria y 9 de Octubre, Edificio Eteco, 6th Floor, Quito, tel 232 660.
Also: 9 de Octubre 109, Guayaquil.
Canadian Honorary Consul: Ave 6 de Deciembre 2816 y James Orton, Edificio Josueth González, 4th Floor, Quito, tel 564 795.
Peru: Ave 9 de Octubre 411, 6th Floor, Guayaquil.
Colombia: Ave Amazonas 353, Quito.

Opening Hours

Most offices and businesses open every morning at 8.30, close for a two hour *siesta* at 12.30, and then re-open on weekdays until 6.30. On Saturdays they are open only in the mornings and are closed on Sundays. Government offices close for weekends, and banks are only open on weekdays in the mornings.

Churches open and close according to God's will, but usually early in the mornings, shutting at midday, and opening again in the late afternoon.

Maps

All Ecuadorean bookshops sell servicable general maps. For specialized or highly detailed maps go to **El Instituo Geográfico Militar**, on Avenida T Paz y Miño, open 8–3 Mon–Thurs and 8–12 noon on Fridays.

Post

The Ecuadorean postal system is mostly reliable—even if not fast—and you will find post offices in all largeish towns. If you want to send postcards home you will find that they are more likely to arrive if mailed in an envelope.

The best way to receive mail, if you have a card, is at the **American Express** office, Aptdo 2605, Quito, Ecuador. But if you have mail addressed to you at a town's post office, make sure that your surname is written in large clear letters so that it will be correctly filed, eg: SMITH, John, Lista de Correos, Correos Central, Quito, Ecuador.

Phone

IETEL offices are open from 10–6 every day and most can make international calls. You will always get a clearer long distance line however if you call direct from any major hotel. Ecuador is five hours behind Greenwich mean time.

Shopping

Ecuador is not renowned for its gold or jewellery, but for its *artesania* (arts and crafts). These are easy to come by, of high quality, and very cheap. Often produced by Indian co-operatives, you will see representative selections of naif paintings, chunky sweaters, shawls, masks, and wall-hangings in all souvenir shops and large markets.

Although Ecuador is especially famous for its Indian weaving (especially Otovaleño weaving) the country's best buy however, must be a Panama hat (see p. 87 and p. 110). Unique to Ecuador, a good Panama costs about US$20 and is so pliable that you can fold it up, pass it through a napkin ring and then snap it with a flick back into its original, pristine, shellac-smooth shape. A Panama not only distinguishes the debonair, but also provides practical shade from the equatorial sun, although a baseball hat is perhaps less conspicuous.

Media

The best highland newspapers are *Hoy* and *El Commercio*; the best coastal papers, published in Guayaquil, are *El Telegrapho* and *El Universo*. All of these newspapers cost around US25c and provide good entertainment listings for their respective cities. US newspapers, such as *Time* or the *Herald Tribune*, can usually be found only in Quito and Guayaquil.

Literature

In the 19th century, Ecuador produced two major literary figures; Juan León Mera (1832–94), whose *Cumanda* must rank as one of the best Indianist novels of Spanish America, and Juan Montalvo (1832–89) a polished stylist and essayist—Latin America's Cicero.

In the 20th century, Ecuadorean literature was largely social and realistic, conditioned by the Russian Revolution. Protest literature reached its apogee with Jorge Icaza's world-famous *Huasipungo* (1934), which is perhaps the most brutal portrayal of Indian misery ever written. Profoundly influenced by Balzac, Icaza is considered to be Ecuador's best novelist, and despite his overweening pessimism, his books continue to move readers through their vivid description of man's inhumanity to man. *Huasipungo* still floats near the top of Ecuador's best-selling books list.

Festivals and Holidays

Most festivals in Ecuador are based around the liturgical calendar, and the list below is only a sample of the country's largest. Nearly all villages have their own days and a complete year's list of the country's festivals would be at least 365 days long. Festivals in the highlands tend to be celebrated with great pageantry and drunken decorum; festivals in the lowlands with a wilder gusto. During festivals all banks and offices close and it may be very difficult to find a hotel bedroom.

January:	1, New Year's Day; 6, Epiphany.
February:	20–30, Ambato's Flowers and Fruit Festival.
March:	Carnival in the last days before Lent.

21

April:	Easter, and the holy days around it, are celebrated with processions throughout Ecuador.
May:	1, Labour Day; 24, National Holiday celebrates the decisive 1822 Battle of Pichincha.
June:	First weeks inthe highlands celebrates Corpus Christi; 24–29, fiestas in the Otovalo area celebrate St John's, St Peter's and St Paul's days.
July:	24, national holiday to celebrate Bolívar's birthday; 25, anniversary of the founding of Guayaquil—a major fiesta.
August:	10, Quito's Independence day.
September:	1–15, Festival of Yamour in Otovalo.
October:	12, National holiday celebrates the Discovery of the Americas.
November:	1, All Saints' Day; 2, All Souls' Day is celebrated with drinking and the laying down of flowers in graveyards, especially in rural areas—a festive occasion, not to be missed; 3, Cuenca's Independence Day.
December:	6, large fiesta in Quito, with bullfights and street orchestras, to celebrate the founding of the city; 24 and 25, Christmas Eve and Christmas Day; 28–31, End of the Year celebrations with street processions and fireworks.

TOPICS

Frailejones (grey friars) on the high Sierra paramo

A Brief *Natural* History

In traditional European thinking, people come to take on the characteristics of the land that they inhabit: if the natural life of the tropics—unfettered by the demands of a hard season that never comes—is wild and extravagant, so too are the people. And if the Andes are denuded and melancholic, so too are the Indians. Unlike in Europe, where nature was flogged into a virtual bowling green by the Middle Ages, one is still ever aware of nature as a protagonist in South America. And ever since the times of the *cronistas* of the Indies, the strangeness and size of American nature has been one of the keys to understanding American differences.

Unlike the colonization of North America, which followed an orderly progression across the continent from a well-established eastern seaboard, South America was conquered in a start. Most of South America's major cities were founded within 50 years of Colombus's first sighting—Havana in 1512, Mexico City in 1521, Quito in 1534, and Bogotá in 1538. The Universities of San Marcos in Lima and of San Francisco Xavier in Sucre were founded before the Pilgrim Fathers even sailed from Plymouth. But, separated from each other by huge distances, these metropolitan centres were as isolated as islands in an archipelago, and it was not unusual for two cities within the same republic to be in closer contact with Europe than with each other. Journeys between them were wearisome and interminable. In New Spain (Mexico) voyagers would travel with a compass or astrolabe in hand, as if travelling the oceans. And the famous 16th-century expeditions of the *Paulistas* across the wastes of South America in search of gold, precious stones and Indian slaves were voyages neither of conquest nor of colonization; they left as little trace behind them as the passage of a ship through the sea. Nature—full of opportunity and hindrance—dwarfed everything; land was plentiful, but labour was scarce. To fuel the European development of the New World, the slave trade began. And so the haemorrhage of one continent—Africa—fed the rape of another—the New World. It took the Spanish only 30 years to overcome the Amerindian civilizations. Thereafter the struggle was against an empty landscape with its strange and powerful nature, or against peoples still living in the Stone Age. Naturally, the European imagination boggled.

The Venetian Giovanni Batista Ramusio was the first European to be entranced, specifically, by South American nature. His *In Delle Navigatiore et Viaggi*, filled with naive and elegant drawings of sea monsters, scenes of Indian life, men and beasts of other climes, and of panoramas executed in the most minute detail, was a 1550 European best-seller. But he was only the first in a steady stream of European scientists and amateur naturalists to be lured across the Atlantic by the promise of a nature vaster and wilder than any known before. Seen from the boxed hedges and tidy fields of Europe, South America was a naturalist's El Dorado, with something new to be discovered by everyone who visited the continent. Who knew what might survive in the lost worlds of the Amazon, or in the wild and infernal south?

La Condamine, during the French expedition of 1735, measured the globe from Quito, mapped the river Amazon, collected vegetable samples and saw the sea cow (of mermaid myth) in the Rio Marañon. In between his endeavours, he faced local accusations that he was a spy. But it was the notes, drawings and highly accurate reports of the journeying German scientist Baron von Humboldt, in 1799, that truly stirred Europe's intelligentsia. Although the foundations for his work had already been laid by the Colombian botanist Celestino Mutis, Humboldt opened up a period of investigation whose excitement has often been compared to that of Colombus's first voyage. Humboldt rediscovered South America.

With his botanist collaborator, Bonpland, Humboldt travelled through the South American continent collecting, mapping, measuring and sketching as he went. He was tireless and precise. After his return, it took nearly 30 years to compile and publish the 30 volumes of his studies, along with its 1500 illustrations. Apart from his impact on South American political life (when asked in a European drawing room by Simón Bolívar whether he thought South America was ready for independence, Humbolt had replied, 'Yes, all it needs is a great leader, and the continent will produce that man') Humboldt's project laid the basis for the modern study of physical geography and ecology. Stressing the accuracy of his observations and measurements, Humboldt was the first man to relate ecology to altitude when he recognized the three major ecological zones of South America: lowland (hot/torrid), central (temperate) and highland (cold). His drawings emphasized the inter-linkage of the natural world, of cultures in their natural setting, and of plants and animals in their proper context. In one famous illustration of Mount Chimborazo, he drew all of the plants at their correct zonal heights.

Humboldt's tropical descriptions and peripatetic narratives inspired a legion of European naturalists. He wrote: 'When a traveller newly arrived from Europe penetrates for the first time into the forests of South America, he beholds nature under an unexpected aspect in a vast continent where everything is gigantic . . . if he feels strongly the beauty of the picturesque scenery he can scarcely define the various emotions which crowd upon his mind ... everything in nature appears new and marvellous.'

In 1831, Darwin began his epic voyage of exploration with HMS *Beagle*, writing, on the voyage's completion, an historic account of the continent's natural history and, of course, his Theory of Evolution. The English naturalists Henry Bates and Russell Wallace explored South America concurrently from the land, mapping and identifying the species of the Amazon with a rigour that has left little work for taxonomists ever since. It was their discoveries that fuelled the Victorian fashion for greenhouses and hot-house plants.

But after more than 400 years of European influence and a century and a half of scientific exploration, the field of South American natural history has still been touched only superficially. New discoveries of species and animal relationships are continually being made. Naturally, South America remains as surprising as a conjurer's hat.

The Paramos

The natural life of the Galápagos has been well studied, as has that of the Amazon, and you will find more details in their respective sections. In the higher valleys of Ecuador, such as those around Quito, much of the vegetation—the eucalyptus tree, for example— has been imported, and can seem like that of home, as does the weather. But there is another type of highland zone that is unique to South America: the paramo. These harsh, cold, and often snowy tablelands lie between 3200 and 4000 m, and are as flat as tortillas. You will often drive through them, recognizing them by their harsh conditions and scanty animal life. If you are lucky, and look up, you might see the 3-m span of the largest flying bird in the world, the condor.

Condors, noble in name and flight, are in fact birds of carrion; the tourist eagle. Their beaks are hooked for tearing at flesh, and their pink heads and neck are bare of feathers. They are most easily identifiable in the air by their flat gliding flight with fingered wing tips, silvery patches on the upper surface of their wings, and white ruff. A good condor-spotting area is Cotopaxi National Park, or anywhere in the highlands during lambing, when they come down to feed on placentas.

Probably the most remarkable group of birds found in the Americas are the humming-birds. There are at least 129 species in Ecuador alone, and you are bound to see them at least once, probably in the garden of your hotel, working over the blooms of a flowering shrub. Francisco Pizarro described the hummingbird feathers on the Incan emperor's cloak thus: 'There were deposits of irridescent feathers, some looking like fine gold and others of a shining green colour ... each feather is little larger than a fingernail. Quantities of them were threaded together on fine thread and were skilfully attached to agave fibres to form pieces over a span in length ... Clothes were made of the feathers and contained a staggering quantity of these irridescents.' In fact, the pigments of the feathers are dull, and most of the colours of the hummingbirds' plumage depend on refracted light. This is why their jewel-like brilliance only shows when the light hits them at the right angle.

No other bird can match the manoeuvrability of the hummingbird, which comes from its method of flight. Instead of beating their wings up and down like other birds, they beat them to and fro in a shallow figure-of-eight. Insects move their wings in the same way. The figure of eight stroke means that by altering the tilt of their wings, hummingbirds can make rapid transitions from forward flight (speeds of up to 70 mph have been recorded), to hovering, and even to flying backwards. It is the high speed of the beat—up to 80 beats a second—that causes the hum that gives the birds their name. Hummingbirds are also the smallest birds in the world; the Andean hillstar is 13 cm in length, the short-tailed woodstar only 7 cm.

There are mammals on the paramo, but they are rare and hard to spot, preferring the remotest regions of the Andes, such as those around Papallacta in Ecuador. The largest land animal in Ecuador is the tapir, with its heavy brown body and elongated snout. If you don't manage to see one sheltering in a bush, you might see their tracks, four toes in front and three on the rear foot. One of the smallest mammals in Ecuador is the light greyish-brown dwarf Andean *pudu*, which averages out at 35 cm in height. Llamas are rare, unless domesticated or as a kept herd such as exists on the slopes of Cotopaxi. Rarest of all is the Andean spectacled bear.

At 3000 m and above, heat depends so much on the sun that a passing cloud can cause a 15°C drop in temperature in only five minutes. The Jambato toad, for instance, has a bright orange belly, but his back is black to absorb the heat of the sun. Paramo vegetation has adapted in its own way to the constraints of high-altitude life. Hugging the ground as a springy carpet in the search for a more constant temperature and as protection against the wind, the leaves of paramo plants tend to be small and thick, so as to be less susceptible to frost; curved with thick waxy skins, so as to reflect or absorb solar raditation; covered in a fine 'down', that acts as insulation; and arranged in concentric rings, so as to prevent shading. The plants are tough and one of the llama's sister species, the *vicuna*, has lower incisors that grow continuously so it can chew the hard, bunched paramo grasses. The main exception to the stunted paramo vegetation are the *frailjones*, members of the daisy family. You will see them looming in the mist as tall and mysterious as their itinerant namesakes—grey friars—wispy, covered in a fine down, with a splayed head of leaves.

As one early voyager remarked for those who would follow him: 'Traveller, you have come to the most transparent region of the air'.

Manuela Sáenz: The Liberator of the Liberator

Actions can take on a parabolic intensity in Latin America; some are poetry made flesh, mirrors for our own actions. The sad and strange love story of Manuela Sáenz and Simón Bolívar is a rollercoaster example of such seemingly implausible passion.

They first saw each other in Quito, after the Battle of Pichincha, as Bolívar rode into the city in triumph. Manuela caught his eye from a balcony, smiled, and tossed him a flower which grazed his forehead. Later that night they met properly, at a ball, and Bolívar found her the best dancing partner that he had ever had. They danced until dawn, forgetting everyone else, including the lady's husband.

Bolivar was then 39, and Manuela 22, married to a staid English physician, Dr Thorne. She was mischievous, spirited and had a positive genius for finding a character's weakness and mocking it. She showed neither humility nor modesty. She was aggressive, self-confident and volatile, in turn gay, sensitive, quick-tempered, ribald and courageous. Both in Quito, where she had been born, and in Lima, where she had spent much of her life, she had always been an ardent plotter in the patriot cause. She was also beautiful. Bolívar had never met anyone like her; nor she, him.

At first they were inseparable. During the year of campaigns in Guayaquil and the Province of Quito, Manuela went with Bolívar wherever he rode or fought. Mounted on a stallion and dressed in the uniform of a dragoon with a lance in hand, she charged into battle with the other Colombian troops. The men made her presents of the moustaches that they cut from the faces of the fallen Spaniards, and she collected them, stitching them onto a silk scarf. 'La Libertadora', the patriot officers called her; whilst to Bolívar she was his 'amable loca', the lovable fool.

Manuela's husband Thorne wrote to her constantly, begging her to return. In one famous letter, which shows more than anything else the kind of woman she was, she replied:

> 'No, no, no, never again, por Dios! What do you gain by forcing me to answer... no? Señor, you are excellent, you are inimitable—that I shall never deny... But Englishman of my heart, I am more honoured by being the mistress of General Bolívar than the wife of any living man. I do not worry about the conventions invented by men for tormenting themselves.'

She carried on in the same excellent vein:

> 'In heaven you and I shall marry again; but not on earth. In Paradise we shall live an angelic, an entirely spiritual life (for, as a man, you are a bit heavy). Everything there will be in the English manner, for monotony is the exclusive right of your people (in love, I mean, for none are more enterprising in practical things). Their love has no pleasure in it, their conversation no grace. Their walk is hurried, they get up and sit down with caution, they do not laugh at their own jokes. And I, miserable mortal, who laugh at myself, at you, at all this English seriousness, how shall I suffer in Heaven!... the English are tyrants with women. However, you were never that with me—on the contrary, you were more solicitous than a Portuguese. Am I in bad taste? But enough of jokes. Without laughing, with all the sincerity, truth and purity of an Englishwoman, I tell you that I shall never go back to you again. That you are an Anglican and I am a Pagan is the greatest spiritual obstacle; that I am in love with someone else is a still greater reason. You see how exact my reasoning is?'

Bolívar and Manuela truly loved each other, of that there can be no doubt. But their love was far from ideal, and they were frequently separated by war, political dissent and, as often, by Bolívar's infidelities. In one incident in Peru, Bolívar entered his bedroom to find three of the best-looking girls in the province, corralled next to his bed by his faithful major-domo.

'Who,' asked Bolivar, 'are these?'

'These,' replied the major-domo, 'are et cetera, et cetera, et cetera.'

Although hundreds of miles away, Manuela heard of the affair. Alone, bored and angered, she wrote to her friend Juan Santana: 'Misfortune is with me; all things have their end. The General no longer thinks of me. In nineteen days he has scarcely written to me twice. What is wrong?'

They came together, and parted. Bolívar fought, Manuela waited. The cycle repeated itself endlessly. They met again. But Bolívar was unfaithful and Manuela's 'pretty nails' made such scratches on his face that he had to remain in his room with a 'very heavy cold'. They parted again.

On 11 September 1827 Manuela received the following letter sent by an ailing Bolívar from Bogotá:

> 'Manuela, the memory of your enchantments dissolves the frost of my years... your love revives a life that is expiring. I cannot live without you. I can see you always even though I am far away from you. Come. Come to me. Come now...'

Manuela replied immediately, making her position very clear:

> 'I am very angry, and very ill. How true it is that long absences kill love and increase great passions. You had a little love for me, and the long separation killed it. But I, I who had a great passion for you, kept it to preserve my peace and happiness. And this love endures and will endure so long as Manuela lives... I am leaving for Bogotá the first of December—and I come because you call me. However, once I am there do not afterward suggest that I return to Quito.'

Bolívar never suggested that *she* leave for Quito, but *he* was frequently called away around Gran Colombia and they continued their romance through letters and infrequent meetings. Manuela continued an incessant round of loyal mischief in his absence. On one occasion she set up on the walls of her *finca* a stauette of Santander, Bolívar's arch political enemy, and had it blown to bits by a round of cannon fire. Bolívar was politically compromised, especially as he had just succeded in molifying Santander and his factions. In an apologetic letter to General Cordova he wrote:

> 'I see now the calculated stupidities committed by my friends... as for Manuela—that lovable fool—what would you want me to say to you? You well know from times past how often I have tried to separate myself from her. But this I have been unable to do, she is too resistent.'

Bolívar's republic was now in a delicate state. In Bogotá there were plotters and discontent. On more than one occasion Manuela saved her lover's life from assassination attempts. In January 1829, Bolívar had to leave the capital because of an invasion from Peru. Inevitably, there were squabbles while he was away, with Manuela taking much of the flak. The Liberator's dream of a united Gran Colombia slowly began to fade and he returned to the capital, in bad health, a year later on January 15 1830. Manuela nursed him back to health. But on January 20, broken by his efforts, Bolívar resigned from office and two months later rode out from the capital of the republic into a self-imposed exile. Manuela did not accompany him and they were never to see each other again. Bolívar died at the end of the year.

Manuela remained true to the memory of Bolívar for the rest of her life, and lived to see him awarded the official recognition that she always believed he had deserved. She spent her last years in the little town of Paita on the Peruvian coast, selling cigars for a living. In 1841 she met a 21 year-old Herman Melville who had stopped at port on the 38-ton, New Bedford whaler *Acushnet*. Much later, Melville remembered Manuela: 'Humanity, thou strong one, I worship thee not in the laurelled victor, but in the vanquished one.' In 1854, the great Italian patriot Garibaldi visited her; in his memoirs he described her as the the most gracious lady that he had ever known. She died of the plague in 1856, an often forgotten part of the legend that is Símon Bolívar.

Food Glorious Food

Colombus had been lured by the promise of spices; the conquistadors by silver and gold. Atahualpa's easily-raised ransom had been worth £3 million alone at today's prices; and the amounts of silver mined in Mexico and Peru were so fabulous that they led—so the Chicago economists will tell you—to 500 years of global inflation. But although the Spaniards could never have guessed it, food was to be El Dorado's greatest legacy to the world. Sixty-five per cent of all crops now in cultivation originated from the Americas, and it has been estimated that the annual worth of the world's potato harvest alone is many times the value of all the treasures and metals that ever originated from South America.

As with all things that came from the edge of the world, the discovery of South America's new foodstuffs and 'miracle crops' raised more than eyebrows on their introduction to Europe; they divided opinions. Linnaeus, the founding father of tax-onomy and scion of 18th- century Europe's classificatory frenzy, took the genus name for chocolate—Theobroma—from the Greek for 'food of the Gods'. On the other hand, the Russian Orthodox Church, among others, initially banned potatoes and tomatoes because they were unmentioned in the Bible.

The first reference to the potato had been made by Jiménez de Queseda in 1536 as he quested south for El Dorado through the mountains of Colombia. But it took nearly two centuries for the spud to become popular in Europe. No edible plant in the Old World had been grown from tubers rather than from seed, and no other plant had such mysterious, white or flesh-coloured nodules. Potato tubers seemed to people, at first, to be deformed, like the feet of lepers. Many indeed, thought that the potato caused leprosy, and then when that disease vanished, the tuber was blamed for scrofula. Balkan peasants would not eat 'that cursed food hidden in the earth'. And as the men of Kolberg in Prussia said to Frederick the Great in 1774, 'The things have neither smell nor taste. Not even the dogs will eat them, so what use are they to us?'

By the mid-18th century, however, the potato's image had taken a 180-degree turn. Glamorized in Europe, it became the characteristic crop of the Enlightenment. The English historian Hugh Thomas wistfully suggests that when Voltaire desribed Candide retiring to 'tend the garden', it 'surely would have been potatoes that he would have dug'. The reformer Turgot served it ostentatiously at his table when first minister of France, and the enlightened Duke of Parma cultivated it in 1765. Shakespeare's Falstaff had made an aphrodisiacal reference to the tuber with: 'Let the sky rain potatoes... hail kissing-comfits.' And basing his researches on the observation of prostitutes and labourers imported to London from Ireland, the British economist Adam Smith, two centuries after Shakespeare, judged that it made men stronger and women more beautiful.

The potato was now thought to resemble a phallus. Or a truffle—that extravagantly expensive delicacy of the rowdy and gluttonous aristocratic rich. People saw it as an aphrodisiac, an enhancer of life—*but really*—the spud as a love potion? Nevertheless, since its uptake by the Old World in the 18th century, northern Europe's population had started to boom.

American foods—but especially the potato—brought about the miracle that prayer, work and medicine had been unable to do: they cured Europe of the episodic famines that had kept its populations in a Malthusian check. Previously, Old World staples had been based around grains. And for centuries, inclement northern countries—such as Russia, Germany, Scandinavia and England—had suffered from the periodic famines that followed the failure of a crop due to bad weather. In 1660, London—the richest city of Europe, had been so short of food that 50 out of 250 people died in a prosperous, central parish, for while winters had always been severe, it was due to lack of food rather than great cold that people had suffered.

The historian of the plant, Professor Redcliffe Salaman, has argued that the subsequent widespread cultivation of the crop saved mankind (by which he meant Europe) from starvation in the 18th and 19th centuries. The tuber provided a much needed winter source of Vitamin C, and it also produced more food, more reliably and with less effort than any field planted with grain.

In the history of banalities such as the vinegar-soaked, greasy chip there lies a microcosom of universal history. At least eight cornerstones of western food culture—chewing gum and chocolate, pop-corn and cornflakes, coca-cola, the barbecue, tomato ketchup and french-fried potatoes—owe their existence, even if not their proliferation, to the Americas. At the time of the conquest, 3000 varieties of potato were being cultivated in the Andes. And in your travels you will find them varying in size from an egg to a small rock, and in colour from a translucent yellow, through to purple.

HISTORY

The Inca ruins at Ingapirca, near Cuenca

Until Independence, Ecuador's history was written by outsiders and conquerors: in the 15th century by the invading Incas, and 50 years later, by the conquistadors. In the torpor of the colonial years administrators dispatched from Spain replaced the conquistadors, and in the 18th century, revolutionary *criollos* replaced the governing *peninsulares*.

Even during the wars of South American Independence, Ecuador played only a peripheral role. But, as if to make up for such backwater peacefulness, its modern history has been turbulent, and the 19th and 20th centuries have seen a succession of warring civil governments seeking power over each other.

From each of these changes, the bulk of Ecuador's aboriginal population, the highland Indians, has usually benefited little and often suffered greatly. Only recently has their lot improved.

Pre-History

Halfway between the Caribbean and the Incas of Peru, Ecuador is not associated with any great aboriginal civilization. Although Stone Age tools found in the Quito area have been dated to 9000 BC any significant traces of the Indian groups that lived in the mountains were all but obliterated by the Incan conquest in the middle of the 15th century. All that now remains of these peoples are the names associated with archae-ological sites: the Cara and Quitu peoples around Quito, the Puruhuas around Ambato,

31

and the Cañari, the southernmost group, who lived around Cuenca. Archaeologists believe that at the time of the Incan conquest, the Caras were in ascendency, challenged by the Puruhua, with the Cañari moving within an independent orbit to the south.

There were also significant pre-Columbian coastal civilizations. The most notable of these were the Valdivians, who flourished around 3000 BC and were the earliest group in the Americas to develop ceramics. Unfortunately even less is known about the coastal and Amazonian groups than those of the mountains. Then, as now, Ecuadorean history largely revolved around the Sierra.

1450–1526: The Incan Conquest

It is a prevalent attitude to imagine primitive man as limited and timid in his movements, but nothing could be further from the truth. When the Incas began their conquest of Ecuador from Peru during the second half of the 15th century, they often met with fierce resistance.

The Cañari, for instance, so pleased the Inca Tupac Yupanqui with their talent for war that he fathered a son, Huayna Capac, by a Cañari princess, and re-settled a group at Cuzco to act as his personal bodyguards. In turn, Huayna Capac's advance on the Cara Indians to the north of Quito was so slowed by their fighting that he eventually ordered all of their chieftans to be beheaded at the edge of a lake, renaming it after the occasion, Yahuarcocha, the 'Lake of Blood'. Fifty years later, the conquistadors were also to find that some of the most vigorous resistance to their own conquest was to come from the Ecuadorean Indians in the professional Incan army.

The Incan occupation may have been brief—only fifty years or so—but they were administrative geniuses and their success as imperialists lay in bringing together disparate people under their own flag. Instinctively adopting some of the most successful devices of modern colonial regimes, they generally avoided bloodshed and sought instead to preserve and consolidate, rather than re-model, those social and technological features of conquered territories that they found useful. Sometimes they would resettle vanquished tribes, now loyal to them, in newly conquered areas. Called *mitimaes* these Quechuan-speaking colonists brought with them the benefits of Incan colonization, so accelerating local integration into the empire.

The expansion of the Incan empire had begun around the 12th century and by the end of the 15th century it was at its fullest and most powerful extent. Stretching over 380,000 sq miles, it included present-day southern Colombia and northern Chile, most of Ecuador, Bolivia and Peru. Consolidating their position in Ecuador in the late 15th century, the stone road from Cuzco was brought up to Cuenca and finally Quito. And along the banks of the Tomebamba River, in the heart of Cuenca, the Incas built a huge stone cathedral called Tumipampa. Unfortunately the road station at Ingapirca is the only Inca ruin that remains in Ecuador today.

In Quito, or 'Tumibamba', Huayna Capac strengthened his northern position in true Incan style with a marriage to Princess Paccha, the daughter of the defeated Caran Queen Duchicela, and the princess bore him a son, Atahualpa, Quechuan for 'Heroic Turkey'. He was to be the last true Incan king.

1526–32: Arrival of the Spanish

1526 was a watershed year: the first Spaniards landed near Esmeraldas on an exploratory mission; and the Inca Huayna Capac died in a delirious fever withour leaving a clear heir. The disease, which consumed much of the Incan court including Huayna Capac's most likely heir, Ninan Cuyuchi, may have been malaria, but it could also have been smallpox. Brought from Europe by the Spaniards, smallpox spread fiercely around the Caribbean among peoples with no immunity. It could easily have swept from tribe to tribe down through Colombia, and struck the Incan armies long before the Spanish sailed down the coast.

The unwieldy Incan empire was already divided into two administrative units, ruled from Cuzco in the south and Quito in the north. Atahualpa, ruler of Ecuador and holder of the formidable title Incap Ranti ('One who stands for Inca'), refused to pay homage to his southern brother Huascar, who ruled from Cuzco. War broke out between them and Atahulapa was captured. But he escaped to Quito, raised an army and eventually defeated Huascar near Ambato around 1530.

The bed for an easy Spanish conquest was made. The magnificent and tenacious leader Francisco Pizarro—hungry for conquest and fresh from Panama—arrived in 1532 and found the Incan empire divided by internal war. The fissures were there. Pizarro exploited them. The pattern of the conquest of Mexico was about to repeat itself.

1532–33: Conquest of the Incas

The beginnings of the conquest of Incan South America were unique in many ways. No traders or explorers had ever visited the Incan court, and there were no traveller's tales. Military conquest preceded peaceful penetration, and the Europeans' first glimpse of the Incan majesty coincided with his overthrow.

The Spanish toiled up from the coast and late in 1532 Atahualpa agreed to meet Pizarro. Atahualpa, although a clever man, was complacent and somewhat arrogant after his recent military successes; prepared to negotiate with the Spaniards, he admitted that he would do away with them later, when he found the time. The Spaniards however were quicker in their betrayal.

The two leaders met on 16 November at Cajamarca in Peru, and at a secret signal the Spanish cavalry charged the Incan troops. Forty thousand Indians fled in suprise and disarray from the tiny Spanish attack. Atahualpa was ransomed for a room full of silver and gold, and as the chamber filled, he whiled away the time learning to play chess with Pizarro's lieutenant, Hernando de Soto. (Here the irony lies in etymology; checkmate comes from the old French, *eschec mate*, death to the king.) The piled Incan treasure finally reached the designated level, the eyeline. But Atahualpa, instead of being released, was put through a sham trial and sentenced to death on charges of polygamy, crimes against the king of Spain, and the worship of false gods. On 29 August, the king of the Incas and the Sun God's only representative on earth—Atahualpa, a deity, a statesman and a soldier—was garrotted, and with him effectively died that fragile confederation of Indian states, the Incan empire.

1533–50: The Quitan Campaign and the Conquest of Ecuador

Peru was quickly mopped up, and the Spanish soon turned their attention to the northern part of the Incan empire, Ecuador. In February 1533, Martín de Paredes had written, 'the riches of this Quito are said to be very great' (an unbeatable carrot) and rumours that Ecuador's wealth rivalled Peru's abounded in Pizarro's camp.

The northern half of the Incan empire was then under the control of Atahualpa's last remaining general, Rumiñahui, and in August 1533 Pizarro ordered his faithful and able lieutenant Benalcázar north to conquer him. Gaining the allegiance of the still resentful Cañari, Benalcázar advanced quickly, forcing Rumiñahui to fall back to Quito. But rather than let the Incan capital fall into Spanish hands, Rumiñahui fired it on 17 June 1534 and the Spanish re-founded the city on top of the smouldering remains. Rumiñahui carried on a guerrilla war from his base in the mountains, but by the end of the year he was captured and put to death. With his execution, organized Indian resistance in Ecuador came to an end.

The Spice Trail

Pizarro's expedition had been conducted in the spirit of a gold rush. Much of the Incan gold had already been collected, assayed, melted down and sent to Spain, but the promise of New World wealth was longer-lasting. In 1536 Benalcázar sortied north on a quest for Colombia's fabled land of gold, El Dorado. And in 1541 Gonzálo, Francisco Pizarro's brother, headed east towards the Amazon and the Land of Cinnamon, a vegetable version of the same.

Spices—especially cinnamon, pepper, ginger and cloves—were part of Europe's obsessive quest for condiments to refresh a diet that was dull and changeless, a monotonous round of meat and mouldy grains. It had partly been the lure of a new trade route to the spices of India that had led to Columbus's inadvertent discovery of the Americas. And it was spices again that drew Gonzálo to conquer the Amazon and discover the Land of Cinnamon.

The expedition was a disaster. Gonzálo quickly floundered and ran out of supplies. After eating their horses, his soldiers were forced to boil and eat the leather of their saddles. Gonzálo's lieutenant, Francisco Orellana, was dispatched downstream to find food but, over-shooting, he ended up floating down the river Amazon, across the continent and out into the Atlantic. Orellana's epic feat constitutes part of Ecuador's claim to being 'El Pais Amazonica'. Gonzálo, of course, found neither cinnamon, nor gold, and his dismal expedition returned to Quito with only their swords.

1550–1810: The Colonial Years

For twenty years the Spanish bickered. But peace was firmly settled in 1550 when the Spanish throne successfully established its authority at Lima and founded the Viceroyalty of Peru, with Ecuador as a province. In 1563, Ecuador became the Audencia de Quito, a more important division. And in 1739, the Audencia was transferred from the Viceroyalty of Peru to the Viceroyalty of Nueva Grenada, present-day Colombia.

Although Ecuador became a political pass-ball, yo-yoing in its official allegiance between Peru and Nueva Grenada, the colonial era brought it some 300 years of peace. Textiles developed as a large industry in the Sierra, and in rural areas various new agricultural products, such as sheep, cattle, horses, cows, bananas and sugar cane, were introduced. In 1590, seduced by such prosperity (as was much of Spain) the father of modern literature, Cervantes, petitioned the President of the Council of the Indies to make him a 'beneficiary of one of the offices of the Indies . . . at present vacant . . . either the paymastership of the Kingdom of New Grenada, Quito, or . . .'. As the Cuban novelist Cabrera Infante notes, if he had been succesful in his application, the course of world literature might have been irreparably changed, with Don Quixote's faithful batman perhaps renamed Sancho Pampa . . .

Native Affairs

One of the most extraordinary facets of colonial life was how it distributed itself. Looking from Europe, Francis Bacon wrote, 'I have marvelled at Spain, how they clasp and contain so large domains with so few natural Spaniards.' Unlike the colonization of North America, which was to be be a family affair, the conquest of South America had been a male venture, with the conquistadors taking Indian women for their concubines and having children by them; a practical, albeit lusty, arrangement. So it was that the arrival of the first European women in 1546 marked the end of the conquering years and the beginning of the colonial. And when it became obvious that the Spanish *señoras* would not, *could not*, share the same status as Indian wives, the social and racial pattern of colonial Ecuador quickly took shape.

The church, by a majority vote, had given the Indians an immortal soul. But it was not enough; Spaniards with Spanish wives were automatically elevated to the elite. There was a great social and cultural cleavage between the Spanish and the Indian, and officially, little inter-marriage. The Indian population formed a fragmented nation within Ecuador, and race is still the country's exposed nerve.

Following the pattern of pacification used in Spain against the Moors in the 15th century, the Spanish elite settled in fortified towns, both for their safety and the pleasures of urban society. Controlling economic life and monopolizing land and trade, they filled all the posts in the army, the Church and the town councils. With a swaggering but impressive sense of self-importance, many began their prayers, 'Mother of God, our cousin . . .'

Those of mixed blood, the *cholos*, formed the majority of the urban population and dominated the skilled trades: they were the barbers, the store-keepers, the artisans, the major-domos, and the scriveners. Living insecurely between the elite—whose status they envied and aspired to—and the masses, whose sullen resentment they feared, they were a pin-cushion of grievances, easily incited to riot. In a society where wealth for those not born to it was only obtained by luck or a sharp deal, the *cholos* placed an emphasis on *viveza*, on being street-wise. To the elite, they were the *chusma*, or urban rabble.

History has often been unkind to the Spanish, but there is no general pattern for the Indian bulk of Ecuador's population as there was, say, in North America, where they were all killed. 'In low animal terms they judged him, in low manner they treated him,' wrote Waldo Frank in *America Hispana*, echoing a common attitude not universally true. Many Spaniards were impressed by the native nobility, and Luis de Morales wrote that 'many Indians are able and of very sound judgement and intelligence. These are being wasted tending horses or guarding cattle'. Sometimes the Spanish tried to preserve native communities, and some of the more remote tribes were only ever partially absorbed into the Spanish system.

The Mexican system of *encomineda* was, however, repeated in the highlands and huge tracts of land, with attendant Indian labour, were shared out by the king of Spain as a reward for the exploits of the conquest. The Indians who worked in serfdom on these great estates formed the bottom of the colonial heap. Unable to cope with the supreme egoism of the Spanisn, unable to understand and unable effectively to rebel, they put their heads in the sand and ignored the conquerors. Deprived of their earthly dignity, aliens within their own land, their spirit became recalcitrant and demoralized. They turned to fermented corn, *'chicha'*—an alcoholic brew no longer associated with traditional practices and so reduced to a means of escape. The Church did little to improve their lot; Indians even had to pay for the ringing of church bells at funerals. Under the 'yoke of peace' they quickly lost what they had been originally, a people living their own culture.

Occupying an equally low social status were the slaves shipped in from Africa to farm the export-orientated sugar and cocoa plantations of the coastal plains. It was commonly thought that highland Indians were unsuitable for work in such hot and humid areas. Although the Africans were few in number, their resistance was widespread and many formed *cimmarones*—palisaded communities of runaway slaves—in the northwest of the country, near the Colombian border. Remote, malarial, and very underdeveloped, these jungled areas still seem African today.

1810–22: Independence

Ecuador is best understood in relation to the rest of South America's Independence history. For 300 years, Spain had kept a tight rein on her colonies, isolating them from the rest of the world. Economic control had been especially severe: officially trade with any country other than Spain was prohibited, and in a typical situation 'two cents of Peruvian cotton sent to Spain became a four dollar handkerchief sold in Buenos Aires.' In the 19th century, European ideas of civil liberty became popular amongst urban intellectuals, and *criollo* grievances slowly grew against Spain. The North American revolution provided a beacon, pointing the way to Independence and successful emancipation.

South America's first popular uprising, in Quito in 1809, was quickly subdued due to lack of support from the other colonies and provinces. But in the following year, when Napoleon deposed the Spanish king and installed his brother Ferdinand as ruler, the whole of Spanish America found in the situation something that they could deplore. Patriotism in the name of the mother country was quickly converted into South American nationalism, and what began as resistance to France, developed into war against Spain. *Criollo* juntas were quickly set up in Caracas, Bogotá, Buenos Aires, Cartagena and Santiago. Bolívar's armies rose in the north. And San Martín's forces swept up from the River Plate Republics in the south.

In retrospect, the Wars of Independence have all the symmetry of a planned attack, a pincer movement with two north and south-moving prongs that would meet and nip off Spanish control at Lima, or thereabouts. In fact, San Martín and Bolívar were finally to meet in Guayaquil.

Even so, Ecuador played only a small role in the history of South American Independence; after more than three centuries of Spanish domination, the whole country was liberated within a few weeks by Bolívar's ablest general, Field-Marshal Sucre. In May 1822, he freed Quito from Royalist control at the Battle of Pichincha. Later, Bolívar entered the city amidst the pageantry that pleased him, but he stayed only a short while. Determined to incorporate the port of Guayaquil into Gran Colombia before San Martín, who was heading north from Peru, could claim it for his own, Bolívar hastened down from the mountains to the coast. When San Martín, who believed that Bolívar was still in Quito, arrived at Guayaquil, Bolívar was already there to welcome him onto Gran Colombian soil.

The two great men met in secret conference on 26 and 27 July 1822, to discuss the impasse. The outcome was inevitable. Genius is egocentric; one of them had to yield, and it was the lesser personality, San Martín. Bolívar was to write of him, to Santander in Bogotá, that, 'he has the type of correct ideas that would please you; but he did not strike me as being subtle enough to rise to the sublime, whether in the realms of ideas or practical matters.'

That night Bolívar danced all night at a grand ball. San Martín on the other hand, depressed, called his aides, told them that he could not stand the noise, left the party unobserved, joined his ship and sailed back to Peru. Bolívar had gained Ecuador for his visionary state. But restive under a military government run by Colombians and Venezuelans, the Ecuadoreans quipped of their Independence, 'The last day of despotism and the first day of the same'.

1830–61: The First Years of the Republic

It took only seven years for Bolívar's dream of a united South America to turn to ashes. The façade of Gran Colombia had certainly been impressive: it had impressed the British Foreign Secretary George Canning, it had impressed the first envoys that he had sent out, and it had impressed those who took up Colombian bonds in the 1820s. But in 1829, Venezuela ceded from the union, and shortly afterwards, on 10 August 1830, Ecuador followed suit. The first officially recognized Latin American republic broke up.

This regionalism, or sense of separatism, existed not only between the newly-founded republics, but within them as well. Ecuador is no exception and in theory the country's history since independence is quite straightforward, with power alternating between two parties—liberals from the coast and conservatives from the Sierra.

Ecuador's *costeños* had always lived with their backs to the mountains, in much closer contact with the rest of the world than with Quito. For the conservative land-owning *sierranos*, on the other hand, the rest of the world might never have existed, but for the fact that most of the government's income was raised from coastal taxes and spent in the mountains. Friction, at least initially, had been softened by the appalling communications. But the Wars of Independence had moved people on an unprecedented scale, the early republic's economy was in tatters, and dissent inevitably grew until there was political and open warfare, with the army alternating in its alliegance between rival blocks. (All too often battles and bankruptcy are confused with full scale war and universal ruin, and it seems worth noting that the Ecuadorean army in the 1830s was extremely small—only 720 infantry and 360 cavalry. Indeed most Ecuadoreans were such reluctant recruits to any pitched conflict that the 19th-century French traveller Holinsky remarked that opposing commanders in Ecuador seemed to hurry their forces into battle for fear of facing each other troopless and alone!)

Nevertheless, between 1830 and 1860, tiny Ecuador drew its political inspiration from the gigantic volcano Chimborazo depicted on its coat of arms. Presidential power swung between anti-Church liberals from Guayaquil and pro-Church conservatives from Quito, and only in 1861, when the arch-conservative García Moreno came to power, did the situation stabalize. Bringing 15 years of peace, Moreno built roads, schools and hospitals, began work on the Guayaquil–Quito railroad, and took steps to promote agriculture and expand agricultural land. He was also responsible for drawing the definitive battle-lines between conservatives and liberals, the Sierra and the coast, the Church and the state.

1861–75: Ecuador is Dedicated to the Sacred Heart

García Moreno was one of the most extraordinary of South American dictators, and certainly the most religious. The last of the crusaders and conquistadors, the Catholics considered him a hero and Father Berthe said of him: 'He is a Christian Hercules, a successor to Charlemagne and Louis.' Very learned, and always dressed in black, faded sepia prints in Quito's Metropolitan Museum show him carrying a crucifix through the capital's streets during an Easter procession.

Moreno's religion was terrifyingly sincere. Holding that the only possibility of national unity was through religion, he insisted on Catholicism as a pre-requisite for citizenship, officially consecrated the country to the Sacred Heart of Jesus, and renamed his best regiments 'Guardians of the Virgin', 'Volunteers of the Cross', and 'Soldiers of the Infant Jesus'. He maintained that 'Ecuador could only be ruled by an enlightened despot.' And, of course, the major landowners—which included the Church—were happy with peace at the price of his authoritarian rule.

The liberal coast baulked at Moreno's rule, which came to a fitting end in August 1875, when he was killed on the steps of Quito's cathedral with a machete thrust and three attendant bullets. Juan Montalvo, an ardent liberal and exiled Ecuadorean pamphleteer who had waged a war of words against Moreno from Colombia, exclaimed with justification and pride on the news of his death, 'My pen has killed him!'

1875–1911: *Alfaro Vive Todavia, Carajo!*

One of the most admired friends of Montalvo—this South American Cicero—was the fifth child of a Spanish merchant who had settled in the hat-making coastal town of Montecristi, Eloy Alfaro. Courageous, noble, quick witted, the embodiment of liberal ideals and completely indifferent to material reward, Alfaro made a fortune in hats in Panama and spent all of it on revolutions. His adoring family were so broke that they couldn't even afford the stamps to send letters to each other. President from 1895–1901 and again from 1906–11, Alfaro was *the* slayer of Ecuadorean conservative hegemony and the man who finally curtailed the power of the Catholic Church, separating its functions from those of the state. Although now a national hero, revered in the tradition of Washington and Lincoln, Alfaro met a violent end: murdered by the mob in 1912, his body was dragged through Quito's streets and burnt in Ejido Park.

1911–75: The Rise of Populism

Alfaro's death heralded a long period of instability, political fragmentation and interim military rule. In only 25 years there were 22 presidents, dictators or juntas. In 1941, when Ecuador was at its weakest, war broke out. Peru had been trying to usurp territory in the upper reaches of the Amazon for many years, and in 1942, the Protocol of Rio de Janeiro, mediated by the United States, awarded it most of the disputed territory. Ecuador lost over 111,000 sq miles and, more importantly, access to the Atlantic. Maps published in Ecuador still show the disputed territory as Ecuadorean, and the country's official foreign policy remains the recovery of all the territories of the Audencia de Quito. But although there are occasional border skirmishes and it is no longer possible to travel by boat down the river to Iquitos, there has not been a serious incident since 1981.

Compounded by a world economic crisis, Ecuador was racked by instability. Social and demographic changes brought about by the cacao and banana boom of the 1920s had also led to the rising importance of the working-class vote and populist politics. Peace would only be achieved by a man who could appeal to both Sierra and coast, to politicans of both traditional currents and, from time to time, the people: José María Velasco Ibarra. His career, charisma and multiple presidencies were to stretch from the late 1930s into the 1970s.

Conducting the first-ever campaign tour of the country, Ibarra raised the techniques of street action to an art, shaping the style, if not the course, of Ecuadorean politics ever since. He has often been copied, but never succesfully imitated. In his *Escorzos de Historia Patria*, the Ecuadorean historian Jorge Salvador Lara gives a good flavour of the remarkable man:

> 'Tall, spare, quixotic... with a high forehead which premature baldness had progressively enlarged and over which he wore a lumpy felt hat in the town, or a straw hat in the countryside... quick bright eyes... cheeks as sunken as a fasting hermit... the long supple hands of a conjurer made for hypnotic gestures... elegantly turned out even in moments of extreme poverty... his voice, now soothing, now inflaming, crackling with steely nuances, with strange inflexions running the whole length of the scale, full of yelps, repetitions, outbursts, quivers, pauses and above all taunts and insults... electrifying momentousness. Such is Velasco Ibarra.'

Ibarra repeatedly pushed his way into the presidency against the reluctance of conservative, liberal and land-owning elites. When they accepted him, it was only as the lesser of

39

two reforming evils; Ibarra or Marxism. But when he frittered away his popular support, or went too far in the direction of genuine structural reform, or even became too cavalier about civil rights, he was overthrown and exiled. Elected president five times, he only ever finished his term once. When exiled, he would run to Colombia, Chile or Argentina, establish residence and wait until he was called back again by 'the people'. 'Give me a balcony and I will be president again!', he once exclaimed.

Ibarra's last term ended prematurely in 1972. In February 1979 he returned to Quito to bury his wife, who had died falling out of a bus. A month later, he died there himself, many say of a broken heart.

Modern Ecuador

The course of Ecuador's politics has always followed the erratic boom/bust cycle of its exporting coffee, banana and cacao industries. Draw a revenue chart of the country over time and it resembles the electrocephalogram of a lunatic. However, the discovery of oil in the Amazon in the 1970s has ushered in an unprecedented period of economic growth and social peace. In the past, the powers of the state were limited by a modest economy, dependent on customs duties and taxes levied on the unstable foreign trade sector. By contrast, recent petroleum revenues have allowed the government to play a more active role, and pursue a set of social and economic goals with little fear of opposition.

In 1978, a new constitution (the 16th since Independence) was approved. It included a guarantee of civil rights, a one-term limit for presidents and the extension of universal suffrage for all literate adults. However, as most Indians are illiterate, they remain excluded from the electoral process, and Ecuador is still only democratic in a fragile sense of the word.

Despite large international debts, Ecuador remains one of the most peaceful and safe countries to visit in South America. Efforts are currently being made to reform the distribution of agricultural land in favour of the Indians, to expand the educational system and to diversify the economy. Rodrigo Borja Cevallos, politically a member of the centre-left, was elected president in 1989, and at time of writing he is still in office.

CHRONOLOGY

9000 BC	Unnamed stone age civilization living around Quito
4000 BC	Valdivian coastal civilization
1300 BC	Machalilla coastal civilization
500 BC	Chorrera coastal civilization
AD 1000	Cara, Quitu, Puruhua and Cañari civilizations in ascendancy in the mountains
1450	Incan invasion
1526	Spanish land at Esmeraldas
1527	Incan king, Huayna Capac, dies
1530	Atahualpa defeats his brother Huascar in Incan civil war
1533	Francisco Pizarro lands in Ecuador and meets and betrays Atahualpa in Peru
	Benalcázar begins Quitan campaign
1534	June: Quito razed by last remaining Incan general, Rumiñahui
	August: Spaniards re-found city on top of the remains
	December: Rumiñhui killed. Organized Incan resistance ends
1536	Benalcázar quests north into Colombia in search of El Dorado
1541	Gonzálo Pizarro explores the Amazon
1542	Orellana floats down the Amazon and into the Atlantic
1546	First European woman arrives in Quito
1550	Ecuador founded as a province of the Viceroyalty of Peru
1563	Ecuador becomes the Audencia de Quito, subject to Lima
1739	The Audencia de Quito is transferred to the Viceroyalty of Nueva Grenada
1745	La Condamine's French expedition arrives in Ecuador
1770	Humboldt's journeys
1809	Quito uprising; the first cry for Independence in South America
1810	*Criollo* juntas set up around South America. Bolívar and San Martín begin to group their armies
1822	May: Sucre liberates Quito at the Battle of Pichincha
	July: San Martín and Bolívar meet in Guayaquil
1830	Ecuador secedes from the Republic of Gran Colombia
1861–75	Theocratic rule of García Moreno
1875	Moreno assassinated
1875–95	Liberal revolution
1895–1901	Eloy Alfaro president
1901–11	Alfaro's second term
1912	Alfaro killed in Quito
1920	Cacao and banana boom
1911–30	'The Waltz of Presidents'
1934/5	Velasco Ibarra president
1942	Ecuador loses vast area of Amazon in Protocol of Rio de Janeiro
1944/6	Ibarra's second term
1952/6	–third term
1960/1	–fourth term
1968/72	–fifth and final term in office
1978	16th and most recent constitution approved
1979	Ibarra dies
1981	Evangelists from the Summer Institute of Linguistics banned from the Amazon
1989	Rodrigo Borja Cevallos elected president

41

Part IV

THE SIERRA

After the damp-laden air of the tropics there is a breathless dizzyness to the mountains. The air has an unnaturally crisp lightness; 'gin-clear' in the words of the German explorer and scientist Baron Von Humboldt. White glaciers are reflected in tiny lakes, as in a Japanese print. Cool breezes rustle through forests of pine and eucalyptus, and mountain streams braid their way through the hills. It's hard to credit at first, but Ecuador's calm Sierra landscape has little in common with what one would normally imagine to find on the equator.

Although only a tiny fraction of Ecuador's land surface, the double north–south slash of Ecuador's Andes, known within the country as the Sierra, forms the social and political core of Ecuador. It also contains almost half the country's population, most of whom are Indian. Five hundred years ago, the Sierra marked the northernmost limit of the Incan empire, and in the deeper regions of the south, towards Peru, a hangover Incan influence is still strong. But even though dispossessed by the Spanish, Ecuador's Indians still seem to possess their mountains: in Quito, by dint of a peaceful but meaningful vigil, and in the capital's surrounding countryside, if only by inaccessible terrain and the weight of their numbers.

In the small cobbled cities that dot the Sierra's high valleys—such as the preserved colonial towns of Cuenca and Ibarra—you can still catch a whiff of Ecuador's feudal and colonial days. Indeed the Andean Indians, squatting by geometric piles of agricultural produce at Saquisilí's weekly market, even look medieval. The deservedly famous market at Otavalo is different, of course; it's brisk, crowded, and bristling with international tourists shopping for rugs and weavings.

There is a road that wriggles through the high valleys of the sierra—the Pan-American. Heaving and bucking, often uncertain, it threads the mountain towns, occasionally giving off unmetalled tributaries. Some of these wander nervously off into the mountains until they vanish. Others dizzy around the skirts of mountains before plunging west towards the coast, or east down into the hot forests of the Amazon. But whilst on a map, or even from the ground, the Andes can look firm and unflinching, these are relatively young mountains, still forming, and many are active volcanoes. Earthquakes are not uncommon, and during your visit you might feel 'a little tremble'. Deep vents in the earth spew up volcano-heated water, forming natural hot pools. Those at the spa town of Baños are the most famous and oft-visited, but there are others too. The baths at Pappalacta are rarely visited by tourists, whilst others are so hidden and local that they are left permanently unattended. You might stumble across one while trekking through the mountains or walking the pine-covered slopes of Mount Cotopaxi's National Park.

Some people describe the Andean Indian's logic as topsy-turvey; others as closer to an oriental rather than an occidental type. But while Ecuador's Sierra lacks Peru's sense of sullen Indian menace, nearly all agree that there is a melancholy to the mountains, a loneliness. The rhythms of Sierran life are not piquant; the pace, instead, is slow. Hot weather Ecuadoreans from the coast like to deride the *sierraños* for their slow wit (it's the low atmospheric pressure that makes everything work at a slower efficency; not only cars and machinery, but people and plants too). But the fact is that you are high, and due to the bulge of the earth at the equator, truthfully on the roof of the world.

When visiting the Sierra most people make Quito their base, foraying out on one- or two-day expeditions into the countryside. However, you might prefer to make a smaller town, such as Baños or Otovalo or Cuenca, your base. If you are hurrying, the best of the Sierra could be covered in ten days or so; otherwise you could spend up to four busy weeks walking and climbing.

Quito

'All of us here smoke the opium of the upper altitude,
voices low, short steps, short breath.
The dogs don't snarl much, neither do the children,
and not much laughter.'

—Henri Michaux, *Ecuador*

Tossed up to an altitude of nearly 3000 metres, Ecuador's capital is so high that its 900,000 inhabitants call it *'El Hueco en El Cielo'*, the opening to the heavens.

The city is defined by its mountains. You can see intimate rings of steep green mountain terraces and foggy peaks from every point. The colonial centre rides the foothills like a rollercoaster, so that the spire of a church in one plaza can look as though it has been bucked into line with the kerbstone of the next. The mountains act on the city like walls, isolating it from the traffic and time of the rest of the world. Ecuador's capital might be one of the oldest and loveliest cities in the Americas, but it is also one of the loneliest in the world; Quito feels far away.

Because of its altitude, the city's days are spring-like and stimulating. But when evening comes, a thin mist—the *garúa*—floats down from the peaks. Newcomers, unprepared for this dramatic change, can find themselves shivering. And as with so many places that are not supposed to have cold weather, but do, there are no radiators to turn on.

The population, drawn from the Andean highlands, is predominantly Indian; guarded and reserved. The city was already an ancient capital when the Spanish arrived as conquerors in the 16th century. But as an important part of the Inca empire, the resisting Indians put it to the torch rather than let it fall into the hands of the Spanish. The Incan city was totally destroyed, and the present capital was founded on the ruins in 1534.

Today, Quito gives the impression of two cities. In the south lies the old centre—preserved by a UNESCO writ—with its colonial architecture, medieval conspiracies, lovers, beggars and thieves. To the north lies the new town, with its well-spaced North American avenues, anonymous offices, plush hotels, banks, tee-shirts, sneakers and jeans.

If you have just flown in from sea level, the high altitude can take it out of you during the first few days. Headaches, dizzy spells, a racing heart and an overwhelming sense of lassitude are common. Take it easy; don't rush; eat lightly; alcohol will make you feel much worse. Your blood pressure is low and oxygen is short.

Every tourist visits Quito—it is their entrepôt to Ecuador—and few are disappointed. The city is well set up for tourism and forms a convenient base for excursions down into the rest of Ecuador. And although there is poverty, Quito has suffered less from the huge rural migrations of other Latin American cities and whilst there are slums, you will not see any rambling shanty towns.

History

The Conquest

'Before the Spaniards there were the Incas; before them the Caras; before the Caras a vague people whom they are said to have conquered: and before them? We do not know. Quito does not tell its past nor its age. It has the air of remembering more years than it troubles itself to reckon. Yes, Quito is old.'
—Blair Niles, North American traveller, 1923

Officially founded only 42 years after Columbus first glimpsed the New World, the original siting of Quito in fact dates from at least a thousand years before the arrival of the Spanish. But long historical views are much like kaleidoscopes—shifting and dependent on who's looking. And ever since the 18th century, those glorious visions of a prosperous pre-Incan 'Kingdom of Quito' have all been based on Father Juan de Velasco's fabulous text, *A Modern History of the Kingdom of Quito*, which more lippy local historians have called Ecuador's 'First Novel'.

According to Velasco, in the 9th century Quito's original founders, the peaceful Quitus, were overcome by the Caras, an expansionist coastal group from the present-day area of Esmeraldas. Imposing their language and religion on the quickly-conquered neighbouring tribes, the Caras went on to establish an Andean empire that lasted five centuries. In his book, Velasco goes into royal Caran genealogy, describes the development of their architecture—'a practical knowledge of the principles of arches and vaulting'—and even of a 12-month calendar. No one can be sure where Velasco drew his information from, and the existence of a Cara empire has never been demonstrated. All one can be sure of is that by the 14th and 15th centuries there were several highly developed political bodies in the Quito area, in particular, the tribes of the Caras and Quitus. Although not empires, these groups were at least well-enough organized to have halted Huayna Capac's invading Incan army for over two years. Spanish historians record that Quito's Indians were still telling of a famous resistance organized by the 'Queen of Cochasqui', otherwise known as 'the Woman called Quilago', in 1631, 100 years after the Incan conquest.

By the 16th century Quito was the seat of government for the northern half of the Inca kingdom, governed by Atahualpa, Huayna Capac's son. Atahualpa liked Quito enough to rebuild it in the precise Incan style, and also to marry a local Caran princess, thereby, theoretically at any rate, binding another reluctant group to the Incan empire.

It was early in 1534 that Francisco Pizarro—the Cortés of Peru—first heard of 'The worthy and very flourishing kingdom of Quito, unrivalled in fertility and abundance and the number of its inhabitants of all the provinces of this New World'. Without pausing for European permisssion, Pizarro hurriedly dispatched his fellow Estremaduran, Sebastián Benalcázar, north from Peru to conquer the area. But as he moved north along the old Incan road, Benalcázar ran into the unexpected: at the foot of Mount Chimborazo, another body of Spanish soldiers. Not reinforcements, but rivals, they were led by the avaricious Pedro de Alvarado, who had levelled the Aztec realm with Cortés. Alvarado had recently grown weary of ruling Guatemala, and was now seeking to increase his fortunes south of the Panamanian isthmus. Benalcázar and Alvarado squabbled. Fighting was only averted by the arrival of Almagro the Blinkered, Pizarro's one-eyed partner, and Alvarado agreed to call off his expedition in return for 10,000 pesos of gold.

Church cloisters, Quito

ECUADOR

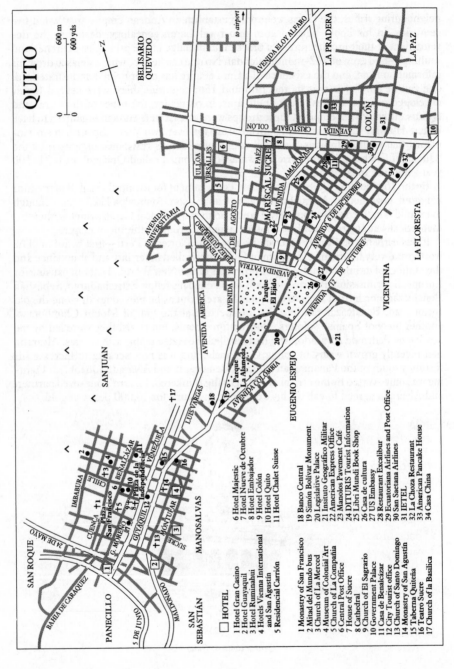

QUITO

0 ————— 600 m
0 ————— 600 yds

N

BELISARIO
QUEVEDO

to airport

□ HOTEL

1 Hotel Gran Casino
2 Hotel Guayaquil
3 Hotel Ruminahui
4 Hotels Vienna International
  and San Agustín
5 Residencial Carrión
6 Hotel Majestic
7 Hotel Nueve de Octubre
8 Hotel Embajador
9 Hotel Colón
11 Hotel Chalet Suisse

1 Monastery of San Francisco
2 Mitad del Mundo bus
3 Church of La Merced
4 Museum of Colonial Art
5 Church of La Compañia
6 Central Post Office
7 House of Sucre
8 Cathedral
9 Church of El Sagrario
10 Government Palace
11 Casa de Benalcázar
12 City Tourist office
13 Church of Santo Domingo
14 Monastery of San Agustín
15 Taberna Quiteña
16 Teatro Sucre
17 Church of la Basilica
18 Banco Central
19 Simón Bolívar Monument
20 Legislative Palace
21 Instituto Geográfico Militar
22 American Express Office
23 Manolos Pavement Café
24 DITURIS Tourist Information
25 Libri Mundi Book Shop
26 Casa de cultura
27 US Embassy
28 Restaurant Excalibur
29 Ecuatoriana Airlines and Post Office
30 San Saetana Airlines
31 IETEL
32 La Choza Restaurant
33 American Pancake House
34 Casa China

Benalcázar renewed his approach to Quito. But on Whit Sunday 1534 Rumiñahui, the last resisting Inca general in the Americas, retreating from the inexorable Spanish advance from the south, razed the city. The dry grass roofs were put to the torch, the stone buildings gutted. Rumiñahui fled to the mountains with the city's treasure, eleven of Atahualpa's relatives and a reputed four thousand women. Robbed of their conquest and the caches of Incan gold, the furious Spaniards slaughtered any of the Indians that remained in the city. Rumiñahui holed up in the mountains, but his attempts to renew the war against the Spaniards fell on deaf ears. He was pursued, eventually caught, later tortured, and finally killed in Quito's main square. But the gold was never found.

Six months later the Royal Scrivener, Gonzálo Díaz, granted the charter, with Benalcázar recorded as the official founder. So it was on 28 August 1534 that the Villa de San Francisco de Quito came into being, municipally complete with mayor, judges, bishops, and a majority Indian population living uneasily under the Spaniards' 'yoke of peace'.

The Colonial Years

The rest of Quito's history is romanticism and gossip. Although a royal *Audencia*, with its own administrative unit, autonomous President and high court, Quito remained an isolated city, ultimately responsible on the South American continent to the Viceroyalty of Peru. It was a provincial city (provincial, in fact, within a province—the Spanish empire) to the extent that for nearly three hundred years caste-ridden colonial life, highly royalist, carried on as if under a glass bell.

Dressed in the fashions of their European counterparts, albeit two seasons late, Quito's dissipated elite led a famous round of gaming and dancing. Supervisory work—farming, sheep raising, and wool production—was delegated to the *cholos*, or mixed bloods; real work to the Indians. Everything was orderly. Quito's gentlemen, exhibiting their rank, were attended by Indians carrying umbrellas. Ladies, in their hooped skirts, were carried in sedans. As a punishment for Quito's sinful ways, one of the snow-topped volcanoes that avenued the Sierra would occasionally erupt, tumble the buildings and bury a good part of the population beneath the rubble. In one famous incident in 1645, when Pinchincha was threatening to erupt again, the nun Mariana de Paredes y Flores offered herself as a scapegoat for the city's vices, fell ill, and died. Pinchincha quietened, disaster was averted, and 200 years later Mariana was canonized by Pius XII. As Ecuador's only saint, she is still a protectress against earthquakes.

The Roman Catholic Church filled every sphere of Quiteñan life. The clergy were extremely strong: they held huge tracts of choice land; profoundly influenced all social and political movements; could and did exercise, through the Courts of the Spanish Inquisition, the rights of life and death; were censors and educators; colonists; missionaries; and, most noticeably today, builders and art teachers—with native artists working under the direction of church-building padres. The clergy transformed the city into an ecclesiastical studio. Quito came to be known as the 'Cloisters of America', the 'Sanctuary of Colonial Art', the 'Florence of the Americas'.

But it was not all work for the Church. Antonio de Ulloa, a man of the world and the Spanish king's secret investigator, reported on one of the busy Quiteñan padres' extra-churchly bacchanals: 'the entertainment is gradually converted into acts of

47

impropriety so unseemly and lewd, that it would be presumptuous even to speak of them, and a want of delicacy to stain the narrative with such a record of obscenities.' Quito's baroque mixture of piety and libido, sin and redemption led the painter Miguel de Santiago, searching for an authentic expression of agony for his Christ, to stab his model. Repentant, he spent the rest of his life doing penance in the San Agustín monastery.

Many missionary priests turned their backs on Quito's society and plunged into the Amazon, introducing themselves to the Indians. They established rest houses along the river and its tributaries where travellers might rest on their passage down-river. The Jesuits alone set up some 32 villages from which they tried to persuade the Amazonian Indians to settle in Christian communities. This early evangelizing must have had some effect. By the end of the 17th century it was reputedly easier to reach Europe via the Amazon, than it was to descend to Guayaquil, run the gamut of fever at Panama, and finally take one's chances with the pirates in the Caribbean.

Independence

Quito was never the same after the French expedition of 1745. Dubbed the Natural Philosophers, this scientific corps had been sent by the French academy to assess the true shape of the earth and so quell a protracted European argument over Newton's theories. The earth was round, but what of polar flattening? Africa was still viewed as the dark continent, Indonesia was relatively unknown, so Quito, the-capital-on-the-equator, was the perfect venue for their experiments. Endless squabbles with the local gentry kept Quito in an uproar, but the corps' calculations of the length of the equator became the basis of the metric system of weights and measures.

More importantly, Condamine and his team of scientists brought a whiff of the world with them. The Old World was undergoing the Age of Enlightenment. France was in the middle of a revolution. Ideas from turbulent Europe began to seep past the Church censors. Voltaire, Paine, Rousseau, and Montesquieu were avidly read.

Quito's first revolt was on 10 August 1809. Quickly subdued by royal troops sent from Lima, all the patriot ringleaders were shot in the back of the head and their hearts burnt in a crucible set up in the plaza. The city was held under iron rule for 12 years by the Royalists, but the movement towards Latin American independence was gaining momentum. Bolívar was leading a successful campaign to the north; San Martín in the south. But the Quiteño house was divided; at least half the city, squeamish at the thought of blood and change, preferred the Royalists. Others, such as Manuela Sáenz, Bolívar's future mistress, were ardent plotters and patriots.

In 1822 Bolívar sent his most brilliant general Antonio José Sucre south, and the battle for Quito's independence took place on 24 May, at 15,000 feet, on Pinchincha, above the clouds. Nothing could be glimpsed through the mist—only when the blue and gold figures of the routed Royalist army were seen running down from the mountain slopes could anyone have known that the patriot army had won. Five days later, Quito swore allegiance and was joined to Bolívar's unified dream-state, Gran Colombia.'

But Bolívar's republic was short lived and in 1829 Venezuela seceded, followed a year later by Quito and Guayaquil. But the country was only a republic in name, and its first years were dedicated to chaos. Regionalism—between the pro-clerical, conservative Sierra and the liberal, trading Coast—was intense. There were civil wars—or rather a series of local battles between rival elites—and a waltz of alternating *costeño* and Sierra presidents through the government palace.

In softer form, the rivalry between Coast and Sierra continues today, filling every sphere of life. In 1939 when the first National Beauty contest in Ecuador was held in Guayaquil, the Quiteños, refusing to demean either themselves or their beauties, sent photographs instead and were awarded a minor prize.

Apart from recent oil finds in the Amazon, most of the national income is still made through the labour and trade of the *costeños*. Through coastal eyes, this makes the Quiteños look like lazy and hypocritical bureaucrats, ever siphoning off money for the capital. But aristocratic Quito remains aloof on its Andean throne, self-important and ever still the hub of Ecuador's cultural and political life.

GETTING THERE

By Plane

Internal Ecuadorean flights are unbelievably cheap and unbelievably chaotic. **Mariscal Sucre Airport** is in a residential suburb about a 20-minute drive out of town and serves both internal and external flights. A departure tax of US$25 is payable on all international flights. *All* flights should be re-confirmed 72 hours in advance, and then again, and again. Some tourist agencies will do this for you. Destinations that have only one or two flights daily should be booked well in advance.

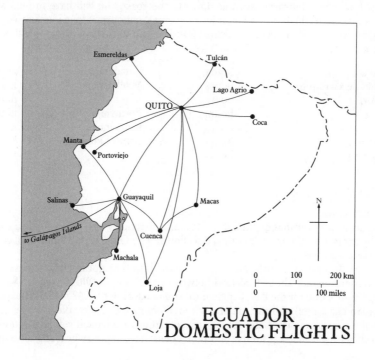

ECUADOR DOMESTIC FLIGHTS

There are TAME and SAN offices in town: **TAME**—Avenida Colón and Reina Victoria; **SAN**—Avenida Colón 535 and 6 de Deciembre. But any good travel agency on the Avenida Amazonas will book you a flight and save you the trouble of finding out which airline is flying and when. There are few, if any, flights on Sundays, except to Guayaquil.

to **Guayaquil**: at least 5–10 flights daily, US$18.
to **Cuenca**: 3 flights daily, US$16.
to **Tulcán** and **Loja**: six flights a week, US$8 and US$10.
to **Esmeraldas**, **Manta**, and **Portoviejo**: daily flights for each destination, US$10, US$13, and US$13 respectively.
to the **Galápagos**: daily flights, at least US$375 for non-residents.
to **Lago Agrio**: daily flights, US$10.
to **Coca**: daily, US$11.
to **Tarapoa** and **Macas**: twice weekly.

By Bus

The **Terminal Terrestre** is just south of the Old City, with a large number of independent companies serving popular destinations on a daily basis. Some places, such as **Riobamba**, have a number of departures every hour—just turn up and listen for the guards' calls (*'RRe-YO-bam-BA!'*). Each office has a board outside announcing destinations. For longer journeys, such as down to the coast, you will have to plan ahead. Below is a list of destinations and their journey times, in hours. A long journey will never cost more than US$8; a ticket for a short journey—up to two hours, say—will only set you back cents.

Ambato	3 hours	Latacunga	2 hours
Bahía de Caráquez	8 hours	Machala	11 hours
Baños	4 hours	Manta	8 hours
Coca	13 hours	Portoviejo	8 hours
Cuenca	10 hours	Riobamba	4 hours
Guayaquil	8 hours	Santo Domingo	$2\frac{1}{2}$ hours
Lago Agrio	10 hours	Tena	9 hours

GETTING AROUND

Taxis and Cars

Driving around by car in the Old City is slow and chaotic by day, so if you have come to Quito by car it is best to leave it in the New Town. The Old City is a small choked area, better visited on foot.

Taxis are the easiest shuttles, and not expensive. If the taxi doesn't have a meter, agree the price beforehand; about US$1.50 between the New and Old Town, US$6 to the airport. To hire one for the day, haggle until you reach about US$25–$30 (cheaper and easier than car rental). All the major car rental companies have offices at the airport, some with offices in town. Land Rovers are sometimes available if you look around. Be sure to check any rented car for its condition: does it have a spare wheel and tools to fit it?

Buses
The buses are privately owned, crowded, and always have space for just one more. Their routes are chaotic and hard to divine. Standard fare is 5 cents. Beginning at the Casa de Cultura and running along the Ave Amazonas are English double-decker buses with routes to the airport (10c). They do not run after dark.

TOURIST INFORMATION
Although Quito's Tourist offices are generally ill-informed they will provide city maps and occasional flimsy brochures. There are three **DITURIS** offices; at the airport, in the Municipal Palace on the Plaza de Independencia, and a main branch at Reina Victoria 514 and Roca (open, Mon–Sat, 8–4:30).

Money Change
Currency laws are loose in Ecuador, so money is easy to change (and many Colombians do). Most **banks**—many doubling as exchange houses—are on the Avenida Amazonas. The **Hotel Colón** changes money on Sundays and is open until 7 weekdays. The **American Express** office is at Avenida Amazonas 339, in the Ecuadorean Tours office.

Visas and Tourist Card Extensions
Visa extensions are available from the **immigration office** at Independencia and Amazonas 877 (open Mon–Fri, 8–12 noon; 3–6). Service can take from 20 minutes to two hours, but first thing in the morning is usually quickest.

Post and Phone
There are several post offices, but the **central office** is on Benalcázar, behind the Plaza Independencia (Mon–Fri, 9–5), in the Old City. This the best place to receive mail and to send heavy parcels (up to 20 kg). The main **IETEL** offices are on the Ave Colón (corner of 6 de Deciembre), at the airport, and most comfortably, at the Hotel Colón.

Travel Agencies
You may well need a travel agency to organize a trip into the jungle or to the Galápagos. **Metropolitan Touring**, tel 524400, at Amazonas 235, is Ecuador's largest tour office and is more of a corporation than an agency. **Etnotours**, tel 230552, Juan León Mera and García, has a list of more adventurous tours and is friendly and efficent. **Galsam**, on Pinto 523 and Amazonas, offers budget tours to the Galápagos.

WHAT TO SEE
The Old City
The Old City is as isolated as a ghetto, basically unchanged and still whispering its past. Two-storey houses built to withstand earthquakes, roughly painted blue or white—some so stained with age that the whitewash has come to resemble dirty linen—lean over the narrow sidewalks. Streets rise up into the hills as steep as stepladders, and give out onto wide, busy Plazas.

During the day, there is an incredible hubbub. Street vendors hawk their wares, anything from toasted maize to boxing gloves. Urchins trip over each other in the chaos. Indian beggars on church steps rattle their cans. Buses, cars and taxis blurt out black

51

clouds of diesel smoke from unadjusted, low-altitude engines. And white-gloved police-men, standing in the middle of this mayhem as self-composed as roosters, wave them confidently on through the colonial labyrinth.

At night the streets are deserted, the cafés and restaurants closed, the shops shuttered. Only the churches are open (after 7.30, sometimes, not always). The sun leaves promptly at six o'clock and it usually rains. The odd car makes mournful whooshing noises as its tyres crease the puddles. And in the Christmas-time air the lights of houses and shanties in the surrounding hills seem to hang between the city's avenues like fairy lights. The least crowded time for a wander through the city is at night and wandering is the only way to get to know it. Purposeful sightseeing is doomed to exasperation.

At the heart of Old Quito is the serene **Plaza Independencia,** a city node and as good a place as any to begin. On one side lies the sombre and unimpressive **Cathedral,** a hodge-podge of architectural styles after successive earthquake damages, and the burial site of the once dashing Sucre. Also facing onto the square are the low-slung arches of the **Capitol,** or **President's Palace,** with its two toytown-esque guards standing outside in blue, gold and white livery. At the time of writing, the Capitol is open for visiting Tuesday and Thursday mornings, although times frequently change; you could look in but there is little to see. Finally there are the **Archbishop's Palace** and a fine old building, once the Majestic Hotel, then lost in a card game, and now turned into shops. Apparently, one president's mistress used to stay there, and spying on him from her windows with binoculars, would interrupt his work at the legislature with inopportune phone-calls.

Three of the streets bordering the Plaza honour sister republics—Chile, Venezuela and Bolivia—and the fourth, in front of the Capitol, is named García Moreno. Following these streets, the old city bucks up into the hills where quieter districts lie.

Rearing to the south of the Plaza and marking the back end of the city is the **Panecillo,** the little bread-loaf, with a huge statue of Quito's curtsying Virgin anchored on top. A ten-minute walk down the rough dirt path that zigzags back into town from the Panecillo takes you past crazy twins on the city edge; the lunatic asylum, barred and silent on one side, and on the other, a noisy crowd of lonely wives haranguing the town jail. The path, now a proper cobbled street, loses itself in the market avenue, El Veinticuatro de Mayo. Left-wing students used to joke, and perhaps still do, that the reason for Quito's Virgin being chained to the crest of the Panecillo was so that she couldn't fly down the hill and join the 10-sucre whores in El Veinticuatro.

El 24 de Mayo was once known as a gathering place for Indian traders, but most have been moved on by municipal restrictions so that now there are only scattered food stalls, some selling roast *cui,* otherwise known as guinea pig. The **market**—as with all markets around the world—is not the best place to flash a camera or other expensive equipment, even though Quito must be one of the safest cities in the world.

The Churches
'It has been said of Quito,' wrote the mocking Bemelmans in his 40s travel classic *The Donkey Inside,* 'that it has one hundred churches and only one bathroom.' Things, of course, have changed, but the churches remain. And whilst Quito's churches are Quito's real museums, they exist not as museums or showpieces, but as places of worship.

The spiritual conquest of the New World required a new Christian iconography to replace the images of Indian deities. The resulting Quiteña school of painting and sculpture, created under Church supervision by Indian and *cholo* workmen, presents a peculiarly baroque syncretism of Catholic and Indian images and beliefs.

All the churches share the same characteristics—skilfully crafted religious scenes detailed along the walls, yards of ornate gilt work, jewelled altars, and paintings as solemn and mysterious as pools of black water. Quito's churches sing, rather than speak, their message, and the total effect is humbling as, indeed, it was meant to be. But the churches that are pointed out with the most pride are always those that were built with forced labour. And outside each, Indians shuffle by, still carrying the country on their backs.

The churches are open in the mornings and early evenings and, as Bemelmans said, there are nearly one hundred. But, to avoid the danger of being 'churched-out', there are three to concentrate on:

La Basílica de la Merced, on Calles Cuenca and Chile, with its domes, great arches of pink and white lacery, is wonderfully monstrously baroque. Non-religious painting was hardly practised in Quito until the beginning of the 18th century, when portraiture became popular. And there is so much religous art in La Merced—at least three dozen gilt-framed paintings from the Quiteña school of art—that it is easy to discount its quality. Paintings by Victor Mideros dominate, and the 14 stations of the via Crucis are by Pinto. La Merced also has the tallest church tower in the city, and the biggest bell. The main altar was carved by Bernardo de Legarda and the central niche is occupied by the Virgin of Mercy to whom Sucre dedicated his victorious sword after the Battle of Pichincha.

The imposing **Monastery of San Francisco** takes up a whole side of the same plaza. Built by Jodeco Ricke, the first man to plant wheat in the Americas, the monastery is South America's oldest Christian institution; construction was begun only three years after the founding of Quito in 1534. Jewelled, painted, inlaid with mother-of-pearl and hung with gold, it drips with fantasy. There is also a small museum next door (open daily 9–11.30; 3–5.30); look for Caspicara's work, especially his neo-classical San Antonio de Padua.

The Jesuit church **La Compañía**, on the corner of Calles Sucre and Moreno, was built by the young Neapolitan architect Marcus Guerra in the 1650s. However construction, in true Quiteño style, was not finished until 1765, on the eve of the Jesuit expulsion from the Americas. The façade is made of drab grey stone relieved with blazing sacred hearts. On either side of the portal are six thick, twisted columns borrowed from St Peter's in Rome. But it is the exaggeration of the interior that stuns. The church is famous as the most ornate in Ecuador and it has been claimed that over seven tons of gold were used to gild the interior, clearly in an attempt to overwhelm and dominate rather than as an offering to God. On the wall, just by the main entrance, is a huge mural depicting Hell, with 'impurity' personified by a monkey vomiting over a naked Indian and 'adultery' by a wolf biting a woman's nipple.

Old Town Museums

Inside the **Church and Monastry of San Agustín** (open Mon–Sat, 8.30–12.30; 2.30–6), one block down Calle Chile from Plaza Independencia and on the corner of

Guayaquil, there is a silent, colonnaded cloister where robed monks plod past oils painted by Miguel de Santiago, the penitent monk who spent his life illustrating the life of St Augustine in the 18th century. There are more sombre masterpieces of colonial art at the **Museo de Arte Colonia** (at time of writing closed for renovation), on the corner of Calle Cuenca and Mejia. **La Casa de Benalcázar** (Mon–Fri, 9–12 noon; 3–6), with its red-tiled roof on the corner of Calle Olmedo, was once the house of the founder of the city and his statue is in the small adjacent plaza.

El Museo del Banco Central (Tues–Fri, 9–8; Sat and Sun, 9–12.30; 3–6.30), at the foot of the Old City, is Quito's pride and has a small but well-labelled exhibition of pre-Columbian ceramics and jewellery on the 5th floor. Some of the jugs have spouts with air holes worked to whistle as water is poured in. Afterwards, go and see the small collection of religious art on the 6th floor. Entrance to the museum is around the side of the building. **The Municipal Museum**, at Espejo 1147, near the main plaza, was closed indefinitely in 1987.

Admission fees for all the above are only nominal.

The New Town
Centred around the Avenida Amazonas—a strip of shops, banks, smart hotels, offices, sidewalk cafés, exchange houses, and tourist offices—the New Town is home to the top end of Quito's bottom-heavy population. It lies northwest of the Old City, on the broad lower slopes of Pichincha. The lifestyle is instantly recognizable—people on their way to and from work, students and university professors, tourists, Peace Corps and Texaco workers, nightclubs, smart cars, embassies and consulates, a middle to upper-class Ecuador, a tranquil and well laid-out suburb; North American, or European, maybe.

It is a pleasant area, but there are no tourist attractions in the conventional sense of the word. However there is one quiet suprise. Behind the Avenida Gonzalez Suarez, below the Hotel Quito, the land drops suddenly into a valley. A statue of **Francisco de Orellana** looks across the hilly pass he took with Gonzalo Pizarro in 1541 on his expedition to the fabled Land of Cinnamon (but which led instead to the European discovery of the Amazon) and **Guapulo**, a semi-rural neighbourhood lies halfway down. A quiet place framed by cobbled streets, the church in the town square has some of Miguel de Santiago's best paintings framing the altar. There is no sense that the capital is only a 20-minute walk away.

New Town Museums
La Casa de la Cultura (Tues–Fri, 9–12.30; 3–6.30) the low, mirrored glass building in a Mexican style on the eastern edge of El Parque Ejido, houses a jumbled (but Quito's biggest) collection of contemporary and 19th-century paintings. It also houses an eccentric collection of antique musical instruments, the **Natural History Museum** (condor and giant tortoise skeletons) previously in the Eloy Alfaro military college, and an exhibition of Ecuadorean costumes.

El Museo Guayasamin (Mon–Sat, 9–12.30; 3–6), houses the eponymous artist's work (some are for sale), and a small collection of religious art. Guayasamin is Ecuador's most famous painter and the founding exponent of 'feismo', a purposefully tortured and ugly style of painting from the 1940s aimed at illustrating the subjugation and dis-enfranchisement of Ecuador's Indian population. A *mestizo* and once radical

Communist, Guayasamin has been a controversial figure: the famous Argentine art critic Martha Traba derided his work, whilst others have slandered him for selling out to the establishment and the international art market. By any standard he has been a prolific, inconclusive, erratic and often derivative painter. See for yourself at Callé Jose Bosmediano 543 in the residential district of Bellavista to the northeast of the city.

Quito's **Zoo**, featuring Galápagos tortoises, condors, and monkeys, is near the intersection of Avenida Amazonas and Avenida Francisco de Orelllana, to the north of the city, with the entrance from Calle La Pradera.

Admission fees for all the above are only nominal.

FESTIVALS
Work in Quito virtually stops at the beginning of December, and begins again at the end of January. In between there are hangovers. The biggest party, when Quito is momentarily transferred into an Andean Cannes, is the **Festival de Quito**, in the first week of December. There are street processions, parties, wandering drunkenness, bullfights (the best day is the last) and open-air concerts. The present-day mayor, keen to impress, has taken to shipping in hot Caribbean bands—Willy Colón, Joey Arroyo; Cuba and Colombia's finest—that play at night in packed but eerie, mist-filled streets. Hyperkinetic Caribbean music is to the stolid reserve of the Andes, as oil is to water. But the two, momentarily at least, and whilst under the influence of a few cups of *canuela* (a filthy good blend of hot tea and hotter cane hootch), do form an emulsion.

SHOPPING
Arts and Crafts
Most of the Indian crafts produced in Ecuador are brought into Quito and can easily be found for sale at only slightly higher prices than in the provinces (but see 'Otavalo' on p. 60). Typical articles—such as chunky Otavaleño jerseys, 'Panama' hats, tee-shirts, wood-carvings, naïf works painted and framed on stretched animal skin, and other knick-knacks (that, economy thrown to the winds, are bought, although two hours later you can't remember why)—can be found in the little shops and stalls along the Avenida Amazonas. Gentle bargaining is expected.

The best and certainly the most expensive artesania shop is **Olga Fisch**, at Avenida Colón 260 (there is also a branch at the Hotel Colón) where you can get anything from wall-hangings and jewellery to painted masks and musical instruments. One year younger than the century, Olga Fisch is the *grande dame* of Ecuadorian folk art, and holds an incredible knowledge of Indian customs and arts. There is a small back room to her store that contains her priceless Corpus Christi dance costumes which, if you are charming or spend enough, you will be allowed to see. Cheaper and also recommended is the **Productos Andinos Indian Co-operative** on Calle Urbina 111 and Cordero. These two shops will give you a good idea of prices should you want to shop around.

Errands and Equipment
The main shopping street in the Old Town is Calle Guayaquil. **El Almacén Globo** (there is another branch in the New Town on Avenida 10 de Agosto Calle Roca) is good for most of the odd bits of equipment—torches, wellington boots etc—that you will need for light expeditions; it is Ecuador's equivalent of Woolworths. **Capitan Peña**, on Flores

200 and Bolívar; **Yanasacha,** at Republica 189 and Diego de Almagro; and particularly **Almacén Cotopaxi** at Avenida 6 de Deciembre 1557 and Baqueadano, are all good for buying and renting more serious hiking and climbing gear.

Literature

For foreign language literature, just off the Avenida Amazonas, at Calle Juan León Mera 851 near Ventimilla, **Libri Mundi** is one of South America's most famous bookshops. With a comparatively large selection of books and magazines in Spanish, English, French and German, what is available largely depends on the most recent import tariffs. It also has Quito's largest selection of books on Ecuador. Open from 9–7 Mon–Fri, 9–1 Sat.

Some of the stalls scattered along the Avenida Amazonas and through the Old City sell international magazines and newspapers; *'Time'*, the *Herald Tribune* etc.

SPORT

Bullfighting, when done well, looks easy and has all the sensuous grace of fluid sculpture. When done badly it is shameful and embarrassing. The most stylish bullfights are always with the Spanish or Mexican bullfighters who arrive for the **Festival de Quito** (see above). Tickets cost around US$3, but you will probably have to buy from touts. See the newspapers for details.

If you would like to make a few passes yourself (and you do!), you can be taught quite safely (the bull's horns are padded) in a rickety 450 year-old bullring at the foot of Mount Cotopaxi, half an hour's drive outside Quito. Phone Xavier Moscoso at Quito 543–405, US$30 per bull, and more fun if you go in a group. With a little booze and so much adrenalin, you feel as though you could fly.

Mountain climbing is one of Ecuador's obvious attractions and there are a number of climbing clubs, both in Quito and the surrounding towns, particularly in Baños and Riobamba. The most famous, **Nuevos Horizantes Club** is on Venezuela 659 and has evening meetings beginning at 7 pm on Tuesdays and Fridays, and will advise on Chimborazo and Cotopaxi. Tourist agencies will also advise. Serious climbers are recommended to buy Rob Rachowiecki's very thorough *Climbing and Hiking in Ecuador* (Bradt Publications, £6.95).

BARS, NIGHTLIFE and ENTERTAINMENT

Quito retires early: dinner, a movie, or the Teatro Sucre perhaps, and so to bed. Most of Quito's entertaining goes on behind closed doors so its nightlife is not the most exciting in the world.

There are some charming tourist traps that host Ecuadorean bands and serve Ecuadorean food in a cellar-bar atmosphere. Starting at around 10 pm and called *Peñas*, the **Taberna Quiteña** is the best known. There are two locations: in the Old Town at Calle Manabi and Luis Vargas, and in the New at Avenida Amazonas 1259 and Colón.

Nightclubs come and go, but at the time of writing, **Vocu** was for young executives, **Gasoline** for sweethearts and a mix of rock and Latin Music, **3.30** for young wastrels, and **Seseribo**, just down the road from the Hotel Quito, for strictly *salsa* and a more humming *ambiente*. The more expensive hotels have discos, which are as you would expect. Mercenaries and Texaco workers go to 'The Pub' opposite the Hotel Quito. And then there is always that strange little wobbly bar on Calama.

Movies are cheap, and show English-speaking films with Spanish subtitles. And the elegant Teatro Sucre often has suprisingly good plays and concerts. The daily papers *El Commercio* and *Hoy* have the details.

All the large hotels have casinos.

WHERE TO STAY

Hotels in Quito are split between the Old and New Towns, with all of the cheaper, more atmospheric and often seedier *residencias* in the old section (with two notable exceptions, see below), and all of the international style modern hotels in the new. There are also, however, some cheaper *residencias* in the New City, which is where you will want to stay if you want to shop, to work, or to escape Old Quito's overwhelming bustle. The best tactic if you have just arrived, as ever, is to check into one of the better hotels, rest and then later look around for what you like and can afford.

New Town Accommodation

You will quickly discover that there are two price tariffs in Quito's more expensive hotels, one for foreigners, the other for locals.

LUXURY

The German-run CEM Hotel group is planning to open a new Hotel Oro Verde (as in Guayaquil) which will be, on completion, Quito's most luxurious hotel, specially equipped for business travellers, with pool, sauna, gym, several restaurants, telex and fax services etc. The Hotel Quito, tel 230300, on Gonzalez Suarez, has the city's best views and is also a social centre of sorts, home in season to the Spanish matadors and their retinues; it has an outdoor swimming pool, and good restaurant. At around US$60–100 it is more fun than the more central business-orientated concrete box, the Hotel Colón International, tel 560666, on Amazonas and Real. Most of the rooms at the Hotel Almeda Real, tel 562345, are in fact spacious suites, good at US$60–68. And the Chalet Suisse, tel 562700, on Calama and Reina Victoria, although in mock Swiss style and used by tour agencies—because they know it to be efficient—is in a quiet but central location, near many of Quito's best restaurants; $37/45, single/double.

MODERATE

The sleek Hotel Embajador at 9 de Octubre and Colón used to be where left-wingers went to stay for a pampering: clean, friendly and efficient at US$20/35 single/double. The Hotel Majestic, tel 543182, in a quiet corner off the arterial 10 de Agosto, is a modern, US motel-style establishment, but pleasant, with clean rooms and baths for US$8/14/17 single/double/triple.

CHEAP

The Residencial Carrion, tel 234620, is highly recommended; it's set back from the road behind a leafy garden, and is geared to long-staying guests at US$7/10. Finally, the Hotel Nueve de Octubre, tel 562424, on Nueve de Octubre, although nothing special, provides fine, cheap New Town accommodation, has some good rooms with telephone (and some not so good without), is clean and friendly and a good choice at US$5/10, single/double.

Old Town Accommodation

MODERATE

La Vienna International, tel 519611, on the corner of Flores and Chile, is a converted colonial house with quiet, dark rooms overlooking an interior courtyard, and noiser but lighter balconied rooms overlooking the streets. All rooms have baths and a phone. Clean, friendly, spacious and very good value at only US$6/12 a single/double. Next door, there is the slightly cheaper and funkier **Hotel San Agustín**, tel 212847, clean, with a more communal atmosphere, most rooms have baths, but no phones; around US$4 per person depending on the room.

CHEAP

The cheaper hotels below come and go, but are all clustered in much the same area. **The Rumiñahui**, tel 211407, on Montafur 449 and Junin is safe, the rooms do not have bathrooms but there is a laundry service and it is not bad at US$2 per person. The **Guayaquil**, tel 511276, at Maldonado 3248 is basic at US$1.50 per person. The famous Gran Casino (Gran Gringo) is awful, the owner a crook (he has appropriated funds deposited for Galápagos tours on more than one occasion) and it should be closed down.

EATING OUT

Cafés

If you are someone who likes to mull over breakfast, read the papers, and really get something *down* for the rest of the day, there is the **American Pancake House** on Pinzon, just a few blocks north of the Avenida Colón. **Manolos** on the Avenida Amazonas is an umbrella'd sidewalk café, always full of tourists writing postcards home. There are innumerable small cafés in the Old City and although a good coffee is hard to find, try a *jugo de naranjilla* (*lulo* if you've just come from Colombia), a tangy fruit juice.

LUNCH AND DINNER

All of Quito's best restaurants are in the New Town. Those in the Old City tend to be cheaper and to serve set-menu meals for around US$2 (*almuerzos*, lunch; *merindas*, dinner) and close early in the evening, not later than 9. However, wherever you eat out in Quito a meal, without wine, will never cost more than US$15. All of the restaurants below are in the most expensive category but, because this is Quito, affordable.

Mountain trout is always available and the *ceviches*—seafood marinated in lime juice and served with a side-order of popcorn—are delicious. **El Ceviche** on Avenida Amazonas and Luis Eloy Alfaro is the best in town. **Las Redes** is the next in line, also on Avenida Amazonas by Colón. If you want to try traditional Ecuadorean food, go to **La Choza** on 12 de Octubre and Cordero and start with *empanadas de morocho* (a deep-fried meat patty), drink *chicha* and fill up on *llapingachos con fritada* (pork with potato cakes and an avocado salad).

The **Casa China** on Avenida 12 de Octubre 1959 and Cordero serves good Chinese food and is very reasonable. The **English Pub**, which has very little to do with an English pub, serves excellent hamburgers. **Adams Rib**, on Juan León Mera, serves ribs of course, and has a good atmosphere, a pool table, all North American style. **La Belle Epoca** on Whymper 925 and Avenida 6 de Deciembre has a good selection of wines and excellent French food. **La Gritta,** at Avenida Santa Maria 246 serves home-made Italian pasta. The **Hotel Colón International** has a very good café and an excellent restaurant, despite the setting. And the **Costa Vasca** on Avenida 18 de Septiembre and Paez has Spanish food with liberal amounts of garlic and delicious prawns. There is a strip of restaurants on Calle Calama, take your pick if you are cruising; **Excalibur** is meant to be good, but the background music and ambience are strictly lalalalalala.

Finally, for a meal with a view at US prices, **El Techo del Mundo**, the Hotel Intercontinental's self-styled Roof of the World, has excellent European cuisine.

SHORT EXCURSIONS

El Mitad del Mundo
'Four Seasons, Two Hemispheres and one Island of Peace' declare the tourist posters. Only 24 km north of Quito, at 10,000 feet and 0 degrees latitude, passes the equator, Quito's most famous tourist excursion. Its exact location was determined by La Conda-mine and his French expedition in the 18th century. A museum and park have been laid out around the monument.

Five km beyond lies the ruined Inca fortress of **Rumichucho**. To get there catch one of the **Mitad del Mundo buses** that leave every half hour from the corner of Calles Chile and Cuenca. A taxi ride there and back will cost about US$10–15.

Pappalacta
These are Ecuador's best **springs**, with a range of hot and cold pools. Situated 90 km northeast of Quito on the road to Lago Agrio, they are open 8–6. The setting is dramatic and on clear days you can see snowcapped peaks looming from the south. There is a small restaurant. But it is not easy getting there, which is probably just as well as in mid-week you could have the pools to yourself. Occasional buses leave from Quito, taking 2–3 hours. Or you could rent a taxi. But the best way is probably to hire a car. Well worth the effort.

Cotopaxi National Park
For a trip to the nature reserve on the world's highest active volcano, see under 'Latacunga' on p. 72.

North from Quito

The surging and falling Pan-American highway runs 250 km north of Quito up to the Colombian border at **Tulcán**. Laid over an original road built by the Incas 450 years ago, the Pan-American is, however, a grand name for a narrow ribbon of tarmac. Neverthe-less, this northernmost tip made the Incan highway the longest arterial road in history until the 19th century; when Pizarro first saw it, it was 5200 km long, with two spans running north and south from Cuzco.

Easily reached on day trips from Quito, the region as a whole is worth visiting for the famous Saturday market at **Otavalo** and, 22 km further on, for the quiet but attractive colonial town of Ibarra, which marks the beginning of the **Ibarra–San Lorenzo railway**.

The highway is now a busy freight route for between Quito and the southern towms of Colombia, and traffic is fierce. Over-laden trucks and over-powered buses swing carelessly around the steep mountain bends; they honk at pedestrians, drive as if to run them over, and chase idle groups back into the side streets of the dusty villages that emerge at every bend. Mountain ranges shelter green valleys, rivers dash through deep gorges, and snow-tipped volcanoes disappear into the clouds. **Cotacachi** (4939 m) rises to the west, humbler **Imbabura** (4609 m) to the east. But it is the massive and extinct volcano **Cayambe** (5790 m) looming above **Lago San Pablo** just 65 km northeast of Quito, that wins the prize for silent drama. The equator passes just south of her peak at the unsurpassed altitude of 4600 m, so providing, as the grandiloquent Humboldt observed, 'an eternal monument by means of which nature has marked one of the major divisions of the globe'.

Although high enough so that everyone seems to live in the clouds, the lake-braided valleys of **Carachi** and **Imbabura** are fertile and densely populated. Agriculture dominates with fields of avocado, potato and alfalfa blanketing the hills in a petit-point of greens. *Chirimoya*, a nobbled green-skinned fruit with a soft white flesh, is a popular cash crop sold at the small roadside stalls. It looks reptilian, but tastes delicious, comparable to a sweetsop or a custard apple.

Otavalo

Twenty-seven kilometres south of Ibarra and 145 km from Quito, the road sign outside the small gridded town of Otavalo welcomes you to 'the friendliest town in Ecuador', which might well be true. Bright, cheerful, confident and worldly, the Otavaleño proudly answers to no one, although history tells us that this was not always so. Subdued first by the Incas and then by the Spanish, the Otavaleños were worked as slaves in the textile *obrajes* of the 16th and 17th centuries; those very same *obrajes* that brought such wealth to Quito in her colonial years. But the Otavaleños quickly learnt the trade and were soon independently imitating European cloth, especially Scottish tweeds. Recognition of their skill at weaving grew and by the 1940s many were making substantial amounts of cash. With cash came land; with land came independence; and with independence came pride and a faith in themselves. The Andean Indians are a telluric people, and without land they are without life.

Otavalo's market dates back to pre-Incan times; now it is the *super*market of regional Indian markets. The time to arrive is on Friday evening and the time to leave is on Saturday afternoon. At least, that is what everybody else does. Trading begins early in the morning, and only fast dawn driving from Quito on a Saturday will get you there in time.

The Otavaleños

In 1941 the arch Bemelmans wrote of the Otavaleños: 'The men have historic, decided faces, and the women look like the patronesses at a very elegant ball. It is baffling that they achieve this effect by just sitting in rows along the sidewalk, their bare feet in the gutter.'

Times have changed. Of sturdy build and aristocratic bearing, the Otavaleños represent one of Ecuador's most remarkable success stories. Known worldwide for the intricacy of their weavings and the expanse of their marketing, it is not unusual to recognize them selling their textiles on the streets of New York and Bogotá, Paris or Buenos Aires. These textiles vary from dark clothes patterned with traditional Indian geometrical designs, to chic embroidered blankets. The women wear long blue skirts and colourful blouses with twists of golden beads around their necks. Traditionally of gold or maize, but more often now of plastic, these necklaces denote wealth. The men wear the sweaters that they weave, and calf-length trousers washed with a local herb to a whiteness that should be the envy of soap manufacturers. Both sexes have long braids of black pony-tailed hair; wear hats whose crowns slope down towards the backs of their heads, and peep-toe rope sandals; have teeth filled with gold and wrists adorned with expensive watches. Children of the most successful traders are educated abroad.

Nevertheless, the area around Otavalo is still one of the purest Indian territories in the Americas and the Otavaleños seem to have successfully bridged the gap between traditional and modern life. Step outside the town and you can find yourself in that other Latin America which thrums below the main square's marketering. The Latin America of traditional lore, ritual purification, witchdoctors and the dream lliana, ayahuasca; the secret Latin America which doesn't reveal itself but has to be found.

GETTING THERE

By Bus
Couldn't be easier: all buses arrive at the **Plaza Copacapabana** and there are regular departures to and from Quito (3 hours, US$1) and Ibarra (20 minutes, 20c.)

By Train
Exact times vary but there are two trains a day to Ibarra; one at midday and another in the late afternoon; 45 minutes and half the bus fare, 10c.

By Taxi
A taxi hired for the day will cost around $50, quite inexpensive if split three or four ways. The journey from Quito takes about 2 hours.

TOURIST INFORMATION
There are no official DITURIS offices in Otavalo, but the town is set up for tourism and many shops even sign their services in English and Spanish. Scattered around town there are also assorted **travel agencies** which will advise and also offer horse treks or camping trips into the surrounding countryside. Some will even change money,

61

including travellers' cheques if, of course, they hold any cash. Two of the many, **INCA** is at Calderon 402 and Bolívar; **Zulay**, which runs very good tours to artisans' homes, is at Sucre and Colón.

The **Post Office** and **IETEL** office—for local and international calls—are both on the western side of the main plaza, flanking the cathedral.

FESTIVALS

Otavalo's best known fiesta, the **Fiesta de Yamor**, is held in the first two weeks of September; there are street dancing, processions, fireworks and cockfights as the Otavaleños flock into town from the surrounding villages.

Between 24 and 29 June, the **feast days of Saint John and Saints Peter and Paul**, there are bullfights, regattas on the lake of San Pablo and fiestas in and around Otavalo.

ACTIVITIES

The Market

Although there is a small market on Wednesdays, and shops open during the week, the spectacle is Saturday morning when all the traders and tourists (especially North American pensioners) arrive. If on a spree, **bring enough cash**—it is not always easy to exchange foreign currency in Otavalo and the rate is lower than in Quito.

The **Saturday market** follows a 12-hour cycle. Indian merchants converge from Peguche, Quichuqui and Iluman during the night and set up their wares. Sales begin with the sun. By 10 o'clock the streets are bulging with visitors—up to 35,000, twice the town's weekly population. But by midday it's all packed-up and over, with only boozy hiccups and drunken staggers to mark the end of another day's sales. Although part of the market is still locally orientated, the bulk of selling is now to tourists.

It only takes a five-minute wander to realize the market's pattern. In a blaze of colour underneath the all-weather concrete mushrooms in the eastern plaza you will find the woollen goods and textiles that have made the Otavalo market so famous: hangings, weavings, chunky-knit jerseys, gloves and socks, blankets, belts, fringed shawls, felt hats and ponchos. Some are still made with traditional patterns, hand-carded and vegetable-dyed maroon, deep blue and purple on old backstrap looms. But powered looms, modern patterns, synthetic fibres and artificial dyes are more and more frequently used.

Bargaining, although hard, is expected. If you buy a number of articles from one merchant, ask for a discount. And if you have come on a large tour from Quito, which you will only want to do if you enjoy panoramic tedium and higher prices, you will have arrived too late! The best choice will probably be already gone for the market is no private affair; it throngs with other tourists and Ecuadorean, Peruvian and Colombian traders.

The **food market** on the outskirts of town behind the cathedral sells household articles: watches, clocks, batteries, radios, torches, fruit, cereals, dark clumps of dried hogs' blood, leather goods, drugs and so on. The **animal market**, just outside town, north along Calle Morales, is over by early morning. The transaction of a pig from one owner to another is always marked by vigorous squeals and snorting protests, so follow your ears to find it.

Museums

The **Anthropological Institute** is a short walk east out of town, behind the hospital. There is a tiny museum of archaeological artefacts and a library open to anyone who cares to browse. Anthropology is a bourgeoning science in Otavalo, a memory of what was and hopefully will still be. After all, the arrival of the Spanish was an education: they taught the Otavaleños that they were descended from Adam and Eve rather than from volcanoes; that God was in heaven and not in idols of wood and stone; that it was no longer necessary to enter the house of a deceased person by the back door, remove all the furniture and tear down the building; and that seeing a snake, thin as a thread and so long that it required all day to pass, did not make it necessary to take to the hills for seven days of fasting before one was purified and could be re-admitted into the community.

If a traveller has any responsibility it is perhaps to impress on the locals that their culture is every bit as sophisticated as his own. Which it is.

NIGHTLIFE

Night-time can be sheer magic in Otavalo. The music of guitars and lonely flutes accompanies a stroll through the formal gardens of the main plaza, and lamp posts straight out of Vienna shed feeble light onto the empty park benches. The Otavaleños have a gift for music and nearly everyone is an adept at the breathless pentatonics of Andean pipe music. Quiet to the point of being closed during the week, the town comes to life as Saturday approaches. The Peña Tucano, on Morales and Sucre, opens on Friday for the weekend, serves long strong drinks, hosts Ecuadorean bands and dee-jayed *salsa*, and on a good night can hum until dawn.

EXCURSIONS

What to do in Otavalo when there is no market, and the town is quiet, even dull, you have just eaten so you can't sit down for a while in front of a meal, the day or afternoon stretches ahead of you, and your book doesn't interest you any longer, is to walk. Ask at one of the travel agencies for routes, or you can sometimes find a *Guida Turistica de Otavalo* in the bookstores. For a four-hour walk, follow the railway tracks out of town, turn right up the stream when the tracks kink north, struggle uphill past the waterfall (**Cascadas de Peguche**), and you will eventually come out onto the shores of the **Lago de San Juan**. From here you can follow the main road back to Otavalo. The lake's water is cold, but you could bathe if you wished.

Cotacachi, is a pretty colonial town 16 km outside Otavalo that specializes in leatherwork. Market day is Saturday. There is one beautiful hotel, a converted colonial house with flowered patios and wrought iron balconies, **El Mesón de Flores**, US$10–15 per person. Buses leave Otavalo every hour from the intersection of Calderon and 31 de Octubre. Most people make day trips.

La Laguna de Cuicocha (3070 m) is a three-hour walk (or you can hire a pick-up) from **Quiroga**, a small village 8 km west along the road from Cotacachi. Three humped-back islands sit in the blue-grey waters of this beautiful mountain lake, which takes about four hours to walk around. You can also camp there.

From the Laguna on, you are in lesser-known country. **Apuela** is 40 km further along a dirt road. The village has hot springs and a basic pension if you feel like exploring this remote area.

WHERE TO STAY

There are a large number of hotels in Otavalo, but all of them fill up quickly on Friday evenings.

The best hotel in the area is the **Hacienda Cusin**, tel San Pablo 305, by the Lago de San Pablo, 10 km east of Otavalo. It is a charming farmhouse with main rooms and upstairs bedrooms overlooking well-tended patios and furnished with period antiques. The food is excellent and horse-riding is available. As sometimes fully booked, check by phoning the San Pablo operator and ask to be connected to Cusin if the above telephone number does not work. Otherwise, write to Señora Crichton at the hotel, San Pablo, Imbabura for a reservation. About US$25 for a double.

The **Hotel Yamor Continental**, tel Otavalo 451, a ten-minute walk outside town, is a large-roomed hacienda set in bouganvillea-strewn gardens. Very picturesque, although hot water is intermittent. Rooms or cabins are $10/13 single/double.

In town the **Hotel Otavalo**, tel Otavalo 416, is a run-down but recommended colonial house on Roca and Montovalo, that fills up quickly and has cheaper rooms if you don't want one with a private bath (US$7/9 for a single/double). The **Hotel El Indio**, tel 004, on Sucre 12–14, is excellent value and has large, light rooms with balconies, good views and a regular supply of hot water, for only $5 per person.

Cheaper hotels spring up in Otavalo like mushrooms and then quickly fade. But there is never any shortage and many are very good. Below are three of the longer lasting: **Residencial Santa Marta** on Colón has large rooms set around a central courtyard and is popular; **Isabelita**, on Roca and Quiroga, is quiet, clean and helpful; **Hotel Riviera-Sucre**, on Moreno and Sucre, is a gaunt but atmospheric, run-down colonial house, also safe and with hot water. There is no one area for cheap hotels, instead they are scattered around town.

WHERE TO EAT

El Mesón de Arrayan on Sucre, is the best in town but is closed during the week. **Guacamayo**, around the corner, has tables set out in the garden and delicious breakfasts and lunches. **Casa de Corea**, opposite the Hotel Otavalo, serves Ecuadorean food and is cheap. **Ali Micus**, in the north eastern corner of the market plaza is a communal style restaurant and the main gathering spot for shoestring travellers. It serves large, long meals. The banana bread is excellent and if you are curious about Incan food, try Quinua, a high protein grain and a staple ingredient of their diet. The **Fuente de Soda** on the market square is popular and serves huge slices of apple and blackberry pie with ice cream on the side.

Ibarra

Ibarra, the somnolent provincial capital of Imbabura, lies roughly half way between Quito and the Colombian border, some 150 km away. Fifty-three thousand people live in this neatly packaged, white-washed colonial town of cobbled streets, wide pavements and gentle mountain views.

Founded in 1606 by Cristóbal de Troya at 2200 m near a small river, the Taguando, Ibarra is one of the most sensibly located towns in Ecuador. It is neither so deep in the 'V' of a valley that you spend all day climbing from corner to corner, nor so far up the slope of a mountain that there is a danger of slipping off a side-street into the abyss.

There is little to do. As with all Andean towns, the good folks go to bed early. And the wildly gesticulating statue of the famous local journalist and diplomat Pedro Moncayo, which stands in the main square opposite the cathedral, is perhaps a 19th-century memory of the last time the town was spiritually or politically roused.

The main reasons to stop at Ibarra are for the Ibarra-San Lorenzo train, as a pausing station between Quito and the Colombian border, and as a base to explore the surrounding villages of **San Antonio**—for its woodwork—and **La Esperanza** for its pastoral relief.

GETTING THERE

By Bus
The bus station is about 1 km south of the town centre; under US$1 by taxi, a few cents on the No. 2 bus. There are frequent departures for Quito (3 hours, US$1.25); Tulcán (2½ hours, US$1); and Otavalo (½ hour, 50c).

By Train
The train station creeps into Ibarra just south of the town centre. Unfortunately, the Quito–Ibarra train has been discontinued, but there is still a twice-daily train to Otavalo in the morning and early afternoon, which is a slow brand of *campesino* fun (45 min, 10c).

The San Lorenzo train (US$1) leaves once a day at 6 am, and is a hairy and exciting trip. You may have to be an astute and charming queue-jumper to get a ticket, so try and reserve a place the day before with the suggestion that you would like to pay a 'reservation fee'.

The train, in fact, is not a train, but a converted a school bus mounted on a railway chassis. With the grace of a pregnant goose it sways down into the valleys through small settlements and muddy railway stations, pauses occasionally to pick up fruit and more passengers, follows the course of the thundering Mira river, and rattles to sudden stops to save the lives of blind cows that have strayed onto the track. The journey is advertised as taking seven hours, but because of de-railments, landslides and assorted dramas, it is always punctually late. Fourteen hours and a trans-section of Ecuadorean topography later, you might arrive in San Lorenzo, and the only way out of San Lorenzo is by boat, or back the same way. It is an extraordinary journey however, worth the discomfort.

TOURIST INFORMATION
There is a helpful **DITURIS** office at Liborio Madera 452 and Flores. The **IETEL** office is on Sucre, just off Parque Pedro Moncayo, around the corner from the cathedral. There are no exchange houses and only **Banco Continental**, at Cifuentes and Moncayo, will exchange travellers' cheques.

FESTIVALS
Holy Week is a big event, but Ibarra's most dramatic annual festival is the rowdy **Fiesta de los Lagos**, on 28 September. Hotels are usually full, so plan ahead.

EXCURSIONS
San Antonio de Ibarra is a small but pleasant town 5 km outside Ibarra, devoted entirely to wood-carving and wood-carving only. The town is overrun with shops: they line the cobbled streets and flank the hushed main square. Apparently this fever for carving and polishing began a century ago when an anonymous woodworker arrived from Quito on a whim. But the San Antonians were keen and—almost, it seems, without exception—eagerly took up his trade.

Most of the work you'll see is only beautiful Amazonian hardwoods turned to kitsch —tortured figurines, anonymous busts, grotesque statuary and replicas of old shoes—but occasional pieces shine through. Try **Galeria Luis Potosí** on the main square.

Regular buses leave Ibarra from the obelisk opposite the railway station. There is one hotel: **Hostería Los Nogales**, one block down from the main plaza overlooking the football field, US$2.50.

La Esperanza is a small village 10 km away from Ibarra, easily reached along the Incan road that continues to **Cayambe**. Buses leave from Calles Sanchez and Cifuentes. The countryside is beautiful and mushrooms are abundant. Try walking up to the summit of the Volcán Cuilche. There is cheap accomodation (US$1) and food at **Aidas**.

WHERE TO STAY
Just over 1 km outside town, on the road to San Antonio at Panamericana Sur km 4, the **Hostería Chorlavi**, tel 950777, is a converted hacienda set in lovely gardens and has a swimming pool. There is also a very good restaurant. Try the white flesh of the *tilapia*, a fish transplanted to Ecuador's lakes from Mozambique. Popular with upper-class Ecuadoreans and high paying tour groups, it is often full, so ring for a reservation (US$15/30 for a single/double). The **Hostería San Agustín**, is also good and set in beautiful countryside although only half a kilometre south of the bus station (US$10/15 for single/double).

In town, the hotel **El Ejecutivo**, tel 952575, on Bolívar and Velasco is cluttered with heavy Spanish furniture and comfortable, although slightly over-priced at US$6/9 for a single/double with bath. The **Residencial Madrid**, tel 951760, on Olmedo 857 is near the main plaza and has clean, carpeted rooms for US$3.50/6. The **Residencial Astoria** at Velasco 809 is popular, central and although not particularly clean is cheap (less than US$1.50 per person), friendly, has hot water, laundry facilities and a huge terrace with sweeping views. The *residencias* scattered around the railway station are noisy and basic. Move a little north west and you will find better value for your money. Try the **Residencial Imbabura** on Oviedo 9–33 (US$1.50 each); the rooms look over a very pretty central courtyard and the hotel is run by a friendly old lady.

WHERE TO EAT
Although hard to find in any restaurant, potato soup with avocado (*locros*) is an Imbaburan lunch speciality, as are nougat (*nogada*) and blackberry ice cream for dessert. Go to **Helados**, on Oviedo near the main plaza, for ice cream, or try looking around the small stalls and street cafés to the south and north east of the town centre.

Ibarra's best is the touristic, folk-band playing restaurant at the **Hostería Chorlavi**. In town, the table-clothed **Restaurant El Dorado**, on Oviedo and Sucre just one block north-east of the Parque Pedro Moncayo, has a large menu and you can eat well for a few dollars. **El Caribe**, on Flores 757, serves set three-course meals of chicken and local fare at a very reasonable price.

The Road to Tulcán

You are only likely to take this road if you are coming into or going out of Ecuador.

North of Ibarra, the Pan-American highway skirts the western shores of **Lake Yahuarcocha**—'Lake of Blood' in Quechuan, so named after the Inca Huayna Capac who reddened the blue-grey waters with his slaughter of the Caran chiefs in the 16th century. A few kilometres further on, the road dips into the **Chota Valley** and the mood changes to tropical. The mountains rise away as dry, grey and wrinkled as an elephant's skin, and the population, suprisingly, is black.

The first black slaves came to the Chota in the middle of the 17th century. At that time, the Jesuits owned immense sugar and cotton-producing *latifundos* in the valley. According to Father Juan de Velasco, the flight of 11,000 Pimampire Indians to the jungle prompted the Spanish landowners to look for other sources of labour. But slaves were expensive. So, in a fit of Catholic casuistry, the members of the Company of Jesus established a breeding farm at the Hacienda Cuajira. There they locked up the finest slaves so that they would multiply and then return with their offspring to the fatigue of the plantations. Slavery moved on in 1852, the Pan-American highway arrived at the turn of the century, but the blacks have ever remained, a displaced slice of African coast in the Indian Sierra.

Tulcán and the Colombian Border

Past the Chota valley and at a chilly 3000 m above sea level, Tulcán is an austere border town that everyone only passes through with pocketed passports and a nod at the graveyard. There is no reason to stay.

A reputation for courage and contraband surrounds the 33,000 inhabitants of Tulcán. Perhaps it runs in their blood. In the 16th century the local Indians fiercely resisted the Incan armies. In the early days of the republic, women disguised themselves as men to fight the Royalists. In the long, forgotten days that followed Independence, bored soldiers with nothing better to do would exchange gunfire with Colombian border patrols, a lethal sport they called *paloleo*. As a point of pride in the 40s, smugglers laid planks across train tracks and slipped past the border patrols in railway tunnels. And during the last uprising agianst Velasco Ibarra, the Tulcenos flung themselves onto the airstrip to prevent military planes from landing. Does it come as a suprise then that the only tourist attraction in Tulcán is a cemetery adorned with painstakingly nurseried, commemorative topiary?

GETTING THERE

By Air
There are daily flights, Monday through Friday, to and from Quito with TAME, US$8. The TAME office is at Junin 315. The airport is a 2 km walk north of town, towards the border; US$1 by taxi.

By Bus
The *terminal terrestre* is an inconvenient 3 km south of the town centre. There are regular daily buses to Quito (6 hours, US$3); Ibarra (2½ hours, US$1.50); and Guayaquil (a very uncomfortable 11 hours; US$6). Occasional buses also go to Otavalo (3 hours, US$1.50).

TOURIST INFORMATION and BORDER FORMALITIES
It is a good idea to exchange all your remaining local currency before leaving Ecuador; the same applies if you have just arrived. Otherwise change only enough money to get to Quito, as the exchange rate is much better in the capital. Men with black briefcases will offer you variable rates of exchange at the border. If going on to Colombia, you will get a better rate for your dollars at the **Banco de la República** in **Ipiales**. In both countries the dollar black market is negligible.

Only Australians, New Zealanders and US citizens need a visa for Colombia and these are obtainable from the **Colombian Consulate** at office 204/5 in the Delegacion de Tulcán building by the Parque de la Independencia. The office is open 8.30–12.30 and 2.30–4, Mon–Fri.

Otherwise you don't need an exit or entry stamp in Tulcán; all formalities take place at the border, four miles outside town. There are regular buses and taxis that make the trip, leaving from *Parque Isidro Ayora* (20 cents and US$2 respectively).

The border is open 8–6 daily, with a one hour lunch-break at noon. Formalities are slight and the crossing is easy. If leaving Ecuador, you have to get an exit stamp in your passport and hand in your tourist card. The opposite applies if you have just arrived.

WHERE TO STAY
It is unlikely that you will spend more than a night in Tulcán, which is just as well as accommodation is scant. There is one good hotel, but it fills up on Saturdays as quickly as the rest. Next to the border, the **Complejo Turistico Rumicacha**, tel 980276, has a restaurant and a swimming pool, US$10/14 for a single/double. The **Residencial Oasis**, tel 980342, which faces onto the town park, is OK at US$5 per person, with bathroom. The **Hotel El Paso**, tel 981094, opposite the Oasis, fills up quickly, has hot water (sometimes) and is the next best at US$3 per person.

WHERE TO EAT
Culinary delights are slim, and your best bet is the restaurant at the **Complejo Rumicacha**. There are also Chinese *Chifas*. Otherwise try the **Restaurant Danubio** on Pichincha for typical Ecuadorean food.

South from Quito

'The paths feather-lined and steep.
Overhead a sky of mud.
Then all of a sudden in the air
the purest white lily of a tall volcano.'
—Henri Michaux

From Quito south to the Peruvian border 600 km away, the Pan-American rolls through the Sierra's inter-montane basins, scattering small towns and villages on its way. You could spend anything from a few days to a few weeks in this area, hiking and climbing Mounts **Cotopaxi** (one of Ecuador's showpiece national parks), **Chimborazo** or **Tunguruhua**; relaxing in the baths at **Baños** on your way to the Amazon; visiting the Indian markets at **Saquisilí** and **Riobamba**; or just passing time in the colonial city of **Cuenca**—after Quito, the prettiest town in the Sierra and also the only site in Ecuador with Incan ruins. The Sierra south of Quito is also the best place in Ecuador to witness Indian life.

For the first 200 km south of Quito, the road passes through a long and gentle valley flanked by two parallel ranges of high mountains and active volcanoes—the 'Avenue of the Volcanoes', so named in the 19th century by the grey-eyed German naturalist Alexander von Humboldt. But although you will see nine of Ecuador's ten highest peaks, the elevated floor of the valley weakens their impression of size and height. The tallest, Chimborazo, bulges out of the plains to 6310 m, and was for many years considered the highest mountain on the globe. Cotopaxi, at 5897 m, is the world's highest active volcano. But the lower slopes of each mountain are farmed in tropical sunshine, and only the highest few hundred metres ever see snow.

Bus services to and from Quito along the Pan-American are fast, frequent and efficient. If you are based in Quito, hiring a taxi for the day is also a good way of organizing trips: you won't have to pay more than US$25, the taxi driver is usually a fount of odd information, will know what to see and where to eat on the way, and his knowledge will be bang up to date.

The Towns of the Sierra

With the exception of Cuenca, the towns of the Sierra are almost generic, repetitions on a theme, with little to tell between them. Try to stop in one, but it is unlikely that you will want to visit more; it doesn't take long to recognize their pattern. Set in the high cup of a mountain valley, their levels of excitement are low. There might be a market tomorrow, a fiesta next month, or a still-talked about earthquake that shook loose half a century ago. Much of the Sierra's colonial architecture has been destroyed by five centuries of tremors and, with the introduction of the concrete breeze-block in the early 80s, adobe houses, known as *chozas*, belong to the past, except in remote areas. Disturbed only by

Cuenca

mists, the standard Sierran town is small enough to cross in a taxi for under a US dollar. Quiet days lead onto the bitter cold and dreamless boredom of even quieter nights. Everyone is in bed by 10 pm. A restful stasis; pleasant for a period, and in its own way.

The Andean Indian and the Markets of the Sierra

Andes comes from *'Andenes'*, a Peruvian-Spanish word for the terraces that steeped the mountain sides of the ancient Indian centres of agriculture. Little has changed in the Sierra over the past five hundred years. The pace is still that of a farmyard—slow. Spanish is mixed with Quechuan, the language of the Incas. Indian attitudes to life remain resigned and fatalistic, a reflection perhaps of the often harsh Andean living conditions. Meals are simple stews or soups with maize, a few greens, some muddy potatoes and perhaps a guinea pig plucked from the hut's dirt floor and thrown into the pot. But while the standard of living is often poor, it is perhaps not as universally brutish as Jorge Icaza related in his famous 1934 *indiginista* novel of the Andes, *Huasipungo*. The colonial hacienda system has been much eroded by recent land reform and peasant collectives. There is generally enough food, much fraternity and, as an offshoot of the above, an intense regional economy: everyday, somewhere, there is a market in the Sierra.

Most of the Sierra's markets are not like Otavalo's—that is to say, for the tourist and retail trades—but agricultural fairs where Indians sell and buy to and from each other, and occasionally, to town traders. Ambato's, although re-housed in modern warehouses, is still Ecuador's biggest regional market. Riobamba's is the busiest. Saquisilí's, however, is the best, and so if you are short on time you should head for this one. Below is a list of the principals and their days:

Monday:	Ambato
Tuesday:	Riobamba, Latacunga
Wednesday:	Ambato, Riobamba, Pujilli

Thursday:	Saquisilí
Friday:	Ambato
Saturday:	Riobamba, Latacunga
Sunday:	Cuenca.

Squatting in the market amidst a riot of colour and surrounded by piles of grain, potatoes and fruits; leather belts, polyester pants and household goods; chickens, hobbled pigs and *cuis* (guinea pigs), the Indian looks like a saturnine medieval page, only with a trilby hat. The colour of a poncho, or of the braid around its edges, denotes the group to which he or she belongs: a red poncho for a Saquisilí Indian for instance, or black for a Salasaca. Come down from remote villages only accessible on foot, the high mountain Indians can be recognized by the many layers of clothes that they shed as the day warms, passes and the drinking of *chicha* begins.

Chicha, described by the English historian John Hemming as 'a pleasant murky drink, like stale cider', is a strong brew of maize fermented in human spittle. On the roads that lead back to the villages after a day in town, you might see family trains of wife (plus a hundredweight of vegetables on her back), children, chickens and squealing pigs, often having to pause while father is sick against a eucalyptus tree. During fiestas and after markets, drinking can sometimes lead to belligerent situations—from which you will have to extricate yourself—although more usually to a roadside snooze. Plastic jugs of chicha will be offered to you, especially in May or June which are good months for fiestas in the highlands, but beware the instantaneous hangover. Romantics who cry 'Lo! behold the Indian!' on first visiting the Andes are often disappointed: the Andean Indians are wonderful and other-worldly, simultaneously timid and airborne, but staying with them for any length of time can lead to a strange species of catatonia.

Latacunga

For most people, the Thursday morning market at Saquisilí and the nature reserve at Cotopaxi are the main reasons to come to Latacunga.

Ninety kilometres from Quito, and built almost entirely of lava foam, or pumice stone, the word for Latacunga comes from the Indian, *'Llacta cunani'*, meaning land of my choosing. A strange choice as only 29 km away, the volcano Cototpaxi has dominated Latacunga with its own no-choice history. In 1742 a major eruption razed the town and it had to be re-built. Twenty-six years later the same happened, as in 1853. After the last eruption in 1877, only the 17th century cathedral remained standing. But each time the undeterred 30,000 Latacungenos re-made their town once more.

GETTING THERE

By Bus

Most of buses on the Quito-Riobamba route do not stop in Latacunga but they will drop you off, or can be easily flagged down, on the Pan-American highway, just outside town: Quito, 2 hours, US$1; Ambato, ½ hour, 40c; Riobamba, 2½ hours, US$1.

It is also possible to travel direct into the lowlands from Latacunga; west through **Pujilli**, up to 3500 m at **Zumbagua** and then down into torrid **Quevedo**; a bumping and grinding seven-hour trip with locals and their chickens. US$2 with Transportes Coto-paxi, and departures all day.

By Train
There are two trains a day from the railway station on the other side of the Pan-American from town: one north for Quito in the morning (2 hours, 50c),the other south for Riobamba in the afternoon (3 hours,50c). Check at the station for times.

TOURIST INFORMATION
The **tourist office** is at Quito 73–12. The **Banco de Pichincha** on the main plaza will change small amounts of cash and travellers' cheques. **IETEL** and the **Post Office** are on Maldonado and Quevedo. The town shuts down by 9 pm.

Apart from the small **ethnographic museum,** the Molinos de Monserrat (open Tuesday through Friday, 10–5) which includes some exhibits on the town's Puruha Indian past, there is little to see in town. But Latacunga is a good base from which to visit Saquisilí, go to Cotopaxi National Park, and hike to the lagoon in the volcanic crater near **Quilotoa,** so salty that it known locally as the 'the eye of the sea'.

FESTIVALS
There are small markets every week on Saturdays and Tuesdays, but Latacunga's biggest and strangest festival, which is well worth seeing, is that of the **La Virgen de las Mercedes,** held in the third week of September. More popularly known as the **Fiesta de la Mama Negra,** there is street dancing, music and fireworks as part of a pagan festival thinly disguised by Christian iconography.

EXCURSIONS
Cotopaxi National Park
'Cotopaxi's shape is the most beautiful and regular of all the colossal peaks in the high Andes. It is a perfect cone covered by a thick blanket of snow which shines so brilliantly at sunset that it seems detached from the azure of the sky,' said Humboldt in 1802, and his description still holds true.

Sixty-three kilometres from Quito and less than 30 from Latacunga, the nature reserve on Cotopaxi is a wonderfully serene and restful place. The park is well organized and, after the Galápagos, is Ecuador's show-piece, similar to the national parks in Europe and North America. There are a large number of camping sites and huts (all free), refuges (that charge a nominal $2 for the night), and wardens to advise you. The park entrance is open from 7–6, and all visitors must register at the entrance.

To get there, pick-up trucks can be hired from Latacunga for about US$20. It is then a one hour drive from town to the **Campamento Mariscal Sucre administrative centre,** which has maps, other good information, two nearby campsites and at **Lake Limpiopungo** (3800 m) a good place to picnic (especially if you are on a day-trip). If you want to ascend the peak, the climber's refuge is 15 km further on, and you will need full climbing gear.

Not everyone climbs the mountain; the area is good for walking, or you can just spend the day lounging. If you want to go trekking it is a week's walk around the base of the volcano. And although huts with cooking facilities are available, if you want to spend the night in the park you must be properly equipped with a sleeping bag and food etc. It was a Don Luciano Andrade Marin who brought the first seeds of the twelve million pine trees that now cover the park's 5500 ha of ancient paramo. But whilst the landscape looks Swiss, with its lakes, pines and snow-capped mountains, the fauna is South American, and hummingbirds, llamas and condors are common.

The climb to the summit is demanding, and takes the longest part of a day from the refuge. You should have prior mountaineeering experience or at least a guide. Consult the **Nuvos Horizantes climbing club** (see under 'Quito') and serious climbers are recommended to buy Rachowiecki's *'Climbing and Hiking in Ecuador'* (Bradt Publications), sometimes available in Quito's Libri Mundi bookstore.

Saquisilí's Thursday Market

Although Sasquisilí is not a tourist market, they do come here. Rated the 'best' market in Ecuador by local economists, it is also one of the most picturesque. Each of the town's eight squares is packed early in the morning by highland Indians in red ponchos and wide-brimmed felt hats. Hunkered down by small pyramids of tomatoes and potatoes—which represent, like a declared bank balance, their wealth—mostly agricultural produce is for sale. But there are also food kiosks every few steps that will sell you, if you have a strong stomach, anything from full *almuerzos* to fried snacks, such as *tortillas de papa*.

GETTING THERE AND WHERE TO STAY

On market days, buses for Saquisilí leave every few minutes from the Plaza Chile in Latacunga: ½ hour, 20c. They return with similar frequency. You can sometimes find a room in Saquisilí, but most people wisely spend the night in Latacunga.

The Quilotoa Crater

The area around **Quilotoa** and beyond is remote, hard and high walking country. In this region Indians tend to be wary, or at least shy, of people who turn up, and you should be self-sufficent (camping gear, food and water etc), self-reliant, experienced in rough travelling and prepared for the strange: there are some radical Indian groups in them thar' hills.

To begin, catch a taxi or a bus to **Zumbahua**, a very small village 80 km west of Latacunga that lies past Pujili, on the road to Quevedo. There is a llama market here on Saturdays, but Zumbahua is also the departure point for the hard (and thirsty) four-hour trek to the emerald lake of Quilotoa (though you might be able to hitch a lift on market days.) Writing of Quilatoa in the 18th century, the French traveller the Marquis de Maenza reported: 'during a night in December in 1740 there rose from the surface of the lake a flame which consumed all the vegetation around and killed the herds of cattle in the neighbourhood. Since then, things have been normal'. The lake however is still an eerie place.

A three-hour walk further north takes you to **Chugchilan**, and beyond that **Sigchos**, a slightly larger village with two buses a day to Latacunga. If the buses are not running, however, you will have to return to Zumbahua. In all of the above, you might be able to scrape together some form of board and lodging by asking around although it will, of course, be very simple: don't count on anything.

WHERE TO STAY

Accommodation in Latacunga is not abundant and there are no more than six hotels in and around town. If arriving on Wednesday, bear in mind that many of the hotels fill up early for the Thursday market at Saquisilí.

The best hotel in town is probably the old **Cotopaxi**, tel 801310, in the quiet town centre, which has rooms looking over the pretty **Parque Vincente León**. You can leave luggage, and the rooms come with bathrooms and hot water; US$4 per person. If full, try the **Residencial los Andes**, tel 800983, by the railway station just off the Pan-American highway; it is brand new and slightly more expensive at US$4.50 per person. The **Hotel Estamboul**, tel 800354, back in the centre on Quevedo and Salcedo, is your next best bet with clean rooms and communal showers (US$2 per person).

Twenty kilometres north of Latacunga the **Hostería de Cienega** is a 400-year-old hacienda, porticoed, white-walled, hung with baskets of flowers and spanned by avenues and beautiful gardens. It was once the resting place of viceroys, then ex-presidents and now tourists. It takes its name from the marshy lake (the *cienega*) that marks a battle won by Sucre during the South American Wars of Independence. There is an excellent restaurant, popular with Metropolitan Tours, who will also book you one of the Hostería's airy bedrooms. Otherwise, phone: Quito 549126/ 541337. At US$15 for a single room, or US$20 for a double, the hotel is 1 km off the Pan-American and there is a sign for the turning at km 72, just south of the village of **Lasso**.

WHERE TO EAT

Apart from the restaurant on the ground floor of the Hotel Cotopaxi, the choice is *chugchucara* restaurants, or Chinese *chifas* (try **Chifa Tokio** at Quito 150). The *chugchucara* restaurants advertise themselves with blazing red-lettered signs and their standard menu is a catch-all plate of roast pork with *fritadas* (fried things), cheese *empañadas*, potatoes, hominys, popcorn, parched corn, a special hot sauce made with the tree tomato and, an absolute necessity, chilled beer. *Chugchucaras* are a religious local tradition and taste better than they might sound.

Ambato

Forty kilometres south of Latacunga, Ambato—the capital of the **province of Tungurahua**—was destroyed by an earthquake in 1949, but was dusted off and rebuilt along modern lines shortly afterwards. A bustling city of nearly 110,000 people and so the sixth largest in Ecuador, **Ambato** breathes the thin air of 2500 m. But, protected from the paramo winds by a ring of black lava-scarred mountains (you can see the ice-cream peaks of Tungurahua and Chimborazo on a clear day), the daytime climate is so pleasant that the city has come to be known as the 'City of Flowers'. Not just a metaphor, flowers are everywhere. The upper-class residential section of town is called *Miraflores*, 'look at the flowers'; and the town's main festival in February is 'The Festival of Fruit and Flowers'.

But all of Ecuador's Sierra is a garden. So why stop in Ambato, unless it is for the fiesta in February or the market on Monday? Most travellers only pass through on their way to Baños.

GETTING THERE

By Bus

The main bus station is 2 km north of the town centre with frequent buses to Quito (three hours, US$1); Baños (45 minutes, 50c); and Riobamba (1 hour, 50 cents). There are several buses a day to Guayaquil (6 hours, US$2.50) and to Guaranda.

The journey to **Guaranda** is spectacular. Passing over Ecuador's highest paved road, the local bus trundles west up the valley of the Ambato River, over the Western Cordillera and through the high desert paramo of La Grande Arenal (4000 m), then around Chimborazo, and back down through the Chimbo valley to 2650 m and the small agricultural town of Guaranda. The trip takes 3 hours, costs US$1 and there is an OK hotel, the **Cochabamba** (US$4), in Guaranda should you want to spend the night. Built on seven hills, Guaranda is nicknamed 'Rome': a misnomer if there ever was one, the town is no tourist mecca.

From Guaranda you can carry on down the western slopes of the Andes and through the back and beyond to **Babohoyo** and **Guayaquil** (5hours, US$2). Or, for an even dizzier ride, take the circituitous road around the skirts of Chimborazo and its sister volcano Carihuairazo, to **Riobamba**; six buses a day, $2\frac{1}{2}$ hours, US$2.50.

By Train

The railway station is near the bus station and there are two crowded trains a day: at dawn for Quito ($3\frac{1}{2}$ hours, 50c) and in the afternoon for Riobamba ($1\frac{1}{2}$ hours, 30c).

TOURIST INFORMATION

DITURIS is next to the Hotel Ambato on the 900 block of Calle Guayaquil; open 8.30–6.30, Mon–Fri, with a two-hour break for lunch at midday.

It used to be quite hard to change money, although matters may now have improved. **Banco del Pacifico** on Calle Sucre will change cash only, **Cambiaria Pichincha** on Darquea and Sevilla, will change traveller's cheques.

WHAT TO SEE

Proud of its scions, Ambato bills itself as the home of Ecuador's three legendary Juans: the journalist Juan Benigno Vela; Juan León Mera, author of the national anthem; and, most importantly, Juan Montalvo. This ardent liberal pamphleteer whose pen brought down President García Moreno, was also the author of the stylish book 'Chapters that Cervantes Forgot'. Montavalo was born in Ambato in 1833 but died, true to tradition, in exile in Paris in 1889. His house, on the corner of Bolívar and Montalvo, is open free of charge to the public.

The **museum** in the **Colegio Bolívar** on the Parque Cevallos has a polyglot collection of stuffed animals (including a six-legged lamb), local relics and a fine collection of photographs taken at the turn of the century by the famous Ecuadorean mountaineeer, Nicolas Martinez—worth a peek and open Mon–Fri, 7.30–12.30; 2–5.

The main Ambato **market** is on Monday, with smaller affairs on Wednesdays and Fridays. Although Ecuador's biggest, and once described as its most interesting, it has been re-housed in a modern and less picturesque warehouse a short walk to the south east of town, just under the hill. One of the main Indian groups that come to Ambato's market are the Salasaca. Plump-cheeked, wide-faced and often wearing three or four hats one on top of each other, the Salasacas are *mitimaes*, that is, a people chosen by the Incas in the 15th century to settle and pacify newly conquered areas. Because of this they do not have a concrete history in the sense of being able to say where they came from nor when, but their music and legends have more in common with Bolivian, rather than Ecuadorean, Indians. Recognizable by their broad-brimmed white hats, black ponchos and white trousers, they are famous tapestry weavers. Their village is only 14 km away from Ambato on the Baños road, and whilst there is no market there, you can buy their weavings at the roadside stalls at slightly cheaper prices than in the craft stores in Quito and Cuenca. Genial haggling is expected.

FESTIVALS
Ambato's famous flower festival, with processions and folk bands as well as harvest festival-style displays of produce, is held in the last two weeks of February. Watch out: hotels fill up quickly.

WHERE TO STAY
Opened in 1985, the modern and eponymous **Ambato**, tel 827598, on Guayaquil and Rocafuerte, is a 60-room hotel and the best in town by a long leap. Highly recommended, it comes with a casino, restaurant and squash courts and charges US$13/18 for a single/double.

In the pretty residential suburb of Miraflores, the **Villa Hilda**, tel 824065, is set in beautiful gardens, has a good restaurant and charges US$12/16 for a single/double room.

All the mid-range and cheaper hotels are around the Parque 12 de Noviembre. The **Vivero**, tel 821100, on Cevallos and Juan León Mera is good at US$6 per person; the **Executivo**, tel 820370, nearer the market at Espejo and 12 de Noviembre, has large rooms and hot water for US$4. And on Juan León Mera, sandwiched between Ambato's bottom-line hotels, is the **Guayaquil**, reasonably clean and friendly at US$2 per person.

WHERE TO EAT
The best hotels all have good restaurants, but if you are interested in local fare, take away from any food-stall or café: *llapingachos*, a fortifying mush of mashed potatoes and melted cheese; *seco*, tasty chunks of chicken, lamb or goat served without gravy or sauce (hence *secos*) with rice and potatoes; or a *fritada y mote*—fried chunks of pork with hominys, wrapped in a newspaper.

The Swiss-owned, three restaurant-strong chain of **Alamos** is very good and serves a mix of international and local food; **El Gran Alamo** on Sucre and Montovalo is the fanciest and a meal will cost you around $8 plus a head; **El Alamo**, around the corner, is inexpensive; and following the progression, **El Alamo Jnr**, on Cevallos and Montovalo, is a cheap self-service place for snacks.

For nightlife and late drinks, try the **Peña Tungurahua Bar** on M. Eguez, east of the market, and open weekends after 10 pm.

Baños

Opinion is divided: some people like it, others don't. But either way Baños is always busy with tourists.

Walled in by mountains and topped by a fleeting cover of gymnastic clouds, Baños is a pretty little green town lying at the foot of a waterfall, halfway between Ambato and the jungles of the Oriente. But as is so often the case in South America, where everything for lack of familiar reference is 'like' something else, Baños looks like an Alpine village, but the international popularity of its thermal baths has leant it the damp and faintly prosperous air of an Edwardian spa. Fed by heated muddy brown water from the entrails of Mount Tungurahua, or by melted snow from its flanks, Baños's baths are not quite the scenic sudsy tubs cut from mountain rock that you might imagine: most have been arranged to look like municipal pools. Nevertheless, following a precedent set in the 1960s, Baños remains one of the most popular destinations in Ecuador. The scenery and climate are splendid, the mood restful. Walking is good, and the town is also a good base for climbing the mountains of **El Altar** and **Tungurahua**; the latter one of Ecuador's most accessible peaks.

Baños is also an excellent place to pause and catch up with yourself when travelling between the central valleys of the cordilleras and the jungle towns of **Puyo** and **Misahuallí**.

GETTING THERE

By Bus

Baños's Terminal Terrestre is on the Pan-American highway, just outside town. Although there are occasional departures to Riobamba and Quito, it is nearly always quickest to catch one of the frequent buses to Ambato (50c, 45 mins) and change there for other destinations.

Baños is also, of course, en route for the treacherous but beautiful road from Ambato to El Oriente. The road, partially metalled, as slippery as soap and sluiced by waterfalls as white and as fine as bridal veils, kitty-corners through the mountains into the jungle. All buses passing through Baños are likely to be full of passengers picked up in Quito or Ambato, and your best bet for a seat is to backtrack to either of the above. Although you can occasionally get a seat from Baños, from Ambato journeys are as follows, with only one or two buses every morning: Puyo, 2 hours, US$1; Tena, 5 hours, US$2.

By Taxi

A taxi to Misahuallí, the main destination for most travellers as it is a good base from which to explore the Amazon, will cost about US$40 and take 4 hours. The views on the way down are unsurpassed.

TOURIST INFORMATION

There is a tourist office on Parque Central (Tues–Sat, 8–12 noon; 2–6), but better information on both Baños and the rest of Ecuador can be had by asking around, especially other tourists. The opening gambit for any conversation is an inevitable dog's nose to tail routine: where have you been? how much did it cost? have you been to … etc, etc? Leading questions such as these can sometimes provide patient adventures in other travellers' blurbdom.

ACTIVITIES
Relax, take a bath, go horse-riding perhaps, or walk. These are the pleasures of Baños.

There are a number of popular walks around Baños. You could try strolling south on the Calle Maldonado until you reach the footpath for the **shrine of San Martín** that tops the the crest of the hill overlooking Baños's waterfall; or walking 2 km east of town along the Puyo road to the **zoo** that, although small, has tapir and rare harpy eagle; or try stepping-out 1 km west of town along the Ambato road, to the **Puente Santa Martia** where the river Pastaza swirls out of the canyon into a huge whirlpool (turn right, off the road, just before the police checkpoint).

Further along this path lies the beginning of the trek to Tungurahua. If you wanted to carry on past the *puente* it would be two hours to the village of **Pondoa**; six more to the refuge; and thence half a day to the summit, which, if unguided, is for experienced climbers only. **Guides** around the area, but especially for the Tungurahua climb, are easily found in Baños and some will rent out equipment; ask at the tourist office, or at the Pension Patty at Eloy Alfaro 554. Siamgal tours are not recommended.

Baños has two sets of **thermal baths**; one in Baños itself, up against the waterfall; and a better second set at **Salado**, just off the Ambato road, a 1-km walk out of town. The gossiping groups of Quiteños, quieting their jangled city nerves in the hot pool, and the rough-hewn Indians scraping themselves clean under the cold showers, make these baths smell of the most pungent smell of all—human funkiness. Open from dawn until dusk, take towels and bathing costumes; entrance costs 50c.

FESTIVALS
The festival in honour of the miraculous Señora de Santa Agua, whose Church fills up one whole side of the town square, is celebrated in October with gales of catcalls, general gaiety, fireworks, bands and processions. On 15 December, Baños celebrates its founding in a similar manner.

WHERE TO STAY
Baños's best, the demi-pension **Villa Gertrude**, tel 740441, is prettily placed amidst lovely gardens on the edge of town at Montovalo 419. It charges US$18 per person and it is best to book in advance. The **Hotel Palace**, tel 740470, is an old gabled house by the waterfall and town pools, has good facilities, charges US$8.50/11/15 and is much better than the damp **Sangay**, tel 740490, across the road, which you might want to use for its swimming pool and tennis courts. Prices are the same.

There is a plethora of cheaper hotels in town. The three-floored **Hotel Flor de Oriente**, tel 740458, above the restaurant on Ambato and V.Maldona is excellent, has big and clean front rooms that look out over the main square, a roof terrace, and charges only US$4/6 for rooms with private bath and an endless supply of hot water.

The **Pension Guayaquil**, on the Parque de la Basílica, is rambling and old, but has good food and a price that makes up for its lack of rooms with private baths (US$2 per

78

person). For US$1 per person, try the family run **Pension Patty** on Eloy Alfaro, near the market. A long-time favourite amongst tourists and travellers, the hotel has clean basic rooms, a laundry service and the helpful owner can offer good trekking advice.

If you ask around you can find simple houses to rent by the month. Try at the **Paisano** restaurant on Martinez and Santa Clara.

WHERE TO EAT
The calle Ambato is filled with small cafés and local restaurants, but for a quiet evening steak for around US$3, go to the **El Marquès No. 1**, just by the Hotels Sangay and Palace. The **Marquès No. 2** on 16 de Deciembre and Rocafuerte, is also good. The **Rincón de Sueca** on Montovalo is run by a German who liked Baños so much that he stayed. Although relatively expensive, the breakfasts are excellent and the menu, with more than a tilt at the health-conscious, has a long salad list. **Donde Marcelo**, on Ambato, is a marker of how Baños is changing; there is a good restaurant downstairs and a balconied room above, from where you watch the goings-on down in the street, with, in pride of place, a long, wooden North American bar.

Riobamba

With just under 150,000 inhabitants, Riobamba, 190 km from Quito, is home on Saturdays to one of Ecuador's biggest markets, and provides a perfect base for excursions up Chimborazo. It is also a nodal point of Ecuador's communications system. Roads span north to Quito, south to Cuenca and west to the coast and Guayaquil. 'All roads lead to Riobamba' declares a sign on the outskirts, and one of the most spectacular ways of arriving there is from Ambato via Guaranda (see p. 75). Unfortunately the famous railroad to Guayaquil collapsed after the heavy rains in 1983 and there are still only *plans* to re-build it.

Life in Riobamba has been peaceful ever since the earthquake in 1797 when the municipality was moved and re-built 10 km away from its original location at Cajamarca. The *tremblores* (little trembles) and *terremotos* (earth shakers) died away. And urban life, rebuilt with squares and gridded streets to a chessboard regularity on the plains below Chimborazo, took on a more dignified air. The capital of Chimborazo province even nicknamed itself 'The Sultan of the Andes'.

GETTING THERE
By Bus
The main bus terminal is almost 2 km north west out of town with frequent northbound buses to Quito (4 hours, US$1.40), and westbound buses to Guayaquil (5 hours, US$1.75).

There are very few direct buses to Cuenca as the road south of **Alausí** is in a bad state. The quickest and most popular route to Cuenca is via the lowlands. Take the Guayaquil bus as far as **El Triunfo** and change there for Cuenca (all in all, about 5 hours, US$5).

Chimborazo Volcano

By Train
There is no longer a train service to Guayaquil, but there is one crowded **autoferro** that leaves for Quito every morning at dawn (5 hours, US$1). The station is near the town centre.

TOURIST INFORMATION
DITURIS has an office at Calle Tarqui 2248 and Constituyente,in the eastern part of town. The IETEL office is just around the corner. You can change foreign currency at the **Banco International** on 10 de Agosto and García Moreno.

WHAT TO SEE
The Market
On Saturdays it can sometimes seem that Riobamba is over-endowed with markets; over-spilling from the newly built covered markets, thousands of Indians fill the streets, pavements and plazas. In the small plaza south of Convento de Concepción you can buy local handicrafts: shawls (*macanas*), embroidered belts (*fajas*), tough woven bags made from agave fibre (*shigras*) and flat-topped blanketpins (*tupus*). If you see something that you like, you should buy it here as it might be difficult to find eleswhere. Combining business with business, some of the women spin thread while they sell to a customer or chat to a neighbour. Leaving their wives to tend the stalls, the men usually take the opportunity to make small domestic purchases around the market or to knock-off for a *chicha* with the boys. **Cockfights** at dusk mark the end of the day's trading; at 6, on the corner of Tarqui and Guayaquil.

Around Town
On Argentino and Larrea, away from the town squares, rests the **Museum of Religious Art**, at the old **Church of La Concepción**. The rooms are well restored and hung with colonial paintings. But pride of place goes to the huge gem-encrusted gold monstrance

80

that has a diamond similar to the one Richard B gave to Liz T between marriages (there is no further connection, apart from their comparable sizes). A walk down Constituente will take you past most of Riobamba's squares and churches. Or, of an evening, you could try strolling up to the Parque 21 de Abril: the mountainous milestone of Tungurahua rises above the small church of San Antonio, and there is a spreading view of Riobamba below.

EXCURSIONS

Chimborazo

'Señor, we understand perfectly, that in an affair like yours, it is necessary to dissemble—a little; and you, doubtless, do quite right to say you intend to ascend Chimborazo—a thing that everyone knows is perfectly impossible. We know very well what is your object! You wish to discover the TREASURES which are buried in Chimborazo...'

—From Edward Whymper's account of his first ascent of Chimborazo in 1880

At 6310 m, Chimborazo is the highest mountain in Ecuador and for many years was thought to be the highest in the world. Due to the equatorial bulge, the peak is at that point on the earth's surface furthest away from the centre (so Europe's 15th-century philosophers were not so wrong after all when they imagined South America to be the lost land of Eden, raised closer to the heavens like the breast of a recumbent woman).

In between battles for South America's independence, Bolívar partly climbed Chímborazo, an experience that prompted his ecstatic poem, *'Delerium Sobre El Chimborazo'*. If you want a closer look at this famous peak, you can hire a pick-up truck by the railway station that will take you to the refuge for about US$15.

The best time of year for climbing the volcano is from June through August, or in December and January. The weather is then favourable, with no extreme changes, but be sure to take top-grade climbing gear. For more information, contact Señor Enrique Veloz, President of the Asociacion de Andinismo de Chimborazo, tel 960916. He can provide guides, not cheap, but fairly priced.

Guano and Santa Teresita

Ten kilometres outside Riobamba, **Guano** is a town of rug-weavers set at the bottom of a small ravine, next to a tiny park that boasts yellow-belled Angel's Trumpet flowers (which they say drive people crazy), and a grove of cypress trees pruned so meticulously that they resemble a rug's high relief. It makes for a good day trip, if only to see the carpet makers. Guano's artisan tradition dates back to the middle of the colonial period when the Duke of Uceda installed the workshops. And even today, the weavers use the same rustic loom; flat with two long horizontal cross bars which allow two or four people to work as a team.

A few kilometres further on, **Santa Teresita** has swimming pools fed by thermal springs and wonderful views of Tungurahua and El Altar. There is a simple cafeteria, but no hotels. A leisurely round trip from Riobamba would take about five hours. There are frequent buses to both villages from the local bus terminal in Riobamba, three blocks south of the main Terminal de Terrestre.

WHERE TO STAY
Just outside town is the luxurious **El Galpón**, tel 960981, a new hotel with only 20 rooms and a first-class dining room. Although comfortable, friendly and probably the best in and around Riobamba, the service is notoriously inefficient (US$20/30 for a single/double).

For long-term stays in town, the **Apart Hotel Liribamba**, on Pichincha and Primera, is spacious, clean and has some rooms set aside as apartments, with attached kitchens. Prices range from US$9 for a single, up to US$20 for a quadruple.

There are several good mid-range hotels in town: the **Imperial**, tel 960429, on Rocafuerte and 10 de Agosto, and **Los Shyris**, tel 960323, next door, are both friendly, safe and clean, with good attached restaurants, charging around US$7 per person.

The **Segovia**, tel 961269, at Primera Constituyente 2226 has some wonderful front rooms, a roof-top view of the volcanoes, and charges US$3.50 for a room with a private bathroom. **The Metro**, tel 961714, just by the railway station on Avenida Borges, is a step into the past and its prices are similar to those of the Segovia.

Residencial Camba Huasi, at 10 de Agosto 2824 is spacious, cheap (US$1.40) and the owner is a mountaineer who can organize trips to Chimborazo.

WHERE TO EAT
El Chuquiragua, 2 km north on the Quito road, is Riobamba's best typical restaurant, but back in town, if you are pining for European tastes, go to the German-run **Restaurant León Rojo**, on the western edge of town on the Avenida DL Borges, which although good, is expensive by Ecuadorean standards (US$10 per head).

The popular **Bistro Cabana Montecarlo** at García Moreno 2410, which has a fine menu and friendly service, is less expensive than it might appear. And for snack bars, Chinese restaurants and fried chicken pit-stops, stroll no further than along the Avenida 10 de Agosto.

South of Riobamba to Cuenca

The Pan-American highway south of Riobamba passes through a deeply rural area and the road is in poor repair, as are many of the towns and villages along it. Ten kilometres southwest of Riombamba traffic whirls by near-forgotten **Cajabamba**. Once the capital of the province, the town was levelled by an earthquake in 1792 and re-founded at Riobamba. The area is still renowned for earth movements, and if you look from your passing bus at the shoulder of hillside that rises above the town, you can still see the landslipped scars of that watershed 18th-century earthquake.

For 4 km after Cajabamba, the road gently climbs up to **Lake Colta**, one of the area's most important historical points, although there is little to see. Local bumpkins will tell you of the legends that connect the waters of the lagoon and its terrible whirlpool to the lands of the netherworld—also, of the junketing students who disappeared just a few years ago and whose bodies would never have been found if the witchdoctor hadn't shown the frogmen where to search! The lake is bordered by cattails and reeds farmed by the poor Colta Indians for cattle fodder. Descended from the once proud Puruhuas, they are now recognizable by their habit of dying the front fringes of their hair a startling gold. Back on the only marginally firmer ground of recorded European history, it was also here that Diego de Almagro tried to found Quito, on 15 August, 1534, as he raced north against Benalcázar towards the fabled Incan city of gold.

Alausí

Eighty kilometres south of Riobamba, almost halfway to Cuenca, and just above the Devil's Nose, Alausí marks the highest limit of the famous railroad from Guayaquil and the beginning of the Inca trail to **Ingapirca**. Alausí used to be a secret place in the mountains to which Guayaquileños used to come by train to cool off. But as the railroad was built around such undependable mountains, and as the terrible rains in 1983 and 1984 washed away so much of the track and buried the railway workers under tons of mud, Alausí's hotels now stand empty, waiting for the time when the trains will come again. At the time of writing the tracks had not been repaired, although they may have been by the time you get here: it is worth checking, since this was one of the world's classic railway journeys.

GETTING THERE
Buses from Riobamba (1½ hours, US$1) drop into town from the Pan-American every hour or so. Occasional buses for Cuenca leave from the main street.

WHERE TO STAY AND EAT
There is nothing luxurious, although for a few dollars you might find yourself in a basic pension more comfortable than a hotel that has cost you fifty times the price. All of the hotels and restaurants are on Avenida 5 de Julio. The **Hotel Gampala** (US$2) is renowned as the best, but you could also try the **Hotel Panamericano** (US$1).

The Road to Ingapirca

(See also p. 90.)
There is still a wonderful journey to be had out of Alausí—a 2–3 day hike along a lost remnant of what was once the greatest road system in the world, the **Incan highway**, to Ecuador's only Inca ruins at Ingapirca.

From Alausí, head for the mountain village of **Achupallas**, 20 km away (several pick-ups a day leave from Avenida 5 de Julio), and from there walk 8 hours southwest along the Rio Cadrul to the **Lago de las Tres Cruces**, a good place for a first night camp. Follow the trail past the lake, up to the pass of **Quilloloma**. Although the trail becomes indistinct, topping the ridge you can clearly make out the Inca road as a straight line through the grass of the valley. The ruins of **Paredones** are half a day's walk from Tres Cruces and a good place to camp. Three or four hours' walking further on from Paredones and you reach Ingapirca.

Cuenca and the Southern Highlands

Cuenca was once Cañari territory. But in the disintegration that followed the execution of Atahualpa and the rape of the Incan empire by the conquistadors, the Cañaris collapsed, as did the rest of the Andean civilizations. Today, only toponymy is evidence of former Cañari greatness. Sigsig, Chordeleg and Pindillic suggest a one-time expanse of tribal empire. But all that remains of the name 'Cañari' today is 'Cañar'—an insignificant town on the road to the colonial city of Cuenca, Ecuador's third biggest and the nub of this region. North of Cuenca, crowning the top of a bare hill, lies the only vestige of Inca greatness in the whole of Ecuador, the ruins of Ingapirca.

Beyond Cuenca, the Pan-American highway is reduced to a rickety wiggle, off the beaten track. And travelling southeast through the southern lowlands towards the Amazon and the pleasant land around Loja, the southern provinces' second city, you feel as though you are moving backwards through history, into a colonial time of small towns, balconied villages and only nominally subdued Indians. A place where time is still like mist, rather than pressurised steam. Beyond Loja, you are travelling in the nowheres, a long way away from the somewheres, indeed the anywheres, which includes this century.

CUENCA

'Of all the earth, as far as I know it, Cuenca has the most perfect climate.
Always cool enough to be mildly invigorating, yet never cold, it is unexcelled as
a place for dreamy loafing.'

—H. Frank, early 20th century vagabond

There is a brisk air to the provincial capital of Cuenca and its 200,000 inhabitants. A convivial colonial town roughly halfway to the Peruvian border, it makes up for its provincialism with a lowland cheerfulness that can only refresh after maudlin Quito's auntie-ness. Chic shops abut onto market squares. Two-storey colonial houses stand firmly over cobbled streets. And sober-looking businessmen in three-piece flannel suits jostle in the liquid mountain air with forthright Cañari Indians, come to town to sell their famously misnamed Panama hats. Despite recent industrialization, feudal Cuencan life is still to be seen.

Ecuador's only Inca ruins lie 60 km outside the city. As does **Las Cajas National Park**—a good place to walk that peculiar, glowing and desolate Paramo beauty. The town is en route to Peru if you are travelling from Quito, and a must-stop en route to Quito if you are coming from Peru. It can also be a resting house on the long road trip from the Sierra to the coast, or from the Sierra to the southern reaches of the Oriente.

In its own right, Cuenca is a pleasant place to pass the days: the colonial architecture is second only to Quito's, there are several small but very pretty museums, what is reputed to be Ecuador's best restaurant, and the weather is perfect, even if at night it becomes a cold city of stones.

Known after Quito as the second home of Ecuadorean culture, Cuenca is nick-named, in a that common classical mode, the 'Athens of Ecuador'. But the town's lazy

84

days have only led to mediocre art and poetry. In a famous incident in 1949 that killed the Lyric Poetry Festival, a group entered a poem by the Nobel Prize-winning Chilean poet Pablo Neruda, and won first prize. So the vagabond H. Frank was right after all.

History

The Cañari, the Incas, and the Spanish: 1400–1550

About the time that Henry V was defeating the French at Agincourt in 1415, the Incas were beginning to expand east into Bolivia, south into Chile, and north into the mosaic of tribes that lived in Sierran Ecuador. Around modern-day Cuenca they met a solid wall of resistance, the Cañari. Armed with only slings, star-shaped stone truncheons and *chonta* spears, this warlike group halted the Incan advance for over 50 years. And although finally overcome by the Inca Tupac Yapanqui, they were so respected for their fighting prowess that a group was resettled at Cuzco, to act as his personal bodygaurds. The Cañari that remained around Cuenca, however, retained a brisk sense of independence.

Cuenca was reputed to be Tupac Yupanqui's favourite foreign capital, and it is thought that he wanted to make it as splendid as Cuzco. He brought the stone road up from his capital in Peru, built sumptuous temples to the Sun, and along the banks of the Tomebamba, in the heart of modern day Cuenca, erected a huge stone citadel called Tumipampa. The Spanish chronicler Cieza de León marched through the place in 1547 and was impressed by what he saw: 'These famous lodgings at Tumipampa were among the finest and richest to be found in all Peru ... The Temple of the Sun was of stones put together with the subtlest skill, some of them large, black and rough, and others that seemed of jasper ... Within, the walls of the Temple of the Sun and the Palaces of the Lord Inca were covered with sheets of the finest gold and encrusted with many statues of this metal.'

Panama hats come from Ecuador

But de León was writing on heresay, for when he saw the town it had already been razed. He commented: 'Whatever the Indians said about these residences fell short of reality, to judge by the remains. Today all is cast down and in ruins, but it can still be seen how great they were.'

It is not clear how or why the city was destroyed, but it might have been by Atahualpa. In the Incan civil war that followed upon Huayna Capac's death in 1527, the Cañari sided with Cuzco-based Huascar against Atahualpa and even succeded in capturing him. But Atahualpa escaped, defeated Huascar's forces at Ambato, and then turned to exact a stiff revenge on the Cañari, ordering his commanders to kill all males. The Spanish were to note fifteen years later that the ratio of Cañari women to men was 15 to 1. So although the Cañari were to be Benalcázar's most faithful allies in the conquest of the Kingdom of Quito, they can only have provided a pitiful force. All that now remains of what must have been a once great Incan architecture are some small ruins in the centre of town, and the way-station outside, Ingapirca.

The Colonial Years: 1550–1820

Tumipampa was ignored for some years following the conquest, except as a way-stop for the conquistadors who came over the old Inca highway between Cuzco and Quito. It was only in 1557, under direct orders from the Viceroy in Lima, that Gil Ramírez Davalos founded the city of Cuenca, borrowing the name from his native city in Spain. Whatever Incan architecture remained was dis-mantled, and the well-chiselled grey stone used to build the Spaniards' own.

Isolated from the rest of Ecuador by mountains and paramos, the Cuencaños developed into a community of fiercely conservative bigots, animated by an intense religious fanaticism and renowned for their intolerance. Their municipal motto still stands: *'Primero Dios, Despues Vos'*—First God, Then You.

The Spanish King's Secret Investigator, Antonio de Ulloa, arrived in Cuenca at the end of August 1739 with Condamine and his band of earth-measurers. Complaining that the town was nothing more than a collection of tittle-tattle busybodies, he grouched: 'The inhabitants here, though of the same classes with those of Quito, differ something in their genius and their manners, particularly in a shameful indolence, which seems so natural to them, that they have a strange aversion to all kinds of work; the vulgar are also rude, vindictive and, in short, wicked in every sense.'

A dramatic murder illustrates Ulloa's sentiments. When Seniergues, the French expedition's physician, stepped into a messy local love affair (although he should have known better), he was killed by a crazed mob at the bullfight to the cries of, 'Long live the King! Kill the French!' His death was of international significance as the expedition was in the Audencia de Quito under royal patronage. But the Cuencaños cared not a flip and even the Grand Vicar denounced the French from his pulpit.

Cuenca remained steadfast in its isolation, unmoved by the revolution in North America, the enlightenment in France, or the rising of Tupac Amaru in Peru. The town even failed to respond to the fervour of the South American Wars of Indenpendence, and was seemingly only liberated by Bolívar as an aside—just a small town in the broad sweep that delivered the rest of Latin America from the Spanish.

After Independence, the Rise of the Panama Hat: 1820–20th Century

Following the revolution, Cuenca continued as before, attached to the world only by slender mountain paths along which had to be carried the whole of its worldly wealth ——mostly on the backs of Indians. A 19th century Cuencan aristocrat historian boasts in his diary: 'I had a grand piano imported from France and carried on the backs of Indians over the Molleturu pass from the port of Guayaquil'. Cuenca's first car was also carried in on the backs of Indians. *After* the first car came a road, but still no great change. Then came the Panama Hat—which changed everything.

The Panama is not produced, of course, in the Republic of Panama. It was merely sold there to canal workers and Californian gold-boomers at the beginning of the century and the name stuck. Cuenca, in fact, is the world centre of Panama Hat distribution, and 'everyone in the trade,' as Tom Miller notes in his hugely enjoyable travelogue, *The Panama Hat Trail*, 'laments the hat's international name'. Ecuadorean consuls were once instructed to attach stickers to all their correspondence, reading, 'PANAMA HATS ARE MADE IN ECUADOR'. But the gambit failed. One consul reported that the only difference was that people now remarked, 'Ahhh. I see that now they are making Panama Hats in Ecuador'.

Straw hat-making began in the colonial period and no Indian in these regions had ever worn one before the arrival of the white man. No one knows precisely how the Panama came to Cuenca, although there is a legend. In the 19th century, following threats of a revolution in the northern province of Esmeraldas, one of Ecuador's presidents, remembering the way in which the Incas transferred troublesome populations to distant parts, had General Molina move his regiments of *costeños* to Cuenca. Amongst these dark-skinned unsoldierly soldiers was a group of men from the coastal town of Manta. As it was their custom to weave Panamas in their spare time, they sent to the coast for toquilla straw—the fine fibre from which the hats are made. Weaving began and the practice spread. By the end of the century over 200,000 people were working in the trade. By the 1940s Panama hats brought Ecuador an incredible 20% of her foreign income, second only to cacao and bananas as the country's main foreign-sector earner. And it was a fortune from hats that fuelled Eloy Alfaro's liberal revolutions in the 19th century.

In Cuenca and its immediate environs most of the Indians own their own piece of earth. Their white-washed homes, made of sunbaked brick and neatly red tiled, are the epitome of cleanliness. All of this has been the result of the independent incomes gleaned from weaving Panama hats. In the northern hemisphere, a Panama used to be a mark of the debonair,but who wears them now? The Panama Hat industry is at a low ebb, returns are slight, cheaper paper hats of a similar style are made in the Far East, and none of the younger Ecuadoreans even wants to know about Panamas. Nevertheless, the best hats in the world—ones that you can fold-up and pass through a napkin ring—still come from around Cuenca.

GETTING THERE

By Air

It is 50c by taxi to the airport 2 km outside town, and there are daily flights to Quito (US$18) and Guayaquil (US$14) with TAME and SAN. There is as yet no SAN office in town, but the TAME office is on the main square. The flight to Quito is meant to have a hex on it. Bumping through, over and around air pockets and mountain ridges, few are those that will travel on Friday the 13th; check your horoscope before flying.

By Bus
The **Terminal de Terrestre** is on Avenida España, 1½ km from the town centre, on the way to the airport. Some of the buses are big, venerable—and slow. So for the quickest journeys catch one of the *busetas*. There are frequent departures for Guayaquil (4 hours, US$2.50); buses every hour for Quito (up to 12 hours, US$4) and Machala (5 hours, US$2.50) and several buses daily for Loja (7 hours, US$3).

Buses to **Gualaceo's** Sunday market leave from outside the terminal (40 mins, 25c).

TOURIST INFORMATION
The **DITURIS** office on Hermano Miguel, between Cordova and Jaramillo, is very helpful and has good city maps for sale. The **IETEL** office is on Benigno Malo, one block south-east from the Parque Calderon. **Money** can be changed at Citibank on Gran Colombia 749, or at the Casas de Cambio around Parque Calderon.

WHAT TO SEE
Evidence of the slower, feudal Cuenca is everywhere, especially by the Tomebamba, the limpid river that cuts the town into two equal sections. Modern suburbs and the University lie to the south, colonial Cuenca to the north. Strolling along the Avenida 3 de Noviembre, which follows the river's north bank, is one of Cuenca's most pleasant walks. Sitting on the river's grassy edges, maids slap their washing against the white stones that lie in the water as smooth as eggs. Peaceful drunks snore in the shade of the willow trees, and the northern banks are lined by crumbling colonial tenements. At the eastern end of the river, against the bridge and just off Calle Larga, lie the city's only Inca ruins—**las Ruinas de Todos Santos**. The site, however, is small beer and the stones—after the ruins of Peru or Ingapirca—lack lustre.

The centre of colonial Cuenca is the **Parque Calderón**. This flowering Plaza radiates from a fine statue of Abdon Calderón, the Ecuadorean hero who fell and died on the point of his own sabre whilst rallying his troops against the Royalists during the Battle of Pichincha in 1822. The Parque's benches are usually occupied by serious young men from the university. Standing and chatting underneath the plaza's topiaried trees are distinguished-looking groups of gentlemen in well-pressed suits. Panama-hatted Indians go about their business. And, as just a hint of the Amazon, on the corner stand traders from El Oriente, selling Amazonian parrots and monkeys from battered cardboard boxes.

On the western side of the park, you can just see the china-blue domes of the lofty **new Cathedral** peeping over its pale pink brick façade. The Ecuadorean journalist and travel writer Filoteo Smaniego wrote of it: 'With all respect to the inhabitants of Cuenca who admire their new Cathedral, I personally prefer the old one. The only adjective which is suitable for this building is undoubtably, "Big".' Opposite the new cathedral lies the old—**El Sagrario**, whose tower was used as a surveying mark for the French scientists' earth-measuring calculations in the 18th century. Recently converted into a small **museum of Religious Art** it is now open to the square and whoever would like to drop in, every morning and afternoon.

Museums

What Cuenca's museums lack in grandeur, they make up for with a soul-lifting intimacy.

The **Museo de las Conceptas**, at Hermano Miguel 6–33 and opposite the DITU-RIS office, was once the infirmary of a convent and is now a small museum of religious art from the 17th and 18th centuries (open Mon–Fri, 9—4.30; Sat, 9–12.30; adm). Most of the exhibits—including a large nativity scene enclosed in a wooden box, with wooden figures adorned in gold and silver brocade—represent part of the dowries presented to the convent by novices entering the Order. The Order's cloistered life of prayer, silence and abstinence carries on next door, the nuns still subject to the strict rules laid down by Pope Julius II in the 16th century. However, they do make excellent chocolate, almost pure cocoa, and this one indulgence is for sale in the arcaded shops outside the museum. Cuenca's **Museum of Modern Art** is also housed in a former religious retreat, on Sucre and Coronel Talbot (open Mon–Fri, 8–12.30 and 2.30–6.30; adm). Most of the exhibitions are touring shows; many are very good. The area around the Museum is slowly turning into a bohemian quarter.

The municipial **Museo de Banco Central** on Calle Larga and Av Huayna Capac, has a very poorly displayed and lifeless selection of archaeological artefacts. The anonymous building has also unfortunately absorbed the eccentric collection of Padre Crespi. A piece of local colour, Crespi believed that the first Ecuadoreans were in fact Phoenicians and other Mediterraneans who came to Cuenca via the Amazon River and its tributaries in the first millennium. He supported his theory with exhibits of Pharaonic chairs and Babylonian statues which he maintained had been gathered in expeditions to the jungle. Since his death in 1982, his collection has been boxed and put away into the dusty corners of the Museo El Banco Central, perhaps never to be seen again. The **Museum of Popular Art**, just off the steps that lead down to the river from Calle Larga, around the corner from Crespi's closed museum, has a permanaent collection of South American *artesania* (open Mon–Fri, 8.30–12.30; 2.30–6.30; adm).

SHOPPING

Most of the craftware shops are on Ave Gran Colombia, near the Hotel El Dorado. High quality **Panamas** can be found at **Homero Ortega**, on Vega Munoz 9–33, and at the shop on the corner of Cordova, at Tarqui 6–93.

Markets

Market day in Cuenca is Thursday, with small markets scattered around the city, each one named for the street on which it takes place. The market on 3 Noviembre, for instance, sells fruits, while that on 12th April has baskets and sweaters. There is a general market in the Plaza Rotary.

FESTIVALS

Independence day is 3 November, which combines with All Saints' and All Souls' Days on the 1st and 2nd, for a *Gran Fiesta*. Celebrations are also notoriously extravagant on Christmas and New Year's Eves when there is much throwing of water bombs, burning of symbolic effigies (some political, others fictional), drinking and eating, drinking and dancing, drinking and fireworks and drinking and singing.

WHERE TO STAY

All of Cuenca's hotels are conveniently located in the colonial section. Overlooking the River Tomebamba, at Calle Larga 7–93 rests a Cuencan institution, the excellent **Hotel Crespo**, tel 835984. The building is lovely and the hotel has a wide selection of rooms ranging from those with river views (at US$20/30 a single/double) to cheaper beds in an annex across the road at around US$6/8. The hotel also organizes trips into the jungle.

If you would rather stay outside town, in a lovely Swiss-run hotel overlooking a lake, try the expensive **Hotel La Laguna**, tel 31200, US$40 per room.

Cuenca's most efficient, and hence most highly starred (and so over-priced) hotel is the **El Dorado**, tel 831390, on Gran Colombia and Luis Cordero; it has a casino, a sauna and a swimming-pool for around US$25 a single and US$30 a double. The **International Hotel Paris**, tel 827181, at Sucre 6–78 is just off the Parque Calderon, has an eastern-European style restaurant, is very good and charges US$11/16 a single/double.

The **Hotel Las Americas**, tel 831160, at Mariano Cueva 13–59, although a little bit out of the way, is friendly and helpful and has a fine, even if standard, attached restaurant. Try to get one of the rooms with windows (US$5/7). The **Hotel Alli-Tiana**, tel 830844, on Presidente Córdova and Padre Aguirre, is slightly over-priced at US$6.50 per person, but has bright rooms, some with balconies, and a discotheque at weekends. Opposite, the **Hotel Milan**, tel 828104, is very popular with travellers and has some very good rooms with bath and phone for only US$3 per person.

The **Gran Hotel** on Torres, between Bolívar and Gran Colombia, has rooms with private bath, that look onto a big, quiet,covered courtyard (US$3/8). The **Residencial Inca** at Torres 8–42, is recommended as a converted colonial house with creaking walkways, clean simple rooms, and occasional hot water for US$2/4.

WHERE TO EAT

It is open to debate but the **Restaurant El Jardín**, on Presidente Córdova, has been described as the best restaurant in Ecuador with a nouvelle cuisine menu; very reasonable at only US$10 per head. There are a couple of Italian restaurants—**La Tuna** and **La Pizzeria**—on Avenida Colombia, opposite the Hotel El Dorado. The **El Dorado**, in its own turn, has two large restaurants with international menus for lunch and supper, and also very good breakfasts. **El Fogón**, on España 2472, serves Argentine-sized steaks, whilst **El Paraíso**, on the third floor of the building at Ordonez 1023, serves vegetarian food.

EXCURSIONS

Ingapirca

A two-hour trip north of Cuenca, and 10 km off the Pan-American road, lies the only vestige of Inca greatness in the whole of Ecuador, the lovely but enigmatic ruins of Ingapirca.

But the ruin is a ruin without folklore and its name gives no indication of what it once was: Ingapirca simply means 'the Inca's wells'. And that no one really knows what Ingapirca is about makes it all the more tantalizing, especially for archaeologists and tour agencies. The presence of granaries suggests that at the very least it was a way-station, or *tampu*, for chieftains and their subordinates as they travelled the conquering road from

Cuzco to Quito. But the recent excavation of chambers that would typically have been used by the Inca, his harem and the upper-class echelons of Incan nobles and priests, indicates that it also had a ceremonial significance. The site was sensitively chosen. When the sun shines, shadows seem to mark off important areas, and standing on Ingapirca's high perch you can see the stretching valleys transformed into a series of tigers' backs—religious in their beauty, if nothing else.

Built between 1450 and 1485 by the Incas in collaboration with the Cañaris, the stonework is typically precise: although mortarless, it is impossible to insert a knife blade between two stones. There are two distinct sites. First a main structure, the ceremonial-looking, elliptical *usnu*, which has a number of trapezoidal arches (the hallmark of Incan construction); and secondly, surrounding it, a low grouping of grassed-over terraced walls, the work of the Cañari, now grazed by skittish llamas.

Unlike Machu Picchu, the ruins have never been lost and La Condamine even drew plans of the site back in 1739. But what is interesting is the site's three layers of religious history. When the Incas arrived, they built on top of Cañari's ceremonial structures as a means of imposing their religion. When the Spanish arrived they, in their own turn, built a small church on top of the Incan structures. Ecuador's present continues to smear itself over the past. Even the great Incan road that used to pass by has been destroyed by local house builders, and you can see that perfect Incan stone incorporated into their homes.

GETTING THERE
The easiest way to get to Ingapirca is from Cuenca by taxi, which will cost about US$20 for the day trip. (See also the walk described on p. 83). To get there by bus is tricky; you have to catch a bus to Cañar—1½ hours and 45c. From there either improvise a lift or walk 15 km to the site (don't get stuck at the site without transport). If you do go by taxi, you can make a short stop on the way back at Biblían whose Walt Disneyish-looking pilgrimage cathedral is cut high into the rocks above the town. The view from the church is worth a climb up the stairs. On September 8 there is a fiesta to celebrate the day of Our Lady of the Dew.

TOURIST INFORMATION
There is a small museum just by the site and a shelter with basic toilet facilites and benches. Guides are available. There is no restaurant.

Las Cajas National Park
Thirty kilometres northwest of Cuenca and at 4200 m , the paramos at Las Cajas make for wild hiking country. The best time to visit is in the mornings—before the afternoon mists rise. The park is administered by the **Ministerio de Agricultura y Ganaderia**, which has offices in downtown Cuenca, on Bolívar and Hermano Miguel, and they can provide you with information, maps and a permit (US$1). You can camp—but take good equipment—or just visit for a day in a taxi (US$15 for the trip there and back). Buses from Cuenca leave from the Plaza San Sebastián early in the morning, by the Modern Art Museum, and there are return trips in the afternoon.

Gualacéo, Chordeleg and Sigsig
These three, adjacent colonial villages just outside Cuenca all have **Sunday markets**. If you left Cuenca in the morning you could easily visit all three and be back in town by the

afternoon. **Chordeleg's** market specialises in textiles and jewellery; **Gualcéo's** in agricultural produce; and **Sigsig's** is interesting because it is off the beaten track. Buses from Cuenca leave for Gualacéo every few minutes on market days; from Gualcéo you can walk the 2km to Chordeleg; and there are hourly buses that will take you on the 40 minute ride from Chordeleg to Sigsig. There are regular return buses from Sigsig to Cuenca.

Baths
There are two good sets of hot sulphur baths 5 km south of Cuenca, US$2 by taxi, or 20c if you flag down one of the buses that pass by on the Ave 9 de Octubre and ask for Baños. One of the baths is rather municipal (open 5–5); the other is for the exclusive use of guests staying at the plush Hosteria Duran (US$20/28 for a single/double).

South from Cuenca

Twenty kilometres south of Cuenca the Pan-American forks at **Cumbe**. The right-hand fork heads west along a good road to Machala and is the quickest route to Peru. The left-hand fork meanders south-east through the dry and dusty, but beautiful, provinces of **Zamora** and **Loja**, eventually reaching the Peruvian border at the one-horse border town of **Macará**. This section begins with a description of the latter, longer and more scenic route, and finishes with details of the former.

On the road to Loja

It is a seven-hour bus journey from Cuenca to Loja and at around the halfway mark, just as you begin the descent from high paramo, you pass through Saraguro country. The Saraguros are Ecuador's most southern Indian community, and wear distinctive broad-brimmed hats and black clothes, fastened across the breast with silver tupu pins. Legend has it that they wear black in eternal mourning for the death of Atahualpa. The Saraguros were one of the first communites to receive a *Cedula Real*, a Royal Certificate that assigned the ownership of land to its community members. Because of this, the Saraguros were freed of the yoke of *haciendas*, and they developed instead into a community of independent farmers, each working his own parcel of land. Consequently, their culture is still intact. Famed horsemen and cattle breeders (in essence, they are sub-tropical cowboys) the Saraguro population now exceeds 20,000. But living as they do in such a quiet corner of Ecuador, they remain almost unknown to the rest of the country.

The road to Loja rolls down and south through a landscape dotted with carob and cotton-silk trees, along the colonial route of the *mitayos*, the forced labourers that were carried off to die in the gold mines of the Zamora, east of Loja.

Loja

Loja lies buried in the Andes, exactly on the fourth parallel south, in the catchment of the Malacatos and Zamora rivers. These break through a canyon of the eastern cordillera to flow into the Amazon basin.

When Antonio de Ulloa visited in the 18th century, he found the town pleasant enough. Loja, he said, resembles 'in extent and the form of its buildings, the city of Cuenca; but the temperature of the air is considerably hotter'. Don't believe him; the weather is merely warm.

With a population of nearly 80,000 and standing at an altitude of 2225 m, Loja was a once important town, but now it's lost in the blue beyond. There is little to see or do, except keep on travelling: either into the jungle, or south along the scenic road to Peru. But the countryside is pleasant, there is a distant purity to the people, and just outside town lies the idyliic village of **Vilcabamba**. Although on first impression this might seem suprising, Loja even takes its own fair slice of world history.

GETTING THERE

By Air
La Tola airport is 30 km outside town, and you will need to leave town at dawn to catch one of the daily morning flights to Quito (US$10) or Guayaquil (US$11). TAME has an office at the centre of Loja's main square.

By Bus
Loja is a long way from everywhere and bus journeys are lengthy. Buses leave from a number of depots, loosely strung out along the Ave Lauro Guerrero east of the river. There are: four daily buses to Quito (18 hours, US$5), Macará (7 hours, US$2) and Machala (8 hours, US$2.50); seven daily buses to Cuenca (7 hours, US$3) and five buses daily to Guayaquil (11 hours, US$3.50). It is best to book your seat at the terminal the day before departure.

There are regular buses everyday to Vilcabamba.

TOURIST INFORMATION
The **DITURIS** office is on the main square, on the second floor of the **Post Office**. You can change cash dollars at the **Banco Central**, on Sucre and Antonio Eguiguren, but traveller's cheques might be harder. There are markets on the weekends.

History

Loja's history is one of stop and go. In ancient times it was an important trading town on the old Inca road that ran northwards to Cuenca and Quito. (But by 1600, like the rest of the Incan systems, it was abandoned.) Shortly after the conquest, gold deposits were found in the surrounding hills near Zamora and Loja's fortunes took an upswing. (But the veins were quickly mined-out or, even worse, buried under a mountain of Quiteñan litigation, leaving Loja again to become just another small colonial town on the way to the Amazon). Finally, in 1650, quinine was discovered and Loja became, for Europeans at least, one of the most important geographical spots in South America; home of the magical powder that cures malaria.

The chroniclers describe the discovery of quinine in the following fashion:

In late 1631, the viceroy Fernandez de Cabrera had arrived in Lima with his young, beautiful second wife, Doña Francisca. They had disembarked at Paita in Peru, to avoid attacks by pirates, but instead had been beset about by mosquitoes. Now the countess was dying of malaria. The Viceroy's physician, Dr Juan Vega—'one of the shining lights of a science which teaches how to kill by prescription'—had tried all his arts, but in vain. The bells of Lima on that afternoon in 1631 began to toll a dreadful knell.

At this point a Jesuit, carrying a jar of russet-coloured liquid, asked to be admitted to the Doña's room. The rouged infusion of cichona bark, as bitter as gall, was given to her. Within hours her fever had dropped, and two days later, when she was fully cured, she vowed to take the bark back home to alleviate the sufferings of the multitudes of Europe. Shortly afterwards however, while passing through Cartagena on her way back to Spain, she caught the Black Death and died.

Quinine became a Jesuit monopoly, and the medicine was known as the 'Jesuits' Bark'. Protestants, of course, would have none of it.

Loja continued to loom large in the botanical and medical worlds. In 1737, La Condamine came to find out more about the tree. Humboldt visited later, in 1802, as did the Colombian savant, José de Caldas. Sagacious Humboldt prophesised that this 'highly esteemed product of the New World will be swept from the country'. And he was right. By the mid-19th century Europe, but especially England, was expanding again into the tropical world, and its soldiers, planters and colonizers needed quinine to combat the fevers. The Andean republics were inefficient in their distribution of the drug, trade was frequently disrupted by internal and external squabbling and, even worse, the Ecuadoreans adulterated the quinine, freely mixing it with the reddish bark of other trees. England couldn't wait; Queen Victoria gave Sir Clement Markham a commission to take quinine seedlings out of South America. And by 1875 the Dutch East Indies and parts of India were producing quinine on plantations under the supervision of botanists, with chemists in abundance. Loja slipped back into the forgetfulness of the centuries.

WHERE TO STAY

Loja's best hotel is the **Imperial** at Sucre 9–45 (US$8–12). The **Hotel Río Amazonas**, on Kennedy and 10 de Agosto, west of the river, is good value and has clean rooms with private bath, phone, TV and the use of a restaurant for only US$4–6.

Most of the cheap hotels are on the waterfront, taking up the three blocks between Rocafuerte and Antonio Eguiguren. Look around for what takes your fancy, each offers much the same, although the **Miraflores** has been recommended.

WHERE TO EAT

There is only one restaurant of note in town: **El Mesón Andaluz**, on Bolívar and Eguiguren. Try the *repe lojano*, a local cheese and plantain soup. As for the rest ... they say that the Lojano that doesn't strum or sing is in a bad way, and so many bars and restaurants keep guitars behind the counter for those that want to use them. This isn't food, but it is nourishing.

Vilcabamba

When a certain suspicious doctor decided to figure out the the age of the old in Vilcabamba and found out that their average age was nearly one hundred, the international press headlined that the Valley of Eternal Life had been discovered. Although the tickler with the scythe still comes round, Vilcabamba is a dreamy place, good for walks and loafing, with a perfect climate that never leaves the temperate boundaries of 17–26°C.

GETTING THERE
Buses leave from and for Loja every hour. The journey takes about one hour and costs 45c.

WHERE TO STAY
In town there is the cheap, basic but comfortable **Hotel Valle Sagrado** (about US$2 per person). On the edge of town is the **Parador Turistico** with a restaurant and bar (US$6), and two kilometres outside town you will find **Madre Tierra** (Mother Earth), which has cabins, horses for hire, full board with home grown food, in a beautiful spot, also very welcoming, blissful at about US$7 per person.

The Peruvian Border via Loja and Macará

As you approach the Peruvian border you enter cocaine country. Rich from the paste smuggled up on the Calvas River, this area of Ecuador has more Mercedes Benzes than any other, more new houses, and also more small towns that carry the tell-all nickname of 'White City'. But that was in the boom years of 1970s and so who knows now?

Macará

The faster and more convenient coastal route carries nearly all the international traffic between Ecuador and Peru, so Macará is a small, dusty and unimportant border town. The main advantage of the route through Macará is the scenic road from Loja.

GETTING THERE
There are daily buses to Loja, Machala, Guayaquil, and Quito, but the the journeys all take at least 7 hours, so it is best to break at Loja.

WHERE TO STAY
The best hotel in Macará is the **Parador Turistico** on the outskirts, towards the border. It has a restaurant and clean rooms with baths for US$4/6 a single/double. The **Hotel Guayaquil**, on the other side of town, is the best of the cheapies.

Crossing the Border
The town is about one hour's walk from the border at the Río Macará with pick-ups leaving from Macara's market once or twice an hour. The border is open at irregular

hours, but generally in the mornings and afternoons. The officials are bored and formalities are relaxed. If you need a visa for Peru, there is a consulate in Macará, on Bolívar, open from 9–1, Monday through Friday.

The Main Peruvian Border Crossing via Machala and Huaquilas

Ecuador's main border route to Peru is through **Huaquillas**. But eighty kilometres back—in prime banana country—the bigger town of Machala is a better base from which to cross the border: it is cleaner, better supplied and there are a number of hotels (as opposed to in Huaquillas).

Machala

Machala handles most of the traffic between Ecuador and Peru and although a major port, it is not an attractive town, so you will probably just be passing through. There is a consulate for those that need a Peruvian visa—at present, for those travelling on French, Australian or New Zealand passports.

TOURIST INFORMATION
The **DITURIS office** is on the corner of Tarqui and Primera Constituyente. The **Peruvian consulate** is at the corner of Ave 3a Sur, on Pichincha and Guyas. The **Banco del Pacifico**, on Rocafuerte and Tarqui, will change bank notes as well as traveller's cheques. If you would like to go to the **beach**, hire a motorized canoe from the old pier in Puerto Bolívar to Playa Jambeli; the return trip through mangrove swamps will cost you about US$10.

GETTING THERE
By Air
There are flights to Guayaquil every morning except Sundays (US$8). From Guayaquil you can easily catch the Quito shuttle and so arrive at the capital on the same day.

By Bus
From the corner of Guayas and Bolívar, there are frequent buses to Huaquillas (2 hours, US$1). Have your passport ready for the checkpoints along the way.

From the bus depots around Ave 9 de Octubre and Colón, there are frequent departures for Guayaquil (3½ hours, US$2), Loja (7 hours, US$3) and Cuenca (5 hours, US$2.50).

WHERE TO STAY AND EAT
For slightly worn luxury, go to the **Hotel Rizzo**, tel 9921511, on Guayas and Bolívar. It has a swimming pool and a casino and charges US$13/20 for a single/double. **El Oro**, tel 922408, on Sucre and Juan Montovalo, has an excellent restaurant and good rooms for US$9/14 a single/double. The **Residencial La Delicia** on Montovalo and Roca-fuerte is safe, has clean rooms and charges around US$3 per person.

All the best hotels have good restaurants and there are some fine sea food restaurants on the waterfront.

Huaquillas

No more than a dusty one-street town next to the Peruvian border Huaquillas is an unpleasant place to linger.

GETTING THERE
There are frequent buses to Machala (2 hours, US$1), and from there connections to the rest of the country.

WHERE TO STAY
If you should need to spend the night here, try the DITURIS-run **Parador Turistico Huaquillas**, 1½ km south of town, US$5/8 for a single/double. In town, the best of the cheapies is the **Residencial Bucanero, US$2 per person.**

Crossing the border

When leaving Ecuador it is best to get rid of your sucres and arrive in Peru with dollars. To leave Ecuador you will need an exit stamp from the immigration office on the main drag, 200 m before the bridge. You will be directed there by *gamines* eager to carry your luggage and it is open every day, 8–12 noon; 2–5. On the other side of the bridge, there are buses and taxis that will take you to Peruvian Immigration, 3 km further on. All very simple, although sometimes a few hundred sucres can speed up the visa-stamping arm of the border officials.

Part V

THE WESTERN LOWLANDS

Economists used to describe Ecuador as a poor man sitting on a treasure chest, but without a key. The key was a road system. The treasure was a world's worth of agricultural produce, with temperate products from the Sierra complementing tropical goods from the coast. With Ecuador's new-found oil wealth, many new roads have been built, linking the Sierra and the coast, and they web the western lowlands. With the exception of the remarkable nature reserve/hotel at **'Tinalandia'** outside **Santo Domingo**, you will probably only be passing through this area.

Santo Domingo de los Colorados

A commercial centre grown from nothing on the back of Ecuador's banana exports and since gone into decline, Santo Domingo has a dispiriting featurelessness about it. Were it not for the highway linking Quito and the Pacific, it is doubtful whether the town would now exist.

Long before the road to Quito had been built, the land that surrounded it belonged to the Colorados, an Indian tribe of uncertain origins. With the push of white settlers west from Quito, the fate of these Indians followed a familiar cycle of subjugation and cross breeding. In the 1970s the local government decreed that the descendants should be given a reserve a few kilometres outside town, on the road to Quevedo. The initiative was taken up. And, in so doing, the administration chose to ignore the fact that the Colorados were neither tapirs nor butterflies in danger of extinction, but a people who had lost the right to choose where to live. The Colorados are easily recognized by their paint-red hair, dyed with the juice of the *achiote* plant. In the way of such things, the reserve is also a tired tourist attraction, not worth the effort, nor the inevitable gloom that follows.

The land around the town is lush and fertile. Taking advantage of Ecuador's lax currency laws, narco-neighbours from the north have bought up plantations around the town; now it's often locally referred to as 'Santo Domingo de los Colombianos'.

GETTING THERE
Santo Domingo forms the hub to a web of roads that radiate out to: Quito ($2\frac{1}{2}$ hours, US$2); Guayaquil (5 hours, US$3); and Esmeraldas (4 hours, US$2.50). Destinations en route to any of the above are also served. Buses leave from their offices around 29 de Mayo and Tulcán.

TOURIST INFORMATION
The Banco International, open Tues–Sat, will change foreign currency.

WHERE TO STAY
The **Hotel Zaracay** is 2 km outside town and charges US$20 for a double room with a bath. The rooms are in jungle-style cabins set amid pleasant gardens. There is also a

98

swimming pool. Closer into town, at the eastern edge, the **Hotel Toachi** has rooms with private bath, a restaurant and a swimming pool, for US$6 per person. For cheaper stays in town, the **Hotels Colorado** and **Amambay** are both recommended, at around US$3 per person.

WHERE TO EAT
The good hotels have the best restaurants. Otherwise, Santo Domingo is distinctly barren of good places to eat. Try the Chinese *Chifas* **Nuevo Hong Kong** and **Nuevo China**.

Tinalandia
Seventeen kilometres outside Santo Domingo, Tinalandia is an extraordinary hotel run by the eccentric, stately and aristocratic Russian emigrée Tina Garzon, the Duchess of Platinov. There is nine-hole golf course (in the manner of a country estate), but the grounds have been otherwise left undisturbed for the birds. Naturalists have counted over 150 species, a list that includes such rarities as squirrel cuckoos, rufous-tailed hummingbirds and the Andean cock of the rock. Accommodation is in jungle chalets set around the grounds, the food is excellent, and the charming Señora charges US$30 per person. At night the clatter of moths the size of plates only adds to the surreal atmosphere. There is no phone and the only way to book a room is to write to the Señora, c/o Tinalandia, Santo Domingo.

Part VI

THE COAST

Flooded Streets in Las Peñas, Guayaquil

Ecuador's coast is settled, but feels lonely, a place to relax and explore. It has some wonderful holiday beaches, of course, and a coast road, of sorts, that roughly follows them. But Ecuador's coast sports neither scuba-divers nor windsurfers, nor all of a beach resort's mod-cons.

With the exception of the resorts of Salinas in the south and Atacames to the north, the coast is mostly undeveloped and rarely visited. There's little to see (or more truthfully, it's just a mite too difficult to get to see what there is). To the north, against the Colombian border, lies virgin jungle and coastal mangrove swamps. To the south, around Guayaquil, lie shrimp farms and cacao plantations. But in between these two poles stretch long and lonely black and white sand beaches. If you have the time, rent a car or travel them vagabond style in *rancheras*; those open-air, wooden frame buses that synchronize their routes with the low tide and use the uncovered hard-packed sands as a road. The vast perspectives on these beaches can warp your own sense of perspective, and more often than not, the nearest person to you will only be on the the horizon, no bigger than a match head.

Those are the geographical features of the coast that can be gleaned from any map, but the Coast and the Sierra also love to hate each other; the two are worlds apart. Where the Sierra is conservative and tight-fisted; the Coast is liberal and opportunistic. Where the Coast is tropical; the mountains are temperate. Where the Sierra is Indian, the Coast is creole. And where the *costeños* are relaxed and open, the *sierraños* are guarded and reserved. Differences pervade every area of life, from economics to matters of toilet. The sierraños deride the *costeños* for the democracy of their loose-fitting, hot-weather clothes and call them 'monos' or 'monkeys'. Un-fazed, the *costeños* retort that the *sierraños* are

100

hypocrites, bureaucrats and that they dress up to look like Christmas trees. 'The Quiteños,' they say, 'don't even have a toilet'.

Unlike the Sierra, the coast has always been a crossroads for world trade: the world came to Ecuador through its ports, and Ecuador went out into the world the same way. Nowhere is this more apparent than in the coast's main city, the busy port of Guayaquil.

GUAYAQUIL

There is very little sleek about Ecuador's largest city, currently home to two million, but growing every day. It's a city in heat; modern, crowded, unattractive and constantly in motion. The air is as thick as cotton wool, and the weather feels like soup, never under 80°C. On the one hand there are no tourist attractions, but on the other, there are no tourists. Whatever value Guayaquil has for the traveller lies with its people and their gay mood; a relief, perhaps, after the melancholy of the mountains.

The city's rhumberos call Guayaquil the last town in the Caribbean. And true enough, it's a hot port with that same sense of careless threat and funky aplomb one normally associates with the Caribbean. The architecture is also recognizably art-deco ocean-going, and the houses have similarly broad concrete balconies, damp-stained saffron walls and cool stone or tiled floors. But Guayaquil is strictly a city of commerce, and instead of Caribbean salsa, the city's favourite sound is the ring of ¡chingo!—cash registers. For this the Quiteños love to deride the Guayaquileños as well-dressed thieves. A more partisan view concedes that they merely love a quick deal.

In spite of such raffish charm, and whatever its dubious merits, Guayaquil's connections with Quito are quick and easy. There are twelve aeroplanes a day (US$15) to the capital, so although not one of the seven wonders of the world, Guayaquil makes for a convenient base from which to visit the coast.

A final note: huge urban migrations are characteristic of Latin American population movements in this half of the century, and as a centre of commerce, unlike Quito, Guayaquil has attracted thousands of people from the rural areas. One third of its inhabitants live in a dirty froth of shanty-towns around the city, and you will see their cardboard villages as you ride into town.

History

1535: The Foundation of Guayaquil

The name Guayaquil was taken in commemoration: the first half from a Puña Indian chief, Guaya; the second half from his wife, Quill. Both committed suicide in 1535 on the approach of the conquistador Sebastián Benalcázar, who founded the city. The roots of Ecuadorean nationalism may lie in the Sierra, but until the advent of the aeroplane, Guayaquil was the customary port of entry into Ecuador, and it was from the Ecuadorean coast that the conquistadors began their penetration of Peru.

1580–1925: Colonialism and Independence

The rest of Guayaquil's history is as equally Hollywood stage-set: three destructions by Indians in the 16th century; two pirate attacks in the 17th; a series of disastrous fires in the 18th and 19th; and in the 20th, the reputation as a disease-ridden pesthole, a death trap of yellow fever, cholera and typhus for the merchant seamen voyaging south from Panama. The North American traveller Blair Niles observed in 1923: 'So clean a city is Guayaquil that the fragrance of drying cocoa clings to our memory of it, as if uncontaminated by anything more gross'. It is hard not to feel that she was trying too hard.

As befits a port, Guayaquil's supreme moment in history came not from itself but from without, with the arrival of two foreigners. In August 1822, General Símon Bolívar, flushed by his triumphant entry into Ecuador, and General San Martín, his more phlegmatic Argentine brother-in-arms, met in secret conference to determine the future of South America. Nobody knows what transpired (see 'History', p. 37); we have only the denoument. Thirty-six hours after he had landed, San Martín returned to Peru without the promise of Bolívar's military support for his campaign against the Spanish in Peru. Bolívar had it all his own way that day, and it is hard to believe that the monument on the Malecon and Avenida 9 de Octubre, which marks the occasion, is an accurate depiction of history. Set inside a semi-circle of columns against the river, it shows the two men clasping hands in an expression of benevolence and political fraternity. The meeting broke San Martín, his campaign collapsed, and he spent the rest of his years wandering sadly around Europe in a half-involuntary exile.

1925–1989: Modern Guayaquil

Quito and Guayaquil continue their historical rivalry, and Guayaquil is still the country's breadwinner and biggest city, even if most of the bread ends up in Quito. When the bridge spanning the River Guayas was completed in the 1960s, the Quiteños—punning on their nickname for the *costeños, monos*—called it the 'missing link'. With monkey cunning perhaps, Guayaquil's most recent mayor—a bombastic and colourful Lebanese—is currently running for president. His campaign, however, has a difference; following allegations of corruption, he is conducting it in exile from Panama. Polls have shown him to be well ahead.

GETTING THERE

By Plane

The airport is 5 km north of town, US$2 by taxi, with good connections to the rest of the country. Airline offices and travel agents are all on Avenida 9 de Octubre, near the river. The list of flights below will give you an idea of what is available:

to Quito: at least ten flights daily, US$15.
to Cuenca: twice daily, US$9.
to Machala (for Peru): one flight daily, Mon–Sat, US$8.
to Manta: daily, US$9.
Loja: one or two a week, US$10

By Bus

Guayaquil's bus terminal is just beyond the airport and, as a hub of Ecuadorean business and communications, there are frequent departures to all destinations.

to Quito: 9 hours, US$4
to Cuenca: 6 hours, US$3

to Riobamba and Ambato: 4 hours, US$2.50
to Manta and Bahía: 3 hours, US$2
to Machala (for Peru): 3½ hours, US$2
to Playas: 2 hours, US$1
to Salinas: 2½ hours, US$1.50
to Santo Domingo: 5 hours, US$3
to Esmeraldas: 7 hours, US$5

By Train
The famous train journey to Quito is no longer operating. If and when the service is ever reopened, trains will leave from Duran, a ferry ride across the river from the pier to the north of the Malecon.

TOURIST INFORMATION
The **DITURIS** office is on the waterfront at Malecon 2321 and Olmedo; up the stairs, on the second floor, and officially open 8–4.30, Mon–Fri. **IETEL** and the **post office** are both contained within the huge building on Carbo and Aguirre.

Money is easily changed at any of the *casas de cambio* on Avenida 9 de Octubre, down by the waterfront.

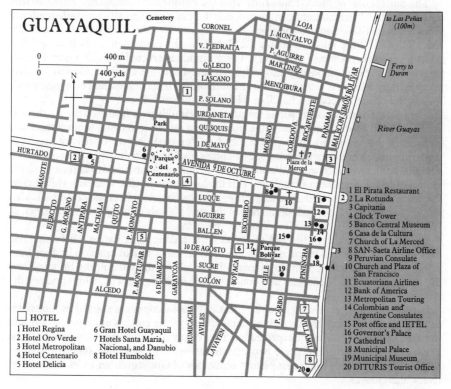

GUAYAQUIL

1 El Pirata Restaurant
2 La Rotunda
3 Capitania
4 Clock Tower
5 Banco Central Museum
6 Casa de la Cultura
7 Church of La Merced
8 SAN-Saeta Airline Office
9 Peruvian Consulate
10 Church and Plaza of San Francisco
11 Ecuatoriana Airlines
12 Bank of America
13 Metropolitan Touring
14 Colombian and Argentine Consulates
15 Post office and IETEL
16 Governor's Palace
17 Cathedral
18 Municipal Palace
19 Municipal Museum
20 DITURIS Tourist Office

HOTEL
1 Hotel Regina
2 Hotel Oro Verde
3 Hotel Metropolitan
4 Hotel Centenario
5 Hotel Delicia
6 Gran Hotel Guayaquil
7 Hotels Santa Maria, Nacional, and Danubio
8 Hotel Humboldt

Tourist cards can be extended at the immigration office in the Palacio de Gobierno; entrance is from Pichincha and Aguirre. The Peruvian consulate is at Avenida 9 de Octubre 411, on the 6th floor, and is open 8.30–1, Mon–Fri.

GETTING AROUND

The area you are most likely to want to cover in Guayaquil is small, so making your way around by foot is easiest and quickest. Buses are chaotic and mainly cover commuting routes. A shuttle journey by taxi should never set you back more than US$2, but to save on later recriminations it is best to agree on the price beforehand.

WHAT TO SEE

Perhaps the most interesting thing to do on a first night in Guayaquil is to stroll down the Avenida 9 de Octubre, the city's main boulevard. Framed by high-rise buildings and cruised by expensive cars, its a Miami-style street with cinemas and expensive shops; a Coca-Cola kind of place, only with a Latin touch. The street is lined with wood-slatted benches set at right angles to the flow of traffic. Night-time strollers get up, sit down, and get up again. Leggy girls flounce by. People are cruising.

The busiest part of the Avenida runs from the Parque del Centenario, where an iron and white marble monument commemorates the city's proclamation of Independence from Spain in 1820, down to the river. Here the Avenida joins the riverside broadwalk, the Malecon. At the junction stands **La Rotunda**, the monument to Bolívar and San Martín's historic meeting (see above). The Rotunda is erected in such a way that two people can stand at opposite ends, whisper, and hear one another. Cooled by river breezes, the Malecon is also the favourite haunt of courting couples, and everyone strolls its length holding someone's hand, or wishing that they did.

The Malecon stretches the whole length of Guayaquil's river front. To the south, near the DITURIS office, it abuts onto the market area on 10 de Agosto, around the Plaza Bolívar. At the other end, to the north, lies **Las Peñas**; an artists' district of tired, but graceful wooden houses with shuttered balconies over hanging the river. In many ways it resembles the finer sections of Washington DC, during quieter days. Plaques mark the homes of past Ecuadorean presidents. But the house where Che Guevara whiled away the years playing chess and dreaming of revolutions has since been destroyed. Hidden away from the traffic and rush of the rest of the city, it's only a short, dead-end street, so you will have to go back the same way that you came.

Above Las Peñas rises the hill of Santa Ana; a dangerous barrio where the avid eyes of *marijuaneros* will calculate your worth in terms of hits of crack. The four fates of the poor surround the hill: the Vernaza Hospital and the old jail, the brewery, and the cemetery, whose Madonnas and concrete doves are the pathetic, white pride of the city.

Beyond the cemetery rises a scrubby, bleak hill whose slopes are scarred by thousands of tiny crosses marking graves with no name. Many of the crosses are toppled over and the whole hillside is simply a projection into death of Guayaquil's crowded slums. Perhaps it is the picture of these two cemeteries—side by side, one stately, the other shabby—that provides the truest picture of the city of Guayaquil, set by its congress of rivers, the Guayas.

Museums
Guayaquil's museums focus on Ecuadorean archaeology. The **Municipal Museum**, on the corner of Sucre and Carbo, is worth visiting if only for the shrunken heads, or *tzantzas*. There is also an archaeological section featuring exhibits from the various coastal cultures of Ecuador, with clay seals and golden masks, and a very good craft collection of Amazonian beadwork, featherwork, tools and weapons. The Museum is open Mon–Fri, 9–12 noon and 3–7; and at weekends, from 10–1 (adm).

The **Museo de Arqueologia del Banco Central**, on 9 de Octubre and Antipara, has a small archaeology exhibition of undistinguished-looking pottery shards, and a suprisingly large upstairs collection of modern art by contemporary Ecuadorean painters. The museum forms part of the bank and is open Mon–Fri, 10–6; and at weekends, 10–1 (adm).

SHOPPING
The black market for general odds and bobs such as shoes, clothes, and radios etc, is on Pichincha, south of Colón, along Olmedo. **English books** are available at The Book Shop, in Urdesa, on VE Estrada. Very good **Panama hats** can be bought at Barberan, at 1 de Mayo 112.

ENTERTAINMENT AND NIGHTLIFE
Guayaquil has the feeling that everyone is looking for a *rhumba*. The only problem is where? There are some heavy-looking sailor bars off the Avenida 9 de Octubre, but most of the city's nightlife takes place in the upper-class district of Urdesa. There are two nightclubs here of age-old fame that have been vying for each other's custom since anyone can remember: **Infinity** and **Etcetera**. Take your neon choice.

The newspapers *El Telegrafo* and *El Universo* carry information on concerts, local events, and cinemas.

FESTIVALS
There are two main festivals in Guayaquil. The first around 12 October simultaneously commemorates Independence and Columbus days. The second, in the last week of July, marks Bolívar's birthday on the 24th, and Guayaquil's Independence on the 25th. The city parties until August and during this time, hotel rooms are very hard to find.

WHERE TO STAY
All of Guayaquil's hotels are well located in the centre of town with good and bad jumbled together. Although prices are set by the tourist board—and as such should be posted by the reception desk—costs are higher here than in Quito and it can be hard to keep to a low budget. Rooms in the cheaper hotels can be squalid and airless, so always ask to see them first.

On the corner of 9 de Octubre and García Moreno lies Guayaquil's most luxurious hotel: the **Hotel Oro Verde**. It's sleek, efficient, has three restaurants, an outdoor pool, a sauna, a gymnasium, a casino, and a full range of business services. Prices for the rooms, which are large and comfortable, start at US$70 (tel 372100; telex 043744).

Guayaquil's other first-class hotels, the **Gran** and the **Casino Boulevard**, don't quite match the Oro Verde's luxury.

The **Hotel Humboldt International** is excellent value; at Malecon 2309 and overlooking the river, it has a wide choice of rooms, a restaurant and a casino. Prices are at around US$11 per person.

The **Metropolitana** on VM Rendon and Panama, tel 305250 can be found an unlikely four storeys up in an office building. But the open Art Deco architecture and the height means that the hotel catches all of the river's cool breezes. Clean, comfortable and reasonably priced (US$5/8 for a single/double) this is a good choice, but the rooms fill up quickly, so call first.

The Hotel Centenario, tel 524467, overlooks the busy intersection of the Avenida 9 de Octubre and the Parque Centenario and can be noisy as a result. On the the other hand, you are definitely in the thick of things. Some rooms come with balconies, US$8/12 for a single/double.

The **Regina**, on L. de Garaycora and P. Solano, although slightly out of the way, has large, clean and simple bedrooms, with quiet views of the street, and probably provides the best bet in the US$5 per night range.

The best cheapie is just by the market, the **Delicia**, at Clemente Ballen 1105. Its staff are friendly and rooms with a private bath can be had for US$2 a night. If full, try the **Danubio**, the **Santa María** or the **Nacional** on Villamil—they have some good rooms away from the busy street, and also some very scummy cubicles. Then again, they only charge US$1.50 a night.

WHERE TO EAT

Cafés
For a beer and a simple plate of fish, or even just a coffee, catch the breeze at one of the boats moored off the Malecon: **La Pirata** is just one, two blocks north of the Rotunda statue.

Lunch and Dinner
Apart from travelling out to Urdesa, the best food in Guayaquil is to be found at the hotels. Try the seafood; the shrimps are large as commas from a billboard hoarding, and are so delicious they can be eaten plate after plate. The prize-winning **El Fortín** restaurant at the **Hotel Continental** serves excellent food. And, apart from **Le Gourmet** and **La Fondue** restaurants the **Hotel Oro Verde's Patio Café** has a wide and reasonably priced menu where you could eat expansively for under US$10.

For a quick lunch, go to **Las Redes** *cevicheria* at 9 de Octubre 1805: it's a few blocks beyond the run of snack bars that line the avenue east of the Parque del Centenario.

For international food, you will have to go to one of the restaurants in Urdesa, a US$3 taxi drive away. **Barandua** on the Urdesa Circunvalacion Norte 528–B has the best in seafood; and the **Trattoria La Carbonara**, at Urdesa Balsamos 108, the best in Italian. However, if you want to cruise restaurants and pick one that suits, wander down the VE Estrada; the Catalonian food at the **Costa Brava**, and the Italian at **Trattoria da Migliorini** are both recommended.

Beaches North of Guayaquil

On the coast to the north-west of Guayaquil lie the beaches, and the further away from the city you go, the better and emptier they are.

History

Yes, these beaches have a history, but one as washed away as the flooded Ecuadorean holiday homes that once lined this stretch of coast. All that now remains of both are faint signals beaming dimly from the past.

The production of ceramics is taken as a key point in the development of any civilization. Remains of the Valdivian culture, found in 1957 around Puerto López, suggests that 5000 years ago there lived around here the oldest ceramic-producing civilization in the Americas. This finding challenged the idea that only Central America and the High Andes of Peru had been epicentres of cultural development in the Americas.

The lifestyle and beliefs of the Valdivians have been hard to divine. As with most Ecuadorean archaeology, all historical reflections are based around imaginative re-constructions gleaned from broken shards and midden rubbish heaps (slim clues indeed, but rootle around in any soft earth and you are almost certain to find fragments). Archaeologists working at Salango believe, however, that the Valdivians were only one in a series of civilizations that developed along the Ecuadorean coast. All excellent sailors, they coursed the Pacific shores of South America on balsa rafts, trading the much valued *spondylus* conch shell from Panama to Chile.

The Valdivians were succeeded by the Chorrerans in 600BC, and by the Manteños in the first millennium AD. The latter culture had the strange habit of deforming their skulls and removing their teeth to emphasize the backward slopes of their foreheads, the prominence of their chins and the hook of their noses. There is a very good and well labelled museum at **Salango** with exhibits of pottery and gold work, if you are interested.

GETTING TO THE BEACHES
Buses for Playas leave from Guayaquil's terminal (US$1, 1 hour). To travel north of the Santa Elena peninsula towards Puerto López, or to go west to Salinas, change at **La Libertad**, the centre for bus services on the peninsula. There are frequent buses to La Libertad from Guayaquil (US$1, 2½ hours).

To travel on towards Manta, change at Puerto Lopez for Jipijapa (US$1, 1½ hours), and at Jipijapa change again for Manta (US$1, 45 mins).

Playas

Playas is only one hour from Guayaquil and is the city's busiest beach resort, often deserted during the week, but frenetic during the weekend, especially Sundays.

The **Hosterias Delfin** and **Gaviota** are both a kilometre outside town and are Playas's best hotels (US$12 per night), even if a bit shabby. In town, the **Hotel Playas** overlooks the beach, has rooms with bath and charges US$7/US$11 for a single/double. **El Galeón**, next to the church, is inexpensive, clean and has a good attached restaurant

(US$2 a night). You can camp at the southern end of the beach. There are a number of restaurants along the beachfront.

Salinas

Salinas is a resort on the tip of the drab and dusty Santa Elena peninsula and has casinos, condos and holiday apartment blocks rearing-up from its wide crescent of sand. This is the resort of choice for affluent Ecuadoreans. There is a yacht club and marlin fishing can be arranged at **Pesca Tours** on the waterfront.

The **Hotel Miramar** has a casino, swimming pool and restaurant. Rooms are air-conditioned and around US$30 a night. The modern **Hotel Salinas** charges US$12 for large, comfortable rooms with bath. The **Yulee** is well placed for the beaches, clean and has a good restaurant (around US$6 per person, per night). If you are staying for a while at Salinas and are looking for an easy excursion, try the **mud baths at San Vicente**, just by La Libertad.

Montanita

Heading 2 hours north along the coast road, **Montanita** is an empty surfers' beach, with high-peaking waves off the point during the late winter swell. There are two small hotels and the mood is ... relaxed.

Stay at **'El Rincón del Amigo'**—a surfing Irish-American's set-up by the point. Accommodation is simple, bunk beds in beach cabins for US$1, but his restaurant serves rich and cheesy prawn pizzas. It is a pleasant spot, and you could linger here.

Salango and Puerto López

As you head further north, the land gradually changes from flat and scrubby desert, to lush and hilly jungle that comes right down to the shore. The road twists for a bus-hour through a string of bamboo villages, passes the architectural museum at **Salango**, climbs a hill, mounts a bend, and then rolls down to **Puerto López**, the nearest town north of Montanita with a beach and accomodation.

There is a small restaurant in Salango where all the archaeologists congregate, **El Delphin Magico**, just three blocks south of the main square; but there is no-where to stay, so if you would like to visit the museum, you will have to stay at Puerto López and visit from there. Having said that, there is almost nowhere to stay in Puerto López, bar the famously mis-named **Residencial Paradiso** on the beachfront. Rooms are simple, but fine, and cost US$2 per person.

But to eat! Go to **Carmita's**, also on the beachfront, and order an *arroz con mariscos* (rice and seafood).

Jipijapa

Beyond Puerto López, the road turns inland and uphill to the drab town of **Jipijapa** (pronounced *Hee-pee-Ha-pa*). Change here for buses travelling further north. The road doesn't touch the coast again until you reach the fishing port of Manta, some 70 km further on.

Manta

Manta has been a town of sailors and fishermen since pre-Columbian times. First on balsa-wood rafts, like the one the conquistador Capitan Ruiz captured in 1526; then in small boats that were hand built with care on the town's gently shelving beaches. And then much later, in the 1980s, aboard large ships owned by international fishing companies.

In the wake of such modernizing zeal, Manta, like much of Ecuador, has swapped its houses of wood and shutters for more anonymous constructions of concrete and zinc. But it is still a pleasant enough resort town of 100,000 people, with two beaches, one at **Tarqui** to the east of town, and the other at **Murcielego**, just outside town to the west. Both are jammed with sunburnt vacationers from the Sierra in February.

GETTING THERE
By Plane
The airport is 3 km east of Tarqui. Tickets for the daily flights to Quito (US$14) and Guayaquil (US$10) can be bought at the TAME office on Manta's waterfront.

By Bus
The bus terminal is at the junction of the muncipalities of Manta and Tarqui. There are regular departures for Guayaquil (3½ hours, US$2); Jipijapa (45 mins, US$1); Bahía de Caráquez (3 hours, US$1); Santo Domingo (6 hours, US$2); Esmeraldas (8 hours, US$3) and even Quito (8 hours, US$3).

TOURIST INFORMATION
The **DITURIS** office is on the second floor of the Edificio Emapa, at the bottom of Calle 8. **Money** can be changed at the Banco del Pacifico on the Manta side of town.

The town is divided in two by an inlet, with Manta on the western side and Tarqui on the east. Only a five-minute walk away from each other, they are joined by a bridge. Tarqui has the better selction of hotels and the nearer beach.

BEACHES AND WHERE TO STAY
The beach at **Tarqui** can be as smooth as milk and in the morning fishermen use it to unload their catch. Their nets look like baskets and are filled with bonito, tunny, and the odd shark—whose fins will go to Japan to swim in famous soups. Birds swirl above their heads, especially frigates, those elegant thieves and dandies of the air.

All the following hotels are on the Tarqui beachfront, which has the best selection. The **Hotel Las Gaviotas** is on the beach and has tennis courts, US$10/20 for a single/double. The rambling **Hotel Inca** has large rooms with ocean views for US$4/7 for a single/double and is a good mid-range choice. The **Hotel Miami**, further along the beach front, has a porch for seaside lounging, is a bit scruffy, but well placed and only US$3 per person.

Murcielego beach is a US$1 taxi drive west of town, has better sand and also dangerous riptides. It is undoubtedly the better-looking beach, but take care, more than 150 people have drowned in its currents. The town also has a small **museum** with exhibits detailing the Manta culture; it's on the 3rd floor of the muncipal building on the corner of Avenida 4 and Calle 9; open Mon–Fri, 9–3, with a break for lunch.

WHERE TO EAT

Some of the best places to eat are at the small restaurants that rim the beach. Try a *sopa marinera*, a seafood casserole, notoriously good at the unnamed restaurant just by the the Hotel Miami. If you are pining for meat after a prolonged fish diet, go to **La Parilla del Che Marcelo**, a 50c taxi drive towards the outskirts of town on Avenida 24 and Calle 20. A good place for carnivores; a mixed grill of meats with beer to drink will only set you back US$4.

EXCURSIONS

Montecristi, a small village half an hour inland by bus (10c),is the land of General Eloy Alfaro, the birthplace of Ecuadorean liberalism, and the home of the Panama hat (see p. 38 and 87). Small shops line the street. Pick up a hat. Unfurl it from its balsa-wood box and snap it into shape. Not a crease. Just shellac smoothness. The best Panamas in Ecuador, US$25 or thereabouts.

There is nowhere to stay, and the town is best visited on a day trip from Manta. Buses stop at 6 pm.

Bahía de Caráquez and San Vicente

These twinned, tranquil towns, are set on either side of a deep river estuary surrounded by high hills. Connected by a frequent ferry service, their beaches are good but the water is marly and clouded by the Rio Chone. There are hotels in Bahía, but most people stay in San Vicente, where the beach is slightly better and stretches north for miles. Pick-up trucks hum along it, into the headland's haze.

WHERE TO STAY AND EAT

Bahía de Caráquez

The **Hotel Americano** has rooms with bath and air-conditioning for US$8 a single. The **Residencias Vera** and **Los Tamarindes** have rooms with bath for US$2.50. For dinner, try the sidewalk restaurant **Los Helechos**, a short walk north of the centre.

San Vicente

Accommodation is better in San Vicente. Almost directly in front of the pier lies the **Hotel Vacaciones**, which, although a little noisy, has large rooms, a pool and a restaurant (US$7/11 for a single/double). On the northern outskirts of town, on the way to **Pedernales**, lie two or three hotels; all quiet, quite secluded, with family-orientated bungalow accommodation—US$5 per person. The only cheap hotel in town is the **San Vicente**, run-down and mosquito ridden at US$1.50 per person.

GETTING THERE

Buses from San Vicente only traverse the northern shore up to **Cojimies**. All the mainline buses leave from **Bahía** with routes to Manta, Guayaquil, Santo Domingo, Quito and Esmeraldas.

TOURIST INFORMATION
There are no banks where you can change money.

North to Cojimies

This is a hard but rewarding nine-hour trip from San Vicente in an open *ranchera*, along the beach, through inland valleys, past desolate fishing settlements, with dust, hungry passengers, agricultural produce and salt-spray for companions. Two buses a day leave from the ticket office by the pier in San Vicente. The villages you pass through—**Jama, Pedernales** and **Esperanza**—are poor and incomplete-looking affairs made of split bamboo. Rudimentary accommodation can be found in all of them, but you don't really want to stay in any of them. Cojimies is the end of the line; from there you have to catch a boat across the estuary to **Muisne** from which it is an easy ride onto **Atacames** and **Esmeraldas**.

Half an hour before Cojimies you pass an unlikely looking place—a lonely hacienda set in coconut groves called **'El Coco Solo'**. It lives up to its name. But it is hard to explain exactly what it is; neither a private house, an hotel nor a conference centre, it looks deserted, but its rooms are often full. If the boss likes you, you can stay there for US$7 a night, in double beds draped with mosquito netting in small, stilted bungalows, for as long as you like. If he doesn't, you're stuck in the middle of nowhere. Its a risk. He's a crazy man. Sometimes he froths at the mouth. Other times he'll regale you with beer and stories about how it used to be a commune. The place is a fantasy. The wind rattles through the trees. The beach is yours. For further information, try phoning Camila Velasco in Bahía de Caráquez at 690531.

The Northern Coast

There are beaches—and good ones too—but in the northern section of Ecuador's coast you will also glimpse a life that seems more African than South American. Around Esmeraldas lives the highest proportion of blacks in the country; a feature associated with tropical plantations throughout the New World. Large black women carry baskets of bananas on their heads, the air smells of peanuts and there is a scrabbling and collective disorder which suggests that no-one is really in charge.

As with every Afro-American region, Esmeraldas has its own music—the airy, rolling rhythms of marimba, a hybrid sound that takes its name from a bamboo xylophone the size of a piano. The songs (*decimas*) are made up of impromptu verses slung back and forth between two singers. Their themes are universal:

Man: 'Oh my Lord! When I see that little black woman well dressed and combed, I want to kiss her little mouth.'
Woman: 'Look! A lot of lovers you've had like the bardolada plant that grows on the beach, but you're never going to find a black woman of my kind.'

Man: 'A good-looking thing you are! If your mother would give you to me for just tonight and tomorrow, I would bring you back!
Woman: 'Bolívar with his sword conquered five nations, and me with my hips I conquer all hearts.'

Esmeraldas is the main port and capital of the province. To the north lies jungle and mangrove swamplands, San Lorenzo and the train ride into the Sierra. South of Esmeraldas are the beaches of Atacames and Same, two of Ecuador's best. The rainy season is from December to June.

Esmeraldas

Esmeraldas has been scarred by exploitation and mismanagement. As Ecuador's only port for the Amazonian oil that is piped over the mountains, the harbour is crowded with squat, aluminium oil terminals and refineries. Heavy commercial traffic has poisoned the surrounding water. And the Pacific—one of the most poetic of seascapes—has been turned into a reservoir of lifeless water; even the most aggressive waves are transformed into an insipid gel. The backstreets are rubbled and run down. Everyone arrives only to leave. Some stay only to pay US$10 for the taxi ride from the airport to the beaches at Atacames and so never even see the town.

GETTING THERE
By Plane
There are daily flights to Quito, except Sunday (US$8). The TAME office is just off the main plaza. Make sure that you get a seat assignation as well as a ticket.

By Bus
Most buses leave from the town square: Quito (6 hours, US$3.50)—quickest with Aerotaxi; Santo Domingo (2½ hours, US$2); Bahía de Caráquez (7 hours, US$3). There are regular buses to Atacames and Muisne.

TOURIST INFORMATION
The tourist office is on the second floor of the Edificio de la Alcaldia, at Bolivar 517, one block from the main square. Money can be changed at the Banco de Pichincha.

WHERE TO STAY
You can either stay in town, or in the faded but breezy beach suburb of Las Palmas. The **Apart Hotel Esmeraldas** at Ave Libertad 407, tel 712712, is the best in town and has quiet, comfortable rooms with TV for US$14/18 a single/double. The best cheapies have just opened next to each other and are also on the Ave Libertad, three blocks up from the central plaza: the **Hotels Sandri** and **Chaver Inn**. Both of them are clean and good value at US$2.50/4 for a single/double.

There are several, more comfortable hotels in Las Palmas—a five-minute taxi drive from the centre. **Hotel Cayapas** on Avenidas Kennedy and Padilla, tel 711022 is set back behind its garden from the beachfront, is low key, and has a good restaurant (US$11/15 for a single/double). The **Hotel Amabato** just around the corner on

112

Avenida Guerra, tel 710344, has OK rooms with bath for US$5/US$7 for a single/double.

WHERE TO EAT
There are no good restaurants in town, so for a slap-up meal, you have to go to Las Palmas; try **Atenas Tiffini** on Kennedy 707, or **Bayardo**, on the Malecon. Try the regional dish—cocado, fish cooked, and sometimes curried, with coconut cream and served with rice and fried plantains.

The Beaches South of Esmeraldas

Atacames

'It was the gring*a*s,' wrote the Ecuadorean journalist Pablo Cuvi, 'who made history at Atacames.' **Atacames** was once a sixties hang-out, an end of the road rest-stop for travellers who had worn themselves out in the Andes and needed a chance to hole up for a while, swim, sunbathe and loll underneath the palm trees. It is still a gathering place, and the beach is good, but there is more of a resort/party atmosphere nowadays with piña colada-dispensing *cassettas* lining the shore. It's a big beach however, and you can enjoy or ignore such diversions as you please.

All the hotels are near, if not right on the beach and generally only salt water showers are available. Hotels tend to fill up quickly at the weekend and during the holiday season, January through March. There is always a wide choice of places, with new hotels springing up as others are closing down, but always check your room to see if it is secure as thefts are not uncommon.

Cabanas del Sol has beach bungalows away from the main strip for US$13 a double. The **Hotel Juan Sebastián**, at the other end of the beach, has a similar set-up only in flower filled gardens.

The **Hotel Chavalito** on the main strip is clean, friendly and secure and has rooms with private baths for US$7. Cheaper hotels are set back from the sea. As they come and go so quickly, the best course is to look around when you first arrive. They are all clustered together and you can expect to pay about US$3–4 for a room.

All the restaurants on the beachfront carry the same menus—whatever was caught that day.

Same

Same, a beach just beyond the fishing village of **Sua**, is quieter, more intimate, and more exclusive.

Try **Las Canoas** tel 246669, or the **Cabañas Isla del Sol**, very reasonable at only US$10 per person per night, with private bathrooms and a restaurant.

Muisne

Muisne, separated from the mainland by a tidal channel, really is the end of the line. There is nothing beyond but ocean. If you want to get away, this perhaps is the place. The beach is almost desolate.

There is only one place to stay in Muisne: straight through the town, on the beach, in one of the simple A-frame huts set back from the shore (US$3 per person). There are some simple restaurants next to them.

GETTING THERE
There are regular buses from Esmeraldas along the coast road. From Esmeraldas to Atacames (US$1, 45mins); to Same, another half an hour; and to Muisne, two hours more and another US$1. When you get to Muisne, you have to take a dugout ferry across the channel, 50c. The beach lies straight through town, down the only road.

San Lorenzo

San Lorenzo is a ramshackle town on the Colombian border that is plagued by mosquitoes and the rank smell of mud. The only way to arrive is by dug-out and the best way to leave is by train, on the *autoferro*, to Ibarra, in the mountains.

The dawn train ride (see under 'Ibarra' for a description, on p. 65) is the main reason to come to San Lorenzo, but you can also occasionally find boats that will take you to Tumaco—another dank town, only in Colombia. Smugglers often make the trip so to avoid any confusion, make sure that your papers are in order.

GETTING THERE
To get to San Lorenzo from Esmeraldas is a dramatic pentathlon event of boats and buses. First take a morning bus to **La Tola** (5 hours, US$3), so obviating any need to stay in La Tola overnight, and from there catch a boat to San Lorenzo (US$2, 2 hours).

The autoferro leaves daily at 6.30 am, costs US$2, and can take up to 12 hours to complete the journey. It is best to try and reserve a seat the night before.

WHERE TO STAY AND EAT
There are no good hotels in San Lorenzo and the best of the bad is probably the **Residencial Ibarra**. At US$2 per person, you do not get a private bath, but the rooms are clean and, most importantly, have mosquito netting. Kids, at the pier or at the train station, will eagerly show you where to go for a small tip. The best restaurant in town is **Jhonnys** (sic). For dancing try **Rumory's**.

Part VII

THE GALÁPAGOS

'Take five and twenty heaps of cinders dumped here and there in an outside city lot, imagine some of them magnified into mountains and the vacant lot the sea, and you will have a fit idea of the general aspect of the Encantadas, or Enchanted isles.'

—Herman Melville, *The Enchanted Isles*

Cut by the equator, 1000 km off the western coast of Ecuador, the islands of the Galápagos archipelago, like all powerful places, feel as though they might be at the end of the earth, or the beginning. Everything conspires to make them seem marvellous.

They look strange; just the picked-off tops of volcanoes coming out of the sea. The horizon around them seems expanded so that claims of the Flat Earth Society do not seem absurd. Their colour is uniform, but uncertain, neither brown nor green, purple nor blue. The land is prehistoric and conjours up visions of a Plesiosaurus gambolling amongst the cacti. The sea is of the palest, most elusive green.

Animals are everywhere. Sunning themselves on dinghies rocking in the bay lie sea lions. Pirate-black frigate birds with their lipstick-red bibs swoop and tangle in the air. Blue-footed boobies dive like stukas into the sea; more magisterial pelicans, flop. Marine iguanas, as mineral-looking as the rocks that they lie on, gather in close groups by the surf. Little-toothed but big-grinning bottle-nosed dolphins ride the bow-waves of tourist boats cruising between the islands. Snorklers hum to themselves through air-tubes whilst watching fish and the underwater antics of sea lions. Everyone has an index finger at the ready—'Look at that!'

The wildlife and terrain of the Galápagos are so unique that the feelings of a first-time visitor can often mirror the opening words of García Márquez's *One Hundred Years of Solitude*, where: 'The world was so recent that everything lacked names, and in order to indicate them, it was necessary to point.' This is no Caribbean-esque, palm fringed resort. But although it costs at least US$900 to visit the islands, nobody regrets the cost.

GETTING THERE

The Galápagos are most usually reached on one of the daily TAME flghts from Quito (US$370) or Guayaquil (US$330) to **Baltra Island** airstrip. As the plane banks to land you get a good view of the islands; a series of arcs and lagoons, low hills, surf and pale marine-greens. Baltra itself sits as dry, grey and low in the water as an aircraft carrier. From Baltra, those with organised tours usually board their ship or yacht directly. Others, who wish to pick-up a boat in **Puerto Ayora** independently, must travel by bus and ferry over to Puerto Ayora on the island of Santa Cruz (45 mins away).

If an independent traveller you can arrange a tour of the islands from Puerto Ayora, otherwise many travel agencies now operate tours to the Galápagos. In Ecuador, **Galsam**, at Pinto 523 and Avenida Amazonas in Quito, is the cheapest, and will arrange a spartan eight-day tour for US$500. **Etnotours**, at Luis Cordero 1313 in Quito, tel 230552, is more expensive but for US$1000 quality is assured. Metropolitan Touring, at Avenida Amazonas 239, tel 524400, is the most luxurious option and can organize a seven-day tour on the 90 passenger *Santa Cruz* for US$120 a day.

In England, **Exodus**, at 9 Weir Road London SW12, tel 675 7996, provides the most comprehensive service for adventure-bound travellers. In the USA, Metropolitan Touring can be contacted through **Adventure Associates**, 5925 Maple, Suite 116, Dallas, Texas 75235.

TOURIST INFORMATION

Do yourself a great service and pack a snorkel and mask in your baggage. The Galápagos marine life is incomparable and whilst most boats stock snorkelling equipment, invariably it leaks.

Changing foreign currency on the islands is extremely difficult—so **bring enough local cash to last your stay**.

There is no best time to visit the islands. The climate is tropically constant, slightly cooled by the Antarctic up-welling of the Humboldt Current, although January to April may be slightly hotter than the misty *garua* season from May to August. Day clothing should be light, but you will need good shoes for walking the lava on the islands—tennis shoes are fine. The sun is *very* strong, so take a hat.

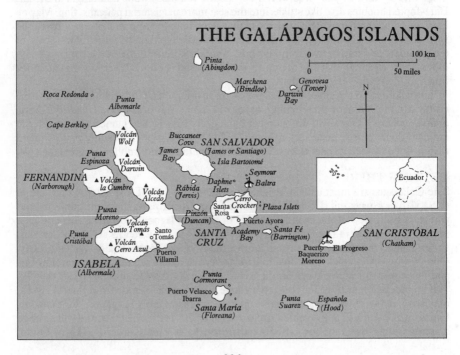

THE GALÁPAGOS ISLANDS

YELLOW EYED GRUNT

MANTA RAY

GALAPAGOS SEALIONS

SERGEANT MAJOR

BLUE EYED DAMSELFISH

GALAPAGOS PENGUIN

GALAPAGOS UNDERWATER

GREEN TURTLES

YELLOW-TAILED STURGEON FISH

MOORISH IDOL

BROWN STRIPED SNAPPER

KING ANGELFISH

BLACK JACK

YELLOW-TAILED MULLET

WHITE-TIPPED SHARK

FLOREANA

BLACK-NECKED STILTS

FLAMINGOS BUILD NESTS LIKE LARGE MUD MOUNDS IN THE LAGOONS, ON WHICH ONE EGG IS LAID

WHITE-CHEEKED PINTAIL DUCKS DABBLE IN THE LAGOONS FOR FOOD

THE YELLOW-CROWNED NIGHT HERON SCANS THE LAVA ROCKS FOR PREY. IT IS MOST ACTIVE AFTER DARK

JOLLY ROGER
POST BO

GREEN OR BLACKISH TURTLES LEAVE THEIR TRACKS ON THE WHITE SANDS OF THE ISLAND'S EASTERN BEACHES

THE ORIGINAL POST OFFICE BARREL WAS SET UP ABOUT 200 YEARS AGO AT POST OFFICE BAY

THE SEALIONS AT PUNTA CORMORANT ARE ESPECIALLY INQUISITIVE

CORONA DEL DIABLO (DEVIL'S CROWN) — SPECTACULAR SNORKELLING

A BLUE-FOOTED BOOBY SITS NONCHALANTLY ON DEVIL'S CROWN

ISABELA & FERNANDINA

THE GALÁPAGOS CORMORANT HAS LOST THE ABILITY TO FLY, BUT CAN STILL BE SEEN DRYING ITS WINGS

THE ENDEARING "SNAKE-NECK" DISPLAY IS PERFORMED BY ALL COURTING CORMORANTS

GIANT TORTOISES ENJOY WALLOWING IN MUD POOLS AT ALCEDO VOLCANO ON ISABELA

JUVENILE BIRDS HAVE DULL-COLOURED EYES WHICH TURN BRIGHT TURQUOISE IN ADULTHOOD

MARINE IGUANAS OFTEN "OVERLAP" TO CONSERVE HEAT AS THE SUN BEGINS TO SET

THE MALE COLLECTS SEAWEED WHICH THE FEMALE THEN ARRANGES INTO A LARGE NEST, IN WHICH SHE LAYS TWO OR THREE EGGS

GALÁPAGOS PENGUINS ABOUND IN THE COOL, FOOD-RICH WATERS OF THE WESTERN COASTS. THEY ARE SOCIAL BIRDS AND SUN THEMSELVES IN LARGE GROUPS, ALTHOUGH EACH HAS HIS OWN TERRITORY

TAGUS COVE, ISABELA

SOUTH PLAZA

SWALLOW-TAILED GULLS GET THEIR NAME FROM THEIR SLIGHTLY FORKED TAILS

THEIR HABIT OF LOOKING AT THEIR FEET IS NOT FULLY UNDERSTOOD ALTHOUGH IT MAY INDICATE FEAR OR UNCERTAINTY

THEY ARE NOCTURNAL BIRDS, AND CAN OFTEN BE SEEN ENJOYING '40 WINKS' IN THE SUN

RED-BILLED TROPIC BIRDS FEED MAINLY ON FISH AND SQUID. THEY ARE OFTEN HARASSED BY FRIGATE BIRDS UNTIL THEY ARE FORCED TO DROP THEIR CATCH

LANDING AT A JETTY COVERED WITH SPRAWLING SEALIONS CAN BE A PROBLEM

SOUTH PLAZA SUPPORTS A LARGE COLONY OF LAND IGUANAS (C. Subcristatus). UNLIKE C. Pallidus ON SANTA FE, THEY TEND TO HAVE DARK MARKINGS. FOR MOST OF THE YEAR THEY CLUSTER AROUND THE CACTUS FOREST, FEEDING ON THE SUCCULENT PADS

A SALT-TOLERANT HERB CALLED SESUVIUM, FORMS A BRIGHT RED CARPET OVER MUCH OF SOUTH PLAZA

ON THE SOUTH OF THE ISLAND, MALE SEA LIONS WITHOUT THEIR OWN 'HAREMS', HAVE FORMED A LARGE BACHELOR COLONY WHERE A RELAXED AND INFORMAL ATMOSPHERE PREVAILS

SANTA CRUZ & SEYMOUR

ESTACION CIENTIFICA
CHARLES DARWIN.
Charles Darwin Research Station

FRIGATE BIRDS DISPLAY
THEIR SCARLET POUCHES TO
ATTRACT A FEMALE.
THEY SIT IN THE LOW
SALTBUSHES, CALLING LOUDLY

DARWIN'S FINCHES
ARE
EVERY WHERE

IN THE LUSH GREEN HIGHLAND
AREA, A SCARLET FLASH IS
OFTEN THE FIRST ONE SEES OF
THE VERMILLION FLYCATCHER.
LIKE THE GALAPAGOS FLYCATCHER,
THEY OFTEN DART AROUND
FOOTPATHS AND
SOMETIMES
ALIGHT ON
TOURISTS

THE BUSY
YELLOW WARBLER
SOON BECOMES A FAMILIAR
SIGHT. ITS SONG IS
PARTICULARLY BEAUTIFUL

GALAPAGOS FLYCATCHER

LARGE NUMBERS OF BROWN
PELICANS LIVE AROUND THE
HARBOUR AND AT PELICAN BAY.
BREEDING BIRDS HAVE A
COLOURFUL CHESTNUT-AND-WHITE
HEAD AND NECK

ALERT LITTLE LAVA LIZARDS
SCUTTLE ALONG THE SANDY GROUND.
BREEDING FEMALES HAVE A
BRIGHT RED CHEST
AND NECK

"LAS GRIETAS" IS A
CHANNEL WHICH
OPENED UP THROUGH
A FAULT IN THE
VOLCANIC ROCK.
SHOALS OF FISH
CONGREGATE HERE
AND HARMLESS
WHITE-TIPPED
SHARKS ARE
OCCASIONAL VISITORS

LAVA GULLS LIKE TO
STAND ON THE BOWS
OF DINGHIES IN THE
HARBOUR TO SURVEY
THE GOINGS ON AND
OBSERVE THE
FOOD POTENTIAL

ESPAÑOLA

MARINE IGUANAS SUN BATHE TO RAISE THEIR BODY TEMPERATURE AFTER SWIMMING

THREE QUARTERS OF THE WORLD POPULATION OF BLUE-FOOTED BOOBIES LIVES ON GALAPAGOS. THE NAME COMES FROM THE SPANISH "BOBO", A CLOWN

...SEA LIONS GREET EVERY BOAT

THEY SPIT OUT EXCESS SALT FROM THEIR GLANDS

ESPAÑOLA MOCKINGBIRDS RARELY FLY BECAUSE THERE'S SO MUCH FOOD ON THE GROUND. THEY ARE SO FEARLESS THEY WILL PECK AT ARTISTS' FEET!

WAVED ALBATROSSES, WITH THEIR 2-METRE WINGSPAN, DO NOT BUILD NESTS, SO EGGS ARE 'MOVED AROUND' DURING INCUBATION.

TOWARDS THE END OF THE ALBATROSS COURTSHIP DANCE, ONE BIRD LEADS THE OTHER IN THIS RIDICULOUS AND RITUALISED "SWAY-WALKING"

CLIFF TOP AT PUNTA SUAREZ'. THE SECOND LARGEST COLONY OF MASKED BOOBY IN THE WORLD NESTS ON THIS CLIFF-TOP. JUST ONE CHICK IS RAISED, EVEN IF TWO EGGS ARE LAID

ESPAÑOLA GIANT TORTOISES ARE OF THE 'SADDLE-BACK' TYPE. THEY CAN WEIGH UP TO 250 kg AND CAN BE SEEN IN THE C.D.R.S. ENCLOSURES

SANTA FE

A GALAPAGOS HAWK PEERS CLOSELY AT VISITORS

THE BULL SEA LION PATROLS HIS LAND AND OFTEN THROWS UP HIS HEAD AND BARKS TO SHOW WHO IS BOSS. THERE IS ONE PARTICULARLY TERRITORIAL MALE ON THE BEACH

THE APTLY NAMED SALLY LIGHTFOOT CRAB CAN 'SKIP' ACROSS POOLS OF WATER

THIS SPECIES OF LAND IGUANA (C. Pallidus) IS FOUND ONLY ON SANTA FÉ. IT HAS A MUCH YELLOWER SKIN THAN THE SPECIES ON SOUTH PLAZA. MALES ARE LARGER AND MORE COLOURFUL THAN FEMALES

GALAPAGOS DOVES HOP AROUND THE BEACH, OR RUSTLE IN THE ARID ZONE, LOOKING FOR SEEDS

THE GALAPAGOS MOCKINGBIRD IS USUALLY THE FIRST BIRD TO GREET VISITORS. IT IS ABOUT THE SIZE OF A THRUSH

THIS GIANT PRICKLY PEAR CACTUS (OPUNTIA) STANDS AT ABOUT 25 FEET HIGH

THIS Dromicus SNAKE IS NON-POISONOUS

BARTOLOME & SANTIAGO

THE COLONIZING LAVA CACTUS IS OFTEN THE FIRST PLANT TO APPEAR ON THE BLACK LAVA ROCKS. LIKE THE TINY, FRAGILE MOLLUGO PLANT, IT CAN GERMINATE WHERE THERE IS VIRTUALLY NO SOIL

THE GALAPAGOS PENGUIN APPEARS ON THE ROCKS AROUND BARTOLOME. THESE BIRDS ALWAYS SHADE THEIR FEET WITH THEIR BODIES, WHEN STANDING AND LOOK QUIZZICALLY AT VISITORS

THE GALAPAGOS HAWK

BROWN PELICANS STAND AWKWARDLY ON DINGHY BOWS, OR PADDLE ROUND HOPEFULLY, WAITING FOR SCRAPS

A TYPICAL BACKWARD GLANCE

JAMES BAY ON SANTIAGO IS AN EXCELLENT PLACE TO SEE FUR SEALS, WHICH PREFER STEEPER, ROCKIER SHORES THAN SEALIONS

FEMALE MARINE TURTLES COME ASHORE, USUALLY AT NIGHT, TO LAY THEIR EGGS IN A SMALL PIT THEY MAKE IN THE SAND WITH THEIR FLIPPERS

FRIGATE BIRDS

THE LITTLE YELLOW WARBLER HOPS OVER LAVA ROCKS

THE VIEW FROM THE TOP OF BARTOLOME OVER TO SANTIAGO

History

During the four and a half centuries since their discovery in 1535, the Galápagos have had a rich and varied human history. Buccaneers, whalers, fur seal hunters, scientists, the military, convicts, fishermen, farmers, and crazed philosophers have all had their stay.

Discovery

As the Galápagos Islands lie at that point beyond which early navigators thought they would drop off the edge of the world, they were only discovered by accident, in 1535, by the Bishop of Panama, when he drifted 500 miles off course on his way to Peru. Writing to Charles V of Spain, he commented on the great tortoises, from which the islands take their name, the iguanas and the tameness of the birds. But the bishop was unable to find any use for the islands. He couldn't find any water either. To dampen their thirst, his crew were reduced to chewing cactus pads.

Pirate Years

The first use of the islands was by English renegades and buccaneers, and in the 17th century Captains Cook, Davis, Dampier and Eaton used them as a base and a retreat for their raids on the Spanish colonial ports. They stocked up on the islands with the water that had eluded the Bishop of Panama, and also tortoise meat, severely depleting the tortoise population as they did so. (Galápagos tortoise was an excellent ship's provision as it could stay alive for up to a year even if stacked in the hold.) It is possible that hidden caches of pirate gold and silver remain to be found. But the most unusual booty so far unearthed has been a cargo of eight tons of quince marmalade.

The Voyage of the *Beagle*

The most famous visitor to the Galápagos was Charles Darwin, in 1835 aboard the HMS *Beagle*, captained by Robert Fitzroy. Darwin described the dreary grey-green thorn brush of the Galapagos as being 'what we imagine the cultivated parts of the Infernal Regions to be.' But the Galápagos provided the intellectual light-bulb to Darwin's long, lulling and meditative trip, and during his stay he made a series of observations that confirmed his theories on evolution. Twenty four years later, he published the classic *'Origin of Species'*, the book that shook the foundations of biological thought and led to profound changes in man's philosophy of nature. Darwin's concept of evolution, through Natural Selection, still provides the basic framework for our understanding of the process today (see below for a further explanation of Darwin's theories).

Floreana Murders

Darwin was the Galápagos's most illustrious visitor, but there have been a number of more infamous residents.

The first permanent resident of the Galápagos was an Irishman, Patrick Walker. Marooned on Floreana in 1807, he spent two years growing vegetables which he exchanged with visiting whalers for rum. In 1809, he stole a whaling ship's longboat and five slaves. When he reached Guayaquil, there were no slaves on board and no-one ever discovered what he did to them.

117

A century and a half later, Floreana was the stage for another murder mystery. The cast was perfect: a German baroness and her three lovers; a crazed Nietzschean philospher, Karl Ritter, and his mistress Dore; and a family of pioneers, the Wittmers. Tensions swung between Ritter, who entertained visions of a Robinson Crusoe-esque paradise and self-determination, and the baroness, who wanted to turn the island into a hotel paradise. The Wittmers kept themselves to themselves. Occasionally a millionaire yachtsman would drop in to inspect the drama. International headlines reached a seventy-point peak in 1930s when the Baroness and one of her lovers disappeared without trace. Another lover later died whilst trying to get to San Cristóbal in an open boat. And Dr Ritter died of food poisoning after eating spoiled chicken—even though he was a vegetarian. A visiting journalist had predicted at the turn of the century that after the other Floreana settlers had 'turned to dust . . . Wittmer will still be sitting in his cosy little house smoking his pipe. The sun will rise and set, and he will forget to count the days.' The Wittmers still live on the sparsely populated island of Floreana and run the post office there.

Penal Days
The islands were officially annexed by Ecuador in 1832 despite attempts by England and the USA to have them for their own, and they were used as a penal colony. On Isabela the convicts were put to work building a wall around a volcano crater. One thousand metres long and five wide, it was called *El Muro de Las Lágrimas*, the weeping wall. At one point the wall dipped and the overseers put a thin plank between the two high points to bridge the declivity. A convict judged in need of the ultimate punishment would be sent across carrying a huge rock on his shoulders. The plank would snap under the strain.

The Present
The Galápagos were declared a National Park in 1959, with the tourist industry as their bread, butter and prosperity. As a tourist you will be pampered, pandered, cosseted, and occasionally rooked. The present population numbers about 9000, scattered in small communities through five islands; the capital island of San Cristóbal, Santa Cruz (the central island), Baltra (the airbase), Isabela and Floreana. Living on remote islands amongst communities so small that they share only three surnames, eccentricities inevitably emerge. In type, the Galápageños range from strong practical people, to the very dotty. Some are even as odd as the animals. Such is the nature of island life.

Conservation
Many visit the islands, more of the many come each year, and everyone wants too much. The Galápagos can only just sustain their natural dream world. In the past the islands' ecosystems have been saved by their isolation, but their present story is an all too familiar conflict between preservation and the economic need of a developing nation. Every foreign visitor must pay a US$40 park entrance fee on arrival and will then be given a full set of park rules. These rules do not impair your visit in any way and are a matter of common sense and courtesy. Do not litter, do not fed the animals, do not buy objects made of sea lions teeth or black coral, and stick to the trails; the wildlife is so prolific that you will see as much from the trails as anywhere else. Tourism is a smokeless industry that can nevertheless pollute, so show a conservationist attitude. As a general rule, take only photographs and leave only footprints.

118

Darwin's Theory

Darwin's theory of evolution is based on the idea that species populations are not static. So whilst plants and animals exist in the environmental framework of the present day, they also have an evolutionary ancestry in which present form is related to what happened in the past. Species continually change with each generation and they are not born in a divine flash, but over time, through the gradual accumulation of genetic variations.

When the tips of the Galápagos volcanoes first appeared above the sea's surface, some three to five million years ago, they were devoid of life. In the 19th century, Herman Melville even went so far as to describe some of the islands' more recently vulcanized slopes as being 'shaved of life'. The ancestors of every plant and animal species native to the Galapagos must therefore have arrived from some other part of the world. Before the advent of man, this could only have been as seeds in the crops of birds blown off course by strong winds, by swimming, or on natural rafts, such as pieces of flotsam. Of course, not every animal on the mainland could survive such a journey and the Galápagos has a distinctly partial ecosystem when compared to the South American mainland; the sea-crossing acted like a sieve. There is a preponderance of reptiles on the islands, but no amphibians (as their skins are too soft to have survived such a long immersion in salt water). There are many birds, but few mammals; only seals, whales, bats and a native rat that Thor Heyerdhal of Kon Tiki fame would be proud of—it holds the world record for sea crossings by terrestrial animals. Amongst plants, there are ferns, grasses and dandelions, but no palms or confiers—species that have very heavy seeds. That the flora and fauna of the islands is species-poor made it easier for Darwin to understand their ecological and evolutionary relationships.

Darwin's theory rested on three simple concepts:

- Organisms vary and these variations are inherited, at least in part, by their offspring.
- Organisms produce more offspring than can possibly survive.
- On average, offspring that vary most strongly in directions favoured by the environment will survive and propagate. Favourable variation will therefore accumulate in populations by natural selection.

In a classic example, a parent bird produces a chick whose bill is slightly longer than its own. This slight difference leads the chick to take better advantage of its environment than its sibling chicks that were not born with different bills. The long-billed chick then has a better chance of surviving—as does its own offspring and the new gene responsible for the longer beak.

Arriving at the virgin and empty land of the Galápagos, the offspring of ancestral animal pairs radiated into niches that would have normally been filled by competing species on the mainland. It is the clarity and delicacy of this patterning on the islands that so delighted Darwin. His most famous example were the islands' 13 species of finches, all descended from one ancestral pair. He wrote of them: there is 'a most singular group of finches related to each other in the structure of their beaks, short tails, form of body and plumage. Seeing this gradation and diversity of structure in one small, intimately related group of birds, one might really fancy that from an original paucity of birds in this archipelago, one species had been taken and modified for different ends.' Darwin saw

119

that some of the finches ate seeds, others insects or leaves, some removed ticks from tortoises, others drank blood from seabirds. There were even two species that used twigs or cactus spines to extract larvae from holes in the dead branches of trees—a food source that might have been taken up by woodpeckers, say, on the mainland.

Darwin argued his case for evolution like a lawyer, using verifiable facts, such as the finches, not the time-bound scholastic approach of beginning with an *a priori* thesis learnt from books and other authorities at home. He had an important philosophical point to prove, namely, that evolution is not purposeful, that there is no Grand Divine Design, and that the process of Natural Selection is based on a mixture of chance and necessity instead of on some evolutionary 'higher purpose'.

Darwin was no moral dolt and he was ever well aware of the higher ramifications of his theory. But A. R. Wallace, the co-discoverer of natural selection, could never bring himself to apply Darwin's philosophical materialism to the human mind, which he viewed as the only divine contribution to human life. Wallace's version might be the truer for recorded in Darwin's deathbed diaries is the strange and curious entry; 'why is it that I feel like a machine?'

Galápagos Wildlife

The bleached vegetation of Baltra island—as dry and fuzzy as an old man's hair—comes as a shock to most visitors arriving at the archipelago's major airstrip. After the verdant madness of mainland Ecuador, the island is drab and low: an inappropriate introduction to one of the world's most famous nature paradises. Plants, after all, form the most basic starting point of any food chain, and unless you include the cactus and the withered and bony *Palo Santo* tree as viable plant food, there does not seem to be any. Although Baltra is one of the drier islands, most of the archipelago is semi-desert, with only the highlands of the bigger islands receiving enough rain to be considered tropically lush. How then do the animals survive?

Most of the wildlife depends on the sea for its livelihood as the marine life of the Galápagos is so exceptionally rich. The combination of cool up-welling waters in some parts (from the Humboldt Current) and of warm tropical waters in others, has allowed for a great diversity of marine flora and fauna. Animal feeding patterns overlap from the sea to the land and back again. For example: marine iguanas dive for algae, hawks feed on young marine iguanas, flies feed on the carcasses of dead iguanas, lizards feed on flies, and snakes feed on lizards. The webs of life on land and sea are inextricably, albeit delicately, linked. This explains why so much Galápagos wildlife is concentrated along the rocky coasts, despite their foreboding, haggard and inhospitable appearance.

Galápageñan wild life appears completely innocent. You can freely approach animals, and they will you. Even lizards on the footpath will not scurry away. The islands' distance from the mainland may have led to some strange and unique patterns of speciation, but it has also meant that colonizing animals have never had to face the majority of their mainland predators. It is probably the absence of large mammalian predators, rather than the only recent arrival of man, that accounts for the fearlessness of the fauna.

Below is a list of some of the principal species that you will see in a relaxed week's touring. The list is far from complete and if you want more detailed information, there are a number of natural history guides you could take with you. Recommended, is M. H. Jackson's *Galápagos: A Natural History Guide* (Univ of Calgary Press). Far and away the best of the general guides on offer, it is usually available in Quito's Libri Mundi book store, if not on the islands.

Reptiles

There are very few terrestrial mammals on the islands. Instead there are reptiles, with the giant tortoises and land iguanas playing the ecological roles of their mammalian counterparts on the mainland. Melville wrote: 'Little but reptilian life is found here. The chief sound of life is a hiss.'

The **giant tortoise**, *Geochelone elephantous*, is the best known of the animals, and Galápagos comes from the Spanish root of the word for tortoise, 'galápago'. Shaped like boulders, giant tortoises can weigh up to 250kg, with the tops of their carapaces, or shells, reaching up to a grown-man's waist. They are mythically slow—workers have estimated that they can travel no faster than 0.3 kph—and they move stiffly, clumsily swinging their leathery-skinned limbs around the edges of their shells like crawling babies. Varying from island to island, there were orginally 14 sub-species of the Galápagos tortoise, distinguishable by the different shapes of their shell. Severely depleted by hunting and the belief that drinking a 200 year-old tortoise's blood would greatly improve your chances of life expectancy, only ten viable sub-species now remain. Of the eleventh, the Pinta species, there is only *one* left, 'Lonesome George'. Living in a much-visited pen at the Darwin Research Station on Santa Cruz island, his name suggests a venerable old man with moss and lichen growing on his carapace. But George is in fact a strapping 60-year old bachelor looking for his other half. To continue his species, a US$10,000 reward is on offer if you can find a Pinta female. Failing that, there are plans to clone him.

Watching giant tortoises mate at the **reserve on Santa Cruz** is a comical affair. Their shells clunk-clunk together in slow time. The male wobbles—he falls off! And the female lumbers away. If he hasn't landed on his back, the fallen male has been known to vent his frustration on the rounded back of any similarly shaped nearby rock. By comparison, the mating of **marine turtles** amidst the mangroves around Black Turtle Cove is one of the most beautiful and mysterious of the Galápagos's sights. The lagoons are as quiet as a secret. The still green surface is only broken when a coupled pair comes up for air and the only sounds are of their little snorts and puffs. Then they disappear again, breaking away underwater from the dinghy, perhaps to re-appear on the other side half an hour later. The marine turtle's breeding season runs from November to January.

The most characteristic animal of the Galápagos's tortured coastline is the lichen-coloured **marine iguana**—the only seagoing lizard in the world. Feeding off algae on the sea bed, their salt intake is extremely high. Glands above the eye secrete the excess salt, which is then expelled with a dragon-like snort through their nostrils. Darwin called them 'his imps of darkness'. And when sitting in large groups near the sucking surf—which is usual—they have all the serious airs of a cabalistic seance in progress.

The brightly coloured marine iguana has a cousin; the torpid **land iguana**. These drab, yellow-greenish lizards live in dry lowlands, such as around the South Plaza islets, and obtain all of their liquid from the prickly pear cactus, their only food source. Darwin commented on their 'singularly stupid appearance' and although large, they are completely harmless.

Lava lizards are the most ubiquitous of the reptiles. You will recognize them by their red throats and distinctive territorial 'push-up' behaviour. Vision is their most important sense, and they are particularly sensitive to movement, especially to objects the size of an insect. Flick a pebble in front of one and he will chase it.

Finally, there are only three species of snake on the islands and they are all non-poisonous.

Birds

The birdlime-streaked rocks of the Galápagos testify to the fact that the islands are an aviary of the ocean. Fifty-eight bird species have been recorded on the islands and of these the most casual visitor will see at least twenty in a week's gentle touring.

Sea birds

As is to be expected, sea birds occupy a prominent place in the island fauna. Of these, **frigate birds** are amongst the most noticeable. As their name suggests, they are pirates of the air and aviators par excellence. They have the greatest wing to bodyweight ratio in the world and you will see their black shapes stall, break, stutter, sweep, swoop, soar and tangle wherever there are fisherman's scraps to be had. Occasionally you will see one harrass another flying bird, such as the **tropic-bird**, recognizable by its long white tail-streamers and coral-red bill. If the chase is succesful, the frigate bird swoops down to catch the tropic-bird's disgorged bolus of food before it hits the ocean. Male frigate birds have large, red gular sacks that are inflated to the size of soccer balls when courting. You will see this mating display at the frigate bird colony on Seymour Island. Sitting plumply in the middle of a safe and appetizing pre-made nest, the males drum their beaks against the pouches in order to attract one of the hovering females and her solitary egg.

The clownish **boobies** are perhaps the most famous of the Galápagos sea-birds. With their pointed, tapered bill, topedo-shaped body and pointed tail, the booby is well equipped for fishing by plunge-diving. Flying in long lines, you will see them twist and dive vertically from a height of twenty metres, folding their wings in a split second. Whole flocks will dive simultaneously on large shoals, emptying, as if on command, a previously busy sky.

Although there are three species of booby—the white-plumed masked booby, and the red-footed booby (which you can only see on remote Genovesa Island)—the most common is the blue-footed. Looking as though they have just stepped out of a puddle of sky-blue paint, their webbed feet are so wide that on land they waddle with the same exaggerated care as swimmers wearing flippers. There is a large colony on Española; watch out for their hooting, honking and sky-pointing mating display.

Also on Española is the world's largest population of **waved albatrosses**. Although aristocratic in aspect and in flight, the albatross is yet to perfect the techniques of take-off and landing. They need a high cliff to launch from and their most common cause of death comes from crippling leg injuries following a crash-landing. Parents are monogamous, will remain coupled until they die, and celebrate their choice of partner with a complicated and frantic courtship dance that has been called an 'ecstasy ritual'. It involves much coquetry, more sky-pointing and no little beak-kissing, and is most common in April and late October. The albatross offspring that are born at the end of August are so grotesque that they have been described as having 'the fascination of only the truly ugly.' You will see them, over-beaked and covered in greasy down, waiting for their parents in shaded nursery groups off the side of the path.

The **Pelican** of Galápageñan zoology is a water bird with a wing span of some six feet and a very long bill whose lower mandible distends to form a pouch for holding fish. His expression is lugubrious, his plumage a dull, ashy colour. The pelican of fable, a much more interesting bird, is known to open its breast and feed its young with its own blood. Blood that gives life to the dead suggests the Eucharist, and so a famous line of Dante's *Paradiso* calls Jesus Christ *nostro Pelicano*—mankind's pelican. The Galápagos brown pelican is often seen at anchorage sitting on dinghies, or flying in sedate chevrons, low over the tops of waves.

The most incongruous bird of the islands must be the **Galápagos penguin**—the only penguin species to live and nest entirely in the tropics. Comical and myopic, to defend itself the penguin resorts to the most endearing of strategies. When on land, it merely turns its white frock-coat away from the predator, hoping that its black back will blend into the lavascape. In the sea, however, it can power along at 40 kph. The sleek, black flightless **cormorant** is another swimming bird of the islands; you can see streamlined members of this vulnerable species on Isabela and Fernandina. Although it has lost many of the attributes of a flying cormorant, it still dries its wings after swimming in the outstretched manner so characteristic of its family.

Land Birds

With few exceptions, the land birds are a dull-coloured lot. But as if to make up for their lack of exciting colour, their tameness is unsurpassed. Curious and impudent, every visitor has commented on their fearlessness. Darwin wrote, 'it would appear that the birds of this archipelago, not having as yet learnt that man is a more dangerous animal than the tortoise or the *Amlyrhynchus*, disregard him, in the same manner as in England shy birds, such as magpies, disregard the cows and horses of the field.' You are likely to see the **Galápagos dove**, with its blue-ringed eyes; at least some of Darwin's dumpy-looking 13 **finches**; inquisitive, thrush-sized, long-tailed, grey/brown **mocking birds**, that will greet you at every landing; and the flashing red spark which marks the tiny, highland **vermilion flycatcher**.

The most fearless of the land birds, however, is the **Galápagos hawk**. In 1845, Darwin wrote: 'A gun here is useless; for with its muzzle I pushed a hawk out of the branch of a tree.' As these mottled brown birds have no natural enemies, they fear no one and may even approach you. You are likely to see them on the beach near any newly-born seal pup, waiting on the blood-rich placenta.

Mammals

Oceanic islands typically lack mammal populations and the Galápagos are no exception. The two weeks or so that it would take for a raft to drift out to the islands is too long for most mammals to survive. With the exception of two bat and rice rat species, the only naturally introduced mammals on the islands are all swimmers. Other mammals that have since been introduced by man, such as pigs, goats, and rats, now constitute a serious problem: they feed on young species and compete with endemic adults for available food sources. If you see a weather-beaten hunter riding around the islands on a trial bike, with a rifle slung over his back, take note, he is the mammal catcher.

Whilst cruising between the islands you will often see **dolphins** riding the bow-waves of your boat. Dolphins are curious, playful, social and very sexy; they're bisexual. They have complex brains which are larger than man's. They have an incredibly refined capacity to form auditory images and 'hear' the texture of objects around them, suggesting that they can look into each other in eerie ways and read emotional states. They once lived on land and gradually, for unknown reasons, took to the seas. One story is that they approached man at around the time of Plato and Aristotle, but the philosophers and religious men rebuffed them, so they retreated into the depths of the sea to await a better time for communication and understanding. Whilst swimming at night, phosphorescing plankton can make them look like guiding lights.

Most obviously present, however, are the **sea lions**, so common in fact that you will trip over them, especially on any sandy beach or gently rocky shore. Honking off the beach will always be a jealous male, cruising the beach's colony on an exhausting and endless round of self-imposed guard duty. The male's harem is less a fixed quota of female seals than a territorial stretch of beach, with females left free to wander into a neighbouring bull's territory. Inevitably there are surplus males, and these form gentlemen's club-like bachelor colonies, especially noticeable on the cliffs of South Plaza Island.

Alternately playful and inquisitive, aggressive and lazy, seals can seem too human. Lonely early settlers are said to have taken females into their arms to alleviate their desert island frustrations. But although the most endearing animal on earth (oh!-how-I'd-like-to-hold-one), do not touch any pup; its mother may refuse it afterwards, or bite you. Also be wary of the bulls.

Hunted almost to extinction in the 1800s, there is also a small population of **fur seals** on the islands. Most easily distinguished from sea lions by their smaller size and large, mournful eyes, the best place to see them is around the grottos in James Bay, on Santiago Island.

Visiting the Islands

It takes at least a week to fully tour the islands. Journey times between islands vary from less than half an hour, to overnight, and it is best to visit a few central islands and inspect them closely, rather than trying to cram as many ports of call as possible into your cruise. If you want to visit the outer-lying island of Isabela, you will have to allow two weeks.

When **choosing a boat**, bear in minds its size; some resemble cigar boxes, others troop ships, only with swimming pools. The best option is the middle course; a small but well-equipped craft—you will not necessarily be sacrificing any comfort; a small group is much more flexible as to how it can behave on shore; you will come into much closer contact with the animals; and you will not feel as though you are invading the islands.

Generally, when **organizing a tour**, you can either: spend money and save time, by booking a trip before you leave, which will cost anything in between US$600 and US$1500; or spend time and save money, by arriving at the islands under your own steam and then joining-up with other tourists in Puerto Ayora to haggle with a local capitan over renting a vessel. This may take up to a week to arrange, but it's a common method and there are always people wandering around looking for a berth. The standard fare for a 10- to 20-berth boat is around US$50 per day, per passenger (including food). But remember that the cheapest option is not necessarily the best. Is the boat clean? Do you like the crew? Is there a naturalist on board, or a guide who can double as a naturalist? (Every boat, by law, must have a naturalist.) If the boat is very high off the water, it will roll more at sea. Do you get seasick? Are the engines loud? Is the boat fast? You don't want to waste all of your time chugging in between islands. Most importantly, what will you be eating—just caught fish? It is also a good idea to get the itinerary down in writing.

As a last option, it is possible to take day trips out of Puerto Ayora, but this will only give you the slightest of Galápagos experiences. The place to be is on a boat, cruising.

Cruise Itineraries

It is hard to go wrong on the Galápagos. Whichever itinerary you choose, you are sure to return with an adventurer's sense of superiority and self-worth, ready to spin tales of sea lions the size of whales, flocks of penguins and dragon-esque iguanas.

The National Park Service has created 45 visitor sites, with marked trails, around the archipelago. These are placed in areas with rich concentrations of wildlife or other interesting features. To visit each site you will travel from ship to shore in a small dinghy, or *panga*, and land either on rocks ('dry landings') or beaches ('wet landings'). Most visits are three to four hours long during the morning or afternoon. This is ample time to walk the trials at a leisurely pace and to study and photograph the plants and animals.

To make the most of a seven-day tour, you could try a circuit something like this:

Española (Hood): although this is the most southerly and oldest of the islands in the archipelago, it is also one of the best endowed: well worth the long boat trip to see the albatross and blue-footed booby mating colonies. The cliffs abound in marine iguanas and at the eastern end of the island there is also a white-sand beach, Gardner Bay, with good swimming, snorkelling, and a sea lion colony.

Santa Fé: on the way back to the central islands, this small island has very good snorkelling off sea lion beaches. If you spent half an hour in the water you would be likely to see sea-lion, marine turtle and sharks. A short walk up to the cliffs takes you to a giant *opuntia* cactus forest and land iguana colony.

Santa Cruz: Santa Cruz has the highest population of the islands and the most tourist facilities. If you never actually stay in town, you will anchor in its bay at least once. In terms of nature-spotting, the island offers the turtle reserve in the highlands and the

Darwin Research Station, just outside Puerto Ayora. For more details, see below under 'Puerto Ayora'.

South Plaza: these small, barren islets, shaped like ramps, are off the east coast of Santa Cruz, and are covered in a hallucinogenic carpet of red sesuvium. There is a colony of long-tailed tropic birds nesting on the cliffs, where there is also a bachelor sea lion colony. At the low end of the island there is also a large colony of land-iguanas.

Seymour: a short journey north from South Plaza, this has magnificent frigate bird nesting colonies.

Black Turtle Cove: on the north coast of Santa Cruz is the marine turtle's mating lagoon, one of the most beautiful of the Galápagos sights, with shark-spotting off the beach.

Rabida: has a flamingo colony in the lagoon just off the *red* beach, where there is also sea lion.

James Bay, Santiago (San Salvador): one of the most picturesque of the bays in the Galápagos. On land, you can either climb the Sugarloaf volcano (395 m) or walk along the shore to see the fur seals playing around the crevices of their lava grottos. The bay was once the home of buccaneers and the site of a crazy and abortive colonization scheme. By the landing site, you can still see the rusted remains of the brothel that the entrepreneurial Victor Egas set up to attract workers to the island. Like so many of the other eccentrics who dot Galápageñan history, he disappeared one day, and nobody knows the true end of his story. Intertidal marine life is rich, and the bay is a good place to anchor for the night.

Sullivan Bay, Santiago: on the western side of the island from James Bay, Sullivan is a huge burnt-sugar-black lava flow, from an eruption at the turn of the century, which reaches right down to the water. The lava field is still uneroded, and you will see lava bubbles and the sharp **pahoehoe** lava formation. Best visited in the morning, the black basaltic rock is like a solar radiator and by the afternoon the air above is warped by the vehemence of the heat haze.

Bartolomé: just across the bay from Sullivan, is the best volcanic walk of the islands. The vista of Santiago from the top of Bartolomé (a steep, but not difficult half-hour climb) has been frequently photgraphed, and justly so. There are two beaches at the base of the volcano where you can relax after your climb. The sheltered north beach has good swimming, snorkelling, and penguins are common; the windier southern beach has turtles and sharks.

*If you had **another week**, you could also visit:*

Genovesa (Tower): this is the most northeasterly of the islands and as such, rarely visited. If you are a keen bird-watcher however, you might want to consider including it in your itinerary. Tower has the largest colonies of red-footed and masked booby, and also large concentrations of red-billed tropic birds, great frigate birds, swallow-tailed gulls, storm petrels, Galápagos doves and short-eared owls. If you went snorkelling, you might also see hammerhead sharks.

Floreana: at **Punta Cormorant** there is a *green* beach (due to crystals of the mineral olivine) with sea-lions and good swimming. On the way to the *white* sand beach 400 m away, there is the island's largest flamingo colony. A *panga* ride around the submerged circle of rocks, the **Devil's Crown**, a few hundred metres from Punta Cormorant, provides one of the most outstanding views of marine life in the islands: the snorkelling is wonderful and you will see fish by the thousand, coral, sea-lion, and, perhaps, shark.

Isabela: this is the largest of the islands in the group, and occupies 58% of the Galápagos' total land mass. The island is shaped like a west-facing 'C', with all of the visitor sites inside the crescent. Getting to the sites therefore takes time—at least a week, so if you are only on the Galápagos for ten days say, visiting Isabela would exclude any of the other islands. It is, however, worth the effort. You can climb **Volcán Alcedo** (1128 m), famous for its giant tortoise colony and steaming caldera. See flightless cormorants at **Punta Albemarle**. And watch the largest penguin colony on the islands at **Elizabeth Bay**, where there are also good opportunities to see marine turtles and rays.

Fernandina: this is the most westerly and youngest of the islands. On the edges of its huge volcanic landscape can be found the largest concentration of marine iguanas on the Galápagos, and also large numbers of penguins and flightless cormorants.

Puerto Ayora, Santa Cruz

Santa Cruz's only port, Puerto Ayora, is a scruffy and incomplete-looking town of two storey houses struggling up to a third, with no hospital and an irregular electricity supply. But it is the main tourist base in the Galápagos, the only town on the islands with accommodation, and the best place for you to hire boats if you haven't already booked a cruise from the mainland.

The port is one of those strange places in the centre of everything, and yet in the middle of no-where. On the one hand, basic amenities—such as food and fresh water—are dependent on irregular cargoes from the mainland and are periodically scarce. On the other, sun-burnt visitors from around the world fill the cafés, bars and discos that line the main street along the waterfront with their Babel.

Stay any length of time and you will realise that life on Santa Cruz lacks the basic frills of living, like space, that mask natural quirks of character. The town is so small that everyone has to say hello to everyone else at least ten times a day. As the saying goes *pueblo pequeño, infierno grande*, the smaller the village the greater the fire, and gossip in Puerto Ayora is more than just a way of passing the time; it's a way of life.

GETTING THERE AND AROUND
You will either arrive by boat—in which case as soon as you dock, you will see your crew zip away with uncharacteristic speed to meet their girlfriends or to have a beer in town—or by bus, over the island's only road, from the airstrip at Baltra on the other side of the island.

Except to meet airflights, there are only very occasional buses up into the highlands— ask at the office on the waterfront for schedules. Occasionally you can convince someone with a car to hire it out to you as a taxi, but this is not cheap.

TOURIST INFORMATION

It is essential to re-confirm your departure flight at the **TAME** office on the main street (open Mon–Fri, morning and afternoon; Saturday mornings only). If you are on a cruise, your crew will do this for you.

If you have not brought enough local currency with you, changing **money** can be very difficult: the souvenir shop on the corner opposite the volleyball park will sometimes help.

If you do go souvenir hunting, please don't buy any black coral. Even though many shops do stock it, it is an endangered species.

ACTIVITIES

Charles Darwin Research Station

Open Mon–Sat from 9 am to 4 pm, the station is one kilometre east of town and is the main base for biological research on all of the islands. There is a scientific library open for public use (mornings and afternoons, Mon–Sat), an exhibition hall with a permananent display explaining the geology, flora and fuana of the islands, and tortoise mating pens. If you are not going to see the tortoise reserve in the highlands of Santa Cruz or Isabela, this is the only place in the islands where you will be able to see giant tortoises, both adult and infant. Look out for 'Lonesome George'!

Turtle Bay

Four kilometres west of Puerto Ayora, a one-hour walk along a rocky path, lies the squeaky, brilliant-white sand of Turtle Bay beach. Melville described it as 'a bare heap of finest sand, like the unverdured mound at the bottom of an hourglass.' True to his description, all there is, is beach and sea. Unlike all the other beaches in Ecuador, there are no drink-dispensing *cassettas*, so it is a good idea to take something to drink with you.

Santa Cruz Highlands and Lava Tubes

Buses occasionally make the trans-island journey on Santa Cruz's only road. It is worth taking one, if only to see how different—lush, well-watered and green—the highlands are in comparison to the coast. A 2 km walk east of **Bellavista**, a small village 7 km north of Puerto Ayora, lie the island's largest lava tubes. The size of a respectable underground subway, these cavernous tubes formed when the outer skin of a lava flow solidified and the inner portion kept on flowing, eventually emptying the shell. If you have a torch, you can walk the tubes for a damp kilometre. Entrance is US$1.

The Tortoise Reserve

West of Bellavista lies the even smaller village of **Santa Rosa**. And below Santa Rosa, half-an-hour's walk down a muddy trail, is the Tortoise Reserve, the easiest place in the Galápagos to see giant tortoises in their natural habitat. You will see their lumpy shapes maneouvring through the long grass. Tortoises are deaf and can be approached freely from behind. As they have no muscles in their chests, their lungs are worked like bellows by their legs and old men's heads. When startled, the withdrawal of their limbs is accompanied by a sharp hiss.

PLACES TO STAY

The best hotel in Puerto Ayora is the **Galápagos**, on the road east of town. With 14 cottage rooms overlooking Pelican Bay, the hotel offers uninterrupted views of the ocean, a library sensibly equipped with a bar, and a good, even if over-priced, restaurant. The charge is US$35 per person per night. Across the harbour, and accessible only by dinghy, the **Delphin** has a private beach and is bookable only through Metropolitan tours.

The **Hotel Sol y Mar** is also on the waterfront and has cabin accomodation for 20 people, divided into singles, doubles, triples and quadruples, at US$10, $15, $17 and $20 respectively.

There are also several good, cheaper hotels and *residencias* in town. The **Residencia** with no name, behind the TAME office, has large clean rooms, even if no bathroom, for US$2 per person. The **Gloria**, on the road out of town towards the research station, is friendly, clean and modern. Señora Gloria also only charges US$2 per person. A little further on, **Residencial Angermyer** is run down but funky, and is managed by one of the kookiest of the island's original settlers—the turbaned and muttering Señora Angermyer. A last choice kind of place, despite its pretty gardens, also US$2.

PLACES TO EAT

There are a number of bars and restaurants in Puerto Ayora, especially on the water-front. **La Panga** and the **Four Lanterns** restaurants are opposite each other on the road to the Research Station and they are both very popular with locals and tourists. The **Pelican Café**, two blocks inland from the Hotel Sol y Mar, is an unassuming place, but very good for breakfast and midday fruit juices. **La Ninfas Restaurant** by the harbour has been a standard meeting place for years; their fresh fish lunches are good and reasonably priced. As already mentioned, the restaurant at the **Hotel Galápagos**, is the best, and the most expensive, in town.

RECOMMENDED READING

Most of the following, and quite a few more, are generally available on the islands or in Quito's Libri Mundi book store.

Natural History
Galápagos: a Natural History Guide by M. H. Jackson (Univ of Calgary Press, 1988).
A Field Guide to the Birds of the Galápagos by M. Harris (Collins, 1982).
Plants of the Galápagos by M. Harris (New York, 1984).

General History
Galápagos; World's End by W. Beebe (1924).
Darwin and the Beagle by Alan Moorehead (Penguin,1977).
The Galápagos Affair by J. E. Treherne (Johnathan Cape, 1983).
Floreana—a memoir by Margaret Wittmer (Anthony Nelson, 1989).

Part VIII

EL ORIENTE (THE AMAZON)

Spider Monkey

'Green, green, green ... water green, moss green, tree with green orchids, green trees with parrots, fallen green tree ... all I have seen is green.'
—Ludwig Bemelmans, *The Donkey Inside*, 1841

Everything is uncertain in the Amazon; it's a world of subterfuge, disguise and deceit, never quite what you will have imagined it to be. The vines look like snakes, the snakes like vines, and the ground is not ground at all but a bed of decomposing vegetation that imitates the contours of solid earth. The burps and whirrups of insect noises seem electronic rather than animal. Even the several ceilings of vegetation ape something else—the curlicues, columns, balconies and false perspectives of baroque cathedrals or theatres.

Ecuador's eastern tropical lowlands, El Oriente (literally 'the East'), were once seen from Quito as being as inaccessible, remote and as marvellous as Paris. Although now easily reached by plane or bus from Quito or Amabato, El Oriente is still Ecuador's wild frontier. Soldiers from the disputed Peruvian border and gold prospectors with their attendant retinues of whores, rub shoulders in the honky-tonk bars of scruffy oil towns such as Lago Agrio and Coca. Oil workers feed coins into old Wurlitzer jukeboxes. And missionaries, specifically the evangelists of the Summer Institute of Linguistics, have only recently been banned. (In the years when they were harvesting souls in the jungle, there was a story of an oil-worker, who, figuring that the Indians deserved a better chance, would dress up of an evening in a priest's black habit with white collar, sweat himself up until his face shone, and then swing through the doors of a saloon shouting, 'Where are the girls?'. A shoot-out can still *seem* possible.)

The history of the forest tells us time and time again of how it has never respected orderly European ambitions. This includes tourism! Don't go expecting the game of a Tarzan adventure; wildlife is scarce. Also, if you are looking for a piquant native touch to your holiday, don't expect to find villages populated by Indians sporting breechclouts and face-paint. Inhabitants of the most accesssible villages are more likely to be wearing tee-shirts and baseball hats, dresses and lipstick. Tourist facilities are sparse. You must be prepared for long waits, and no little boredom. Journeys, by bus or canoe, are arduous but adventurous. Weather is unpredictable, not infrequently rainy and unpleasant. And food is very simple, usually only spaghettis, or some fish chopped up with boiled plantains.

Despite these caveats the jungle is perhaps nowhere more easily reached in South America than in Ecuador, and some of the disadvantages of other parts of the Amazon, such as the inadvisability of swimming in the rivers, are absent. Also, if you haven't been to the Amazon, you haven't been to South America, and when people wistfully sigh, '*Amazoniaaa*' it is not for the lack of any reason.

An Infinitude of Species

Ecologically, the Amazon is the richest area in the world. In the collective imagination, it appears as a vast green swath of forest, mostly flat, that stretches unchanging and without interruption from the foothills of the Andes to the Atlantic ocean. But underneath what looks from the plane like a sea of broccoli, the jungle is inconstant. Spattered here and there, throughout the basin, is an irregular mosaic of different forests, on different soils, with varying climates and species. 'The jungle,' wrote Vargas Llosa, 'is like a hot woman—always changing.'

About 300 million years ago, most of what is now the Amazon basin lay beneath the sea, on the edge of the super-landmass, Pangea. There were rivers, but they flowed west from the ancient rock formations that now lie in Brazil and the Guianas. Some 200 million years ago, Pangea began to separate and the Andes rose, blocking off the flow of the western running waters. A huge inland lake formed, fed by east-flowing Andean rivers that only broke east, into the Atlantic, much later. Some areas in the new continent were left as islands of dry savannah. Occasionally the basin would flood. This, as the brilliant 19th century geographer, de Cunha, explained,' acted like a wet sponge that passes over a poorly done drawing. It obliterates, modifies or transforms the most firm and salient features.'

The landscape of the Amazon has always been in a state of flux. Large areas that were left isolated from each other by rivers or dry savannah would rejoin millions of years later. And it was in these pockets, or refuges, that divergent species evolved in their own time, each eventually contributing to the immense multiplicity of Amazonian species. Everytime you take a step in the Amazon, you tread on about 1500 species of plants and animals, of which only 30 are known to man. The high ceiling on the world's possible number of species had once been set at one and half million. Recent work suggests that the Amazon has at least ten million insect species alone.

Unless you are gliding down a small, leafy tributary, river travel on the Amazon is only horizon and distance; nothing comes close. All that you will see of the shore is the monotonous grandeur of an endless palisade of trees, growing high on the shore's rich and regularly replenished alluvial soils. Conversely, travel within the jungle reveals no horizons or distances. Everything is close. You can never see further than 30 metres. But if you stay quiet and let the forest close around you, all will be revealed.

The most salient features are trees. The great muscled roots of the giant *ceibas* reach out and explore the earth in search of leafy detritus. On the ground stream trails of leaf-cutting ants, their tiny bodies supporting small green sails of scissored vegetation. Primitive agriculturalists, they use the leaves to make hot beds in which they grow the fungi that they eat. Other ants, hating the sun, construct covered passage ways that twist up the trunks. The jungle delights in tricks and vegetable dexterity: burning chunks of certain termite mounds releases a smoke that keeps away insects; another tree's acidic leaves destroys young saplings and, consequently, is always circled by open ground that looks as though it had been swept clean.

The most hidden, but perhaps most important feature of Amazon ecology is the soil, or rather the lack of it. 'The very signs from which we form our judgements are often very deceptive; a soil that is adorned with tall and graceful trees is not always a favourable one, except, of course for those trees', wrote the prescient Pliny in his *Natural History*. Unlike a temperate forest's reserve of nutrients that circulates slowly in deep soil, the Amazon's fertility lies above ground, in a whirling and extravagant pattern of mutually dependent species. Not in fact the verdant madness that it seems to be, this is a system that has come to be organized in a pattern as tight, complicated, and delicate as a spider's web.

Ecologically, the system is closed. Nothing is wasted. Stray nutrients are scarce. Everything is highly competed for. To this end, the *palo santo* tree exhibits a remarkable symbiosis; tap the tree and *azteca* ants with a poisonous bite come running out and swarm over the trunk and surrounding ground. The trunk has small circular channels down its centre which connect to tunnels in all the branches, so that the ants can immediately appear from their subterranean tunnels. Plants cannot afford to lose too many leaves to herbivores, and the ants defend the tree from their foraging. They also nip off the buds of encroaching lianas.

The Amazon—contrary to popular opinion—is not the lung of the world, even though its steamy air might move with the soft turbulence of a held breath. Only 0.055 per cent of the world's oxygen is produced by photosynthesis, and even if the Amazon produces half of it, most is probably reabsorbed by the fungi breaking down leaves.

If you shine a torch into the riverbank foliage at night, and see two red glints lurking in the bushes that look like the glowing ends of lit cigarettes, these are crocodile's eyes. In the Amazon there are butterflies bigger than monkeys, dragonflies that catch hummingbirds, and birds that climb trees. But, with the exception of monkeys, it is unlikely that you will see much game. If you go with an experienced guide, however, he will be able to point out to you, amongst other things, the liana that when cut produces a spout of drinkable water, the red berries of the *achiote* plant that are used as rouge by the Amazonian Indians, the cinnamon trees that prompted Pizarro's voyage of exploration in the 16th century, and the nodes in the leaves of plants that are parasitized as nests by ants. If you are lucky, you might see an anaconda curled around the branches of a riverside tree. But without someone to see and point out the way for you, the jungle can be indecipherable.

The Amazon Indians

Peter Mathiessen's novel *At Play in the Fields of the Lord*, published in 1965, describes the collision of men of adventure and men of God with a native group, and the passion that arises between an Indian woman and the North American narrator. The love proves fatal. The narrator's kiss transmits the disease that destroys her tribe and also signals the fatal irruption of the outside world. The author's message seems to be that to discover Eden is to destroy it, and that by the tales we tell we doom the natural tropical world which we love, and its inhabitants.

For the past 500 years, the Amazon Indians have been alternately romanticized, missionized and killed, sometimes at the same time. In the popular imagination they appear as Rousseauian creatures of the forest, incapable of the exercise of adult decisions. But this is only a vision in keeping with the misleading view of the jungle as an Eden, as an undisturbed and aeons-old cradle of biological evolution. One can well wish that the Amazon Indian had been left alone in the first place. But, as the history of the Amazon tells us, its only natural course has always been change. And, better still, many Indian groups are now organizing themselves into political bodies and lobbying groups to protect their deedless lands from encroaching farmers, planters or oil men. This is most apparent in Brazil, but also, to a lesser degree, in Ecuador.

There are a number of Amazon groups living in El Oriente, and each one differs markedly from the next. Although you are very unlikely to meet any Shuar—they occupy the most south-eastern part of the jungle, in the disputed area nearest Peru—they are Ecuador's largest Indian group and they can at least provide a window onto the country's other Amazon peoples.

Although originally called the Jivaro, of head-shrinking fame, the name carried pejorative connotations of savage, and they now use the name 'Shuar', which means 'man' or 'human being'. They number 60,000, and are divided between Ecuador and Peru. Their language bears no relation to other American languages, but it does have a remote relationship with certain proto-Asiatic languages.

The first reference to them was by Captain Hernán de Bernavente, in a letter sent to Lima, on 25 March, 1550. He wrote: 'I tell you, your highnesses, that these people are more insolent and troublesome than any other I have seen, in all of the time that I have been in the Indies.' Warlike and protected by thick jungle, the name 'Shuar' quickly became synonymous with the word 'indomitable'.

In 1599, they attacked Spaniards encroaching on their territory in the quest for gold. Taking the outpost's garrison, they poured gold into the governor's mouth saying that they wanted to see how much he would need before being finally satiated.

Conquering the Shuar became a Spanish obsession, but the Shuar were never directly defeated or converted. Instead, they were finally subdued by goods and by accepting certain products, such as metal tools, they fell into a cycle of dependence.

Their economic livelihood is part nomadic hunter, part horticulturalist. But generally, they eat as much vegetables as they need, and as much meat as they can.

Excellent ecologists, their houses are just one example of their keen good sense. There is always a fire burning, and the smoke kills insects that might destroy the roof. There are no partitions within the hut, but space is rigorously divided between kitchen, sleeping and conversation areas. One German anthropologist found the construction an optimum dwelling place for the jungle's climate. As just one example; in the hot sun, the roof warms, creating cooling convection currents through its leaves.

Traditionally, the Shuar attribute all evil to the influence of other men moved primarily by envy. Misfortunes, such as disease, are diagnosed by tracing the envy back to the sender. This tracing back is the work of the shaman who often gets to see, or know, the path that the envy has taken through the visions of a drug-induced trance state. Hallucinogenic plants are used. Mythologies such as these—if indeed they are mythologies—are often taken as a collection of ridiculous tales, with eccentric characters, amusing and often obscene. But whilst there is much self-admitted trickery to the witch-doctor's craft, who is to say that there might not be a transcendental plane of Shamanistic knowledge?

GETTING TO SEE THE JUNGLE

A glance at any Ecuadorean map will show it claiming a large section of jungle that extends beyond Peru's Iquitos. Nothing infuriates a country more than losing a square inch of its territory. And Ecuador, which was forced by the treaty of Rio de Janeiro in 1942 to hand over roughly three-quarters of its Amazon to Peru, is no exception. To judge by the misleading maps still being circulated in the republic, Ecuador is in the somewhat uncertain state of a man whose leg has just been amputated. Because he thinks he can feel pain in it, he cannot quite believe that his leg is not still somewhere underneath the hospital sheet. The border dispute affects the traveller in several ways: you should always carry your passport with you as military checks are not uncommon; the south-eastern border is very sensitive—not the best place in which to travel as sabre-rattling continues intermittently; and trying to cross the border into the Peruvian jungle and so descending the Amazon from Ecuador is no longer possible—you will be stopped before you get halfway.

Most travellers follow the **Quito–Baños–Puyo–Tena–Mishualli–Coca–Lago Agrio –Baeza–Quito** circuit, or at least part of it. Using a combination of bus, *collectivo* and boat, the route can be covered in a week, but going at this pace would not allow you to get far off the beaten track. All the places mentioned above are connected to the highlands by road and have regular bus services. However, they are not all connected to each other, so where there is no road, river-boats have to be taken. This is fine; the more time that you spend on the river, the more you will enjoy the Amazon.

Mishualli is far and away the best base from which to make jungle excursions, but other possibilities include: visiting the marvellous **Cuyabeno National Park** from Lago Agrio; making the long downstream journey to **Limoncocha** from Coca; or— and you should definitely consider this option, because however you eventually come to see the Amazon, you will enjoy it most with a well-prepared guide—taking a tour with an agency based in Quito. **Metropolitan Touring** offers comfortable trips aboard the **Flotel Floreana** (see under 'Coca'); **Nuevo Mundo** and **Etnotours** have adventure-style holidays, and the latter's trip to **Cuyabeno** is particularly recommended; or you could take on-board the services of a fly-by-night guide, easily found in Quito by asking at your hotel, in which case—if you are in the mood—anything could happen.

TRAVELLERS' TIPS

The only thing that eats you in the Amazon is the mosquito, and the most common gesture amongst Amazonian travellers is the scratch, so take enough insect repellent. Doctors say that Vitamin B sours the blood and also deters mosquitoes. But you must begin taking the vitamin pills two weeks before you go if they are to have any effect.

The jungle is also marshy and you will need Wellington boots. All guides wear them, even if it does make them look like tropical Christopher Robins.

It also rains, and frequently. If you don't have a waterproof and are caught outside when it begins to rain, the best thing to do is to take off all your clothes and wait for the downpour to pass. Wet clothes can take a long time to dry in the jungle. And besides, it feels great.

Mishualli

Mishualli is a tiny port built on a sandy swimming beach where the Mishualli and Napo rivers join, and is the easiest and most economical place in Ecuador from which to begin a jungle excursion. Ramshackle, but with the charm of the remote although only a day from Quito by bus, there are a number of tour operators on the town square. Tours range from one-day ventures (but if that is all you have time for, it is just as good to wander into the jungle alone) to one- or two-week excursions down the Río Napo towards Coca.

This is not the best place for *deep* jungle excursions, but it is the most convenient. The area has been long settled, and most game has been driven out. (But you can afford to reassure yourself: even in the remotest sections of the jungle, game has a tendency to stay invisible, and Mishualli does offer a true sense of the Amazon.) There are also two comfortable lodges a few hours downstream from the village—the **Hotels Anaconda** and **Jaguar**—that organize trips into the jungle. You might want to consider either of them as your eventual destination. The wettest season is from June–August, the 'driest' around November and December. There is a market on Sunday.

GETTING THERE

By Bus (from Quito)

There are several daily buses from Quito to Tena (a gruelling 9 hours, US$3), via Ambato and Baños. From Tena take one of the frequent buses that leave from beside the river to Mishualli (45 mins, 50c). (If you get stuck in the featureless town of Tena overnight and are looking for a place to stay, try the **Hotel Auca**, 2 km outside town. It has large rooms with bathrooms set in spacious grounds; US$6/11 for a single/double.)

By Boat

There are daily morning departures from the dock just off the Plaza, that make the six-hour, downstream, riverboat ride to Coca. This bus service will cost you US$5, but as the boats are often crowded, you should try to get your tickets a day in advance. Before leaving you must register your passport with the *Capitania*—a simple formality, no more. The trip is worth the discomfort of occasional showers and little leg room.

TOURIST INFORMATION
As ever in remote places, bring enough local currency.

ORGANIZING TOURS
Organizing a tour can take a little time, especially if you are a solo traveller. It is not difficult, however, as there are a lot of travellers passing through; Mishualli is only small and spare places on any expedition can always be filled relatively quickly.

The jungle necessitates a guide. Half a block up from the plaza, next to a kiosk that strangely mixes sewing machines and barbers' chairs, there is a sign pointing the way to, 'Douglas Clark—Jungle Guide'. Son of a North American entomologist and a lepidopterist himself, Douglas Clark is the best-known and most reliable of Mishualli's guides. Browsing through his photo album will give you a good idea of what to expect on one of his trips: tours vary from two to ten-day excursions, prices from US$10 to US$14 per day per person. There are a number of other agencies in Mishualli, and any could be just as good (except Fluvial tours, which has been consistently criticized). However, whilst prices at other offices may be cheaper than D. Clark's, this does not necessarily mean better. A few simple questions can ensure a good time: what will you be eating? where you will be staying? will the guide provide camping equipment? does he know anything of the flora and fauna? has he done this before? how much walking will you be doing? (one hopes not too much). Most importantly, do you think that you could get on with him?

WHERE TO STAY
Outside Town
One hour downstream from Mishualli, on **Anaconda Island** and permeated by the odour of wet jungle, lies the **Hotel Anaconda** Lodge. The rustic bedrooms are thatched huts with palm roofs and mosquito screens, and the US$25 nightly charge is inclusive of food. You can organize trips into the jungle from the lodge, and there are tame monkeys, tapirs and birds wandering freely in the gardens. Half an hour further downstream lies the modern and more expensive **Hotel Jaguar**, bookable from Quito at the agency at Ramírez Davalos 653, tel 239400, although you might also be able to book rooms in Mishualli.

In Town
None of the accommodation in Mishualli is expensive or luxurious: power cuts and water shortages are the rule rather than the exception. Prices hover around the US$2 per night mark, and for that you can expect hammocks and a shared bathroom. Try the **Dayuma Lodge**, the **Residencial Sacha** or the **Hotel Rio Amazonas**; all three are small, wooden, jungle-style buildings with balconies, set just by the river.

WHERE TO EAT
The restaurants at the Dayuma and El Paisano are both good and serve meat and vegetarian dishes. Unfortunately, fish is a rare dish.

Coca

Some 150 km downstream from Mishualli on the Río Napo, Ecuador's main Amazon tributary, lies Coca. A sprawling, dusty, shanty seedy oil town, it is officially called Puerto Francisco Orellana after the conquistador who floated down the Amazon to the Atlantic in 1542. But everyone knows it as plain Coca.

You will only come here to go on to somewhere else: either further downstream towards the Hotel Primavera and the deep jungle around the border town of **Nueva Rocafuerte**; as a stepping stone to the Flotel Orellana; or as a night stop after the boat journey from Mishualli. You can also fly direct to Quito from Coca.

EXCURSIONS AND TOURS

All excursions downstream from Coca, unless with an organized tour, are subject to the presence of Peruvians at the border near Rocafuerte, and also to the whims of the military in Coca from whom you must get a permit to travel. There are irregular boats down the Napo to the missionary villages of Pompeya and Limoncocha and as equally irregular boats returning. If travelling independently you will need sleeping bags and hammocks, and it is a good idea to bring your own food. **Fluvial Tours** organizes trips, or you might be able to arrange something down at the docks, but as very few people sortie independently into the jungle from Coca, there is little to choose from. Nevertheless, the area east of Coca is little travelled, less seen and consequently unspoilt. The most comfortable, and probably the best, way to travel down the Napo is on Metropolitan Touring's Flotel Orellana.

The Flotel Orellana

The Flotel Orellana looks like an old flat-bottomed river steamboat, weighs 440 tons, has three 100 hp engines, a restaurant and a bar. The collection of passengers who sail in it are often worthy of an Agatha Christie novel: honeymooning Ecuadoreans, pensioned North Americans, Canadian families and perhaps a European backpacker who looks like he took the wrong tour. The exact schedule varies, but the boat usually zigzags east of Coca, with day-trips to the shore in dugout canoes. This is no adventure trip, but it is comfortable and well informed: the guides know the jungle and there are also lectures.

Voyages last anything from three days to a week and can be inclusively booked from Quito. Further information can be had by writing to: Metropolitan Touring, PO Box 2542, Quito, Ecuador tel 524400; telex 2482, METOUR ED.

The Hacienda Primavera

Two hours downstream towards Peru, **La Primavera** is a lovely hacienda owned by Otto Rodriguez whose grandfather came to the Amazon in 1875. It offers good home-cooked meals, simple rooms, or camping space. There are a number of good walks around the farm into the jungle. Prices for a room are around the US$20 mark. More information can be had from: Señor Rodriguez, Venezuela 1716, Quito tel 510387.

GETTING THERE

By Plane

There are daily flights, Mon–Fri, with TAME to Quito (US$12). The office is down by the river.

By Boat
All boats leave from the dock. There is a daily canoe to Mishualli—ten hours upstream as opposed to six hours downstream to Coca). Travel downstream, as already described above, can be difficult and expensive. It is an easy haggle for a lift down to the the Hacienda Primavera.

By Bus
There are seven buses a day to Lago Agrio (4 hours, US$1).

TOURIST INFORMATION
Coca's bank will not change money, but you may have more luck at the Alamacen Londono.

WHERE TO STAY AND EAT
Coca has little to choose from. Your best bet is the **Restaurant/Hotel Auca** three blocks into town from the river. A room with bathroom overlooking the hotel's garden can be had for US$3 per person.

Lago Agrio

Lago Agrio (literally, 'Sour Lake') is an oil town, scruffy, with an expanding population (presently 8000), and roads that are covered in black sludge. In between long stretches of dense jungle, the bus journey from Coca gives you the chance to see the impact of oil exploration on the Amazon. If there is a sequence to Amazonian exploration in Ecuador, it might go something like: first the discovery of oil, then a road, next colonizing farmers come down from the highlands, and finally tourists.

Again, there is little reason to linger in Lago, but it does serve as another base for excursions into the jungle, or as a jump-off for the last leg of the circuit back to Quito. Lago also has the best plane schedule from the Oriente to the capital.

TOURS AND EXCURSIONS
Cuyabeno National Park
Cuyabeno is frequently used by biologists as a research station and is a good place to feel in the thick of nature. The park's small shelter is set around clear-water lakes that are rich in animal life: birds, small Amazonian rodents, crocodiles and piranha. The Park is not easy to get to; first you have take a four-hour bus journey, then a further two hours by canoe. The best way to get there is with **Etnotours**, who can arrange a week's tour for around US$60 per day. For further information, go to their office in Quito on the corner of Juan León Mera and Luis García, tel 230552.

Dureno
Dureno is a small Cofan Indian village, about an hour east of Lago Agrio by bus or dugout. You will be able to find a roof over your head for a nominal fee, but bring a hammock or sleeping bag, and your own food supplies. Do not expect anything in the way of comfort here. The Cofan are excellent nature guides, and have an intimate knowledge

of the jungle. To get there, take a bus with Transportes Putamayo to **Tarapoa**; there is no sign, so ask the driver to let you down when the time arrives. From here, follow the path to the **Río Aguarico** 200 m away. The village is on the other side, and a dugout can take you across.

GETTING THERE

By Plane
The airport is 5 km out of town, US$2 in a taxi. There are daily flights to Quito with TAME (US$10), but you should try and book well in advance. The TAME office is in the centre of town.

By Bus
There are daily buses that make the gruelling 11-hour journey to Quito (US$3), and they leave from the centre of town. Eleven hours is 11 hours too long to my mind and you could break the journey at the small town of **Baeza**, roughly halfway to Quito, and stay at the **Hotel Samay**, US$1 per person. There is also a regular service to Coca (4 hours, US$1).

TOURIST INFORMATION
There is an exchange house on the main strip that will change dollars.

WHERE TO STAY AND EAT
The **Gran Hostal del Lago** is the best in Lago, thankfully 1 km outside town. There is a good restaurant, and the cabined rooms are clean, comfortable and have running water at US$10 per person, per night. In town, the **Cofan** is your best bet—the rooms have air-con and private bathrooms, and there is a restaurant (US$8 per person). Otherwise try **La Mexicana**, clean and fair value at US$3 per person. If you are looking for louche entertainment, and what are euphemistically called 'Colombian nights', go to '**La Tropicana**'—in the past it has been very popular with both missionaries and Peace Corps workers. Asking for directions will lead to lewd and conspiratorial smiles.

COLOMBIA

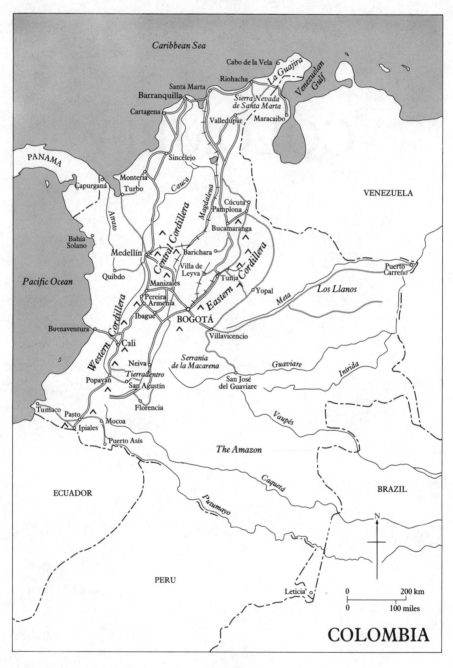

INTRODUCTION

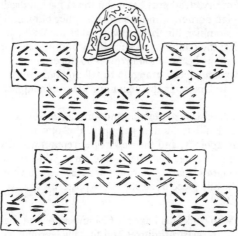

Pre-Columbian gold from the Museo del Oro

Few tourists ever see Colombia; if South America remains the world's least discovered continent, Colombia is perhaps its least discovered country. For the adventurous traveller, at least, this kind of isolation has its merits, for in a place untamed by travellers' tales, you can find yourself stumbling through semi-mythical landscapes and cities, feeling like a trespasser.

If America is a woman, Colombia lies by the belly-button, just below the waist cinched tight by the Panama Canal. It covers an area twice the size of France, and is the only South American republic with Atlantic and Pacific coasts. Within its borders are represented all of the world's races—the white, the black and the Indian; all of the world's climates—from tropical to desert and temperate; and, smeared over its rugged landscape, nearly all of the stages of mankind's history—the Stone Age, the medieval and even, occasionally, the future.

Historically Colombia was the land of emeralds and El Dorado, and it is still a country of extremes and contradictions, criss-crossed by invisible borders that change everything; a place where time and race suffer a bewildering and exciting confusion, where the sophisticated lives cheek by jowl with the primitive, where anthropologists and historians can and do study nearly all types of human society without ever setting foot outside.

The dramatic beauty of the countryside is such that it can get inside you and feel like a pain. Bogotá, the capital, lies 2600 m above sea-level and is a cool, grey city beneath a sky more often gloomy than bright, and an international centre for the arts. Cali stretches languidly under its palm trees in the warm hollow of the Cauca Valley, and rings to its own particular brand of salsa—*romantica*. The fortressed port of Cartagena on the Caribbean coast is a frozen explosion of lyricism. Whilst Barranquilla, the main Atlantic port further to the east, smells of coconut oil and diesel fumes, and runs on a heady mix of

143

Caribbean surrealism and tropical malice. The snowy peaks of the Sierra Nevada de Santa Marta are the refuge of the last pre-Colombian group in the Americas to retain their priestly class—the Kogui. And then through the Llanos, those wide plains of the east with their scent of dry, dead grass, you can travel for hundreds of miles, up to and through the Venezuelan border, without seeing another human being.

It is a feature of Colombian life that everyone likes to join in, and this gives even the shortest journey within the country a strange but wondrous alchemy. Colombians take greedily from life (perhaps because tomorrow is so uncertain) and as all Latins anyway abhor a distance, you can expect strangers to talk to you, events to pass and intimate situations to escalate. In Colombia the uncommon is commonplace, the surreal and the wild the norm.

Finally, because Colombia is so quixotic and sensual, and because it is so full of grace, courtesy, laughter and old-fashioned gallantry, the obvious is left until last. This introduction is not an apology, and the newspaper reports which you might have read about the country are all true. But then—one must add—so are the resonant oral histories from which Gabriel García Márquez has drawn so much material for his books. And so too this worthwhile piece of advice left to posterity by a North American author travelling in the 1950s:

> 'The traveller who packs his bags for Colombia does wrong to think that he will be living amongst primitives and that his learning would be best left at home. In actual fact, he will have difficulty keeping up with the Colombians, who know more about his authors than he does, more concerning the economy of his nation, and overwhelmingly more about its politics. This is true of the college professor with seven degrees and the *campesino* who is unable to read.'

This last remark is not a confusing of quick wits with intelligence, although it's true; in a country where history is such a forceful teacher, people do tend towards the philosophical.

The Lie of the Land

Only 50 years ago, the journey to Bogotá from Colombia's Caribbean was a three-week mountain odyssey on mules and ferry boats. Now you need only pack a sweater and board a plane. But at night, especially for anyone born in Europe, this one-hour journey can still be an unforgettable experience. Looking down you can see the lights of some town shining like an outpost in the darkness that stretches ahead, and you realize that this is still a country only very partially settled and developed, a place where human effort is a tiny thing in comparison to the terrain. The lie of Colombia's land is everything.

Colombia's landscape—as crumpled as bed-clothes, with someone lying in them—can be divided into two parts; the mountainous and the flat. The central highlands—a leaf-shaped region—are temperate and cool, more reminiscent of Tuscan Italy than of a warlike, tropical South American republic. These are the most prosperous and industrialized areas of the republic, and hold most of the population. Passing from east to west, the roads are like dizzy roller-coasters, with journey times across them reckoned in hours rather than kilometres. The Caribbean (or as it sometimes referred to, the Atlantic) coast is low-lying, hot, and studded with walls and fortresses that have been captured, rebuilt and dismantled innumerable times during their 500 years of pirate history. The Pacific, on the other hand, is pioneer territory, jungled, mangroved, malarial, inaccessible, and—populated by the descendants of escaped slaves—African in mood. To the east of the country lie the plains and the beginnings of the Amazon jungle. And then up through the middle runs the fickle Magdalena—*the* river of the country, which sometimes vanishes into its own sands, whilst on others, overflows its banks for several kilometres and floods the plains.

Colombia's topography defines the climate (Humbolt was only the first person to picture a man with a thermometer in his hand, choosing the perfect living temperature by climbing up or down). It has steered the course of the country's history. And it has been responsible for Colombia's intense cultural regionalism. Unlike the Sierras of Peru and Ecuador, which have created a barrier between the men of the coast and the men of the mountains, Colombia's cordilleras have more ambitously divided the country into five, six, seven, even eight parts. There are at least 14 centres of population in Colombia and they are all completely different from each other—racially, geographically and economically.

As in Italy (and there are many similarities between Colombia and Italy, not just the Mafia), in Colombia you are where you come from, and wherever you come to live, this never changes. The man from Medellín, for example, is always the man from Medellín, even if he's been living in Barranquilla for a generation. This, of course, explains everything. It explains why he's so hard-working and such a bad drunk, and doesn't know the meaning of the word laziness. The same for the *costeño* living in Bogotá—he's the sybarite, the drunk, the one that tears around like a Ferrari.

Defined by regionalism and climate, every Colombian, from the Motilone Indian to the professor of political economy, feels that his town is the best. Colombians travelling within their own country are tourists, perhaps even ambassadors. They might admire other villages, regions or cities—but envy? Or even love? Never! (There is one exception perhaps—Pasto, in the extreme south of the country by the Ecuadorean border. 'Oh you're from Pasto?' Thinks: not enough Caribbean blood, Pastusos are notoriously dim.)

The Current Situation

Colombia overturns the received wisdom that social conflict and a climate of insecurity undermines economic activity. Despite the well-advertised drug and guerrilla wars of the 1980s, the economy managed to thrive, with confidence generally bullish and foreign companies content with their profits despite the risks. Over the past two decades annual economic growth has averaged about 5 per cent—a remarkable economic resilience considering the number of crises that the country has had to sustain. Colombia is now the world's second largest exporter of cut flowers and coffee, the third largest coal exporter, as well as being the region's second largest gold producer and oil exporter. In 1990, government elections went ahead as planned, despite Mafia threats, and the liberal candidate Gaviria was elected.

Much of Colombia's current instability—you will have seen the headlines about the 'Cocaine Wars'—is rooted in a history of violence and civil war. As one Colombian politician recently said in interview to a North American journalist, 'In Colombia the situation has always been serious, or very serious.' So, one must ask, has anything really changed?

Colombia is renowned as the most violent country in Latin America today, even though it is not quite as bloody as Guatemala. But the Colombians are not a violent people. Like the Irish, another country with a violent history, they are gentle and courteous. Caught in the cross-fire, the vast majority still manage to pursue orderly lives. They are devout in their religion, conservative in their tastes, loyal to the family and firm believers in their country's long-standing democratic tradition (which dates from 1820, making Colombia the second oldest democracy in the Western hemisphere). It is as if two different societies—one of violence, the other of peace—share the same state. As the wonderfully humane North American historians Will and Aeriel Durant once wrote:

> 'Civilization is a stream with banks. The stream is sometimes filled with blood from people killing, stealing, shouting and doing things historians usually record; whilst on the banks, unnoticed, people build houses, make love, raise children, sing songs, write poetry and even whittle statues.'

It is the latter peaceful society of unapplauded and unnoticed daily life that the traveller is most likely—unless he or she is looking for the other—to see. As far as safety in South America goes, you are more likely to meet with mishap in Peru or Brazil.

The Best of Colombia

Beaches: Deserted beaches—Providencia, Tayrona National Park, Cabo de la Vela, Bahia Solano.
Party beaches—San Andrés, Cartagena.
Climbing: Sierra Nevada de Cocuy.
Colonial Towns and Cities: Cartagena, Mompós, Villa de Leyva.
Festivals: Caribbean Music Festival in Cartagena.
Hotel: Hostal Doña Manuela in Villa de Leyva.
Indian Statues: San Agustín.
Islands: Gorgona, a remote Pacific paradise.
Museums: Bogotá's Gold Museum, and Museum of Colonial Art.
National Parks: Tayrona, for beaches; Puracé for mountain fauna.
Rain forest retreat: Amacayacu National Park, in the Amazon.

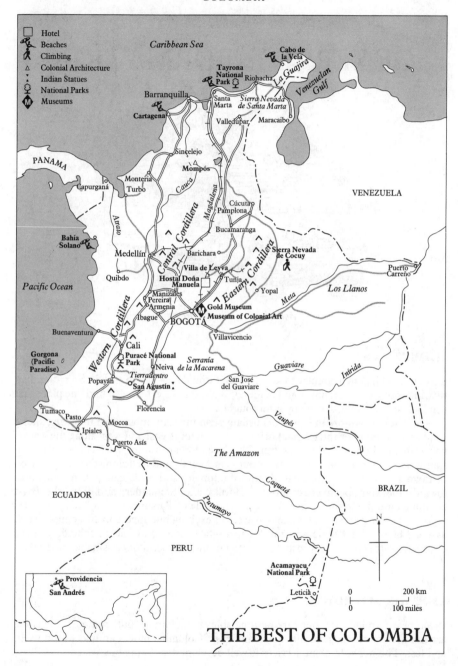

THE BEST OF COLOMBIA

Part I

GENERAL INFORMATION

Antioqueñan escallera ladder bus

Itineraries

Colombia is big, but a country to savour, and it would be a pity to rush it. So rather than wearing yourself out on buses and planes, it is always much better to find one place that you like, stop a while, and enjoy it thoroughly.

Nevertheless, visitors to Colombia usually rush through, most often following a long south-north route (or the reverse), with looping detours east and west along the way. If you were to do this, beginning from the Ecuadorean border, you could then visit southern Colombia—and the areas around San Agustín and Cali along the way; move on to Bogotá—from where you can fly into the jungle, and back again; then tour north towards the Caribbean coast through Boyacá and Santander; and from the coast continue onto the island of San Andrés, Venezuela or Panama.

Journeys into peripheral Colombian areas of exciting but uncertain attraction— such as the Llanos, the Pacific and the Guajira—take time, and just as they don't have classifiable attractions, they also don't really fit into any kind of classifiable itinerary.

Getting Around

If you bear in mind that there are no timetables in Colombia, only rumours, travelling around the country is generally quick and easy; Colombia moves around within itself, and fast. The network of air services is well developed, as is the bus system.

By Air

The fastest and most convenient way of covering Colombia's vast distances is of course by air. **Avianca, ACES** and **SAM**, amongst others, provide regular shuttle services to most destinations on a scale rarely equalled in South America. **Satena**, the military airline, provides inexpensive flights to non-commerical destinations. Even if not in the habit, you will save yourself both time and money by booking tickets and flights through a good travel agent, such as TMA.

Avianca also offers a very good **'Get-to-know-Colombia'** ticket; for US$324, it offers unlimited travel within the country for 30 days, but it is only purchasable outside the country.

Every flight in Colombia is subject to a US$5 airport tax.

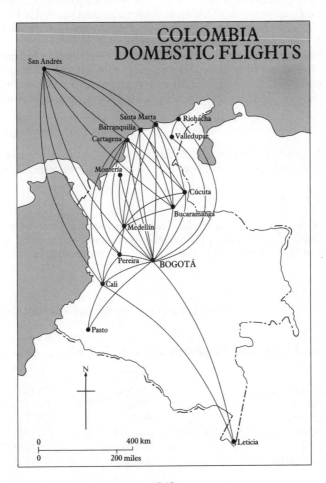

149

By Bus

Colombia's bus system is extensive and well-run, especially by the **Copetren** and **Expresso Brasilia** bus companies, and for all long journeys you should head for their offices.

Buses run the full gamut of types: 'Pullman' buses are usually very comfortable, with air-conditioning (which can make them very cold, so take a sweater), reclining seats, and on-board movies; local buses on the other hand can be nothing more than pieces of tin wrapped around an old Ford engine. Luggage compartments are usually locked, but nevertheless keep an eye on your bags. Breakdowns are frequent, as are police checks. Be prepared for great climatic changes in the course of a journey; you might begin in the tropics, stop for a meal in the icy highlands, and then carry on back down into the heat again, all in the course of a few hours.

A slightly more expensive alternative to the bus, is the **collectivo**. A cross between a bus and a taxi, collectivos are faster and more comfortable than buses. They usually carry no more than five or six passengers, leave from central bus stations when full, and charge one and a half times as much as the Pullman bus service.

All towns have long distance bus terminals, and seats on buses can be booked before the journey. If you are in a hurry, however, just turn up and listen out for your destination; major routes have regular departures and it is likely that you will be away within a few minutes. To dismount from a bus, tell the driver, *por acá, por favor*, over here please.

By Train

There is only one train line in Colombia that still operates a passenger service; the **Expresso del Sol** service from Bogotá to Santa Marta (see under 'Santa Marta', p. 205).

Car Hire

Petrol is cheap in Colombia, but car hire is expensive, at European rates. All international car hire companies have representatives throughout the country, and provide well-maintained, late model vehicles. You will need both international and home driving licences.

By Taxi

If the taxi does not have a car meter, always negotiate the fare in advance!

Altitudes and Average Temperatures in °C (°F)

	Altitude	*°C*
Barranquilla	sea level	28 (82)
Bogotá	2600 m	14 (57)
Bucaramanga	960 m	23 (73)
Buenaventura (Pacific Coast)	sea level	28 (82)
Cali	995 m	24 (75)
Cartagena	sea level	27 (80)

Leticia (Amazon)	961 m	27 (80)
Medellín	1490 m	22 (71)
Maicao (Guajira)	50 m	28 (82)
Mompós	33 m	28 (82)
Popayán	1740 m	19 (66)
San Agustín	1300 m	20 (68)
Santa Marta	sea level	27 (80)
Tunja	2780 m	12 (54)
Valledupar	170 m	27 (80)
Villavicencio (Los Llanos)	470 m	25 (77)

Tourist Offices

Apart from the national **CNT** tourist offices in every town, that sometimes stock handy local maps, **Inderena** will be your most useful port of call. Responsible for the running of the country's National Parks, Inderena issues the permits that you will sometimes require to visit them. The central office is in Bogotá and is the only office that can issue permits to visit La Isla Gorgona or the Lost City in the Sierra Nevada.

Colombia has three tourist offices abroad:

Paris: 9 Boulevard de la Madeleine, 75001, tel 260 3565
Madrid: Calle Princesa No.17, Tercero Izquierda, tel 248 5090
New York: 140 East 57th Street, tel 688 0151

Opening Hours

Stores follow banking hours; open 9–12, closed for siesta and then re-opening 2.30–6.30. Government offices are open 8–3.

Maps

General maps of Colombia can be found at any good newsagent; local maps at tourist offices. For specialized maps, go to the **Instituto Geográfico Agustín Codazzi**, Carrera 30 No. 48–51, Bogotá.

Post

Avianca is in charge of Colombia's postal system and is very efficent; airmail letters take less than a week to reach their destination. If you want to send postcards home you will find that they are more likely to arrive if mailed in an envelope.

The best way to receive mail is probably at the Poste Restante of your local **Correo Aéreo Avianca**. To ensure correct filing, make sure to have your letters addressed to you thus; SMITH John, c/o Poste Restante, Correo Aéreo, Avianca, City, State, Colombia.

Phone

Telecom offices can be found in nearly all towns and villages and are generally efficient. You will always get a clearer long distance line however, if you call direct from any large hotel. Colombia is 5 hours behind Greenwich Mean Time.

Shopping

If you have an itch, Colombia can scratch it. Good Colombian buys include emeralds (see p. 162), filigree goldwork, gold replicas of pre-Colombian figurines, and local artesania such as hammocks, and Indian pottery and textiles. Leatherwork is also excellent, and you can have a pair of bespoke boots made up for around US$20. Bogotá is the best place for shopping; go to the state run **Artesanias de Colombia**, Carrera 3 No 18–60 for a representative collection of handicrafts from around the country.

Note: Colombia abounds in fakes, its a national speciality, and even experts have been fooled by re-constituted pre-Colombian pottery. The cunning fakers powder found, genuine fragments and use them to build and fire replicas that defy all known Carbon-14 tests.

Indian Groups

The present population of Colombia stands at around 30 million people. Of this, only 1 per cent can be considered pure-blood Indian (about 300,000), spread amongst over 50 Indian groups scattered throughout the country, in the Amazon, on the Pacific coast, in the Sierra Nevada de Santa Marta, on the Llanos, and in the high southern areas of Colombia. Some, such as the Kogui and the Arhuaco (see p. 210) have shunned the white, the mestizo and the black man, and have retained a strong cultural identity and religion. Others, such as the Páez (see p. 281), have been assimilated by the dominant culture. The greatest threat that Indians face in Colombia is from *colonos*; mestizo farmers who gradually erode the Indians' deedless lands. This problem is especially prevalent in the Amazon and the Chocó.

Media

The Colombian press has a long tradition of excellence, is erudite, and also often brave; many journalists have staked their lives on an anti-Mafia article. All major cities have local newspapers, although the national newspapers gravitate around Bogotá. *El Tiempo* is the country's power-broking newspaper. But *El Espectador*, apart from being at the forefront of the anti-Mafia crusade, is perhaps better written and more incisive. In *El Tiempo* look out for political analysis by Ivan Santos and Plinio Apuleyo Mendoza, and for cute but literate comedy by Daniel Samper Pizano. In *El Espectador*, read articles by García Márquez and the radical columnist Antonio Caballero.

The radio waves are awash with music, but by some hidden logic, classical music stations occupy the left-hand part of the FM dial, with popular stations pushing-out chugu-chugu music over the rest. Radio Caracol is the equivalent of BBC's Radio 4.

Culture and the Arts

Literature

It has taken a while for Colombian letters to find its feet. For although García Márquez now represents only the tip of modern Colombian culture, for the first 50 years after independence, Colombian literature was unremarkable. On the main part it reflected the traditionalism of a conservative society proud in its pursuit of linguistic purity and the imitation of European models. Nevertheless Jorge Isaacs' *María* (1867) was the most important romantic idyll of its time in Spanish America, and José Asunción Silva helped originate Spanish America's first autonomous movement in prose and poetry; Latin American *modernismo*.

After 1910, Colombian literature began to take off. Tomás Carrasquilla (1858–1940) wrote masterly stories and novels, based around his observations of local life in Antioquia; José Eustacio Riviera's *La Voraigné*, a highly lyrical account of man's struggle against nature in the Amazon, was published in English in 1935 to international acclaim; and Porfirio Barba Jacob (1883–1942) invigorated Colombian poetry with a high emotive content—'*Cancion de la Vida Profunda*' is his most famous work.

Poetry and fiction truly flourished in the period following the Second World War. The sonnets of the satirist Luis Carlos López (1879–1950) mocked the solemnity of conventional lyric poetry with subtle and ironic humour. Also important were León de Greiff, Eduardo Cote Lamus, and Eduardo Carranza. In fiction, following on in the tradition of Carrasquilla, writers began to transform the pathos of regional life into a new and innovative literature. The Nobel Prize winner Gabriel García Márquez is the most famous of this generation, but the ball does not stop with 'Gabo'. For important, demanding, and *exciting* modern writing, read the novels of Rafael Humberto Moreno Durán and Alvaro Mutis.

Painting and Sculpture

Perhaps there is an equation: $CA=2DV$, where C is creativity, A the number of artists, D difficult times, and V violence? As Colombian violence has grown, so commensurately have artists proliferated. There are supposedly over 100 art galleries presently in Bogotá. Colombian artists appear to need to suffer, and this is reflected in much Colombian work, which is often expressive, painterly and violent, with the English painters Bacon and Auerbach as important models.

But maybe the explanation is simpler. The Colombian Mafia, like gangsters everywhere, crave respectability. They need something to spend their money on and 'Art' is suitably expensive and mysterious. It is also socially respectable and, what's more important, socially improving. But paradoxically, artists that have ridden the boom would rather not sell to the Mafia; they pay high prices, but are indiscriminate buyers, and once a painting is bought it is hung on the walls of a hideaway and never seen again.

The years from 1950–80 produced the most famous generation of Colombian painters and sculptors, including such internationally celebrated figures as Enriqué Grau, Fernando Botero, Ramiro Gómez and Alejandro Obregón. But other younger and just as talented artists are also at work. See the work of Gustavo Sánchez, Ricardo Villabuena, Rodrigo Callejas, Diego Pombo and Juan Camillo Uribe. For a window onto the Colombian art scene, buy the glossy magazine 'Arte en Colombia', available from the bookshop in the Museum of Modern Art in Bogotá.

Festivals and Holidays

Partying is a true Colombian speciality. The tourist office lists over 300 festivals for each year; everyday, somewhere, there is a holiday or festival. Some are just excuses for a party. Others follow the liturgical calendar. The rest are true celebrations.

Below is a calendar of some of the most popular annual events; all of those of particular interest are listed inthe text. For many you will have to check at the Tourist office for precise dates, which change each year.

January:	*Carnaval de Blancos y Negros* in Pasto: lively throwing of paint with dancing in the streets
February:	*Carnaval de Barranquilla*; Colombia's most rumbunctious carnival.
March/April:	Cartagena's International Music Festival, a gathering of Caribbean musicians in the old city
	Holy Week (*Semana Santa*) celebrations in Mompós and Popayán; Catholicism at its most baroque and solemn
	Folklore and vallenato music at the *Festival de Leyenda Vallenata* in Valledupar
May:	1 May, Ascension Day
	Bogotá's International Book Fair.
June:	Cartagena International Cinema Festival
	Music, beauty parades and dancing at Neiva's *Bambuco* Festival
July:	20 July, Independence Day
August:	7 August, Battle of Boyacá
	Medellín's *Desfile de Silleteros* (Flower Parade)
	Manizales' well attended International Theatre Festival
October:	12 October, Discovery of America Day
November:	1 November, All Saints' Day
	11 November, Independence of Cartagena, with music and beuaty contests
	Reinado de Coco, folklore and beauty contests in San Andrés
December:	Salsa orchestras and vivacious dancing at Cali's Sugar Cane Festival, between Christmas and the New Year

Part II
TOPICS

A gaitero

The Discovery of the Americas
Some suggestions as to why the letters in Colombia are sometimes inverted to Locombia and some stray hints for travellers who have never been there before

South America feeds on myth, mistakes and a quixotic sense of optimism. The Spanish philosopher, José Ortega y Gasset, once wrote:

> 'Everyone arriving on these shores sees, first of all, the "afterwards": wealth, if he be *homo oeconomicus*; successful love, if he be sentimental; social advancement, if he be ambitious ... The horizon is ever making gestures of abundance and concession. Here everyone lives on distances. Scarcely anyone is where he is, but in advance of himself. And from *there* he governs and executes his life *here*, his present life. Everyone lives as though his dreams of the future were already reality.'

Columbus was no exception. With inspiration as his only capital he bravely sailed into the unknown territories that had only been marked by dragons in 15th-century maps. But his discovery (by an *Italian*, of the *Spanish* Americas) was the result of a mistaken enterprise to the East Indies. An admiral who couldn't sail and a sailor who couldn't swim, he held only little knowledge of the newly discovered sextant and of the more eternal stars.

155

'In the carrying out of this enterprise to the Indies,' he wrote to King Ferdinand and Queen Isabella from the Orient (as in Oriente Province Cuba, not Far East), 'neither reason nor mathematics were of any use to me; fully accomplished were the words of Isaiah.' Paradise had been revealed to him in a triumph of poetry over science.

Of course, the Admiral's co-ordinates were wrong. The silver-capped bay he first sighted in the distance was glinting—not with the Eden of riches he had read about in Marco Polo's *Milliones*—but with the light reflected by the white, shining leaves of the ilam-ilam trees, turning in the breeze. The Khan's wealth at Cypango (Japan) lay thousands of miles—a continent and an ocean—away. But fervent, feverish Columbus did little to belittle the myth of a promised land that had been gaining stature since the Greeks. And looking to the hysterical literary models of Pliny's *Natural Wonders*, the romances of chivalry, epic Renaissance poetry, and the oft-told myths of Amazonian women and mermaids, Columbus disguised his correspondence with the fantasy that has fuelled the rampant logic of Latin American writing ever since:

> 'It is a desirable land, and once seen never relinquished... There are many mountains and streams... and all are most beautiful, of a thousand shapes, and most accessible, and filled with trees of a thousand kinds and tall, and they seem to touch the sky... And there the people are born with tails.'

Perchance he was heady with that aboriginal weed—discovered by the Spanish, but popularized by the English and French—tobacco. Not likely, Columbus was busy besides, doggedly pursuing the gold promised in Marco's tales from another place. ·

'We came here to serve God and to get rich,' wrote the missionary chronicler, Bernal del Castillo. And from the moment the Columbus had signed the articles of agreement with the Catholic Kings, he had promised them gold; his expedition, after all, had been financed with their venture capital. Eager to please, his account of the first ten days in the islands mentions the word 'gold' no less than 21 times. ('Money makes the world go round (and can make you go around the world),' quips the Cuban novelist G. Cabrera Infante.) And in the plans for the New World's colonization that he presented to Queen Isabella on his return, settlers were to pay levies; one fifth to the king, one tenth to Columbus and another part to the Church. Wrote Columbus in his log-book, 'of gold is treasure made, and with it he who has it does as he wills in the world and it even sends souls to paradise.'

The year 1492, in which Columbus sighted the New World, was also one of domestic European conquest, or rather reconquest; in a union of church and sword, the Spanish recovered Granada from the Arabs and Islam. The discovery of America can also be understood in the context of these crusading wars that prevailed in medieval Castile. The church needed no prompting to provide a halo for the conquest of unknown lands across the ocean. The Pope was Spanish, he had ordained Queen Isabella as proprietor and master of the New World, and the expansion of the Kingdom of Castile overseas also extended his, and God's, reign over the earth.

South America promised instant wealth. Myths akin to that of El Dorado flourished, prompted by the Indians who answered the discoverers' and conquistadors' eager questions with an obliging series of 'Yes it's over there's'. Sir Walter Raleigh was one of the first to make money out of these vaporous myths; in a fabled wager with Queen Elizabeth he bet that he could measure the weight of smoke. Weighing some tobacco before he smoked it in his pipe, and then weighing the ashes, he claimed that the difference was 'the weight of smoke'. The Virgin Queen paid, but only after remarking that 'she had known alchemists who could turn gold into smoke,'but Raleigh was the first to reverse the process.'

Back in Europe, the bound volumes of Columbus's correspondence were a literary success; eight editions in the original Spanish, a Latin version read all over Europe, and a paraphrased Italian. His Utopian visions heralded a springtime of dreams. Compounded by Amerigo Vespucci's tales (the namer of America, but only because of a punning German cosmographer) the New World inspired Thomas More's *Utopia* and Voltaire's *Candide*. Shakespeare turned Cuba's Carib cannibals into a Caliban *Tempest*. And Montaigne ruminated about natural grace, the noble savage, and the habits of eating flesh and not wearing clothes (the fashions of late 15th century Europe dictated that women be heavily dressed from head to foot).

The civilization from across the ocean that descended on Latin America was undergoing the creative explosion of the Renaissance; along with gunpowder, printing, paper and the compass, Latin America became another invention to be incorporated into the bubbling New Age. For armchair Europeans, America's destiny took on the meaning of a field trial where justice could be made more equal, liberty more real and happiness more complete and better distributed. The Mexican essayist Alfonso Reyes wrote that its discovery was akin to the 'opening of a theatre for every experiment in human happiness and every adventure in well-being.' The lawyer Antonio de León Pinelo devoted two entire volumes to demonstrating that the Garden of Eden was in America. In *El Paraíso en el Nuevo Mundo* (1656) he had a map of South America showing, in the centre, the Garden of Eden watered by the Amazon, the Rio del Plata, the Orinoco, and the Magdalena; the forbidden fruit was the banana; and the map showed the exact spot from which Noah's ark took off at the time of the flood. Columbus believed that at South America the globe had a bump on it, like a woman's breast, in order to bring Terrestrial Paradise closer to heaven. And the 16th century philosospher, Ulrich Hugwald, prophesisied that following the colonization of the New World, humanity would return to 'Christ, to Nature, to Paradise—a state without war or want.' And all this because of a mistake, a dream!

The myths have changed, but their power remains. William McFee wrote in his 19th-century travelogue *Sunlight in New Granada* that, 'the first great law of travel [is]—you find in a place exactly what you bring to it.' Ever since the first Europeans landed on the shores of what they thought to be India, Latin America has been an imaginary and uncertain place: the horizon is unknown; everything is negotiable; precise plans go precisely wrong; The Book of Rules is yet to be written.

Spanish Caribbean Music

Salsa! Music and the Caribbean are synonymous. The principle of Brownian motion tells us that smoke particles suspended in a closed cell of air move faster, experience more random collisions, and caroom off each other at ever zanier angles as temperature is increased. Applying science to life, tropical heat actually speeds things up! And you can see this in the Ferrari-esque rate of growth of tropical vegetation, and the turn-over of street-corner dramas—a series of sultry adagios punctuated by sudden scherzos and florid trills—that accompanies any stroll through any coastal Colombian town. But this is not necessarily a frantic affair. When Colombians dance, they do not leap about, thumping the ground with their feet. They move from the ground upwards. Their feet softly paddle and their hips begin to sway. Each part of the body moves within its own orbit, independently of the others, counter-pointing rhythms. Children wriggle like elvers in a spring tide. The old yield gravely, like trees to the wind. And the young dance as angels might make love, their hips close, fluent and inexhaustible, their feet hardly touching the ground.

Music is a constant backdrop to the Caribbean, and the belief that music incarnates the most characteristic elements of Caribbean culture is an assumption that the region's literature has made since the 1920s. But to understand how music came about in the Caribbean, and what it means, one has to go back over 400 years, remembering as one travels through time that Africa didn't create voodoo; the Americas did.

When plantation owners Christianized African slaves as a means to subdue them, the two religions blended. Christian saints were re-interpreted, the Yoruba pantheon of gods took Christian names, and Afro-Caribbean moral values came to take their orientation from a concept of God and reality different to that of the strictly Christian faith. Europe rubbed off on African culture, and Africa rubbed off on European culture. With this syncretion came a concomitant blending of musics; salsa after all is only a waltz, but with a religious, African, background drum.

The son, the guajira, the danson and the rumba were the earliest Afro-Caribbean rhythms to flourish in the Caribbean basin. More specifically, they were actually Afro-Cuban, since Cuba was the dominant musical influence in the Caribbean at the time. These were pure, root rhythms played by simple trios on improvised guitars, with a drum, maracas, and the ever-present 1–2–3/1–2 wood-clack background beat of the claves. In the 1940s these rhythms, in their own turn, were mixed with big band, North American-style sounds—most famously by the Cuban band leader Benny More—and so arose the mambo, conga and cha-cha-cha orchestras. Mixing, turning and adapting, Caribbean music was ever ready to incoporate new elements. Cu-bop came next, a fusion of Afro-Cuban music and hot be-bop jazz: American jazz players picked up on the Cuban rhythms, and the Cubans picked up on North America's jazzier rhythms and chord progressions. The complex African-derived percussion, the melodic sweetness and the startling virtuosity were still there, only now it was Charlie Parker who was going nuts over those extended vamps that were called *montunos*, and not a creole blower from the Caribbean. A British jazz critic once described music as juggling, only with harmonies instead of oranges. So while the Caribbean is sometimes seen as little more than a ceaseless party, this is only part of the truth. The joy is lofty and hyperkinetic, like mathematics, engineering or chess.

The Cuban son formed the base to salsa. But Colombia has its own root rhythms too; specifically the cumbia and the vallenato. The cumbia is a courting dance with a clip-clop rhythm that originated amongst slaves on the Atlantic coast, especially around Cartagena and Cienega. Early versions have a rough, but recognizable, ska beat. The traditional dance pattern describes a man slowly circling a woman, who stays still in the middle with a spray of lit candles held high above her head, like the torch on the Statue of Liberty.

The man hops around, dragging one of his feet like a bird with a broken leg, historically because it would have been weighed down with a ball and chain.

But the plangent rhythms, swirling accordions and yearning voices must make vallenato the most characteristic of Colombian sounds. Sung with a reckless joy plaintively offset by the sincere but mournful constraint of saying in a hundred different ways, 'I love you', vallenato originates from around Valledupar, a swaggering cowboy town south of the Sierra Nevada de Santa Marta. Although a regional genre, it has come to spread across all of Colombia's social and geographic boundaries; from Bogotá brahmins to Caribbean swingers, from white urban bourgeois to mixed blood pueblo. And because Colombians, if not politicians, are lyric poets, the songs are meant to be listened to, not danced—despite their infectious swinging beat. The lyrics of early vallenatos tended to be male boasts ('I just got myself a girl, whey-hey!'); newer ones lament ('Ohh my girl just left me and so it goes'). The vocals are nasal and old-timey twangy; a Latin country-and-western blues. Traditionally it is played with only three instruments; a ridged stick of cane, the *guacharaca*, that gets scratched like a salsa gourd; drums; and an accordion. Legend has it that the music began when a German cargo of button accordions was shipwrecked off the Guajira peninsula. The noises and wheezings that the Indians made experimenting with these novel, washed-up squeeze boxes, were the very first songs. Which goes some way to explaining the Colombian joke: 'What's worse than a vallenato?' Answer: 'Another vallenato'.

Music in Colombia is not just to party to; it's also a tuneful grapevine. The words are important. Songs can sometimes provide political commentary, social satire, and a run-down of current events. Often they are just plain touching. Take a popular local rendering of the famous song 'Guantanamera'; Cuba's unofficial national anthem and a tune sometimes chanted—although with a different lyric—at English football matches. The Colombian version tells of a Juan Ramón who finds out that his wife has been cheating with a neighbour. In a blood rage he gets out his machete, sharpens the blade on a whetstone and steeling himself for the task ahead, tells his wife:

'You know what I must do. Now I'm going to do it.'

He disappears into the tropical night. Stanza by stanza his wife's terror increases as the inevitably murderous end draws near. She passes a sleepless night. In the morning Juan Ramón returns. Red, covered with small scratches and drying sweat, he tells her:

'There. I have done it. Now I can see. *Never Again* will you lie with your lover in the long grass. I have just cut it all down.'

If you want to buy some records, the choice can be bewildering. Here are a few suggestions:

Portovales is a Cuban musician, who settled in Colombia, and his *'Best Of...'* record includes some resonant, beautifully arranged and classic drawing-room guajiras, as aromatic as any Cuban cigar. La Sonora Mantancera is *the* classic Cuban band from the 1950s, that played with all of the singing greats, such as Celia Cruz and Daniel Santos. Still with the old guard, Pedro Vargas sings slow, sentimental boleros and Mexican ballads.

Joey Arroyo is a Barranquillero, currently Colombia's most famous, whose band 'La Verdad?' plays spikey, up-beat, party music. Groupo Niche play quintessentially slinky

Calena salsa. Binomio de Oro are current leading vallenato musicians, while Rafael Escalona is a classic vallenato composer and one of the originators of the genre. Finally, the recording companies Discos Fuentes and Col Discos also make some very good compilations on cassette and record, such as *Siempre Salsa*, *Lo Mejor de Vallenato*, or *Cumbia, Merengue* etc.

Simón Bolívar—The Liberator

Streets, squares, towns and provincial departments bear his name. His busts and statues are everywhere: Bolívar on a horse, with a sword in his hand, and with an arm across his heart. Wherever you look you can see him. Bolívar fever! What's all the fuss about? What was he like? And does he really represent the spirit of Latin American know-how? It's hard to know, for if there is a curse on Bolívar, it is that everyone enjoys projecting their fantasies onto his life. In 1953, when the distinguished Colombian historian Germán Arciniegas published a review of two famous Bolívar biographies, he titled his piece, 'On two famous *autobiographies*' by Salvador Madariaga and Waldo Frank.' As José Palacios, Bolívar's faithful manservant, once said: 'That what my master thinks, only my master knows.' The rest can guess, or impute, for then, as now, the man is an enigma.

Born in Caracas in 1787, Simón Bolívar came from a line of wealthy criollo ancestors, but his tutor—Simón Rodriguez—used *Emile* as a text book, and Bolívar was raised in the spirit of the Enlightenment. He was a voracious if eclectic reader, well versed in Homer, Plutarch, Caesar and Virgil; recent English, French, Spanish and Italian classics; and the French Encyclopaedists. Voltaire was one of his favourites; apparently he used to read the French satirist at mass, hiding the book within the bindings of a Bible.

After travelling abroad, dazzling Europe with his Latin sense of etiquette and courtesy, Bolívar returned to South America in 1807. He was immediately struck by the contrast between his ideals of justice and liberty—reinforced by his visits to Europe—and the apathy and lack of ideals prevailing in his own land. In a European drawing room, he had once asked the German geographer and naturalist, Baron von Humbolt, whether he thought that Latin America was ready for Independence. When Humbolt had replied yes, and that the continent would produce the man to bring it about, Bolívar had no doubts as to who that man would be. As early as 1795, when he was 12, Bolívar insisted that his sole aims in life were to free his country and to win glory for himself—not the traditional glory of power, fame and riches, but the glory of 'being great and useful'. In later years he said, 'My one ruling passion, my one inspiration, is to be known as a lover of liberty'. And in 1810, he helped set up the first revolutionary junta in Caracas; in 1819 he liberated Bogotá; in 1821, Caracas; in 1822, Quito and Guayaquil; and finally in 1826, Lima and Peru. After nearly 15 years of hard campaigning, South America was free. Bolívar was at once romantic and practical, a visionary and a soldier. His limpid writings reveal a man of extraordinary gifts, of talents that amount to genius. Although slender, he had an extraordinary vitality, and was always in movement, avid for fame. He campaigned ceaselessly and his endless crossings of the continent, on mule or horseback, earned him the respectful nickname of *culo de hierro*, iron-arse, amongst his llanero soldiers. A United States representative in Bogotá reported that 'there is an intrinsic moral force to the man, that awes the disaffected and inspires courage in the patriot.' His soldiers were devoted to him. His enemies heaped abuse and calumny on him. His style was inimitable. He found the charm of women irresistible, as they did his. One adjutant reported:

> 'In the time of his military campaigns, when his headquarters were in a city, town or village, dances were arranged nearly every night, and his pleasure was to dance and valse, then vanish from the room to dictate some orders and dispatches, and again dance, and work again. In this way his ideas became clearer and stronger, and his style more eloquent. In a word, dancing inspired him and excited his imagination... When the bad weather prevents our going out, H.E. gets his own back by lying on the hammock and rocking fast, or walking along the corridors of the house sometimes singing, sometimes reciting verse, or conversing with others who walk with him.'

Bolívar had a complete disregard for material gain, and often rejected huge gifts of money. When he served Peru and Colombia jointly as supreme commander, he received no salary whatsoever, and wrote to Santander, 'Incidentally, I am in a strange position at the moment... I have no means of support, though I am both President of Colombia and Dictator of Peru.' His life was short, explosive and brilliant. But after Independence his political ideals were quickly usurped by regional prides, local elites and 'smooth philosophers', and his dreams of a just, thorough and integrated Latin American revolution turned to ashes when Gran Colombia collapsed. He said: 'There have been three great fools in history: Jesus, Don Quixote and I.' And shortly before his death, added: 'America is ungovernable. He who serves the revolution ploughs the sea.'

At one o'clock in the afternoon on 17 December, 1830—the same month, day and hour that 11 years earlier he had signed the agreement uniting Venezuela and New Granada to create Gran Colombia—Bolívar breathed his last. When it was discovered that he had nothing in his wardrobe but shabby clothing, General Silva came to the rescue. Rejected and in poverty, the Libertor of Venezuela, Colombia, Ecuador and Peru was buried in a borrowed shirt.

Fruit

Colombia is a haven for exotic strands of Vitamin C. There are bananas and pineapples and mangoes and paw-paws and passion fruits—so called because of the thorns on the vine and the arrangement of pistils on the flower, which are reminiscent of Christ's passion and so nothing, after all, to do with love. All of these are already known about in Europe, of course. But then there is a hallucinatory array of other fruits, some delicious, like the silky curuba and the bubblegum flavoured zapote, others astringent and medical, like the borojo.

The borojo is a 'super fruit', that only grows wild on hermaphroditic trees in the wettest place in the world—El Chocó, on Colombia's Pacific coast. It is very expensive, smells of high cheese, tastes of soap and looks like a gloating brown snooker ball. Its skin apparently shrinks from any knife and scientists from around the world have prodded it and declared its red flesh to have near-magical medicinal properties. The borojo can, apparently, cleanse your liver, reduce your blood pressure, stabilize your blood sugar levels, cure your cancer and—apart from being the source of a plenitude of useful vitamins—also be effectively used as an aphrodisiac.

Then there is the delicious papaya, which is sometimes packaged powdered in western supermarkets as a meat tenderizer. Because of its animal protein-digesting enzymes it is also, incidentally, very good for upset stomachs. A papaya is prepared by cutting it into thick slices, so when someone says, 'don't give him papaya' it does not mean let him go hungry, but is instead a caution: don't reveal yourself, or give too much away to him, or else he will use it against you and slice you up, as if you were a papaya.

Star-apples, marmalade plums, tree-tomatoes and honey berries, but the superlative taste award must go to the ugliest looker of them all; the green, bulbous and warty guanabana. The skin is encrusted with spiky protrusions and excrescences. But inside, delicious soft white meat is packed around large black pips. It has a very fine and elusive taste, something like a heavenly version of wild strawberries. Or is it peaches, or mangoes? It is hard to say, but try it, and ask for a *jugo* anyway.

Emeralds

> *'Of all the precious stones, this is the only one that feeds the sight without satiating it. Even when the vision has been fatigued, it is refreshed by being turned upon this stone.'*
>
> —Pliny

Colombian emerald production goes back long before the Spanish conquest. The stones were first mined by the Chibcha Indians and other minor tribes, and used for trade, as well as for personal adornment and religious ceremonial offerings. Emeralds also have a long history in western religion and folklore. The ring of a Catholic bishop bears an amethyst, a cardinal's a sapphire, but it is the Pope's that carries the emerald. According to the Bible, the emerald is the 'fourth stone', and as such assigned to the fourth apostle, John the Evangelist. An emerald was also used as the fourth foundation stone of the City of Jerusalem.

The magical properties of emeralds are supposedly legion. Emeralds can: cancel magic spells; reveal the truth and the infidelities of lovers; improve the memory; enable eloquent speech; sharpen the wits; quicken the intelligence, and promote good health. Caesar used to wear emeralds around his neck to prevent epileptic fits. And the medieval Bishop Marbodius, whose life was dedicated to the study of nature, said that emeralds favoured the function of the liver, relieved dysentry, promoted easy childbirth and healed the bites and stings of venomous creatures.

The emerald is the legendry gem of lovers, controlled by the planet Venus. It is the present-day birthstone for the month of May, whose star-sign is Taurus. It is the talisman for Mondays and the second hour of each day, and the gem for celebrating 55 years of marriage. Emeralds are the most expensive stones in the world, but while they have always had a value attached to them, at first it was spiritual. The pyramidal emerald of the Mexican Tezcuco Indians, for instance, was placed on the foreheads of human victims to soothe them before sacrifice.

It seems quite appropriate that such a strange, sensual and quixotic stone should come from such a strange, sensual and quixotic country. Nowhere else are they found in such high quality and quantity. Nowhere else are so many people involved in the trade and everyone, it seems, is in the business. Every cabbie, hairdresser and bootblack in Bogotá has a 'brother' who can guide you to the best deal and the best stone. But emeralds are personalities. They don't have quantifiable properties like diamonds. And if you want to buy one you will soon discover that your own eyes and your own good taste will be your best guides.

Buying Emeralds

First some definitions. A carat is a unit of measurement, one fifth of a gram. A point is one hundredth of a carat. An inclusion is any imperfection contained in a gem. And a natural is any inclusion that reaches the surface of a gem.

Emeralds are judged by their colour, brilliance, clarity, weight and proportion. Depths of colour are matched against degrees of brilliance—one cannot have both colour and brilliance, except with the semi-mythical *gota de aceite*, the oil-drop, which to look at is 'like falling in love'. The Oriental and Arab markets generally prefer brilliant stones, with fewer inclusions, while European and North American markets prefer the warm glow of a deep colour over a brilliant sparkle. The choice is yours. The clearer the stone and the fewer the inclusions, the better. Inclusions are *not* proof of a natural emerald; and opaque, cloudy, or black-spotted emeralds in particular are not recommended.

When looking at emeralds, insist on a lupe (a 10x magnifying glass) and use it to detect imperfections on the surfaces of the emerald. Practise focusing and then get the light to flash off every surface. Slight 'naturals' not on the top face are marginally acceptable. Broken or chipped stones should never be bought.

Prices can be estimated at a rate of about US$1000 per carat for a medium-light to medium-green stone with considerable sparkle and few inclusions. If the colour is better than medium-green, double this price. If the stone weighs under one carat, deduct 30 per cent. You could for instance, pick up a nice, light-green pair of emeralds, each about 0.2 of a carat, and make up a pair of earrings for about US$150. Mounted next to diamonds, their fire would be considerable.

Where To Buy Emeralds

You could go to the mines at Muzo to the north-east of Bogotá of course; but the only reason to do so is to get emeralds, to get rich, and to die. The Emerald Mafia are every bit as fierce as the Cocaine Mafia, and only marginally less powerful. Feuds are so violent that even the Colombian army stays out. F-2 undercover agents stationed at Boyacá's emerald mines had bus tickets slipped under their bedroom doors with notes advising them that they had 15 hours to leave or face certain death. Natives to the area come and go at will and these few privileged people do all the negotiations in towns such as Borbur, Guateque, Muzo or Chiquinquirá. Most of the clan heads do not come out for fear of enemies. Nearly everybody has been responsible for at least a few deaths.

Cab driver recommendations of emerald dealers and jewellery stores are always suspect, and the street market in front of the Banco de la República is as equally uncertain. Your best bet is to shop around the quality stores; **Sterne's**, at the Taquendema Centre in Bogotá, is one of the most famous, or, for a more intimate buy, try **Origenes**, on Calle 82 No. 14A–17, Oficina 601. Telephone Bogotá 257 1045 first for an appointment. Picking a shop with a reputation for quality will save you money in the long run: a reputable source guarantees the gem that you buy, can handle any problems that you might encounter, and will protect you from more unscrupulous practices. Emeralds sold in Colombia retail at a price between one-and-a-half and two times cheaper than in the USA.

La Malicia Indigena: a Note on Personal Security

Emeralds, Marlboro cigarettes, car parts and marijuhuana: Colombia has a history of smuggling and violent entrepreneurship. Everyone—but especially the Barranquilleros—will tell you about La Malicia Indigena—a term not translatable as native malice. It's a national, perhaps even Latin American, trait, but no-one knows exactly what it means. Like love, happiness or the English Reserve, it is a quality easily recognized, but harder to describe:

'My daughter learnt how to use a computer in two days, with a manual. But her cousin, who lives in the US, had to take a course. La Malicia Indigena!' declares a happy architect.

'It's a social intelligence, a meta-paranoia, derived from the Indian trait of seeing a feint within a feint in the gestures of life,' says an Indian specialist.

'It's an opportunistic business sense,' suggests a foreign diplomat.

'It's when I tell a joke and everybody else laughs but you don't because you didn't understand,' says a wag. And finally:

'It's a street sense; the ability to immediately intuit all of the possibilities inherent in any given situation,' says a streetsharp.

One of the most characteristic elements of life in underdeveloped countries is that it becomes a series of reactive reflexes to unrelated events, which is anarchic. The difference in Colombia is that the reflexes are remarkably well-honed. One does not experience any overt sense of danger in Colombian cities. But there are those sudden winces of paranoia—La Malicia (a contagious hustle, you seem to be catching on). Or queue-jumping—La Malicia again—which makes getting to the front another form of Latin expression.

Somewhere in between paranoia and self-preservation, but definitely occupying a niche of its own, lies La Malicia Indigena. One hundred years of internal conflict have left the Colombians on their toes. In poetical terms it leads to a tendency to springboard from the concrete into the abstract. In street terms, like New York's, it leaves Colombians relaxed but attentive, cruising by the guidance of a built-in radar. Colombia is renowned for its petty crime (perhaps unfairly when compared to Brazil or Peru). But crime is also a battle of wits. Professor Moriarty used to goad his arch-rival Sherlock Holmes with the jeer that the criminal mind, by definition, is more intelligent than the police brain. Colombia is a place of reveries, most of them romantic, many misplaced, but none innocent or inattentive. If you bear this in mind, nothing will go wrong for you as you will always be a step ahead of—or at least anticipating—the possible. And whilst this might sound silly, people will bend over backwards for a smile. Latin manners are exquisite, and charm can be used in the same way and for the same purpose as an octopus squirting clouds of ink.

Time

The classic attitude is that Colombians, and Latins in general, are always late. Perhaps one can learn more about the Latin approach to hours by following the Indian clock below, which divides the day into 17 very sensibly allocated stations:

The first crowing of the rooster.
The second crowing of the rooster.
The third and last crowing of the rooster.
The break of day.
The first light.
Dawn.
Sunrise.
Middle of the morning.
A little before noon.
Middle of the afternoon.
The sun turning westward.
Hour of the sunset.
Coming of nightfall.
Night.
A little before sunrise.

If Latins are late it is usually because—God willing—something was broken, or fixed, or worse, or better, or more promising, amusing, or profitable, you understand. But the Latin sense of time is, in fact, always spot on. 11.50 am, for example, always warrants a *buenos días*, whereas five minutes after noon, a punctual *buenas tardes*.

Part III
HISTORY

Pre-Columbian statue, San Agustín

As Gabriel García Márquez once wrote: 'For Europeans, South America is a man with a moustache, a guitar and a revolver': Colombia's history is complex, and perhaps not what you might expect it to be.

Colombia has never been, nor ever will be, a banana republic, even though in the 1920s it was the world's largest exporter of bananas. Democratic elections have been held, on and off, since the 1820s, which makes Colombia the second oldest functioning democracy in the western hemisphere. The country has always concerned itself with the values of cultural distinction and intellectual activity, and Bogotá was once described by the Nicaraguan poet Rubén Darío as a place 'long famous for its cultivation of intellectual disciplines, a city of Greek and Latin'. In the 17th century Colombia was the land of El Dorado. In this century it has consistently exhibited freedom for newspapers to publish, with no persecution of writers, and only briefly, on one rare occasion, a period of military rule. Yet, despite this, and the degree to which it contradicts all South American stereotypes, modern Colombia has also exhibited some of the highest levels of political violence in the world.

Geography and landscape provide some explanation; whilst active protagonists in all spheres of Colombian life, they have exerted themselves particularly forcefully in the country's history. Colombia is so torn and divided by its rugged terrain, that it is difficult to talk of a national history: instead, there are the histories of the Caribbean coast, the mountains, the plains, the jungle, the Pacific and the three cordilleras, all quite distinct from one another. Like all South American countries, Colombia has been conquered, colonized and freed, but often the effect of each of these major happenings has been local, and what has been true for one area, might not have been true for another. In some parts of the country, the conquest is still going on, or more incredibly, only just begun.

Colombian Pre-History: 7000 BC–AD 1500

The very beginning however—Colombia's aboriginal prehistory—lies on the Caribbean, with simple hunting and gathering groups, pot-sherds and axe-heads, time-date 7000 BC. But Colombia's Indian cultures did not leave strong traces behind them, and most of the country's prehistory has since been worked out from a combination of on-the-spot reportage conducted by the conquistadors 500 years ago, and intelligent guesswork by anthropologists extrapolating backwards from work done in the field today. So, as Fernando Portuondo ironically notes, 'History begins with the arrival of the white man, whose deeds it records.'

At the time of the conquest there was no embracing imperial Indian empire in Colombia comparable to the Incas in Peru. Instead, each new corner of Colombia's landscape held a new and different group. The list of their names is long—Quimbaya, Calima, Tumaco, Tolima, Narino, Paez, Sinu, San Agustín, Chibcha, Tayrona and Guane—but little is known about them. Many of the groups were small. Mostly they farmed. Occasionally they traded with each other along slim mountain paths—cotton for corn and salt for gold. They left no records behind, and only few spectacular monuments; the mysterious sculptures and sarcophagi around San Agustín (see p. 267), the burial chambers of Tierradentro (see p. 275), and the lost city of the Tayronas in Santa Marta's Sierra Nevada (see p. 213) are the country's three biggest and there aren't many more.

The most important cultural unit within the Indian population of Colombia in proto-historic and historic times was the Chibcha, who occupied the highland areas around what is now Bogotá. In the 16th century they numbered about 500,000, a figure which makes them as populous a nation as any that then existed in Europe. They had a well-developed religion, moral code, system of justice, and stratified society. They had a system of coinage, based on gold, and were skilled jewellers. But they had no wheel, no domestic animals bar the dog, and no talent at engineering or masonry. Their thatched towns were ruled by chieftains with names like 'Ruler of the Heights' and 'Song of the Forest'. Their temples to Sua and Chía were gilded (although they 'esteemd gold no more than dross, yet for the colour's sake adorned themselves with it'). And they seem to have been a more philosophic than practical race, and as such quick to lose out against the impact of European imperialism. Their temples and records are now all gone, and they were felled as a people, not by the conquistadors' swords, but by the diseases that they brought with them; by 1580, just one generation after the arrival of the Spanish, 90 per cent of Nueva Granada's aboriginal population had perished to a combination of smallpox and influenza. What has been left behind however, is their highly crafted gold, and along with the finer work of the Quimbaya and the Tayrona, you can see it in staggering array at the Gold Museum in Bogotá today.

The Colombian Indians' talent at making gold statuettes, masks, rings and bracelets delighted the conquistadors and served to confirm their belief in the myth of El Dorado. To the penniless potential conquistadore in Europe, thinking about seeking his fortune in the Indies, El Dorado was a mythic city where the buildings were lined with gold and the streets dotted with emeralds. In their search for this hallucination, the Spanish quested madly over Colombia, and indeed nearly all of South America, subduing as they went, but leaving only partially settled areas in their wake.

The Conquest and the Quest for El Dorado: 1500–1550

Although the country is named after the Admiral, Colombus never set foot in Colombia. His pilot Alonso de Ojeda was the first, at Cabo de la Vela in 1499. However, the first firm foothold in South America was not established until 26 years later, in 1525, at Santa Marta: the first port on the southern continent—until it gave way to Cartagena—and also the main coastal base for excursions into the Colombia interior for El Dorado.

El Dorado, however, does not mean the Golden City, or the Land of Gold. It means exactly what it says, the gilded man. Indian informers had told the Spanish in Santa Marta of a highland lake called Guatavita, in a land called 'Bacata', where several times a year a gold-dusted chief (the golden man) made offerings and sacrifices. European wish-fulfillment, however, quickly turned the fact of a man into the myth of a place.

In April 1536, Capitán Jiménez de Quesada led 875 men out of Santa Marta on a year-long trek up the Magdalena, to Bacata. In hunger and constant danger, tormented by fever, insects and stifling heat, by the time his expedition reached the highlands, the wadded cotton 'armour' that they wore against the poisoned arrows of the Indians had long since rotted away. They had already eaten the leather of their shields, straps and belts, and when they finally reached the Sabana they were on a slim ration of 40 parched grains of maize a day. Vasco Núñez de Balboa, who had explored the country twenty years earlier from the Gulf of Uruba while looking for the Pacific, had experienced similar difficulties. In 1513 he wrote to King Ferdinand II:

> 'The country is difficult to travel through, on account of the numerous
> rivers and swamps... where many men die owing to the great labour they
> endure... for every day we are exposed to death in a thousand forms...
> I have thought of nothing, by day and night, but how to support myself
> and the handful of men God has placed under my charge.'

Quesada endured the same. Many was the time when his expedition was almost abandoned, but, like Balboa, he persevered.

At the outskirts of Bacata, Chibcha Indians barred Quesada's way. One of them, armed with a lance and broad arrows, came out to offer single combat. The Spaniard who accepted the challenge charged at a gallop, and seizing the Indian by the hair, bore him away. The rest of the Indians ran. The Chibcha were already divided into two rival groups—one ruled to the south from Bacata (Bogotá) by the Zipa, the other to the north from Hunza (Tunja) by the Zaque. The Spanish exploited the rivalry. And any that did resist were hampered by their semi-supernatural view of the Spanish, and were easily overcome.

The Spanish obssesion with crosses puzzled the Chibchas; for them, a cross signified 'death by snake bite', and a sad Chibcha verse recalls the moment of their defeat:

> *'Surubu Loma, Nevin Ra, Canan Cruz, Nigua Ra.'*
> (I climbed the mountain, I sat down, I found a cross, I started to weep'.)

The Foundation of Santa Fé de Bogotá: 1538

Quesada had at last reached the true land of El Dorado. But after inspecting the lake at Guatavita, and finding less gold there than legend had led him to believe, he considered continuing his expedition south to Peru to find more. Two startling arrivals quickly changed his plans. The first was by Sebastián Benalcázar, journeying north from Quito; the second, by Nicolás de Federmann, journeying west from the plains of Venezuela. Both had arrived almost simultaneously; both had also been looking for El Dorado; all three now formed an uneasy alliance as they jockeyed for legal ownership of Bogotá and the Central Colombian lands.

Benalcázar's men were fresh and well attired. 'Having come from Peru, a very rich and prosperous country,' they had 'rich clothes of silk, and fine cloaks, silver ornaments, coats of mail, and many servants ... and a great quantitiy of pigs to sustain them.' Quesada's and Federmann's were tired and in bad condition. Quesada's troops had long lost their armour and now wore the fashioned clothes of the Indians; Federmann's only had the skins of the animals that they had killed. (Rather tactlessly, 'the soldiers of Benalcázar made fun of the clothes and habiliments of the men of Quesada') But Quesada was a lawyer by training and, juggling possibilities, managed to draw the weakened German jungle expedition onto his side against the superior might of Benalcázar. Inevitably there was squabbling, and ownership was only finally ascertained back in Europe by King Charles of Spain, 14 years later. Quesada got Bogotá; Benalcázar Popayán, Cali and a thick wedge of land between Bogotá and Quito; whilst poor Federmann only merited a lawsuit and a creditor's prison chains.

The conquest has been tagged with the label of unique greed, savagery and obdurate cruelty. It was ruthless, but it was not unique—except in daring. The Spanish conquistadors were instruments perfectly adapted to their ends, and if they took naturally to the adventure of the Indies it was because they had been conditioned to it, for centuries, at home. Since the first millenium the Spanish had fought Arabs, the Berbers, the French and each other; there had been civil wars and crusades, quests and fighting (the only honourable occupations for Spanish gentlemen of the time); and finally, during any rare intervals of peace, duels that were sparked off by the Spanish, famously hair-trigger, sense of honour.

The conquistadors despoiled the Indians, but were genuinely concerned about their immortal souls. They constrained them to labour in the fields, but did not drive them from the land. They exploited them, but also married them. Nor were the abuses suffered by the vanquished natives condoned by the Spanish government, which from the start had: established the rights of Indians as free subjects of the king; forbidden forced labour; enjoined free dealing and kindness; and even established formal reserves of Indian land. This was the official version, anyway, which considering the social conditions of Europe at the time was a miracle of liberality. Of course, New Granada was a long way away from Spain, and the rulings were not always effective across the Atlantic.

But the Indians did have one or two champions of their own in the New World. Most notable of these was the pious padre Bartolomé de Las Casas. According to the Argentine writer Borges, Casas took 'great pity on the Indians who were languishing in the hellish workpits of the Antillean gold mines and suggested to Charles V a scheme of importing blacks, so that they might languish in the hellish workpits of Antillean goldmines'. Because of this influx of Africans and African culture into the New World,

169

Casas was also responsible, according to Borges, for other human woes galore. To name a few: the American Civil War, Uncle Tom's Cabin, Nigger Jim on the raft with Huckleberry Finn, Faulkner's novels, Black power, Afro hairdos, Cuban music, the Tango, and all that jazz.

But all of this is much later. The history is getting ahead of itself. And whatever the faults of the Spanish administration, which were many and glaring, Colombia first passed through an indolent period of empire that was to last for just over three hundred years.

The Colonial Years: 1550–1810

If the period before 1550 was one of conquest, the one after was of administration. To control the lawlessness of conquest the Crown conceded an Audencia to Santa Fé in 1549. In 1564, the colony became the Presidencia del Nuevo Reino de Granada, with dual military and civil power radiating from a Capitán General based in the capital. And in 1717, following Philip V's decision to further divide the increasingly cumbersome Virreynato del Peru, Nueva Granada became a fully autonomous Virreynato, a more important division comprising a huge area; the territories of what are now Colombia, Panama, Ecuador and Venezuela.

A central administration had been established, but the colony was still poor and its economy frugal, even though gold was the main export item. Although ranking far behind the silver-rich Viceroyalties of Mexico and Peru, New Granada yielded more gold than any other region during the colonial period. By the late 17th century, gold accounted for 90 per cent of all registered exports, and paid for such Spanish imports as fine cloth, wine, cooking oil and flour. Gold was Nueva Granada's life-blood and it was gold that lubricated the economic ties of the colony.

The gold trade did not, however, fashion any strong sense of 'national identity'. Communications to and from the capital were restrained by the terrain, which acted like a tourniquet on administrative control. Apart from Cartagena and Santa Fé, Spanish presence in the provinces was shadowy. Inter-regional trade was scarce, and from the economic standpoint most regions remained basically autarkic. Villagers and peasents knew litle more than the tiny world of their valley, the wealthy only slightly more. People did not move: it was difficult, often novel. Humboldt, travelling in the late 1700s, wrote:

> 'As few persons in easy circumstances travel on foot in these climates—
> through roads so difficult, during fifteeen or twenty days together—they
> are carried by men in a chair, tied on their back, for... it would be
> impossible to go on mules. The whole of the province of Antioquia is
> surrounded by mountains so difficult to pass that those who dislike
> entrusting themselves to the backs of a carrier must relinquish all
> thoughts of leaving the country... I was acquainted with one inhabitant
> of the province, so immensely bulky that he had not met with more than
> two mulattoes capable of carrying him, and it would have been
> impossible for him to return home if these two carriers had died...'

New Granada was marked by a greater number of regional divides than the Andean colonies. But racial differences were softer and there was a greater blood mixing; Indian with white in the highlands, black with white on the Caribbean coast, and Indian with black wherever the two populations met. By the mid-18th century, the population of the eastern highlands in the heart of Colombia was predominantly mestizo. But this is not to say that great prestige was not associated with paler skin, and at all levels of society. To quote Humbolt again, only this time on the whiter shades of pale amongst his chair-carriers:

> 'No humiliating idea is annexed to the trade of *cargueros*, and the men who follow this occupation are not Indians, but mulattoes, even whites. It is often curious to hear them quarrelling in the midst of a forest, because one has refused the other, who pretends to have a whiter skin, the pompous title of Don, or Su Merced...'

By the 18th century, legal authority was everywhere present through the colony, at least in theory, for it was still local views and local men that actually controlled Nueva Granada's isolated communities. It must be understood that this was not a lawless society, but one comprised of a large number of tiny societies, usually carrying out the law in the interests of local elites. Santa Fé was too distant a capital for its influence to be felt in any meaningful way in the provinces. It only had a very small administrative budget, and no effective police force. In addition, it was one of the few Spanish colonial capitals that had no real importance with respect to trade between the provinces. The north-east supplied the western mining camps of Antioquia with wheat products, cheeses, tobacco and sugar conserves. Cloth came northwards from Quito, wine and brandy from Peru, and Spanish imports directly via Cartagena. Santa Fé did not even have the distinction of being an entrepôt. The colony looked not so much to Santa Fé, as *through* it, to Europe and Spain, and the capital was seen more as the convenient outpost of a greater authority, the Crown, rather than an authority in itself.

The Awakening: 1780–1810

The history of Colombia is easily divided into sections. First it had been conquered, then it had slumbered, now it awoke: 1780–1810 was the period of the Botanical Expedition, a special time when the country was enlightened by European ideas.

The Botanical Expedition does nothing at first to raise one's interest: it has a Victorian ring to it, suggesting a group of young ladies under the guidance of a droop-whiskered, tight-trousered professor engaged in a genteel day with nature. Actually, it was an achievement of the first magnitude. It accumulated a library of 6000 volumes that made Humbolt's mouth water, an herbarium of more than 20,000 plants and some 3000 carefully coloured botanical plates. It lent itself to the study of geodetics, geography, and zoology. And it also earned the admiration of scientists from all over the world. José Celestino Mutis was the Expedition's boss.

Apart from directing the Expedition, Mutis was also a savant of European reputation. Bringing radical views, the bound volumes of the French Encylopedists, and fresh ideas on education, Mutis came to be mentor to Bogotá's information and knowledge-hungry criollos. His indirect influence on Nueva Granada's politics cannot be underestimated: a whole generation of his students would later provide the intellectual leadership for the independence struggle against Spain.

By 1800 newspapers were beginning to circulate and ideas were growing at a tropical rate. Books were smuggled in from Europe as if contraband, which they were. *Tertulias—*

those semi-formal politico-literary salons where ideas were discussed as if they were fireworks—took on a torch-bearing tone. And without plan, almost without consciousness, the revolution began to take shape.

The Wars of Independence: 1809–19

The Spanish empire had resembled a solar system, with the colonies revolving around the Crown like minor planets. But by the end of the 18th century, the colonies had begun to shine with their own light and the Spanish presence was increasingly felt by the American-born criollos to be stultifying and irksome. Their list of complaints was long: no responsibility had ever been delegated to them (of the 170 viceroys that had ever governed Spanish America, only four had been American-born); they perceived the viceregal administration as being morally and spiritually bankrupt (which it was); and the English–Spanish war had brought them increased taxation. There was the impetus of revolutionary ideas from Europe. In 1794 Antonio Nariño had translated into Spanish the *Declaration of the Rights of Man*, a touch paper of revolt. And then there was the beacon of the successful North American revolution. The final straw, however, came in 1810, when Napoleon deposed the Spanish king and installed his brother Ferdinand as ruler in Spain instead.

Revolution, which had long been possible, now seemed probable. Patriotism in the name of the mother country was quickly converted into South American nationalism, and what had begun as resistance to France, quickly developed into war against Spain. By early July 1810, the town councils of Cartagena, Mompós, Cali, Pamplona and Socorro had all taken full power of their respective districts. And a few weeks later a new government was set up in the capital, at Santa Fé.

Such an easy beginning seemed auspicious—Bolívar had had a series of spectacular sucesses in Venezuela, and Spanish authority had seemed to melt away in the face of the patriot cause. But one vital element was still missing from the New Republic—a patriotic sense of unity needed to conquer the scattered remaining centres of royalist support. Unity, unfortunately, was a rare commodity. Cartagena refused to send representatives to the government in Bogotá—advocating regional autonomy instead—and the other provinces were sympathetic to Cartagena's federalist leanings. This division between centralists and federalists was to be a continuous feature of post-Independence Colombian politics and now, while the Republic dithered, the Spanish readied themselves to advance. In July 1815, a Spanish force of 11,000 men, under the orders of General Pablo Morillo, landed at Santa Marta. The inevitable denouement now began.

Morillo's Reign of Terror: 1815–19

If the fortunes of the patriot cause during the Wars of Independence fluctuated as wildly as a profile of the Andes, the Spanish General Pablo Morillo's reign of terror can be seen as a plummet-drop into the deepest valley.

General Pablo Morillo was called the Pacifier—in the same sense that the conquistadors were pacifiers of resisting Indians. He arrived with promises to forget the past, but stayed in order to supervise wholesale executions. Only bad transportation and difficult terrain slowed his path of retribution. First he took Cartagena, executing 400 prisoners on the beach after promising amnesty. Bolívar, meanwhile, fled the Colombian coast for Jamaica. Then Morillo re-took Santa Fé in May 1816, after the Virgin of Chiquinquirá had been invoked in vain by the Santafereaños. Finally he set about refining his cruelty, sending out a general order to his troops to: 'Burn cities, behead their inhabitants, ravage the country; respect neither sex nor age; replace the peaceful farmer with a ferocious warrior, the instrument of vengeance with a king'. His campaign report sent back to Spain chillingly declared: 'The Kingdom of New Granada is on its way to extermination', and colonial rule was re-established in 1817.

If Morillo's re-conquest had been undertaken with greater sensitivity, and if pardons had been more freely given, then perhaps the war-weary and disillusioned patriots would have accepted the return of colonial authority for a few years more. But Morillo's savagery killed any hope of winning the colony back to Spain, and in 1818, the pendulum began to swing again. In December, Bolívar returned from his Caribbean exile and quickly set up operations in the lower reaches of the Orinoco basin. Within a year he had won the support of the renegade plains cowboys. Led by the 'murdering tiger', the brutal and valorous José Antonio Páez, the *llaneros* had already beaten the Spanish once, a few months earlier; Morillo's first and only defeat since he had landed on South American soil.

The two rebel forces of Páez and Bolívar joined in April 1819, and in May Bolívar started his famous march from the plains up to the Bogotá Sabana. Two squadrons of horse and four battalions of infantry (one of them the famous British Legion) floundered and strained across the flooded *llanos*. At Tame, Santander joined them with an equal force. Together, some 5000 men strong, they faced the horrors of the Cordillera—in winter, with troops unused to mountains, by a back trail considered impassable in the rainy season. Half dead they took Paya in June; then they took Paipa; at Vargas Swamp, on 25 July, they defeated the forces of General Sámano, Morillo's successor; and at the decisive Battle of Boyacá in August, they beat him again. Sámano fled. Bogotá was easily taken soon afterwards. But as Morillo had said of Bolívar, 'He is the Revolution', and the Liberator did not stop at Bogotá. Carrying on to Venezuela, he won another victory as Caraboba in 1821. And, although Royalists continued to put up a rearguard action from the coast, he finally went on with Sucre, after working his way over from Venezuela and Colombia, to liberate Ecuador, Bolivia and Peru. On January 23 1826, the last Spanish flag in South America was lowered and Independence was finally secured.

Post-Independence: 1821–30

The differences between the Spanish and English colonies in the Americas were immense. The Spanish colonists had committed many horrors, but at least they had not committed the gravest of them all: that of denying a place, even at the foot of the social scale, to the people who composed it. There had been classes, castes and slaves in colonial Spanish America, but no pariahs, no persons lacking a social position, or a legal, moral and religious status. The War of Independence did not change this. The revolt had been more a civil war than a radical revolution in the modern sense of the word. There had been no upheaval of the proletarian masses, no huge and inarticulate stirring. It had been essentially aristocratic and intellectual, with freedom the work of the *tertulias* and the upper-class criollos, who had conducted a revolution *de minoría*. The patriots had broken away from Spain, but would they be capable of building a new society with 'liberty, fraternity and equality for all'? It would be difficult; the lot of the majority was yet to change. Culturally, much of South America was still in the Middle Ages.

In 1821 a revolutionary Congress was held in Cúcuta with Bolívar's vision of a united Republic made-up of Colombia, Ecuador and Venezuela briefly prevailing over Santander's looser federal arrangment of sovereign states. Reality, however, was soon to shatter all of the Liberator's projects. The process of disintegration within the Spanish empire proved itself stronger than his clairvoyant desire for unity. And on 10 August 1830 Gran Colombia dissolved into its constituent parts. Bolívar died disillusioned in Santa Marta shortly afterwards.

Fifteen years of war had left the country poor and in debt. National unity was still only an uncertain notion, not a likely fact, and Colombia threatened to do the same as the larger 'Gran' version had just done before—dissolve. The factions that had come to the fore at the Revolutionary Congress in Cúcuta coalesced into two rival politcal factions, the centralist Conservatives and the federalist Liberals, and their political opinions were passionately held, articulately delivered and often violently expressed. As the English historian Malcolm Deas has noted, 'A poor country makes poor wars', but the rest of the 19th century was marked by conflict and any sense of national development was obscure. Between 1830 and 1886, the country changed its name, and constitution, five times. One Bogotáno politician remarked: 'In the political life of all peoples progress is slow. As with the tides, the waves alternately advance and fall back, but the land conquered is always greater than the land lost; there is a constant advance.' The advance may not have been clear to many of the participants, but at least there was hope in such inglorious and apparently austere times.

Modern History: 1890–the Present

In 1890, Colombia was governed by the Conservative—recently converted from the Liberal ranks—Dr Rafael Núñez. This ravaged intellectual—a poet, philosopher, and president, only recently returned from the fleshpots of Liverpool where he had been consul—exerted his influence from a breezy summer house in Cartagena. The mundane day-to-day business of government was meanwhile left to the Virgil translator and polymath, Miguel Antonio Caro, in faraway Bogotá. Under the rustling palm trees, Núñez read the journals of the times—such as the *Economist*, the *Revue des Deux Mondes*, Freud's early paper on cocaine . . . and, with a more avid interest, poetry. He also wrote, most notably four years earlier, the Constitution of 1886. Battered, but still just in force one hundred years later, this legislative piece of lyricism was read and commented on at the time by Victor Hugo, who described it as having been 'Written for Angels'.

One day, sized by a fit of literary enthusiasm, Núñez had the rising star of Latin American literature, the young Nicaraguan poet Rubén Darío, cabled from Bogotá. Darío was to be offered the post of Colombian consul in Buenos Aires, a posting he duly accepted. In his appalling sonnet of thanks to Núñez, Darío began 'Colombia is a land of lions . . .' Darío went into ecstasies over Bogotá ('A paradise for the spirit!' he exclaimed). But what must have most puzzled him was: how was it that this large and warlike tropical republic could be governed by such unlikely literati, with scarcely a peso to their names?

We can wonder too—and not only about lions and angels. The problem of Colombia's post-colonial order was complex. The country's current political situation is rooted in this complexity (not least in the paper first hinted at by Freud). And in order to

174

understand Colombia's present we must begin to ask, what was this early 20th century disorder like, how did it come about, and why?

From Independence until the beginning of this century, Colombian political life was entirely dominated by Liberals and Conservatives. These parties bear no relation to the English concepts: instead they are based around a few strong families and Colombia's traditional voting patterns. In Colombia you are born 'with a political identity card around your navel' and if your father is a Conservative, so too are you. Although ideological differences between the two parties were so slim that people joked that their only real difference lay in the fact that Liberals went to the 9 and Conservatives to the 10 o'clock mass, open pitched conflict between the two parties was common: following the 15 years of the Wars of Independence, Colombia experienced eight general civil wars, 14 local civil wars, countless small uprisings, two international wars with Ecuador and three coups d'état. Violence also spanned the centuries: sparked by a liberal revolt, the 'War of A Thousand Days' (1899–1902) caused nearly 100,000 deaths in a country with a total population of less than 4 million.

In 1903, taking advantage of Colombia's weakened state, the USA encouraged a group of Panamanian dissidents to declare their independence. From under the shadow of a battery of naval guns, Panama ceded in 1904 and in return the North Americans received quasi-sovereign rights. Bogotá only acknowledged Panama's independence in 1921, and the USA compensated them with a belated US$25 million.

Liberals v Conservatives: So What's the Difference?

'Liberals! The words we know so well have a nightmarish meaning in this country. Liberty, democracy, patriotism, government—all of them have a flavour of folly and murder. Haven't they doctor?'

—from *Nostromo*, by Joseph Conrad

The conflicts that marked the first 100 years of the republic seem odd at a first glance; they were based around party groupings whose ideologies hardly differed. The Liberals were vaguely federalist and anti-clerical, the Conservatives vaguely centralist and pro-church. The parties governed from Bogotá, a city whose life, political or otherwise, had little to do with the rest of the country. The fighting was never popular, nor the recruitment. Much local writing of the time was even a lament against these struggles. Yet party elites consistently managed to mobilize large parts of the population, from all classes, in support of their struggle for power. Can one fall back on some sort of political Magical Realism as an explanation of the violence? There is no clearer picture of the seemingly absurd extent to which party ties could reach than of the Mayor in García Márquez's *In the Evil Hour*, staggering around a small town, crippled by a toothache, but unable to see the dentist because he is a Conservative and his mouth-saver a Liberal.

It was out of these party alliegances that Colombia's famously violent modern history grew. An historical report from the Bogotá news weekly *Semana*, gives a good indication of how they formed. For the preservation of their life and property, peasants of the time—isolated by impassable terrain from any other political choice—had to align themselves to whichever group was strongest in their area. However, come peacetime, Colombia's centralized system of government meant that national changes in rule were faithfully duplicated at a local level. A new Liberal governement in Bogotá, for instance, ushered in a new liberal local council in what had previously been a Conservative town. This meant that:

> '*The mayor would turn into a dangerous enemy; that the official of the branch of the Agrarian Bank would refuse the loan, that the new teacher would look with disfavour on one's child attending school, that the official of the Department of Health would first attend his fellow partisan of the other party... and that it was necessary to remain a prudent distance from the police.*'
>
> —*Semana*, 1958

More often than not, Colombia's political violence stemmed from old and personal vendettas that were reflected in the traditional political *labels* of Liberal or Conservative, rather than in Liberal or Conservative ideologies. So it was that hereditary hatreds—created and confirmed in civil wars—prevailed over any rational differences, with party allegiances and violence persisting along an evolutionary ratchet from which there was no going back...

The First Phase of La Violencia: 1948–53

Although competitive, democratic elections had been held, on and off, since the 1820s, power still remained in the hands of the professional Conservative and Liberal politicians in Bogotá, not with 'the people'. Jorge Gaitán represented 'the people'. He gathered great crowds, struck resonant chords, mobilized the rural and urban poor, gave hope to the humble, and his lunchtime assassination in Bogotá on the 9 April 1948 unleashed a hurricane. First the *Bogotázo*, a looting of the capital and any of its symbols of power. Then, a spread of violence into the countryside.

The two periods of civil war between 1948 and 1966 were so terrible that they are simply known as 'La Violencia' and the precise dating of the period, its causes, development and subsequent influence on Colombian history remain a source of controversy, as does any attempt to attribute responsibility. The events have been the subject of intense scrutiny by sociologists, political scientists and military analysts. But there is general agreement, at least, that the period was one of exceptional bloodiness and cruelty. Nearly a quarter of a million people died, some from new methods of horrible death; the *corte corbata*, the short tie, for example, left the tongue hanging from a slit neck.

The 'War of a Thousand Days' had represented the last attempt by one side or other of the Colombian political divide to win power through conventional 19th-century battlefield warfare. Now, however, armed conflict ceased to be 'a matter of ill-equipped rebel armies of peasants confronting ill-equipped government armies of peasants', and instead assumed the form of street riots, isolated clashes between civilians and government authorities, coup d'état attempts, and guerrilla warfare. But especially guerrilla warfare.

During the 1950s a strong 'power to the people' spirit arose in the countryside. The campesinos, who had long borne the weight of Colombia's violent history, formed self-defence groups, often teaming up with liberal guerrillas and, in some areas, small communist groups—the first to operate in the western hemisphere. The language of these defence groups came to take on a revolutionary fervour—which worried many Bogotá politicians—but a traditional verse of the times perhaps better sums up their attitude:

'I'm just a campesino,
I didn't start the fight,
But if they come asking for trouble
They'll get what is coming to them.'

Many of the defence groups have since dissolved. Others, such as the FARC, have consolidated, forging themselves into a powerful left-wing guerrilla group that still controls large portions of the country.

The Second Period of La Violencia: 1954–66

In 1953, in a coup d'état supported by nearly all the national political groups in Colombia, the Army Commander General Rojas Pinilla took power. An amnesty was offered to those involved in the violence. Six thousand peasant fighters, mostly from the *llanos*, surrendered their arms and the scale of conflict was, at least initially, drastically reduced. Rojas's government has been the only military intervention in Colombian politics this century, and the relief that it offered was short-lived: in 1954 the violence began to escalate once again as the army instituted a systematic repression of both Liberals and Conservatives.

In this second period of the Violencia, traditional partisan rivalries tended to become secondary as the political parties strove to unite against the threat posed by the military government. The Colombian political elites drew together, realising that continued inter-party struggle could only threaten their collective hold on power. An agreement was reached to form a kind of Liberal-Conservative coalition government in 1957, and the dictator Rojas was brought to heel in 1958. Thus came into being what was known as the National Front, one of the strangest experiments in the democratic history of the world.

The National Front: 1958–74

In the National Front, the Liberals and Conservatives agreed that elections would continue to be held, but that the competitive element which had led to so much violence at election time would be removed by deciding the results of the election in advance. Only the two main parties were to be included and, however the votes were cast, the two parties would split them evenly. Thus, at the national level, Conservatives and Liberals would have equal representation in the two Houses of Congress, and, at the local level, parity in all departmental assemblies and municipal councils.

The National Front was scheduled to last from 1958–74 and has been described as 'the world's first attempt at a two-party dictatorship'. One political analyst accurately summarized its workings as follows: 'Instead of representing the political hegemony of the Liberals *or* the Conservatives, the Frente Nacional was the exclusive hegemony of the Liberals *and* the Conservatives.' It is easy to deride the experiment, and it certainly stretches the definition of a 'functioning democracy', but within the context of Colombian politics it was not entirely absurd. The arrangement was less monolithic

177

than might appear: the persistent factionalism of Colombian politics rapidly led to the proliferation of dissident groups within the Front, and there was some judicious bending of rules to allow this. And insofar as the violence in Colombia stemmed from inter-party competition, the National Front did contribute to its diminution, although the persistence of violence into the 1960s suggested that there were now other causes too.

Death Squads and Guerrillas: 1974–88

Levels of violence did drop during the years of the National Front. The period was also one of great economic growth, with 'King Coffee' at last providing the economic potential energy for the diversification of the rest of Colombia's economy . Yet Colombia remained one of the more violent countries of the world as conflicts from other sources became prominent. Drug-related violence in the early 1970s led Liberal governments of the time to adopt wide-ranging powers in the name of a crusade against the drug cartels, powers which simultaneously furnished a context for the repression of all forms of radical political protest, such as the communist guerrillas. Two security measures taken in 1978 illustrate the problem. One, adopted without parliamentary consultation, exempted the police and armed forces from all responsibility before the law for actions taken against violence and drug-trafficking, and also authorized the use of arms by civilians in similar circumstances. The other provided for terms of imprisonment of up to five years for 'disturbing public order'; up to one year without trial for the possession of subversive literature; and trial by summary court martial, with limited right of defence and appeal, for offences such as printing slogans.

However, the most disturbing and sinister innovation of recent years has been the proliferation of paramilitary death squads. Financed by the drug trade, and apparently enjoying the complicity of some elements of the security forces, the most widely publicized of these, known as MAS (*Muerte a secuestadres*/Death to kidnappers), appeared in October 1981. It was formed ostensibly as a response to the activities of guerrilla groups which kidnap the wealthy in order to raise funds for their operations. However, the principal victims of MAS have been the same as those of death-squads elsewhere in Latin America: trade unionists, peasant leaders, left-wing lawyers, and the like.

In the mid-1980s, the liberal president Betancourt sponsored the formation of a left-wing party, the Union Patriotica, in an attempt to give the guerrillas a legitimate, national, political voice. But the UP were notably unpopular on some fronts, and many were assassinated by the narco-financed paramilitary squads of above. The logic behind the cartels' support of the death squads is that there is no more fervent a capitalist than a cocaine Mafiosi. Elected members of the unarmed left thus found themselves playing an ideological game of hopscotch in which they had to defend the theory of the 'people's war' whilst at the same time demanding increased protection from the government against whom the war was waged. In the lurch and hurtle of Colombian politics, guerrilla conflict proliferated throughout the 1980s, as did peace talks, and both have become a regular feature of Colombian political life. Left-wing support within Colombia has subsequently united under the banner of the maverick, urban and *unarmed* communist group, the M-19. The armed guerrillas have mostly lost both their popular support and ideological commitment and have become instead more like rural bandits, operating,

178

true to bandit tradition, with a fast-fading tinge of romanticism in the distant hills and jungles of the country.

Behind all of this—the guerrillas, the prolonged Conservative–Liberal political rivalry, and the extreme right-wing death squads—and apparently divorced from human agency although exacerbated by all of them—lies the unruly, pinched, chaotic and febrile improvisations of underdevelopment that prevails throughout most of Latin America. Not without reason have Colombian politics been described as as complicated as a Gordian knot, and in the late 1980s, many of the country's unresolved problems came to a head in the cocaine wars.

The Cocaine Wars: 1988–90
Cocaine has received its fair share of media attention, much of it wrong, and nearly all of it exaggerated.

Colombia does not grow much coca, nor does the cocaine trade employ many Colombians, nor do cocaine earnings in any way dominate the Colombian economy; the trade has damaged the economy more than it has benefited it. From the late seventies, Colombians have controlled the processing and transportation of cocaine, elaborated from coca paste produced in Peru and Bolivia and chemicals produced in West Germany and Brazil. The Colombian hold on the trade derives partly from geography, and partly from traditions of violent entrepreneurship in emeralds, marijuana and the contraband import of Marlboro cigarettes. Much of Colombia's history has been pirate history, and most of it, at that, European piracy.

As Stephen Minta notes: 'There are interesting similarities between this narcotics bonanza and the 'banana fever' which affected Colombia in the early decades of the century (See 'Ciénega' on p. 209). Both have involved substantial transformations within the rural economy to adapt to the demands of a largely North American market; both have generated very large sums of money which have been very unevenly distributed; both have caused serious social dislocation in rural areas; and both have been a source of violent conflict in one form or another.'

As far as the drug trade is concerned, however, its effects on Colombian society have been uniformly disastrous. In September 1989, Luis Carlos Galán, the Liberal Party's presidential candidate, was assassinated by the Medellín Mafia. Galán was comparable in his charisma to a latter-day, Latin John. F. Kennedy. The country was rocked, and President Virgilio Barco declared an all-out war on the Mafia. The Mafia responded with bombs.

During the drugs war what was at stake was the character of a country that, for all of its problems, had always been a pleasure to live in. The drug barons exerted their subtlest and most pervasive pressure on this point. Life will not be worth living, they said, if the government does not negotiate. The spate of bombings at the end of 1989 were less designed to cause casualties, which would only have further united the country against them, than to cause panic. Placed in banks, building societies, schools and supermarkets at night, when the buildings were empty, they were designed to make people think, 'Where will this all end?'

Where indeed might it all end? This is how it worked in 1990: Colombians have been understandably cynical and indulgent about cocaine. The trade began along a hostile but precise imitation of North American marketing principles (there's a demand; so supply),

179

and anyway, cocaine was not their poison. For a long time the country was complacent about the trade, and in the beginning it could afford to ignore it. However, the intensity of the conflict during the 'Drugs War' indicated a new position. So while it seems unlikely that drug smuggling will end—despite the country's efforts—as long as the magnet of drug consumption continues in the USA, what one can hope for is that the behaviour of those engaged in the trade will change. Everyone in Colombia is tired of the war. Perhaps, probably, there will be, or already have been, negotiations between the government and the cocaine cartels. Narco-traffic is not necessarily perceived as a crime; narco-terrorism, however, is.

CHRONOLOGY

10,000 BC	First Indian groups arrive in Americas.
3000 BC	Date of pottery remains found near Cartagena.
300 BC	Chibcha expand trade network through the highlands.
100 BC	Period of best San Agustín sculpture.
AD 500	Peak of Tayrona civilization.
1470	Chibcha rivalry begins between the Zipa and Zaque.
1499	Alonso de Ojeda lands at Cabo de la Vela.
1500	Rodrigo de Bastidas explores Caribbean shoreline.
1509	Alonso de Ojeda founds first mainland settlement in the New World at San Sebastián de Uruba.
1514	Vasco Núñez de Balboa crosses the Darien, bound for the Pacific.
1529	War with the Tayrona in the foothills of the Sierra Nevada de Santa Marta.
1533	Cartagena founded
1536	Jiménez de Queseda sets off inland from Santa Marta, questing for El Dorado. Benalcázar founds Cali and Popayán whilst moving north from Quito.
1537	Queseda, Benalcázar and Federmann jockey for legal possession of Bogotá.
1538	Bogotá founded.
1549	Charles V creates Audencia de Santa Fé.
1564	Presidencia del Nuevo Reino de Granada created.
1586	Cartagena sacked by Francis Drake.
1594/6	Indian land reserves created.
1610	First Court of Inquisition founded in Cartagena.
1739	Vice-Royalty of Nueva Granada formed.
1741	Vernon defeated by Don Blas at Cartagena.
1781	Communero revolt against Spain in Socorro.
1783	Celestino Mutis leads Botanical Expedition.
1794	Antonio Nariño translates 'Rights of Man'.
1810	Napoleon replaces Ferdinand VII with his own brother, Joseph, on the Spanish Throne.
	Cali, Pamplona, Cartagena and Socorro declare Independence
1811	Rebel state, 'The United Provinces of New Granada', formed.
1815–16	Pablo Morillo, the 'Pacifier', crushes criollo revolution.
1817	Colonial rule re-established in Bogotá.
1819	Páez and Bolívar join forces and defeat Spanish at Paipa, Vargas Swamp, and, decisively, at Boyacú.
	First Revolutionary Congress held at Angostura.
1821	Bolívar defeats Spanish at Coroboba, in Venezuela.
	Second Revolutionary Congress held in Cúcucta
1826	Last Spanish flag in Americas lowered.
1830	Bolívar dies, and confederation of Gran Colombia dissolves.
1849	Centralist and federalist factions formalize into Conservative and Liberal parties.
1853–85	The years of Liberal Government.
1885–1930	The years of the Conservative Republic.
1886	President Rafael Núñez ratifies his centralist constitution.
1899–1902	The Thousand Days War.
1903	US foments Panamanian separatism in order to build canal.
1921	US settles with Colombia over Panama.
1928	Cienega banana strike.

181

1948	Assassination of Jorge Eliecer Gaitán, the populist liberal leader, leads to outbreak of 'La Violencia'.
1948/53	200,000 die during worst years of 'La Violencia'.
1953	General Gustavo Rojas Pinilla chosen by Liberal and Conservative politians to lead coup d'état.
1954	Campesinos organize into self-defence groups.
1955	Repressive period of military rule under Rojas Pinilla.
1958	National Front established and Pinilla brought to heel.
1958–65	Second stage of 'La Violencia'.
1966	The Revolutionary Armed Forces of Colombia (FARC) is officially formed.
1974/78	National Front dissolves and Liberal President Alfonso López Michelson elected.
1978/82	Liberal government of Julio Cesar Turbay launches repressive period against guerrillas.
1982/6	Conservative government of Belisario Betancur begins peace process with guerrillas.
1984	Minister of Justice, Rodrigo Lara Bonilla, assassinated by drug barons.
1985	M–19 holds hostages for ransom in the Palace of Justice.
	Volcano El Nevado de Ruiz explodes and 20,000 die at Armero.
1986/90	Liberal President Virgilio Barco elected, and establishes 'party in power and party in opposition' system for the first time.
1989	Liberal presidential candidate Luis Carlos Galán assassinated; conflict between government and drug barons intensifies.
	M–19 guerrillas sign peace agreement; Cocaine baron Rodrigo Gacha killed
1990	Liberal candidate Cesar Gaviria elected President.
1991	Conditional surrender of Cocaine baron, Pablo Escobar.

Part IV

THE CARIBBEAN

The old Spanish fort of San Fernando guards Cartagena's harbour

There has always been a cultural and poltical rift between Colombia's coast and mountains; their rivalry is famous.

'Those Bogotános, those *cachacos*,' say the *costeños*, 'are uptight and only think to work.'

'Those *costeños*,' comes the reply, 'are informal and loud mouthed and only think to drink and dance.'

Music is everywhere in the Caribbean; this is rock' n' roll South America and it's the area's dominant trait. It's in the dancing imagination of its most famous writer, Gabriel García Márquez. It's in the over-heated marine light that banks, reels and ricochets, throwing its lurid hues on colours that grow almost poisonous in the shade. And it's even in the luscious open faces of the coastal people—a toffee-coloured racial mixing initiated in the Caribbean basin by the slave trade 400 years ago.

Colombia's Caribbean is a country within a country, a country within its own right. It's an area where everything is a story and everyone a storyteller. It's 600km of tropical surrealism, unclassifiable sights, threat, carelessness and charm. Pot-holed roads criss-cross it. Forgotten villages dot it. There are palms, beaches, trees hung with heart-shaped leaves, vertiginous cliffs and, always, a buzzard drawing circles in the sky.

After the mountains, you could spend happy weeks exploring its diverse terrain. To the east lies the highest coastal range in the world, the Sierra Nevada de Santa Marta, and, among its wrinkled heights, a lost Indian city. At the feet of the mountains lies the sleepy bays and beaches of Santa Marta, and beyond Santa Marta, the scrubbed desert badlands of the Guajira peninsula. In the far west, the coast rises towards the jungled

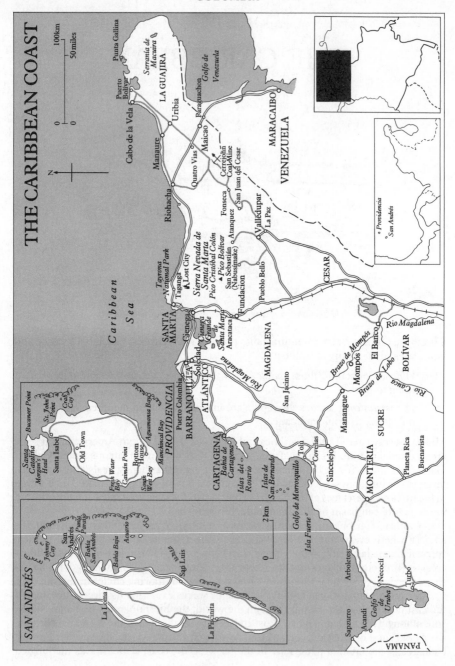

THE CARIBBEAN COAST

beginnings of the Panamanian isthmus like the spout of an upturned tea-pot. Eight hundred kilometres out at sea lie the idyllic coral islets of San Andrés and Providencia. Winding north through the marshy central lowlands, and eventually spilling out into the Caribbean through Barranquilla's Mouth of Ashes, runs the river of the coast and the country, the gravel-grey Magdalena. And then finally, plumb in the middle and 4000 km due south of New York, lies the beautiful fortressed city of Cartagena.

The coast is not all beaches—although there are these too. Nor is it all gaiety—tropical heat and the Caribbean appetite for laughter mask a profound seriousness. In fact, as the northern trading nub of Spain's American empire, the coast can often feel more like Mediterranean Morocco than Caribbean South America, filled with the same gossip, malice and intrigue that you would more normally imagine filled Arab bazaars. Márquez once admitted that in order to write *The Autumn of the Patriarch* he had to return to the Caribbean to 'breathe in the smell of the guayabas rotting in the sun.' The real question however, as he later added, was: 'Why did I ever leave?'.

Cartagena

Cartagena is a frozen explosion of lyricism, a town of half a million people, come upon unseen. There is something delirious in the air—an exotic perfume, or pollen perhaps. The *Cartageneros* have a gift for happiness. Everything is so easy. And it's not uncommon for a newcomer to arrive for a stay of days and to linger for years.

The town is shaped like a crab with pincers outstretched. To the south, arcing across the bay, lies the Bocagrande; a free-wheeling peninsula of modern hotels fringed with beaches and gridded with boutiques, discos and pavement cafés. At the base of this claw lies El Muelle de los Pegasos—the fishermen's wharf. Here men in ragged clothes, hair matted over faces of polished wood, wander through the moorings and small stalls selling, with a casually insistent banter, drugs, or women, or boys; all illusions and anyway everyone's seen it all before.

But the nub and main attraction of Cartagena, the southern pincer, is the Old City, still shaped by its fortressed walls. Passing through the gates is akin to falling, like Alice, through the Mirror. Inside, everything is tall, narrow and close: the cobbled streets are lined with deeply-eaved, off-white or saffron-painted colonial homes. The doors are massive and nail-studded. In quiet parts the city feels like a spectral, run-down Seville; in the trading areas more like a Turkish casbah.

The Caribbean plays hide and seek, flashing from wall entrances. Balconies rise and stretch like the dizzy brass notes of salsa. Sultry eyes watch from grilled windows. Heart-stopping carnival-eyed creole belles ride side-saddle on their boyfriends' motor-cycles. At dusk, during the hour of vespers, a breeze whips up, breaches the walls and stirs the dust. And at night, courting couples fill every stuccoed corner. In Cartagena there is an air of romantic mystery, of *embruja*, a spell, and everything is a flirtation.

Cartagena is a party town, geared for tourism, a neutral ground where other Colombians go to holiday and feel safe. Caribbean cruise ships, with their canned gaiety and cargoes of tourists, now turn away, scared by newspaper headlines. So Cartagena's streets will still be dotted for at least a few years more with bouquets of rocking chair-bound men, T-shirts rolled up, scratching their bellies, shooting the breeze. After all, what the traveller wants is adventure, not development, although both, unusually, are available here.

History

The history of Cartagena is not the cold history of the printed page. The city feels like a stage still set for a faded drama played long ago; at every step there is a tangible reminder of the past. On top of a high hill overlooking the city, the convent of La Candelaria once served as a fort and today houses a religious order; the massive castle of San Felipe rises like a behemoth on a huge boulder right outside the city walls; and the bay is guarded by the twin forts of San Fernando and San José, built to catch invaders in a deadly crossfire. One king of Spain is reported to have spent so much money on Cartagena's fortifications (the then fantastic sum of 59 million pesos) that when he looked west out of his palace windows, towards an imagined ocean horizon, he expected to see the citadels of the port rise between the meeting of sea and sky. Altogether, in the city's heyday, there were 29 forts and bastions, nearly all called after the great Saints of the Church. Fifteen were set in the inner circle of walls, and six around the outer, a ring of stone which, persistently Biblical, was named Gethsemane. As the story goes, when the English historian Arnold Toynbee first saw the fortifications, he remarked: 'So this is why South America doesn't speak English'; clearly the Spanish exported their country's might and God with the clear intention that it should stay.

The Pirate Years: 1533–1811

For nearly 340 years there were only three trading ports in the whole of mainland Spanish America: Portobello on the Panamanian isthmus; Vera Cruz in Mexico; and Cartagena, the only port on the South American mainland. Throughout the year goods accumulated in each port, filtering through from the interior. And because neither the Spanish Main nor the Atlantic was a safe place for a lonely caravel with gold in its hold, there was just one heavily convoyed shipment to Spain, each year, from each port.

Cartagena was founded in 1533 by Pedro de Heredia and its main shipment was the wealth of a gold and silver-rich continent. Mined in far-off Potosí and Puna, these precious metals were symbols of Spain's power, and a constant temptation to the covetousness and piracy of her neighbours. Hawkins bombarded the city in 1568, but it was his pirate nephew Sir Francis Drake who inflicted the most damage: he captured the city in 1586, looted it for a month, burnt some two hundred houses, destroyed the half-finished cathedral and finally made off with 107,000 gold ducats.

Admiral Sir Edward Vernon, aka Old Grog, best remembered for having introduced the naval rum ration, arrived off Cartagena in 1741 with orders to capture the city. He brought 50 men of war, 130 transports and 25,000 troops and, after a huge bombardment, made a landing. Confident of victory, he sent a message to England to say that Cartagena had fallen. His opponent, Don Blas—a Spanish Admiral famous for his courage in 21 major naval engagements, in the course of which he had lost an eye, an arm and a leg—hunkered down behind the city walls. Meanwhile, Vernon's friends in London, on the strength of his message, had medals cast showing Don Blas kneeling in submission to Sir Edward. Fever struck Sir Vernon's troops. He tried a direct attack on the Fort of San Felipe, and failed. The Spanish rushed out in a surprise bayonet charge and killed and captured 2000 British troops.

Don Blas was killed in the seige. But Vernon sailed away in ignominy, to be mocked by both the Spanish and his countrymen when news of the medals became known and now that grog has been abolished, his name does not survive as he had hoped in the proud annals of naval history.

Degrees of Colour—Colonial Life: 1700–1810

Cartagena of the 18th century was not very different from the walled city of today. There were churches with square bell towers, cloisters filled with trees, green plazas and hidden patios. Don Antonio de Ulloa desribed them all in 1735, and there they are still today. Luckily, he also filled his notebooks with endless descriptions of the criollo's less-enduring local customs. He describes ladies in their hammocks who smoked small cheroots the wrong way round, with the lighted end in their mouth, and how they would sally forth to mass at dawn, heads covered with a handkerchief, a *panito*. He tells of their remarkable habit of taking hot chocolate, laced with cinnamon and accompanied by bread and honey, one hour after a full meal; and of how the men, before lunch, would take a glass of spirit, a habit called *hacer las onces*, literally elevenses, because of the hour and the number of letters in the word for the local anisette, *aguardiente*.

Cartagena's upper classes lived in the now touristic areas of El Centro and San Diego. Artisans, soldiers and traders lived in the rougher quarter, El Getsemaní. At the bottom end of the social scale were the slaves. The Spanish crown had forbidden Indian slavery, so African slaves were needed to build the city and work the empire's plantations. The first blackbird ship to arrive in the New World came in 1564; its shareholders included Queen Elizabeth I. Cartagena was already one of the most important centres of the Spanish overseas empire. Now it rapidly became the most important African slave market in the New World.

Huge fortunes were made. The trade was massive. Between 1616 and 1650, the Spanish monk San Pedro Claver, the 'slave of slaves', is alone said to have baptized 300,000 new arrivals before they were branded at the Customs house and then sold to South American buyers in the Plaza de los Coches. Some escaped and formed palisaded enclaves called *palenques*, or *cimarrones* in the jungle. Others stayed and blended, and by the time Ulloa visited the colony the variety of Cartagena's mixed bloods was bewildering. The offspring of white and black were known as mulattos, and those of Indian and white, mestizo. The children of Amerindian and African parents were called zambos, from which the term 'sambo' is derived. Then there were quadroons and a perplexing series of ever paler gradations known as terceroons and quinteroons, the child of a quinteroon and a white being called a Spaniard, so completing the circle. It is easy to forget that the death penalty for slave-trading and slave-holding was in force in Colombia 40 years before the 13th amendment abolished it in the United States.

In the 19th century, Cartagena attracted a new wave of immigrants from Europe and the Near East, including Jews, Turks, Lebanese and Syrians. At the beginning of this century, this typically American mixing of bloods prompted the Cuban anthropologist Fernando Ortiz—who knows about such things—to write: 'there is no such thing as race.'

Independence 1811–21

Indomitable Cartagena was the second city in the New Realm to declare absolute independence from Spain, in November 1811, after Caracas. The city sponsored Bolívar, even though he was a Venezuelan, and was a hot-bed of revolutionary activity. In 1815 however, when the Spanish General Pablo Morillo beseiged the city, her inhabitants paid dearly for their rebellious federalism. Every able-bodied citizen between 16 and 60 was called to arms; the nearby towns were burned to prevent supplies reaching the enemy; women gave their jewels, churches their silver, and patriots destroyed their own haciendas to deprive the advancing Spaniards of food and livestock. With 11,000 well-equipped veteran troops and a large squadron of ships, Morillo blockaded the city for three and a half months. The patriots fought off the Spanish army, but as the weeks passed, famine and disease came to stalk the town. People ate 'rotten meat and flour, rancid codfish, horses, mules, burros, dogs, rats and skins... Foreign speculators profiteered without mercy.' The dead mounted into thousands, and there was no-one to bury the putrefying corpses. On the day that the tottering survivors spiked their guns and attempted to run the blockade, 300 men and women died of hunger in the streets. When Morillo and his army finally entered the city, they found it a stinking desolation, so horrible that the Spanish general Montovalo said it was difficult to breathe. Over 6000 people had already perished. But, under the promise of amnesty, Morillo gathered 400 more and shot them on the beach.

Cartagena remained under the rod of Spanish control until October 1821 when a patriot force re-took the city by sea. The Spanish governor surrendered and his troops, for the first time, saluted the tricolour of Colombia; Nueva Granada was free.

The Modern Years: 1821–Present

Cartagena's descent to a secondary Colombian city has been steep, even if gracefully bittersweet. The city has been a seaport, a trading market, a centre of government and a symbol of empire, but it has never been a country seat. In mood it is still as distinguished as a baroque seigneur. The port at Barranquilla may have gained in stature during the late 19th and 20th centuries, taking away some of Cartagena's trade, but the city's special character continues to be marked by courage, generosity and an easy hedonism; in short, all of the faults and virtues of an aristocratic and unquestioned rank.

Low on municipal funds, much of the city has been recently renovated and bought up by inland—Antioqueño and Bogotáno—money, and the city has become something of a holiday resort. The Cartageneros are understandably peeved when *cachacos* come to town and act as if they own the place. So late at night, and always after a few drinks, the *costeños* have taken to re-designing Cartagenan flags. Cartagena still feels like a country apart from the rest of Colombia—a place to holiday and enjoy—which is why so many people come.

GETTING THERE

By Plane

Most flights into Colombia land at Bogotá or Barranquilla, and there are good daily services from these airports to Crespo, Cartagena's airport: 1½ km and a US$5 taxi ride from the city. However, there are occasional direct flights from Miami or New York, and you can arrange for a stop-over en route, at no extra cost, at the island of San Andrés (see

p. 219). The **Avianca** offices are at the Edificio Fernando Díaz in La Matuna, tel 647405, and Centro Pierino Gallo in El Laguito, tel 650053. Otherwise flights can be booked at any good travel agency, such as Tierra Mar Aire on the Bocagrande at Carrera 4 No. 7–196, tel 655322.

By Bus

All long-distance buses from the interior, or other coastal cities, arrive at Calle 32, with Avenida Pedro Herrera, near the foot of San Felipe fortress. The long-distance **Expresso Brasilia** terminal is the only exception; it's at Calle 32 and Carrera 20E, 500 m further on. There are three buses daily to Bogotá, 24 hours, US$20; several to Medellín, 16 hours, US$15; and regular buses to Sincelejo, 4 hours, US$3. For Barranquilla or Santa Marta catch one of the shuttles, a costenita, 3–4 hours and US$3–4 respectively.

By Boat

Some of the cargo boats moored at the Muelle de los Pagasos will take passengers. These banana boats all head for the towns east along the Gulf of Uruba, such as Tolu, Turbo, Acandi and Capurgana. Departures are irregular and depend on the whim of the Capitán, with whom you will have to bargain for the fare; expect to pay around $20 for the 36-hour trip. It's a crazy, perhaps dangerous, but memorable journey. All of the boats are laden up to the gunwales with crates of coca-cola and beer. The Caribbean whips up storms. You will need to take your own food and hammock.

GETTING AROUND

The only time that you will need a taxi or bus is when travelling the short distance between the old city and the beaches that lie along the hotel-lined Bocagrande. Taxi fares are set at around US$2; bus fares at about 20c—flag one down by the harbour and pay the driver. Otherwise it is best to get about on foot; the distances are small.

TOURIST INFORMATION

The **National Tourist Office** in the Casa del Valdehoyos, in Calle de la Factoría, does not have much in the way of information, but can provide city maps. The local tourist board, **Promatora de Turismo de Cartagena**, is on the Plaza Bolívar and is open Mon–Fri, mornings and afternoons, and on weekends in the mornings only. Otherwise, all good hotels have tourist information and also stacks of innumerable brochures.

The **Post Office (Correo Aereo)** is in La Matuna, just off the Avenida Venezuela, next to the Avianca building. There are two Telecoms; one in La Matuna in the Edificio Mariscal, the other on the Bocagrande at Cr 3 with Calle 6.

Money

The **Banco de la República** in the Plaza Bolívar will change travellers' cheques. If you are bothered by the inevitable long queue, any of the **Casas de Cambio** around it will change cash, as will any of the street sharps who will approach you offering 'good rates of exchange'. But beware *El Paquete Chileno*; an umbrella term for any raw deal, but in this case, an envelope containing a neat wad tied up in a rubber band, with a 5000 peso bill uppermost and every other a blank sheet of paper. There are variations on this theme, of course.

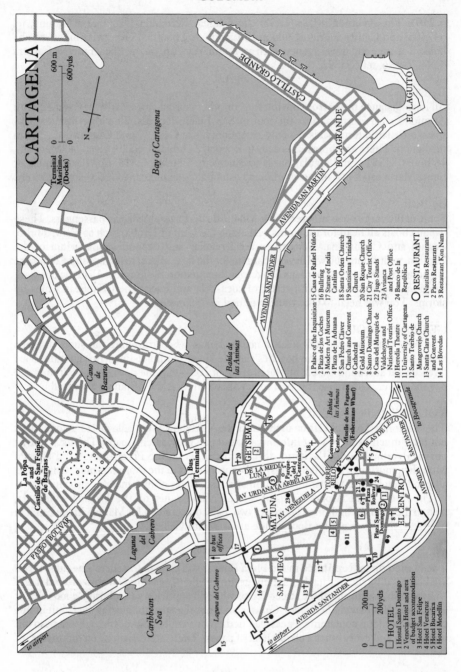

CARTAGENA

600 m
600 yds

N

Terminal Marítimo (Docks)

Bay of Cartagena

Caribbean Sea

to airport

La Popa and Castillo de San Felipe de Barajas

PASEO BOLÍVAR

Caño de Bazurto

Laguna del Cabrero

Bus Terminal

to bus offices

Laguna del Cabrero

Bahía de las Ánimas

1 Palace of the Inquisition
2 Plaza de los Coches
3 Modern Art Museum
4 Plaza de la Aduana
5 San Pedro Claver Church and Convent
6 Cathedral
7 Gold Museum
8 Santo Domingo Church
9 Casa del Marqués de Valdehoyos and National Tourist Office
10 Heredia Theatre
11 University of Cartagena
12 Santo Toribio de Mangrovejo Church
13 Santa Clara Church and Convent
14 Las Bóvedas
15 Casa de Rafael Núñez
16 Bullring
17 Statue of India Catalina
18 Santa Orden Church
19 Santíssima Trinidad Church
20 San Roque Church
21 City Tourist Office
22 Jugo Stands
23 Avianca and Post Office
24 Banco de la República

○ RESTAURANT
1 Nautilus Restaurant
2 Pacos Restaurant
3 Restaurant Kon Nam

AVENIDA SANTANDER

AVENIDA SAN MARTÍN

BOCAGRANDE

CASTILLO GRANDE

EL LAGUITO

GETSEMANÍ

Bahía de las Ánimas

Muelle de los Pegasos (Fishermans Wharf)

Convention Centre

C. DE LA MEDIA LUNA

Parque del Centenario

AV URDANATA ÁRBELAEZ

AV VENEZUELA

LA MATUNA

SAN DIEGO

EL CENTRO

TORRE DEL RELOJ

Plaza Bolívar

Plaza Santo Domingo

AV BLAS DE LEZO

to Bocagrande

AVENIDA SANTANDER

to airport

SANTANDER

200 m
200 yds

☐ HOTEL
1 Hostal Santo Domingo
2 Venecia Hotel and area of budget accommodation
3 Hotel San Felipe
4 Hotel Veracruz
5 Hotel Bucarica
6 Hotel Medellín

WHAT TO SEE
The Old City
Cartagena's fortressed walls still shape the feeling of life in the old city. It is a small area, full of dead ends, so an aimless afternoon wander through the cobbled labyrinth of colonial streets provides the best orientation. There are no dominant landmarks, so you are bound to get lost. But specific names and functions don't seem to matter on a first turn, and anyway, even the best-laid sightseeing plans quickly dissolve into the heat, like melting ice.

All visits begin, however, at the **Puerta del Reloj**, a yellow clock tower that looks over the fishermen's wharf on one side and the triangular **Plaza de los Coches** on the other. It was, and still is, the main entrance to the city. The plaza was once the slave market of Cartagena, but in the cloisters around the square, vendors now sell 10-cent *dulces*.

Leading off from the square, to your left as you came in from under the clock tower, lies **Plaza de la Aduana**. A statue of Colombus stands in the middle of the parade ground that is flanked by all the administrative and governmental buildings of the colonial city. On the left lies the old customs house, now the **Museum of Modern Art**. Touring shows are put on and the museum is open Mon–Fri, 9–12 noon and 3–7 and Sat mornings; entrance is 50c. In the opposite corner of the square lies the **Iglesia y Convento de San Pedro Claver**. Built by the Jesuits, originally under the name of San Ignacio de Loyola, the 17th-century church and convent was later re-named in honour of Pedro Claver, who lived and died there. Called the 'Apostle of the Blacks' or the 'Slave of Slaves', Claver was the first person to be canonized in the New World. He spent his whole life minstering to the slaves and his body now lies in a glass coffin beneath the high altar. It looks curiously small, hardly larger than that of a child. In the adjoining convent, through the patio where palm trees reach almost to the top of the triple-arched cloister walls, is the room, now a chapel, in which he sat watching for the ships from Africa to come into harbour. Almost before they tied up, he was on the dock; a 'hound of God', he did not rest until he had brought them to Christianity. The church is open 8–6 daily.

Kitty-cornering a few hundred yards back west into the Old City, you will come across the **Plaza Bolívar**, a small but elegant square, coursed by coffee sellers, shaded by smooth-limbed royal palms and flanked by balconied colonial buildings. In the far corner lies the simple limestone facade of the **Cathedral**, built in 1612, and next to it, the air-conditioned **Museo del Oro y Arqueología**. The museum has a good collection of Sinú gold and pottery which, although not as dramatic as the collection in Bogotá's Gold Museum, is still well worth a visit. Open from Mon–Fri, 9–11.45 and 2.30–6; Sat, morning only. Entrance free.

Opposite both the Cathedral and the Gold Museum lies the grandeur of the **Palace of the Inquisition**, where Spanish God and Spanish Might most obviously met. In contrast to the medieval Inquisition, which was primarily a religious affair in the hands of the clergy, the Spanish Inquisition blended politics, economics and spiritual hygiene. More or less under royal control, its initial aim had been to destroy Judaism, then Islam and finally Protestantism. But it was also a handy instrument with which the Spanish crown—in the name of the Catholic church—could crush every type of colonial subversion, and sieze every embarrassing pamphlet or publication. Cartagena's Tribunal had jurisdiction over Ecuador, Colombia, Venezuela, Central America and the

Caribbean, and its influence was huge, not only geographically, but politically, socially and religiously. In the course of two centuries, it carried out 12 *auto-da-fés*, or burning ceremonies, in which a total of 767 people were condemned to death. The legend, as it has been passed down, exaggerates its diabolical and terrifying effects, but its disappearance with Latin America's Independence in 1821 no doubt freed men's minds.

The Palace took 150 years to complete and is a larger edition of the other colonial houses that frame the square. Walk through the baroque entrance, under the blazing Spanish coat of arms, and you will find an interior of courtyards, interconnecting walkways, and bare wooden-floored rooms, as cool as caves. A number of instruments of Inquisitional torture—including the rack and thumb-screws—are on display. The Palace is open Mon–Fri, 8–11.30 and 2–5.30; Sat, morning only. Entrance 50c.

Coming out of the Palace, head for the Cathedral in the far left-hand corner of the square, turn left, then left again, and the street empties out into the **Plaza Santo Domingo**. The square is dominated by the church of the same name. Built in the 16th century, it is probably the oldest in the city. 'Legend has it' that the church's tower was knocked crooked by a 17th-century devil who then jumped into the well in the middle of the square, thereby poisoning it, but also trapping himself. The well is now capped by a lantern.

If you turn right in front of the church, and carry on down the Calle de la Factoría a block, you will pass the **Casa del Marqués Valdehoyos** on the left hand side, a gem of colonial architecture. The Marqués made a fortune in the slave trade, but his mansion now houses the tourist office. There is a viewing tower worth climbing. The house is open Mon–Fri 8.30–12 noon, 2.30–5.

Carry on down the street and you will reach the city walls—where everyone goes to stroll and muse and enjoy the calm of the periphery in the evenings. Turn right along the walls and you will eventually reach the **Bóvedas**, a yellow arcade of bomb-proof strongrooms that were used to house munitions in the 18th century, then prisoners, and now, finally, curio shops. Under the acacia tree in the dusty square below, a painfully bored policeman will strike up conversation with a student, flirt with a girl, or give instructions to you, a stranger.

Walking the walls at night creates the strongest sense of the past, when Spanish soldiers guarded these same ramparts, staring out to sea to discern the leaning sails of a friend or foe. The moonlight is bright, but the shadows ink-black and concealing. The air feels as soft as honey. The Caribbean sighs. And the silvered cathedral towers rise from dark tiled roofs. Now surely, *this*, one feels, is it: the something-else almost-felt.

Outside the Old City
El Castillo de San Felipe de Barajas is the most important single fortress in South America. A bunkered stronghold of battlements, terraces, guard-houses, casemates, tunnels and underground passageways, its plans were first laid in 1639 by the Spanish architect Antonio de Arevalo, but it took another century to finish. The batteries were positioned so that they could destroy each other if the castle fell to the enemy, and strategic points were linked by a labyrinth of tunnels which allowed provisions to be brought in or troops to be evacuated. You can walk these electrically-lit subterranean passageways; some have fiendish niches for prisoners cut into the walls, others are

humorous blind alleys designed to trap uninformed enemies. But each one is constructed so that the slightest sound—whether a message or the passage of an enemy's feet—becomes an echoing reverberation. A statue of Blas de Lezo stands outside, and needless to say, the castle never fell. Guides are available, and the fortress is open Mon–Sat, 8–6; entrance 50c.

La Popa, where Morillo's soldiers were repulsed at the bayonet by the defending Cartageneros, stands like a sentinel outside the city, a little beyond San Felipe. Its name was bestowed because of the hill's apparent likeness to a ship's poop. The building that crowns the hill is the **Convent of Nuestra Señora de la Candelaria**; Our Lady of the Candlemas, the Patron Saint of Pirate Attacks and hence of the city. The monastery and chapel were built in 1608 by Fray Alonso, an Augustinian priest commanded to do so in a vision. He only realized the urgency of his task when he climbed the chosen hill and found a gathering of natives intent on worshipping a large goat. Wasting no time, staff in hand, he drove the animists down the hill and the four-footed deity over the cliff, in the place now called the Goat's Leap.

The view from the convent is spectacular. The city below is reduced to a complex design in white, carved into curves by the greens of the inner bay and the lagoon, and certain sounds inexplicably detach themselves from the hum of noise below; a car's horn, a shout, faint laughter, sometimes music. Inside the convent there is a small museum of religious relics which includes the bones of the founder, some dresses and hairpieces used to adorn the Virgin on Feast Days, city maps faded into sepia, penitential whips, and other religious paraphenalia. The convent is a half-hour walk up the hill from the base, or a US$2 taxi ride—there are no buses. It is open daily from 9–5; admission 50c. On 2 February, the day of the Virgin, there is a procession down the hill and through the city.

The breezy *casa* just outside the city walls, by the Bóvedas, was the place from which Rafael Núñez once used to govern the country (see p. 174). The modest wooden house is now a museum and some of the poet-president's documents and personal possessions are displayed. The chapel opposite, known as the **Ermita del Cabrero**, holds his ashes.

SWIMMING, BEACHES AND DIVING
Cartagena's beaches lie a short taxi or bus drive to the south of the Old City, along the hotel-lined Bocagrande. Strutting on the sand are fruit-selling *palenqueros*, descendents of the runaway slaves who founded breakaway African communities along the Caribbean coast. Languid musicians sit in deck chairs, squeezing their accordions; they are available for hire but until that moment comes, play vallenatos anyway. Their music sounds as if it comes in off the waves, rolling in with each bar of surf. The sand on the Bocagrande is only white-ish, and the sea not always clear. But the Islas del Rosario, an archipelago of coral islets—now a national park—are only a short boat ride away.

Islas del Rosario
The best way to get to the islands is on a group tour. But the tour feels more like a renegade expedition than an organized tourist excursion. With this in mind, the early morning trip to the Islas del Rosario is worth every effort. The coral reefs around the islands are the largest and the best in the Colombian Caribbean, comparable only to those in San Andrés, and underwater life is prolific—this is a paradise for snorkelling. The water is glass-clear, ranging in colour from purple to turquoise; the cruise through

the islands is spectacular; and the sand on the beaches is squeaky white. Boats leave early at 7 or 8 am from El Muelle de los Pagasos.

The boats make a standard trip: across the bay; through the Bocachica between the Spanish forts of San José and San Fernando; and then out into the open sea with an hour's stop for swimming and relaxation on the Playa Blanca at Barú. After Barú you'll head for one of the larger islands for lunch, swimming and snorkelling, and be back in Cartagena by 4 or 5. Tickets cost about US$18 and include a lunch of platanos, coconut rice and freshly grilled red snapper. Choose to go on one of the high-powered launches—much better than the larger cruise ships—and if you buy tickets from sharps on the waterfront, you will be throwing money away; buy from one of the agencies on the Bocagrande, or your hotel instead. If you want to stay on the islands, there are one or two hotels; try **Margaritaville**, a tropical paradise run by a Colombian and her Swedish husband. It costs US$30 per night, including food, and is bookable from Rafael Pérez, Manga, Callejon Ferrer No. 25–108, tel 62198.

Diving
There is diving off an old Spanish wreck, in about 15 metres of water; US$45 for two dives with Bill More, contactable through the Hotel del Caribe in the Bocagrande.

FESTIVALS
There is a large Caribbean music festival in the third week of March. The bands come from all over the Caribbean and bring with them their rhythms; merengue, reggae, soca, salsa, cumbia, vallenato, calypso. Held in the Plaza de Toros, a 10-minute taxi drive from the city, tickets cost about $5 and are available from the Tourist Office. On the last day there is a crowded free concert held on the city walls. Be prepared, Colombians like to party... There are also street festivals, with fancy dress and beauty contests, from November 11–14, to celebrate the independence of Cartagena.

SHOPPING
Cartagena has a wide choice of tourist shops, but the best selection is at the Bóvedas, in the north-eastern corner of the walled city. Each store is like a national closet, stocking hammocks, coffee bags, pottery, gold replicas of Indian figurines, *mochillas*, Indian fabrics, summer shirts, giant beetles from the Amazon, stuffed iguanas, powdery coral, both the useful and useless, the good gift and gew-gaws. For between US$10–20, depending on their size, hammmocks are perhaps the best buy; they fold up small and make indispensable travelling companions—you can sling one up at the beach, or in your hotel bedroom.

NIGHTLIFE
By big city standards, Cartagena does not have a serious nightlife, but what it does roars and thumps. Most of the clubs are on the Bocagrande, and **La Escollera** on Carrera 2, a beach-facing discotheque, is open late into the night. **Anoranzas**, a pavement café on Calle 8, plays Latin golden oldies; tangos from the thirties, steamy boleros from the forties and cry-in-your-tequila Mexican ballads. In the Old City, go to **La Vitriola**, the bar next to the walls on the western side of the city, behind—more or less—the Plaza Santo Domingo, in the Calle de Buloco. It does not serve beer, but has a good choice of wines and spirits, and the mood is tolerant, tropical, creole, and Cuban.

WHERE TO STAY
Although there a number of cheap places to stay within the walls, nearly all of Cartagena's quality hotels are on the Bocagrande. There have been plans to turn the old city's hospital into a luxury hotel, but these have been momentarily—indefinitely?—shelved.

Expensive
At the far end of the peninsula, a late addition to the city's many fortresses, stands the **Cartagena Hilton**, tel 650660, a butterfly-nut shaped tower of steel and darkened glass; US$50 for a single—write to AA1774, or telex 37645. Halfway down the peninsula and facing the beach stands the colonialesque **Hotel del Caribe**, tel 650155. The original Bocagrande Hotel, and a node of social life for the city, the Caribe has large flower-strewn grounds, a swimming pool with open restaurant, and good access to the beach. Prices are around US$30 per night. The postal address is AA 1530 and the telex number is 37749. Other up-market hotels include the **Capilla del Mar** and the **Decamaron**, which are nearby.

Moderate
Set back a couple of blocks from the beach on Carrera 2 lies the **India Catalina** at No. 7–115, tel 655392, and the **Succar** at No. 6–40. Both are clean and pleasant and charge around US$10 per person. If these are fully booked, try looking in at one of the small hotels clustered around Carrera 3 between Calles 5 and 6. Finally, the business hotel, **San Felipe**, even if rather starched and bare, is well situated in La Matuna at Carrera 9A No. 31–72, and has air-conditioned rooms for US$10/15 for a single/double.

In the Old City, the **Hostal Santo Domingo**, tel 642268, on Calle Santo Domingo, is an old colonial home (in fact it used to be a bordello) renovated in a simple style. The rooms are fresh and cool and there is a small attached restaurant; US$7 for a single, US$12 for a double—a good choice, but rooms are limited, so call first. The **Hotel Veracruz**, tel 641521, on Calle San Agustín is clean and safe but can be noisy from the disco downstairs; US$7 per person. The **Hotel Bucarica**, also on San Agustín, is cheap (around US$4.50 for the night) and popular among travellers; check the rooms first. As a final bet, try the **Medellín**; one block north of the Plaza Santo Domingo, it's another shoestring travellers' delight, but the management is friendly and singles/doubles are US$3.50/5.50.

Inexpensive
For cheap (US$2 or less), even if seedy accommodation, go to the Media Luna, the red light district at the edge of Gethsemaní. The **Hotel Venecia** is the best; in many of the others, midnight interruptions will quickly reveal that your hotel doubles as a brothel.

WHERE TO EAT
Nearly every restaurant serves delicious fried, broiled or iron-grilled seafood. **Pacos**, a saffron-painted colonial restaurant in the old city's Plaza Santo Domingo, where the mood is flavoured with a glamorous sense of Caribbean funk, is particularly good. The rum and limes are strong and long, and on weekends a small and venerable Cuban band play sentimental boleros; an average meal will cost about US$15 a head. For other restaurants in the old city at about US$10 a head try: **La Quemada**, a wood-panelled restaurant a few steps away from the Plaza Bolívar with a very fine *cazuela de mariscos*—

seafood casserole—on the menu; or the seafood at **Nautilus,** a two-floored restaurant opposite the Fortress de San Felipe. Otherwise, the **Kon Nam** in Matuna, just off the Avenida Venezuela, serves the best chinese food in Cartagena at around US$5 a head.

On the Bocagrande there are Italian restaurants, pizza joints, hamburger places, all clustered around Carrera 2 between Calles 5 and 6. For juicy Argentine steaks, go to **La Pampa** on Carrera 3 and Calle 5; and for unbeatable Brazilian food, go to **Rio d'Enero,** on Carrera 2 and Calle 8, and try the *rodizio brasilero* for US$7.

Snacks

In chaotic and dense array around the Parque de Centenario you will find *osterias*—seafood cocktail stands. Strolling by are other vendors, tapping forks against bashed tin bowls which contain iguana eggs (in season from February and April and threaded together like rosaries), or *butifarras*—a small meatball.

For really quality snacks, however, go to the best *jugo* stands in Colombia, just along the harbour front. Tin-topped, whirling with trade, always excellent, they serve fruit juices—banana, passion, orange, lime, lulo, nispero, guanabana, pina, zapote—and tapas (such as boiled eggs and baked potatoes) around the clock. A dose of any of the above exotic strains of Vitamin C relieves most morning sluggishness.

Back in the old city and good for a light lunch, there is a palm-shaded, French-run **crêperie** on the Plaza Bolívar; and around the block, **Sandwiches Cubanos,** which serves sandwiches with cheese melted over ham, turkey and pickle, in a flat toasted bun for about US$2.

Cartagena Excursions

Mompós

> *'Sir,' he said, 'we are in Mompox'.*
> *The General replied, without opening his eyes, 'Mompox doesn't exist…*
> *Sometimes we dream it, but she doesn't exist.'*
> —from *The General in his Labyrinth* by Gabriel García Márquez

Isolation has its merits. Mompós is one of them. Two hundred kilometres south of Cartagena the Rió Magdalena divides into two branches, the Brazo de Loba and the Brazo Mompós. Between the branches lies a large island, and on its eastern side lies this small town of three wide dusty streets running parallel to the river.

It looks like a colonial fairy tale. The Caribbean is just a faint phosphoresence on the horizon. The town has the musty smell of long-locked rooms. Every square is criss-crossed by the careless zig-zag flight of yellow butterflies. And on certain clear nights, when the stars are just *so*, its dusty bat-swooped streets present the possibility of time travel, for pickled in solitude, nothing has happened, nothing has changed, for nearly two hundred years. One local joke runs that if the ghost of Bolívar were to return, he would stroll around and ask, 'So what's new?'.

History

Founded in 1537, Mompós (or Mompox) took its name from the last cacique of the

La Media Calle, Mompós

Kimbay Indians to live there before the conquest. During the colonial period, it was the commercial bridge between the Caribbean coast and the interior of the country, the epicentre of Magdalena river life through which all merchandise from Cartagena passed on its way to Santa Fé. When Cartagena was attacked by pirates, Mompós also served as a refuge for the families of the defenders.

At first the town flourished. Large churches and mansions were built, and it became a centre of coastal learning, religion and justice—a university town, the Bogotá of the Caribbean. Bolívar stayed there during his liberation campaign, and each of the many statues to him in the town carry the same legend; 'While to Caracas I owe my life, to Mompós I owe my glory.'

But the Magdalena is a fickle river. At the end of the 18th century its currents shifted drastically, leaving Mompós stranded on what now became a shallow and un-navigable eastern channel. Neither the big river boats from the coast, nor the hydroplanes from the interior, could stop. Trade slowed, finally ceased, and, pickling itself in languid river heat, the town closed in on itself like a heavy wooden door. Seventeen thousand people live there today. But immersed in solitude, all that now remains of Mompós's passage through history are the worn stone steps down to the river, a faint but lingering air of prosperity, and some stray memories of ghosts and glories past.

GETTING THERE
Mompós is off every main route, but can be reached by an irregular plane service with ACES from Cartagena or Barranquilla (around US$22), or after a day's hard bus and boat journeying from Cartagena.

By Bus
There are occasional direct buses from Cartagena, but this is a very irregular service, so check first. More usually one must take the arduous road and river trip outlined below.

From Cartagena take an early morning Unitransico bus to the river port of Magangué

(US$6 and 6 hours, but you might have to change en route at Sincelejo). From Magangué take a fast river launch, a *chalupa*, which will deliver you to Mompós as you would have arrived two centuries ago, which is by river. Magangué's pier is only a short walk from the bus station, and launches leave up to 3 pm, which is why you have to catch an early bus from Cartagena. The ride takes about 2½ hours and costs around US$4. Riding the river at dusk feels royal.

TOURIST INFORMATION
There is no official tourist office, but the **Hostal Doña Manuela** can provide information, as can the **Casa de la Cultura** on the Calle Media, open Mon–Fri, mornings and afternoons, and on weekends in the mornings.

WHAT TO SEE
So perfectly preserved is Mompós's colonial character that the town was used as a stage set for Rossellini's recent film adaptation of García Márquez's novella *Chronicle of a Death Foretold*, a story set anyway in Mompós. At communal screenings of the movie, everybody laughs; there's José, Cecilia, Pepita... But, even more comic, there's the English lead who never sweats. No damp patches? Can't be! Mompós is too hot. So hot in fact, that you can fall asleep at will. And even down by the river, where the breeze is freshest, the leaves of the tamarind, guayaba and eucalyptus trees hang limply off their branches, like damp washing.

Momposina architecture is colonial, but with a strong Moorish strain. The main street, La Calle Media—curved to stop an attacker's cannonball volley—is lined with colonial homes whose windows are covered with finely worked metal grilles. Elaborate metalwork, especially of gold, is a Mompós tradition, and the tale of those intricate fishes over which Colonel Aureliano Buendia consoled himself in *One Hundred Years of Solitude*, owes its existence to this tradition. If you rootle around you will soon find someone with a makeshift display, willing to sell.

The town is small, and an evening stroll quickly familiarizes. Down by the river, fronting onto a small square, stands the **Iglesia Santa Bárbara**. Built in 1630, the church has a Moorish-style tower circled by a balcony—a unique feature in Colombian religious architecture. The town has five other major churches, each one peeling, pillared, circled by bats, but still standing with the faded grace of a dowager down on her luck. Mompós's greatest dowager, however, was the Marquesa. Her home down by the quay, now closed, gives the truest sense of Mompó's distant glory; once a major house, it has fallen into disrepair. An independent, handsome and headstrong widow, La Marquesa owned huge tracts of land, but freely admitted that her life was lacking in something. During the Wars of Independence she picked out a good-looking second husband from the ranks of a visiting general's staff. She remarked as she did so that as she already had everything that she needed, bar a husband, this seemed the perfect opportunity to remedy the situation. The general was best man.

FESTIVALS
Holy Week in Mompós is high Catholicism, with Christianity at its most dramatic, serious and solemn. Hotels fill up quickly, so arrive early to ensure a room. In the second week of June there is also a recently inaugurated festival of Caribbean folklore, with

processions, live music, street theatre and poetry readings in the town square. The mood is warm, not raucous; it's a family affair and by the end everybody is holding hands.

WHERE TO STAY

All of Mompós's hotels are converted colonial homes, with arcaded patios and period furniture. This is not the result of deliberate interior decoration, it's just the way the houses have always been. The town's best is the **Hostal Doña Manuela**; the rooms are large and cool, in the back patio there is a swimming pool, and it also has Mompós's best restaurant (US$12/15 for a single/double). At around US$4 per person, go to the **Residencias Unión** or **Aurora**; both have clean rooms with bathrooms set in colonades around luxuriant patios. Slightly cheaper is the friendly **Residencias Gloria**, which has an attached bakery so that every morning your room is filled with delicious smells and a doughy heat.

WHERE TO EAT

There is not a large choice and the fare is simple—river fish or meat. The restaurant at the **Doña Manuela** is Mompos's best. **El Galileo**, just down by the quay, is cheap and lively and serves good corrientes for US$3. Whilst **Tebe** on the main square, although it has slightly less good food, has a cool and breezy backroom.

Barranquilla

Barranquilla operates at a high level of fantasy, and the four-day carnival that precedes Ash Wednesday each year is only the most obvious symptom of this.

Otherwise, most tourists don't stop at Colombia's biggest port, unless it is for supplies. Its seedy tropicality is a torrid and unlikely mix of heavy industry and Caribbean sentiment, of posturing and fancifulness, of simultaneously futuristic and retrograde architecture. It's a dirty town, with little dignity, but everyone agrees that it does, at least, have great style.

The city lies eight miles inland from Las Bocas de Cenizas, the Mouth of Ashes, the river delta through which the curried waters of the turbulent Magdalena dirties the Caribbean. On a first impression, the town looks like nothing more than a dirty great armadillo of dockside derricks and tacky skyscrapers, with a hinterland of indistinguishable suburbs rinded by unappealing shanty towns. But a closer inspection only reveals that the city is almost proud of this lack of redeeming virtues and its pervasive air of mañana collapses. So although Barranquilla's two million inhabitants are among the friendliest (or at least, most vivacious) in Colombia, the Cartageneros like to disparage the city, calling it a place of pirates and thieves, of *mucho cuchillo*, a lot of knife, which, of course, is exactly what Cartagena used to be.

History

Founded in 1629, Barranquilla has a two steps forward, one step backward kind of history, dictated by the fickle vagaries of the Magdalena. In 1500 the river's discoverer, Rodrigo de Bastidas, was nearly shipwrecked amidst the tricky currents and sand bars of the Boca. At this time Barranquilla was only an unimportant hamlet, described simply as being, 'one league from Soledad.' However, 300 years later, at the beginning of the 19th century, local conditions changed, and winds, calms and tricky currents stopped dominating the entrance to the river. Ships came up to cast anchor on the banks of the Magdalena, and Barranquilla became Colombia's front door and a place of some importance. It was the first town in Colombia to have a telephone (one wonders whom the owner called), and soon became a cosmopolitan port with Turkish, Arab, German and Italian populations. It was also the birthplace of commercial aviation in South America, in 1919, under a German concern, later called Avianca, with only one route—to Bogotá and back.

(The only other reasonable method of travelling into the interior at the time was to toil upstream on steam boats. In a fine piece of tropical surrealism, it was the hard push of the river's downstream waters that brought an exotic strain of monetarism to the fortunes of the foundling Avianca. With only the rapids as competition, the inland flights, at US$200, were highly priced. Travel upstream, after all, was a lengthy business, so people were prepared to pay for the convenience. On the coast bound journey the cost fell dramatically to US$50, as travellers could simply float down from Bogotá and still make good time. Result? Avianca flourished and the Mississippi paddle steamers are now all gone.)

In 1880 the Bocas silted up, leaving the chief port of Colombia a port without a sea. But just as suddenly, in 1935, the Bocas de-silted itself, and Barranquilla's fortunes rose again. Barranquilla today is once again an important port—the coast's concrete capital—and its life continues in that same careless and raffish, stop-start fashion.

TOURIST INFORMATION

Barranquilla is not a tourist city, and commensurately, the city's **Tourist Office**, at Carrera 54 No. 75–53 is not very helpful. The **Banco de La República** is at Calle 34 No. 43–31, just off the Plaza Bolívar. The **Post Office** is at Carrera 45 No. 34–01. Check the newspapers *El Heraldo* or *El Diaro del Caribe* for information about films and concerts in town.

GETTING THERE

By Plane

The international **Ernesto Cortisso airport** is about 10 km from the city, a US$5 taxi ride from the city centre. Avianca has regular flights to Bogotá (US$55), Medellín (US$45), Cali (US$65), and San Andrés (US$50). ACES has once a week flights to Mompós. The Avianca office is at Carrera 45 No. 34–01; the ACES office next door at Carrera 45 No. 34–02.

By Bus

Short-range buses for Cartagena and Santa Marta leave from the *Costenita* depot on the Plaza Bolívar; Cartagena (3 hours, US$2), Santa Marta (1½ hours, US$1.50).
Long-distance buses leave from the Copetran and Expresso Brasilia terminal on Calle 44 and Carrera 35, with six buses daily to Bogotá (20 hours, US$23); and Medellín (15 hours, US$17). Buses for Valledupar leave every other hour (6 hours, US$6).

GETTING AROUND

Buses ply up and down the Calles and Carreras. But when they deviate off course it is confusing, so if you just want to travel a few blocks, flag one down, and pay the driver 25c. Taxis are easier and a crosstown journey should not cost you more than $1.50. Cruising through the city in a perfectly restored Chevy '55—bedecked with saints, furry mats, boxes of tissue paper—and with the radio on full, is also a rare species of bliss.

WHAT TO SEE

Barranquilla, like Casablanca, is a city of myths but no obvious charm. There is no beach, nor any real focus to the town—it sprawls. Nothing works and when it rains the streets are turned into gutters and people and cars are washed out to sea. The main downtown area around the Plaza Bolívar is choked with hubbub, smoking tin buses, and rattling cars that more often resemble battered cardboard boxes than automobiles. The **Cathedral** at Calle 53 and Carrera 46 is squat, geometric and unappetising, and the park in front of it was cleared, in a rare burst of civic pride, when the Pope came to visit and even now you are not allowed to walk on the grass. Rain has stained away most of the town's peach and pistachio painted art-deco architecture. And while Calle 72 is the main upper-class shopping street, and a pleasant place to cruise, it is still only a shopping street. (Calle 70, on the other hand, is 'crack' street, which might be more interesting—*¿Quiere hacer una programa Señor?*).

The up-town residential area in the north-west of the city, around Carrera 70s and Calle 80s, is an indistinguishable tesselation of replica North American suburbs, only with acacia trees. And it is too hot to tramp around anyway, especially when everything is so much the same. But laid over such an unpromising urban plan lies an invisible but buoyant human geography of stories, rumours and little dramas. Over there García Márquez used to drink with his friends from the Cueva, and at this corner such and such happened to so and so, and so it goes ... Barranquilla is a city of people and incidents, which are, in their own way, sights and marvels.

ATTRACTIONS

The Zoo

El Jardín Zoológico at Calle 77 No. 68–70 is the best in Colombia. It holds some two thousand animals, belonging to about 350 species, some of which are South America's strangest. Go to see the Perro de Monte or mountain dog, the quizzical Harpie Eagle, and the ligre—a cross between a lion and a Bengal tiger. The zoo is open from Mon–Fri, 9–11.45 and 2–5.45; Sat–Sun, 10—5.45. Entrance is 50c.

Museo Romántico de Barranquilla

This permanent historical exhibition on Barranquilla, set in a beautiful old house, conjures up times past and is good for a dopey wander. Faded daguerreotypes, sepia prints and period clothes add to the drowsy atmosphere. The Museum is at Carrera 54 No. 59–199, open Mon–Fri mornings and afternoons. Entrance is 50c.

FESTIVALS

Each year, for the four days that precede Ash Wednesday, Barranquilla is the *Ciudad Loca*. The city torques itself up with *aguardiente* (it has been estimated that more than

100,000 cases are drunk), goes wild, and locks itself into a spasm of dancing, music, jungle masks and ragged costumes. The streets are full of vital suprises; floats, balls, orchestras, sound-systems, water-bombs, and hysterical revelry. If you are asked to join a *parranda*, go along, keep an eye open and don't ask questions—this is mad Colombia's maddest carnival.

The Carnival begins on Saturday with a chariot parade, *La Battalla de Flores* (the Battle of Flowers) and continues on Sunday with a grand fancy dress procession. On Monday there is *El Festival de Orquestas*, a music marathon. And then on Tuesday there is a strange, half understood ceremony, the Death of José Carnivalito, when everyone runs after the Carnival Queen in her big shiny Cadillac. Suddenly it's all over, and everybody is strolling around again in their clean-pressed work-a-day clothes as if nothing had happened the day before.

SHOPPING
San Andrecito, on via 40, is where smuggled goods are sold at very competitive prices; any taxi driver will take you there.

WHERE TO STAY
The Barranquilla hotel, and the focal centre for the city's social life, is the **Prado**, at Carrera 54 No. 70–10, tel 456533. Looking like the best of any of Hollywood's many glamorizations of the tropics, it has a large swimming pool, three restaurants, business services and large, cool rooms for US$30/50 for a single/double.

Slightly more mid-town and mid-range, is the excellent saffron-painted **Hotel Majestic** on Carrera 53 No. 54–51, tel 320152. Its style is Casablanca-cool, and it has a quiet swimming pool in an interior courtyard, and a remarkable restaurant inlaid with Moroccan tiles. With rooms costing US$10/$15 for a single/double, this is a good choice. Downtown and comfortable (an unusual combination), is the **Hotel Caribaña**, on Carrera 41 No. 40–02, tel 414277. Well located for downtown chores, it has a swimming pool, and is good value at US$8/15 for a single/double. Just off Barranquilla's main, family, shopping street, is the pleasantly located and quiet **Aparta Hotel Sima**, on Carrera 49 No. 72–19, tel 450055. The rooms are good and prices reasonable, again about US$9/13 for a single/double.

Cash keeps Barranquilla at bay and the less money that you spend, the more you must be prepared for unwarranted interruptions, incidents, and little dramas. Bearing this in mind, cheaper accommodation can be had downtown. The **Victoria**, at Calle 35 No. 43–140, is an old house with a fine facade and comfortable rooms, each with private bath, US$7/9 for a single/double. **El Turista**, at Carrera 43 No. 33–35, and **El Zhivago**, at Carrera 44 and Calle 36 are both near the Plaza Bolívar and can therefore be noisy. But they are both clean and safe,with rooms costing about US$2/4 for a single/ double. Any cheaper than the above and you are most likely to find yourself in a *puteria*.

WHERE TO EAT
A shaded and breezy place for lunch is on the leafy veranda of the **Barranquillerato**, opposite the Hotel Majestic, on Carrera 53 and Calle 54. At about US$8 a head, the restaurant is quite dear, but the meals—traditional *costeño* food of thick soups and fried or broiled fish served with plantains and coconut rice—are huge and delicious. **El**

Calderito, at Carrera 54 No. 72–125 also serves typical food, but in a tropical garden atmosphere. For French food go to **Devis**, on Carrera 56 No. 72–110, and for excellent fish go to **El Mesón de Morgan**, on Carrera 46 No. 64–14—both are high quality and high priced.

For snacks, two special mentions must be made. Firstly of the *fruteros*—the fruit stalls that you will see dotted around the uptown area which serve fruit salads, juices and snacks. And secondly, the wandering *tinto* salesmen; stop one, pay 10c and get a sweet and restorative thimbleful of Colombian coffee. Both are Barranquillero institutions. Otherwise, for cheap eats and filling *corrientes*, try any of Barranquilla's many cafés; a soup, followed by a platter of meat, rice and beans will cost no more than US$2.50.

EXCURSIONS

Puerto Colombia
Twenty kilometres west of Barranquilla, Puerto Colombia is a rough town with a broad, white, clean beach—Barranquilla's main town beach, even if the water can be muddy. The place is quiet and deserted during the week, but at weekends the arrival of the *Barranquilleros* completes some hidden electric circuit and the town whirrs into life; restaurants open, vendors cruise the sand, and radios and makeshift sound-systems are turned up loud. The easiest way to get there is to hire a taxi from Barranquilla—expect to pay about US$6. Buses leave from around the Plaza Bolívar and cost 50c, but while a taxi might be ten times as expensive, it is at least ten times easier. The bus back into town, however, is hassle-free; the last one leaves from Puerto Colombia's main street at dusk, so don't get stranded.

Cangarú
Cangarú is a beach on the mangroved Isla de Salamanca, a national park 27 km east of Barranquilla, towards Santa Marta. There is good bird spotting, and during the week the beach is usually deserted. The best and almost only way to get there is in a rented car—take the turn-off at 27 km. Otherwise, for swimming, go to **Santa Marta** where the beaches are much better.

SANTA MARTA AND THE SIERRA NEVADA

Paired with the resort at Rodadero, Santa Marta is one of Colombia's most pleasant holiday towns, with a welter of recreational pleasures such as beachcombing, fishing, swimming and scuba-diving. Colombia's best beaches (palm fringed, white, secluded, always empty and with jungle coming right down to the shore) also lie only 15 km outside town, at the Tayrona National Park. And then soaring above Santa Marta, a world apart from such frivolous holidaymaking, rises the Sierra Nevada: the highest coastal range in the world and also the refuge for two of the most significant Indian groups in the Americas.

Santa Marta

Santa Marta's tropical langour quickly overcomes any scruples you might have brought with you from the wintery north. As Charles Nicholl wrote in his excellent travelogue *The Fruit Palace*, 'Santa Marta pampers your vices so attentively that they begin to feel like virtues'. Now clearly—one feels—this is a good start.

Nestled between the mountains and a deep natural harbour, Santa Marta is a small, halfway-colonial and indolent provincial capital of just under 200,000 people. On clear days you can paddle in the Caribbean and see the snowy peaks of the Sierra rising in the distance. Bathed in chalky haze, the town fits promisingly into the palm of your hand. At midday the streets are as barren and hot as dry rivers; in the afternoon they are filled with light and bisected by shadow. Stay for a while and your sense of time becomes drowsy; things do happen, but slowly and probably tomorrow. In the 1970s it had a cowboy atmosphere and was a smugglers' den, a pivotal point in the south-north marijuhana trade. But now that the boom has moved on, the town has been re-christened Santa Muerto, a double-edged nickname denoting the deathly slumber into which the town has fallen, and in mourning for its long-vanished marimba trade. Most of Santa Marta's villains have since retired, investing their money in hotels and resort facilities instead. But the feeling of a subterranean pulse remains, and small-town dramas still come in off the sea on the breeze.

History

True to form, Santa Marta's early history is lazy. In 1524, Rodrigo de Bastidas signed a contract with Charles V to colonize a tract of his own choosing on the Colombian coast between Cabo de la Vela and the mouth of the Magdalena. But 21 years in Santo Domingo on a plump crown pension had dimmed Bastidas' spirit, leaving him slack around the waist. A conquistador turned capitalist, he hoped to do his colonizing by remote control: he hired 800 men, equipped them, and prepared a ship that would take them off to Colombia. On a fine day in February 1525, he went down to the wharf to wave them good-bye. But fearing that without his authority the expedition might dissolve into squabbles, his men bundled him aboard while he was still in cheery mid-wave. So it was that a shanghaied conquistador founded Santa Marta in late 1525.

Towards the end of the 16th century, Santa Marta was used as a base for Spanish expeditions into the interior. It was from here that Jiménez de Quesada set off on his quest for El Dorado—that arduous mountain trek which ended with the founding of Bogotá. Santa Marta was then an important port, although overshadowed by Cartagena, but during the colonial years it led the same feudal and somnolent life of the other New Granadian towns. Occasionally, however, its patrician repose was rudely interupted by French and British pirates. Between 1550 and 1600 Robert Baal, the Cotes, Sir Francis Drake and the slaver Hawkins all sacked and burnt the city. But each time, unruffled, Santa Marta merely shook itself, buried its dead, rebuilt and continued as before. (With one small exception: the anonymous, but big-bad-wolf of children's cautionary tales was converted in Colombia into a cannon-firing and marauding Sir Francis Drake—Queen Elizabeth's favourite looter, otherwise known as 'The Master Thief of the Unknown World'.

Santa Marta was steadfastly Royalist during the Wars of Independence, and in 1821 a lean, gaunt and very sick Simón Bolívar rode into town to die. Neglected and impoverished, it took 12 years for him to receive the official acknowledgement that he deserved. In 1833, amid great pomp and circumstance, his body was disinterred from its common grave and transported to Caracas in a Venezuelan warship, escorted by the navies of Britain, France and Holland. His heart, however, stayed in Santa Marta, in a lead casket that has since mysteriously disappeared. All that remains of him in the city where he died are the things that were lent to him during his last ten days, kept in the well-preserved Quinta de San Pedro Alejandrino, a 20-minute bus drive out of town. The Quinta only compounds the irony of Bolívar's death: although he is now worshipped by the five countries he freed from the Spanish, the only roof that the dying liberator could find to shelter him was that of a Royalist Spaniard.

GETTING THERE
By Plane
Avianca operates regular flights, from the airport 20 km out of town, to; Cúcuta (US$40) and Bogotá (US$53), with connections on to Cali ((US$65) and Medellín (US$45). A taxi to the airport will cost about US$4, a bus from Carrera 1C, about 50c. The Avianca office is at Calle 17 and Carrera 3.

By Bus
The bus station is on Carrera 8 and Calle 24, a 15-minute walk from the beachfront, and has good connections to Bogotá (20 hours, US$20), and all of the towns en route, such as Bucaramanga and Tunja.

To Barranquilla, and thence on to Cartagena, there are frequent departures (1½ hours and US$2). One of the ways to get to El Parque Tayrona is to catch one of the many buses to Riohacha (3 hours, US$3), and signal the driver to let you off opposite the park entrance.

By Rail
The railway station is at the centre of town at Carrera 1 and Calle 9. There is meant to be a daily train to Bogotá but, bearing in mind that there are no timetables in Colombia, only rumours, you should go to the station and check first. The journey is slow, hot and dusty, and the train arrives when it arrives, at Bogotá, US$20 and maybe 28 hours later.

GETTING AROUND
Santa Marta is conveniently arranged for the tourist. Everything that you will need—shops, banks, chemists and restaurants—lies within a small area bounded by the sea and the main shopping street, Avenida Campo Serrano (Carrera 5), which runs parallel five blocks back from the beach. The best way to get around town is on foot.

To get to Rodadero—the Colombian resort 6 km south of Santa Marta—catch one of the buses from the beachfront (50c, 15 mins) or catch a cab, about US$3.

TOURIST INFORMATION
The **Tourist Office**, at the former Convent of Santo Domingo, Carrera 2 No. 16–44, is open Mon–Fri, mornings and afternoons. One of the tour agencies that have recently sprung up around town might be more useful, however. **Correcaminos**, at Calle 15 No.

3–42, has a wide choice, including tours to Tayrona Park and the Ciénega Grande. **TMA** at Calle 15 No. 2–60 has well-organized treks to the Ciudad Perdida. And the **Hotel Zulia** on the beach front has daily tours to Tayrona National Park, with minibuses leave at 9 am in the morning, returning in the afternoon (US$4 for the round trip). Joining one of the Zulia tours is prehaps the easiest way to get to the park; you can leave the tour when you arrive and return on another day.

WHAT TO SEE

By Day
Sun and sand are the main attractions of Santa Marta, and most people go swimming in the daytime—either north to Taganga or south to the beach at the nearby resort of Rodadero. There are some sights in and around town, however. The **Museo Arqueológico Tayrona**, on the main square at Calle 14 and Carrera 2, is a beautiful colonial mansion that houses a small exhibition of Tayrona gold with adjacent displays of Tayrona life and the Lost City. Open Mon–Fri, 8–12 noon, and 2–6, entrance free. The **Quinta de San Pedro Alejandrino**, where Bolívar died, is a fine colonial hacienda that has been converted into a museum with paintings, furniture and clothes from the period. There are guides, and the museum is open Mon–Fri 9.30–4.30, entrance US$1. To get there, take the Mamatoca bus from the seafront (Carrera 1C) — 20 minutes, 50c.

An Evening Stroll
The best time to promenade is in the evening, at the hour of vespers. Down by the bay stand palm-draped benches at cross angles to the broadwalk. The beach faces west into the setting sun. Banana boats bound for Europe announce themselves with a deep horn that sounds across the bay. *Jugo* trolleys dot the pavement, their attendants ready to whisk up a juice at the flick of a wrist, and at weekends, at the Pan-American restaurant, a vallenato band kicks out music and a rubber-necking crowd gathers. Invariably a 'businessman' approaches, 'Pssst. Hey you . . .' (Take care, the police do this too.)

Past the bay's bars and small cafés, towards the railway station and the wharf, lies the seedy warren of the red-light district, a dangerous area. And then, in the smooth, cool backstreets, loose groups sit in rocking chairs on the pavement outside their homes. Gazing through a window's iron grille, you will see a family moving about inside: the children look like twittering canaries fluttering around inside an airy bird-cage.

SWIMMING AND BEACHES
There is always the town beach, or the beach at Rodadero, but the best sand and water lies a short way outside Santa Marta.

Taganga
Taganga is a small fishing village set in a deep horseshoe bay, 5 km north of Santa Marta. To get there, flag down a bus on the beachfront (Carrera 1C). It's a beautiful drive: the bus crosses the railway tracks, Santa Marta falls quickly away as the road climbs the hills north of town, you top the rise and suddenly you are above a glorious bay, rimmed by hills, with a small beach crowded with fishing boats below. You can arrange short boat excursions with the fishermen to other beaches further north along the coast, or walk—the hills are threaded with paths.

There are some small restaurants by the beach that serve freshly caught fish, or you can eat at the **Ballena Azul**, an idyllic hotel that is the realized dream of a quixotic Frenchwoman. Rooms here cost around US$15/25 for a single/double and the Hotel also organizes tours to the **Lost City**. At the southern end of the bay you can rent hammocks at a young family's house (US$2 for the night).

Playa Blanca
Playa Blanca is a wonderful sandy cove that lies a 10-minute boat ride across the headland from Rodadero. The return boat journey costs about US$6 from the pier at Rodadero beach and it is better to pay on the return trip. There are some simple restaurants at the beach.

Parque Tayrona
The first question one asks on arriving at this Caribbean paradise is 'Why didn't I come here before?'. For more information, see below, under 'Excursions'.

WHERE TO STAY
You can either stay in town, where accommodation is generally cheap, or over the hill at Rodadero. The advantages of staying in Santa Marta proper are that you have all of a town's conveniences—such as banks—close at hand, and the town is not a resort. Conversely, the advantage of staying in Rodadero is that it is a resort, if you like that sort of thing. A few kilometres west of both, however, just before the airport, lies **Irotama**, tel 27643. The most luxurious hotel in the area, it has 60 cottages set back from a beach and no sense of town, or any other, life around you. To get there, turn off at KM 14; rooms work out at about US$25/30 for a single/double.

In Santa Marta
The **Yuldama** on the beachfront is a tall, modern building, nothing special, but the most luxurious in town with rooms at around US$20/25 for a single/double.

The **Andrea Doria No 2**, at Carrera 2 No. 19–61, is only 50 metres from the beach, has fine, light, clean rooms with balconies, and is run by a friendly, helpful and extensive family of brothers. A good choice and also good value at US$5/9 for a single/double. The **Sol Hotel Inn** (sometimes known as the Zulia) is on the beachfront and has spacious rooms for US$6/8 a single/double. It also organizes tours to the Tayrona National Park. The **Residencias El Trebol**, on Carrera 2, is a brand-new venture as smart as a new lick of paint, but its comfortable bedrooms have no windows. Nevertheless, it is good value at US$3/3.50 for a single/double.

For budget travellers, the **Miramar** on Calle 10C No. 1C–023–59 has become very popular, and is the only true 'gringo' hotel in town. The US$5 a night rooms are simple, but large and have baths; the pigeon-hole rooms on the second floor are hot and poky, but only US$1.

In Rodadero
The pink-painted **El Rodadero** just by the beach has a pool, a casino, good ground-floor rooms, an excellent restaurant and very friendly English-speaking service; good value at US$15/20 for a single/double. The **Tamacá Inn**, on Carrera 2 No. 11A–023–98, offers much the same as the Rodadero, with rooms at US$20/25 for a single/double.

La Riviera, on Carrera 2 No. 5–42, has rooms with TV and air-conditioning for around US$10/20 a single/double. The Valladolid, at Carrera 2A No. 5–67, is helpful, has large clean rooms, and is good value at around US$8/16 for a single/double.

You can also rent apartments in Rodadero at Condominio La Mansión; for bookings call Bogotá 2126646, or Rodadero 27408.

WHERE TO EAT

In Santa Marta

There are a lot of bars, cafés, and small restaurants along the beachfront. All of them serve seafood and most of them are good. The Pan American is certainly the best, with delicious fish and meat dishes (try the mysterious *Guapinahaca*—a 'little meat thing'.) The Real Parilla on Calle 2 No. 2–28 serves grilled meats; and the Oriental Restaurant, also on Calle 22, but across the street, has delicious Chinese food with refreshingly light and grease-free soups at about US$3 a head.

For snacks, the fastest hot-dog-stand-in-the-west operates with furious efficency on the corner of Calle 22 and Carrera 3. And then there are always the *jugo* trolleys on the beachfront...

In Rodadero

Karey's, Pez Caribe and Pinchos are all on Calle 2A, the main cruising strip, and have large menus and good, albeit slightly over-priced food. La Gran Parilla at Carrera 2A No. 8–41, has very good grilled steaks, served in the traditional manner with a banana and an *arepa* on the side, for about US$3. For lunch in pleasant surroundings, go to Ranchito's, which doubles as a discotheque at night.

Santa Marta Excursions

Parque Tayrona

Tayrona National Park lies on the jungle-bordered Caribbean coast, under the shadow of the Sierra Nevada, and stretches for 35 km from the Bahía de Taganga in the west, up to the mouth of the Rio Pedras in the east. Completely unspoilt, the park is a Caribbean paradise, a nature reserve and an archaeological park, all rolled into one. It offers quiet sandy beaches, walking in the hills, and the remains of a small Tayrona Indian village—El Pueblito, an hour's walk up from the shore at Arrecifes. You could spend anything between three days and three weeks here. There is no rush—time tends to tie itself up in knots.

GETTING THERE

The easiest way to get to Tayrona Park is to join one of Santa Marta's Zulia Hotel tours; these set off every morning, but you should buy a ticket the evening before (US$4). The bus leaves you at Canaveral, the park's administrative base. From there you can then set off at your own pace, re-joining the tour back to Santa Marta on another day. Alternatively a taxi to the park will cost about US$15/20. Or you can catch a bus to Riohacha, and signal the driver to let you off at El Zaino, the main entrance, which is open daily 8–5. Admission to the park costs 50c and Canaveral lies 4km below the gates.

WHAT TO SEE

At **Arrecifes**, an hour's walk west of Canaveral, you will find the park's most splendid beaches. You can also camp or hire hammocks here (US$2 per night) in quieter conditions than at Canaveral. There is also a simple restaurant (the 'I Come and I Go'). Beyond Arrecifes lie only beaches, and more beaches, linked by narrow paths that skirt the shoreline's graceful coconut groves.

Finally, an hour's steep walking uphill from Arrecifes lies **El Pueblito**, the park's most important archaeological discovery. It is only a small site, a mere taste of the Lost City, and there is little to see. But the undulating stone avenue that sweeps through the village and the groping cottonwoods that surround it, make this an idyllic spot. The walk up there, along an old Tayrona road, is also spectacular; set off in the morning, before the heat gets up.

WHERE TO STAY

At Canaveral you can stay in an Eco-hab, a reconstructed Tayrona hut, or camp. Each Eco-hab has a bathroom on the ground floor and a stilted bedroom on the second, with a balcony running the full circumference. They provide 360° views of the sea and two-star, ecologically-sound comfort. Each cabin costs US$20 per night and can sleep up to five people. During Holy Week and the June and December holidays they can be fully booked so make reservations at any Inderena office first—the one in Santa Marta is at Carrera 1C No. 22–75. Camping space costs US$5 per tent, and has baths and water facilities. The centre also has a small restaurant.

Aracataca

The town's south of Santa Marta are built around the rivers that flow down the western slopes of the Sierra. One of these is Aracataca, birthplace of Gabriel García Márquez, or 'Gabo', Colombia's Nobel Prize-winning novelist and cultural folk-hero. Aracataca is the Macondo of Márquez's stories, the little village where South America's rickety dreams and exotic despairs are played over and over in miniature. There is now a small museum to the writer in town, but little else. It's just another dusty grid of freshly painted pastel streets lined by more sun-baked almond trees. Another steel bridge, over another grey river with women slapping their washing against the rocks. As Charles Nicholl wrote, 'Aracataca is only an hour or two away from Santa Marta. It is close to the foothills of the Sierra, close to the lagoons of the Ciénaga, close to the fertile plains of the Magdalena. Yet the feel of it is somewhere far, far from everything.'

Ciénaga

Ciénaga lies half an hour outside Santa Marta. In 1928 it was a boom town in a thriving region, *La Zona Caramba* the banana zone, a narrow and humid elongated triangle on the lower slopes of the Sierra Nevada. Since the turn of the century, the United Fruit Company of Boston Massachussetts—*La Mama United* as it was known in Colombia, or the 'Octopus' as it was known in Honduras—had been making big business out of bananas, controlling over 60 per cent of the world banana trade. In Colombia they owned three-quarters of the banana-producing land, and exercised considerable rights over the rest. This near-monopoly left them free to leave huge tracts of land uncultivated as a means, among others, of controlling the world price of fruit. The company's political influence was huge, and inevitably corruption followed upon the necessity of maintaining their free flow of profit. Ironically, imported African folklore invested the banana with certain magical and religious associations; bananas had the power to cure poverty and illness, and were also the preferred food of the devil. The Bantu name for banana is also Makondo.

Money rolled in. But the local workers continued to live in a neglected circle of poor housing, bad education and scanty health care. Their only benefits were scripts issued for the goods that were stocked in the company shops. The goods were brought in on the otherwise empty return journeys from the US of the banana boats. But the appealing symmetry of this arrangement was lost on the plantation labourers. Unrest grew and a strike was organized.

On 6 December 1928, some ten thousand people—workers and their families—were camped out in the square by the railway station in Ciénaga, listening to the speeches of the Union organizers, waiting for the news of the negotiations in Santa Marta. Maybe they thought that the army was there to protect them. When General Cortez Vargas ordered the crowd to disperse, it responded with cries of 'Long live the Army! Long live Colombia!'.

In the dead of the night the army's machine guns opened fire. At 8 o'clock the next morning the square was empty save for nine bodies and an assortment of medics and officials. Officially the death toll was nine; an event of no great historical importance, meriting not even the briefest entry in the history books. The stories of the thousands dead were discounted and a conspiracy of silence developed over what had taken place. The Colombian government had nothing to gain from a revelation of the truth, and the people living in the banana zone were understandably reluctant to expose themselves to further reprisals.

In *One Hundred Years of Solitude*, García Márquez tells an exaggerated version, that nonetheless conveys a true sense of the weight of the event:

> 'There must have been three thousand of them.'
> 'What?' The woman measured him with a pitying look. 'There haven't
> been any dead here,' she said. 'Since the time of your Uncle, the
> Colonel, nothing has happened in Macondo.'

Sixty years on, Ciénaga's fine colonial buildings have decayed. The boom years have moved on, taking away everything they brought, leaving less somehow than there was before. The old railway station has gone—but the tracks still cut across the streets, and bananas still move through the town. There is now a monument to those killed, the work of Rodrigo Arenas Betancourt.

Out on the actual Ciénaga, the lagoon where the Magdalena has its estuary and which you pass through on the road between Barranquilla and Santa Marta, there are some small stilted fishing settlements. The fishermen who eke out a living among these mangroves recall again García Márquez. Men slouch on creaking verandahs; figures are barely discernible moving about inside; children leap into the water and rise, giggling and spluttering next to the boat, to ask for a 'pesito'. They have the look of a people, condemned to one hundred years of solitude, who will not have a second chance on earth.

210

Canoe tours of the lagoon are available with **Correcaminos** in Santa Marta (see p. 205).

The Sierra Nevada de Santa Marta

Everything about the Sierra Nevada is anomalous. It's the highest coastal range in the world and also home to the Kogui and Arhuacos, the only Indian groups in the Americas to have maintained their priestly class. Separated from the Andes by the valley of the Rio César, it looks like a pimple on the map. Roughly triangular in shape, each side is 160 km long, with the base of the triangle to the north, running parallel with the Caribbean coastline between Santa Marta and Riohacha. This northern face is the sheerest, coming right down to the sea in steep, densely forested foothills. At the shortest point, the mountains rise from sea-level to over 19,000 feet in 28 miles, a gradient only surpassed by the Himalayas.

On this face of the Sierra, the trails are arduous and easy to lose, and once you get lost you are likely to wander into someone's marijhuana plantation. The slopes to the south-east, around Valledupar, rise more gently. The Indians of this corner of the Sierra are the Arhuacos. These are the most numerous of the Sierra's mountain tribes and about 15,000 of them live in small, nucleated settlements in the high valleys of the south and east, occasionally coming down to market at Valledupar. Naturally reticent, intensely introspective and imbued with a deep mystical sense, the Arhuaco are only marginally more acclimatized to the white man than the fiercely isolationist Kogui who live on the inaccessible northern slopes.

The Arhuaco

The Arhuaco wear generic clothes; what look to be judo suits, tied around the waist with a rope, peep-toe rope sandals, and domed white hats that sit high on their heads like the unbroken half of a hard-boiled egg. Their faces are shaped less by wise ideas than by ancient blood, but by comparison, European features look panicked and hawkeyed. Their language sits uncomfortably in the western ear and, rich in 'mmmmmm' and 'vvvvvv' sounds, is especially well suited to speaking with a mouth full of coca leaves, which is often. Every adult male has a cheek distended by thick quids of coca. And whilst each man tends a small plot of the bright green-leafed shrub behind his house, only his wife is allowed to pick the leaves, and only he is allowed to chew them.

The hit from chewing a mouthful is like a cup of coffee, only more elastic, and the Arhuaco can walk for miles chewing only this cud. But the leaves make for more than just a good walking head; the coca leaf is a central part of Arhuaco religion, a stiff spiritual discipline administered by the Shaman *mamas*. A forgotten British nurse's medical report notes that the Arhuaco do not suffer from rigor mortis when they die—they surrender life peacefully, resolved and without struggle—which suggests that the Arhuaco shamans are perhaps privy to something that the West is not.

Most middle-class Colombians prefer not to think about the Arhuaco, but, around dinner tables in Bogotá, it is increasingly fashionable to at least pretend that they do. Conversely, the Arhuaco only laugh at sentimental, post-industrial yearnings for a simpler age. So perhaps this is a balanced equation, especially as in this rare case, the Arhuaco seem to have been politically agile enough to save themselves from the fate of

211

their downtrodden, and largely lost, Andean cousins. Most visits to the Sierra are carefully monitored and the Casa Indigena keeps knuckle-cracking capitalism at bay, or at least tries to.

The Tayrona

Both the Kogui and the Arhuaco are descended from the Tayrona, a far-flung Carib community of about 700,000 people that flourished for perhaps 1000 years before the Spaniards arrived in the 16th century. If the Incas were the engineers, the Mayans the mystics, and the Aztecs the bloodiest of the Amerindian civilizations, the Tayrona were the hippies: fanciful, baroque, creative, not a little radical and, also, master-ecologists. They cultivated maize, beans, yucca and other staples on irrigated fields and terraces that the Spanish chronicler Oviedo compared to those of Lombardy and Etruria. They fished the Caribbean for tuna, snapper and fat-eye. They wore cotton, kept bees and chewed coca leaves. Their ceramics and stonework were decorated with elaborate figures—warriors in feathered headresses, monstrous fanged humanoids, jaguars, snakes, bats, foxes, birds, turtles and crocodiles. They were also master gold workers, with a vigorous vein of phallic and sexual representation that enabled the Spaniards to plunder them in the name of godliness and cleanliness. The worthy chronicler Gonzáles Fernandez de Oviedo saw a Tayrona gold piece weighing 20 pesos that depicted 'one man mounted upon another in that diabolical act of Sodom'. (Later he relates that he smashed this 'jewel of the devil' to smithereens at the smelting house in Darién, before shipping it, melted down, to Spain.)

But although the Spanish search for gold left little room for appreciation of the Tayrona's highly advanced culture, their civilization did not go unnoted. Brother Pedro Simón wrote: 'And if there is an earthly paradise in these lands of the Indians, this must indeed be it . . . Everywhere is crowned with high peaks . . . slopes and mountains covered by populous towns of Indians.' He also spoke of their cities' 'cleanliness and neatness, as shown in their courts paved with very large, dressed stone . . . and also in their paths made of slabs.'

Initial contact between the Tayrona and the Spanish had, in fact, been friendly. But by the end of the 16th century, any sense of amnesty had faded and the coastal foothills of the Sierra became the scene of bitter skirmish warfare. In 1599, the Governor of Santa Marta, Juan Guiral Velón, led a final campaign of attrition into the hills. The chiefs were hanged and burned, and the great Tayrona townships—Tayronaca, Posigueca, Betoma—were put to the torch. The last remnants of the tribe retreated to the higher slopes, into valleys too distant and inaccessible for the Spaniards to follow. The jungle reclaimed the abandoned terraces and temples, and covered the intricate pathways that connected the villages, guarding the Tayrona gold even more jealously than the Indians had before.

A small vestige of Tayrona greatness can be seen at Pueblito, an archaeological site in the Tayrona National Park (see p. 208). But *the* Tayrona city, La Ciudad Perdida, the lost city that was alluded to in the chronicles, was only found in 1970s by a grave-robbing *guaquero* and his two sons, one of whom is now buried at its foot. A miniature Machu Picchu, its discovery marked the most important American archaeological find this century. It is a hard six-day trek up to the city, but you are only sometimes allowed a permit. In April 1987 the Kogui lodged a protest with the government that visitors were tramping over and robbing their ancestral gounds and miraculously, the protest was upheld, and the city was placed off-limits to visitors.

Recent History
Since the days of the conquistadors, other settlers have lapped around the lower edges of the Sierra: banana growers and coffee planters during the boom years at the beginning of the century, political refugees during La Violencia of the 1950s, and, most recently, marijhuana planters. Hard-bitten treasure hunters—*guaqueros*—still comb the rugged mountain slopes in search of lost temples and burial sites, but none of the *mestizos* have penetrated higher than 5000 feet. The heart of the Sierra remains Indian country, the world of the 'other' South America that moves to an older and more mystical pulse, and the Arhuaco and the Kogui Indians continue their old ways undisturbed. To the average *mestizo*, the Indians represent poverty and underdevelopment and not much else. They are *gente baja*, low people. To this the Indians respond with their ancient, disconcerting, stonelike gaze, and with the inner conviction that apart from the minor inconvenience of colonization, the continent is still entirely theirs.

Visiting the Sierra
This is not easy. You will need a guide, and you will need time. And you should not travel here unless it is with sensitivity. Following the precedent established in colonial times, travellers have come to this area for a variety of motives besides *conocer la región*. Foreign tourists and climbers are among the least harmful of visitors, but they do leave litter and have a tendency to ignore the Indians, rushing by their farms and settlements like thieves. If you do visit, be a guest, not an intruder; this is their land. It is always better to face up to the people you encounter; greet them, let them look at you and hear your voice, and bring small gifts such as pens, soap and sewing needles. Don't take pictures unless invited to do so; the Indians do not believe that their souls can be captured by mechanical means—which puts paid to that old chestnut about taking photographs—but they are a proud people, not animals in a zoo.

Travellers who wish to experience solitude, nature, or to climb, would do better to skip this troubled area in favour of one of the many other ranges in South America (such as the Sierra Nevada de Cocuy, see p. 253) which are no longer the vital centres of a living culture. Remember: outsiders are not welcome in the Sierra and you should bear in mind the Kogui greeting, which is a succinct, 'When are you leaving?'.

The Lost City
La Ciudad Perdida lies on the northern face of the Sierra and was known to the *guaqueros* who discovered it in 1975 as *El Infierno Verde*, the Green Hell. There are two ways to get here; by helicopter,or on foot. The former takes three hours, the latter three days of stiff trekking.

Founded between AD 500 and 700, the city was the most important centre of Tayrona culture, a city of as many as 15,000 people in its heyday. The remains stand on the steep slopes of Cerro Corea, on the northern slopes of the Sierra, and consist of a complex system of buildings, terraces and platforms linked by paved footpaths and flights of steps. As with Incan stonework no mortar was used, and the walls are only held together with judiciously chiselled and well-placed stones. Above the city rises the umbrella canopy of

213

the forest. Everything is perfectly integrated into the surrounding environment and the architecture flows with the natural curves of the mountainside. The atmosphere is strong.

GETTING THERE

You will need two permits; one from **Inderena**, the other from the **Instituto Colombiano de Antropología** in Bogotá (Carrera 7 No. 28–66). If you do not have these permits, you will most likely be turned back by military patrols. The area is an important marijuhana growing area, bounty hunters abound and occasionally guerrillas hide in the hills. This is wild west country.

By Helicopter

Aviatur operates 3-hour helicopter tours out of Santa Marta airport on long weekends and national holidays. The tour costs US$150 per person and is bookable through any good travel agency, such as **TMA**. The Aviatur office in Bogotá is at Calle 19 No. 4–62; the office in Barranquilla is at Carrera 54 No. 72–96.

On Foot

You will need a guide for this hard three-day trek. Tours are available from the **Hotel La Ballena Azul** in Taganga (highly recommended), from **TMA**, and occasionally from the **National Tourist Office** in Santa Marta. Tours set out from Santa Marta, and prices hover at around the $200 mark; for this you should expect both food and an informed guide. You will need hammocks and/or sleeping bags, one set of warm clothes and some good shoes (good shoes are particularly important). Tours offered by Robert Ospina and Miguel Ramirez have not been recommended, but they may have improved.

The Southern Sierra

San Sebastián, or Nabusímake as it is more properly called by the Arhuacos, is a ceremonial Arhuaco village, and their occasional administrative centre. It lies on the Sierra's southern slopes and to visit it you must first get a permit from the Casa Indigena in Valledupar.

A village of 50 low thatched huts set in a stunning, deep-green valley, Nabusímake is no ordinary Colombian village; surrounded by a stone wall it is neat, clean and well laid-out. Most noticably, there are there are no hard sounds, no radios, no cars, no metal. Nor is there is any electricity. Nor are there any hotels or restaurants—you must bring your own food and sleeping bag or tent.

You can camp down by the river and there are good walks to be had up into the hills that surround the village. If you want to trek further into the mountains you will need another permit from the village chief—inquire about the procedure from the small shop just outside the village. From San Sebastián onwards, you are on your own, but if you would like a guide, write to Gustavo Sánchez, AA51071 Barranquilla.

GETTING THERE

To get to San Sebastián you must first catch a jeep from Valledupar to Puerto Bello. Jeeps leave from Carrera 7A and Calle 18 in the mornings when full (3 hours, US$3). At

3600 feet, Puerto Bello is the last *mestizo* village before Arhuaco country on this flank of the mountain. It is not well named; there is only one village street and it is lined by a straggling double-line of sagging houses. From Puerto Bello occasional jeeps continue onto Nebusímake, otherwise it is 22-km hike. However, if you were to set off walking you might be able to catch a lift—there is some irregular traffic betwen the villages. If you should need to spend the night in Puerto Bello, there is a simple, cheap but clean hotel, **El Hogar de Miami** (US$2 per person).

Valledupar

Valledupar is a frontier town with a broad Texan swagger. In the plusher areas ranchers' houses are wide and modern. More modest neighbourhoods are tidy and freshly painted. Downtown is an area of wooden boardwalks and cowboy-hatted men. Downtown is also the only place that I have ever seen a man thrown into the street through the flapping swing doors of a saloon.

There are two reasons to come to Valledupar. Firstly, as a jumping-off point for the Sierra Nevada. And secondly, for the Festival de Leyenda Vallenata that is held each year over the last three days of April.

GETTING THERE
By Plane
Avianca has an office at Calle 16B No. 9–46 and has flights to Bogotá for US$50.

By Bus
There are regular buses to Barranquilla (5 hours, US$5); Bucaramanga (12 hours, US$9); Maicao (5 hours, US$4); and Riohacha (5 hours, US$4).

Daily jeeps for Puerto Bello leave from Carrera 7a and Calle 18 in the mornings when full (3 hours, US$3).

TOURIST INFORMATION
The tourist office is in the Casa de La Cultura.

THE FESTIVAL DE LEYENDA VALLENATA
Between 27 and 30 April every year, Valledupar is given over to vallenato music. The festival is a competition, and allegiences are fierce. People drink chilled anise-flavoured *aguardiente* for the whole week, and by the end of the celebrations the mood is high.

Vallenato floats *everywhere*. It's sung and played in fierce competition for the best accordionist. It's in fierce stomp in the small bandstands that dot the town square where the bands are judged. And it's still swirling in the morning whilst you nurse a hangover after an excess of Colombian pleasures.

Vallenato has become a bullish local industry and successful musicians enjoy a great local prestige; some have become ranchers, others political dignitaries. It is no secret that Colombia's new wealth also enjoys the music and this, in turn, has been good for business; vallenato is everywhere, and in turn, everything is in vallenato (see the 'Caribbean Music Topic' on p. 157).

WHERE TO STAY

The two-star **Hotel Sicare** at Carrera 9 No. 16–04 has large air-conditioned rooms, a swimming pool and charges US$18/25 for a single/double. **Apartamentos Exito** on Calle 17 No. 7A-19 has clean rooms with private bath and fan US$5/7. **El César** at Calle 18 No. 9–39 is much the same, only slightly cheaper. The cheapest residencias are on Carrera 7 between Calles 18B and 19A, but most of them are whorehouses, so you would be wise to invest a little more and stay a few streets uptown.

WHERE TO EAT

There is little to choose from. The best hotels have good restaurants. Otherwise there are street cafés. Try roast kid with plantains, or a *sancocho*—an inclusive stew that contains most of the local flora and fauna.

LA GUAJIRA

Colombia is criss-crossed by invisible borders that change everything, but La Guajira is one of the country's most startling frontiers. More of an afterthought than a true extension of the Caribbean coastline, La Guajira is a 240-km long, 48-km wide snout that guards the Venezuelan gulf and ends at Punta Gallinas, the northernmost point in South America. It has just two towns of note—Riohacha, the department's capital, and Maicao, on the Colombian/Venezuelan border. Apart from these towns and a few minor hillocks towards the tip, it is as flat as a runway; a hot, arid spit of rock, sparsely dusted with rock and thorn. It is populated by semi-nomadic, goat-herding Indians; by vast flocks of flamingos up around Cabo de la Vela; and by a shifting army of contrabandistas that use its open but inhospitable spaces for their airstrips and its deserted and silent coastline to land their boats. Romantic and strange, La Guajira is one huge hide-away, an old-fashioned badlands, and you should take extreme care when travelling here.

The Guajiros
The Guajiros, or Wayuu, curently number about 80,000 and carry themselves with a pride and an opulence that looks to have floated in from somewhere in the Middle East. They have leather-skinned desert faces—leaner than most *costeños*—with high cheekbones and deep-grained wrinkles etched around their eyes by a lifetime of squinting into the sun. Too warlike to have ever been subdued by the Spanish, they are a proud, fierce and self-determining people; quick to take offence, quicker to take advantage and as opportunistic as any of the world's other pastoral nomads—such as the Kenyan Masai, the Russian Cossack, or the Saharan Berber. The women wear colourful *mantas*—soft-flowing cotton robes wonderfully unsuited to the peninsula's thornbrush country; while the men wear mostly western clothes, sometimes with a ·45 tucked under their belt.

The Guajiros have only recently become integrated with Colombian society. Firstly, through the growing fortunes of the Cerrejohn, the huge coal-mining development that lies in the middle of the peninsula which has led to the building of a paved road and railway across the desert. And secondly, through the new wealth gleaned from the marijuhana trade of the 1960s and 1970s. Partially integrated they maybe, but civilized? Police in the Guajira are virtually non-existent and the Cerrejohn/Guajira interface handbook advises all coal workers, 'Do not make eyes at Guajiro women. And do not to join in Guajira drinking or shooting competitions, and if you must, lose, and with grace.'

WHAT TO SEE

La Guajira is slowly losing the Harlem-don't-go-there-reputation that it had in the 1970s, but there is little worth seeing. Riohacha is the peninsula's capital, and Maicao a contraband town that you will have to pass through if on your way to Maracaibo and Venezuela. In Cabo de la Vela however, right to the north, there lies a magnificent beach—'The flourish on the top of Colombia!' as the poet Aureliano Mutis exclaimed.

GETTING THERE AND AROUND

There are a number of deluxe coaches that ply the roads between Venezuela and Riohacha, Santa Marta or Barranquilla. Otherwise travel through the desert is in Toyota Land Cruisers and Chevrolet pick-up trucks. These bump and grind along dusty trails or sandy tracks: the Guajiros get on, the Guajiros get off,then they melt into the desert shrub. Small, open sided thatched huts along the road mark places which sell soft drinks or 'Polar Beer'. And the painted billboards by the roadside, signed in Wayuu, are reminders to the Guajiros not to let their sheep and goats stray onto the Cerrejohn railroad or the commercial expressway.

Riohacha

At the beginning of the 16th century, Nuestra Señora de los Remedios de la Rio Hacha was founded as one of the first Spanish settlements in South America. But its position was so arid and desolate that the town declined and gave way to Santa Marta and Cartagena. Renowned throughout the New World for its pearls, the town was razed four times; once by Sir Francis Drake, twice by Guajiro Indian armies, and finally in 1701 by the English pirate Peter Horne (Pedro Cuerno), a rapacious filibuster who, appetite unsatisfied, immediately afterwards sailed west along the coast and sacked Ciénaga as well.

Today only the easy-going beach front area gives any inkling of the town's Spanish ancestry. The rest of the town is made up of peeling two-storey houses, with a rubbish-strewn market just off the main road. Even Riohacha's police cars are smuggled North American, made in Detroit, and carry Venezuelan number plates.

GETTING THERE

The bus terminal is 1 km out of town—US$1 in a taxi. There are regular buses to Maicao along a good road (1 hour, US$1); Santa Marta (3 hours, US$3) and Valledupar (5 hours, US$4).

TOURIST INFORMATION

The **National Tourist Office** is on the beachfront, at Calle 1 and Carrera 4, and is open Mon–Fri 8–12 noon and 2–6. It has good information and maps. The tour company

Guajira Viva have an office on the ground floor of the Hotel Delicias on the beachfront, and organize tours around the remoter parts of the peninsula; if you want to explore, it would probably be best and easiest (but not cheap) to go with them.

The **Banco de La República** is on the beachfront at Calle 1 and Carrera 7.

VISAS
The *Venezuelan Consulate* is in the El Ejecutivo building at Carrera 7 No. 3–08, and is officially open Mon–Fri, 9–2. This is your last chance to get a Venezuelan visa before the border.

FESTIVALS
There is dancing and drinking in the streets from 28 June–1 July, at the **Festival y Reinado Nacional del Dividivi**.

WHERE TO STAY
The state-owned **Hotel Gimura**, a 10-minute walk east along the beachfront, has a swimming pool, and air-conditioned rooms that overlook the beach for US$20/23 for a single/double. The **Hotel Delfines** on Calle 2 and Carrera 9 is one block away from the beach, is clean and friendly and has a good annexed restaurant across the road. Budget accommodation can be had at **Central**, on Carrera 6 and Calle 5; it has simple rooms with fans at US$2.50 per person.

WHERE TO EAT
Your best bet is at the hotel restaurants.

Maicao

The best part about Maicao is leaving it; 80 km south-east across the desert from Riohacha and 12 km north of the Venezuelan border, this contraband city is one big, sleazy downtown market area. Because of the heat, trading begins in the cool of dawn, midday is moved forward to 10 am, and all the shops are closed by 4 pm. The town is a tower of Babel with French, English and Spanish-speaking traders from the Caribbean, Wayuu-speaking Guajiros from the desert, Colombians and Venezuelans. Each brings what he has to sell, always at the 'cheapest price' (Johnny Walker Black Label is US$10 for a litre). No shopping paradise, by the early evening, the town has surrendered itself to drunken cowboys—a perfect time to get into trouble and have all of your belongings stolen. As they say, everything is changing hands in Maicao, which includes other people's luggage.

If going onto Venezuela, come to Maicao early and leave the same day. If going to Cabo de la Vela, get off before Maicao at *Quatro Vias*, a desert crossroads easily noticed by the Cerrejohn railway bridge that crosses the main road, and pick up a connection from there.

GETTING THERE
Maicao has a lot of bus traffic, but the bus companies are inconveniently spread over a wide area. Buses to Santa Marta and Barranquilla are with **Expresso Brasilia** on

Carrera 9 and Calle 13, **Cope Tran** on Calle 13 and Carrera 16, and **Rapido Ochoa**, on Carrera 15 and Calle 13 (6/9 hours, and US$4/7 respectively). All buses pass through Riohacha. There are also buses to Valledupar and early morning buses to Bogotá. Pick-up trucks go to Uribia—a desert town en route to Cabo—from the corner of Calle 12 and Carrera 17.

WHERE TO STAY
El Dorado, at Calle 12 and Carrera 10, is one of the best in town and has air-conditioning and single/double rooms for US$11/15. **Venecia**, on Carrera 13 and Calle 13 is good and has its own restaurant—single/doubles are US$4/6. **Don Blas** on Calle 14 and Carrera 10 charges US$2.50 per person.

ON TO VENEZUELA
The border is 12 km south of Maicao, on the road to Maracaibo. You will need a visa—have one ready before you get to the border. There are four daily buses to Maracaibo from Maicao that leave from Carrera 14 and Calle 13 with **Expresso Gran Colombia** (4 hours, US$3).

Cabo de La Vela

Cabo is a flourish on the top of Colombia, a haven in the Guajira, Alonso de Ojeda's first landing place in South America, and one of the most picturesque spots on the Caribbean coast. The only problem is getting there.

Overlooking a broad bay, the village is a simple collection of fishermen's huts and lean-tos set, with their backs to the constant peninsular wind, in an entirely mineral landscape of sky, sun, sand, rock and sea. The village looks like something out of Hemingway's *The Old Man and the Sea* and is a good place to swim, eat fresh lobster, swing in hammocks, let things slide for a while, and take eerie walks through a land from which the sun and wind have erased all colours. Occasionally, coal workers come down from the Cerrejohn and buy seashell necklaces from black face-painted Guajiro women. This is an ironic and complete reversal of South American history, when 500 hundred years ago the *conquistadores* first exchanged shiny baubles for Indian gold.

GETTING THERE
Unless you go on a tour, the only way to get there is on jeeps, irregularly scheduled, so set off early. On the Riohacha/Maicao road, get-off at Quatro Vias, a crossroads where the Cerrejohn railway bridge crosses the main highway. From here, there are occasional direct jeeps to Cabo (5 hours, US$5). If none are forthcoming, catch a pick-up to Media Luna (aka Puerto Bolívar), 4 hours and US$6 away, and from there try to convince the driver to make the last extra half hour leg on to Cabo (expect to pay up to another US$6 extra). Otherwise, from Puerto Bolívar, it is a 3-hour walk through desert; head along the dirt road towards the pyramid shaped hill with the statue of the Virgin Mary on top and Cabo lies 5 km further on, in the next bay.

WHERE TO STAY
There is only one place to stay; the friendly, very clean and family-run **El Caracol**. They

have simple rooms for US$8, or hammocks, overlooking the sea, for US$2. You can leave luggage in reception. The hotel also has a small dry-goods store, and a restaurant—try the freshly caught and cooked lobster, only US$6.

SAN ANDRÉS AND PROVIDENCIA

You would need an Admiralty map to be able to pin point these two tiny Caribbean islands, and a spy satellite to peer closer and see what they were like.

Lying some 700 km north-west of the Colombian mainland, and 200 km east of the Nicaraguan, both San Andrés and Providencia are archetypal Caribbean paradises; surrounded by balconies of coral and a clear turquoise-blue sea, covered with coconut palms, and rimmed with white coral beaches. The southern island, San Andrés, is the most important, and is also a duty free zone; a miniature Caribbean Hong Kong. Providencia, the smaller island 90 km to the north, is quieter, undeveloped and the kind of place that you might want to head to if you wanted to be right off the beaten track. Both are holiday islands, with a friendly population of mixed English, French and Spanish ancestry; a typically Caribbean-creole mix, only more so.

There is virtually no local industry on the islands and agriculture is scarce, so almost everything, except for fish and some fruits and vegetables, has to be shipped in. This makes the islands quite expensive. The tourist peaks are in late December and early January and booking a flight on or off the islands at this time can be difficult. The climate is tropical, but sea-breeze fresh, with temperatures rarely ranging outside the limits of 26°C and 30°C.

History
We are prone to think of pirates, semi-official or otherwise, as ranging the seas alone, a Jolly Roger at the masthead and a cutlass between the teeth. Most of them, however, organized their banditry on a solid commercial basis, and many lived in Jamaica and Santo Domingo as landed gentry between expeditions. Henry Morgan for instance, the most brutal of the Caribbean's pirates, was knighted and thrice made governor of Jamaica. But then that was after he had made both his name and his fortune from raiding the Spaniards out of his strategically chosen Caribbean base: San Andrés.

Discovered by Colombus during his fourth voyage, the islands were partially settled by the Dutch, but it was only after the English arrived in the late 17th century that they were effectively colonized. San Andrés and Providencia were perfect bases from which to raid the Spanish caravels that sailed to Europe from Panama. John Equemeling, doctor and companion to the pirate Morgan, wrote that, 'no place had seemed more propitous to Morgan as a hiding place for the fruits of his piracy than the islands; for their proximity to Cuba and the Spanish trading routes.'

It was on 15 November 1671 that Sir Henry Morgan lead his most profitable attack. At the head of 40 ships and 400 men, he bombarded, razed and looted the Spanish port at Panama. Making off with the booty, he headed back to his island base, 400 km away. The story goes that after they had landed he asked his men, whilst still on the beach, 'Who loves me most?'. Four men stepped forward. Shouldering the chests, they set off to the other side of the island to bury the treasure. Then Morgan killed them. It was an act of love—he explained in his own defence. He had wanted to mount a guard over the treasure, and who better than the loving ghosts of his four best friends? There are still regular searches for Morgan's US$1-billion worth of bullion; no-one has found it yet. The more folkloric prospectors employ young children to help in their quest as apparently dreams of gold only appear to those under seven years old.

The islands' sovereignty remained in dispute between Colombia and Nicaragua until 1928, when a treaty decided in favour of the Colombian claim. But as the islands didn't have any consistent form of communication with Colombia until the advent of regular aeroplane services in the 1950s, the English-West Indian influence on language, architecture (wooden, gabled, and gaily painted) and religion (Protestant, but especially Baptist) remained. The local inhabitants, descended from the Jamaican slaves of the 18th century, still speak the musical patois of the English Caribbean and the mood of the islands is commensurately... relaxed.

GETTING THERE
All access to the islands is by plane through San Andrés airport; there are no boats. The airport is a 15-minute walk or US$3 taxi ride outside town. Checking in can take hours as Colombians pile up box upon box of duty-free goods, all of which require an inspection.

From Colombia
There are daily flights to Bogotá (US$74), Barranquilla (US$50) and Cartagena (US$50) with Avianca and SAM. There are also weekly flights to most other Colombian cities. The SAM office is on the corner of Avenida Duarte Blum and Ave Colombia. The **Avianca** office, a few metres away, is also on Avenida Duarte Blum.

From Abroad
An exit tax of US$8 is payable on all flights abroad, increased to US$20 if you have been in Colombia for more than 60 days. Avianca has a Sunday flight to Miami for about US$250. And there are regular flights with other airlines to most Central American countries, and to Mexico.

San Andrés

San Andrés, the main island of the archipelago, has around 33,000 inhabitants. It is 13 km long, 3 km wide, ringed by a road, covered in palm trees, shaped like a seahorse, and mostly flat. The main town—El Centro—is in the north and has all of the hotels, shops and restaurants of the island. This is the tourist centre, busy with Colombian shoppers. In the centre of the island lie the quiet hamlets of La Loma, and below it, San Luis. As soon as you leave El Centro, the pace of life drops quickly.

TOURIST INFORMATION
The **Tourist Office** is on Avenida Colombia, towards the airport, and is open from Mon–Fri, mornings and the afternoons. The **Banco de la República** is on Avenida Colón, but some of the shops around it will also change travellers cheques. Costa Rica, Guatemala, Honduras and Panama all have consulates on the island and they are all open Mon–Fri; the first two in the morning and afternoon, the last two only in the morning.

SWIMMING AND DIVING

Most of the shoreline is rocky and there are, in fact, only two beaches on the island; a good one at El Centro, and the other at San Luis. However, a few hundred metres opposite the beach at El Centro lies Johnny Key—a small coral islet with a good white sand beach. It is best to go on a Sunday, when there is a fish-fry on the quay with music and gentle drinking; invariably it turns into a rhumba, just for fun. Around the point from Johnny Key lies El Acuario, a shallow natural aquarium, excellent for snorkelling. Boats for both Johnny Key and El Acuario leave from El Centro's beach front, US$2 return, or you can make a combined trip to both. Snorkelling gear is easily bought or hired on the island. And diving on the reef can be had for US$50—arrange a trip at the **Aquarium** diving shop or the **Sea Horse Inn**.

AROUND THE ISLAND

Bicycles are a popular way of getting around and can be hired for US$6 a day from the shop in front of the **Hotel El Dorado**—check on brakes and tyres first. Motorcycles can also be hired for about US$4 an hour, US$25 for the day. The drive around the island is splendid; stop at any kiosk for a cold beer and a breeze. There are two sites that mark the journey around the island. At the southernmost tip lies El Hoyo Soplador, the blowhole, and halfway up the western side, a cave rumoured to have once been used by Henry Morgan.

WHERE TO STAY

Expensive

All of the best hotels in San Andrés are on Avenida Colombia, facing the beach. **El Acuarium** is the best of the best; a delightful place with 12 bungalows set on pilings over the water facing El Acuario Key. It also has an excellent restaurant. Bookings can only be made in Bogotá, tel 282–0691. Rooms are about US$40/60 for a single/double. **Los Delfines**, tel 4803, back in town along the Ave Colombia has 23 air-conditioned suites and the hotel has a swimming pool and very good service; rooms cost about US$18/28 for a single/double.

Moderate

For more mid-range accommodation, try **Las Antillas**, on Avenida 20 de Julio No. 1A–81, and **Rifas San Andrés**, which is hidden away down a small pedestrian passage two blocks back from the beachfront. Both are good, safe, and clean, and have rooms with private bath for US $7/10 for a single/double.

Inexpensive

The cheapest hotel in town, just by the airport and right underneath the flightpath of landing jets, is the famous **Restrepo**—a 'gringo hotel', as only gringos go there, and the only one like it in Colombia. Some of the rooms are ragged, others fine, but at least most of them are clean—it all depends on pot luck which you get. The prices however are constant: US$2.50 per person.

WHERE TO EAT

Seafood is locally known as *sifú* and the most delicious restaurants are, again, all along the beachfront. Go to **La Tortuga** for excellent turtle soup and seafood dishes with an

Italian twist at around US$8 a head, or try the cheaper fish and meat menu at the **Fonda Antioqueña No. 2** on the corner of Avenida Colombia and Avenida Nicaragua (about US$4 a head). For juices go to **Jugolandia** on Avenida 20 de Julio, and for a cheap *corriente*, try **Miss Bess** on the main road west out of town and order a *rondón*; a typical local soup prepared with coconut milk, vegetables, fish and prawns (US$3).

Providencia

Providencia, traditionally known as Old Providence, lies 90 km north of San Andrés. Volcanic rather than coral-based, it is older, smaller, and hillier than San Andrés, and also less visited and hence less tourist-spoilt. The names of some of the island's hamlets—such as Lazy Hill—are indicative of the mood, and English is more widely spoken than on San Andrés ('So hot today that the sun come down and melt me-up like butta!'). Life is very sane and in the graveyard at Lazy Hill it is impossible not to notice that the minimum age of death is at least 90.

The water is marvellous and there are three wide-beached bays strung along the shore. The first is at Aguadulce, the second is at South West Bay—just beyond the point, and third lies a little way beyond South West Bay, at Manzanillo. Co-operatives make boat tours of the island for about US$5 a person and these are worth joining. Most circle the island before making for Santa Catalina, a small island just off the northern tip. Walking up to El Pico (320 m) is also popular and takes about an hour and a half from Casa Baja, the southern most settlement on the island.

GETTING THERE

By Plane

There are three flights daily with SAM to and from San Andrés (US$17). In the high season you should book well in advance. Flights land on the opposite side of the island to Aguadulce bay, but pick-ups will be waiting to take you there after you have disembarked.

By Boat

Small cargo ships make a weekly run between San Andrés and Providencia, and charge about US$10 for the 10-hour trip. Ask in San Andrés at the harbour, in the last small white house in the port.

TOURIST INFORMATION

Providencia has neither tourist office nor bank, and the island is expensive, so take enough cash.

WHERE TO STAY

There is nothing to be had in Providencia for under US$8 a night and the norm is around US$10–15 a night. In Aguadulce the **Hotel Royal Queen** has clean rooms with bath for US$8 a person. Right on the beach is **Cabañas El Paradiso**, a pretty collection of small wooden cabins at US$10 per person; it also has a good restaurant. Away from Aguadulce, in Aguamansa, sitting on the eastern coast of the island, you will find the lovely and very quiet **Dutch Inn**; US$30 per person, with breakfast and dinner included.

Camping

Camping is easy on the island—just ask for permission from the nearest house first. Your most comfortable bet is up in the hills; camping on the beach leaves you prey to mosquitoes, especially on South West Bay.

WHERE TO EAT

Eating is best at the hotel restaurants, from menus almost entirely given over to fresh fish, lobster, king prawn and conch. **Cabañas El Paradiso** is the best (about US$9 a head); **Miss Elma's** the cheapest (US$3 for a *corriente*). On Manzanillo beach you can have good fresh fried fish for around US$3.

TURBO AND THE GULF OF URUBÁ

'Tus ojos son dos Dabeibas   'Your eyes are two Dabeibas
Tu boquita un Pipinta   Your mouth a Pipinta
Tu cintura un Darien   Your waist is a Darien
con su Golfo de Urubá.'   And your Gulf is an Urubá.'

—Local ditty

The Caribbean coast to the west of Cartagena is less well known, less explored and much less developed than the coastline to the north-east. There are two or three seaside villages here—Tolu, Covenas and Arboletes—that have been developed for local tourism (*tourismo marron*, literally brown tourism). And inland lies Sincelejo and Montería, the capitals of the Sucre and Cordobá provinces respectively. All of these towns fall within Dr Johnson's dictum of worth seeing, but not worth the effort of going to see. Way to the west however, lies the Gulf of Urubá; a great 80 km inlet via which the Atrato river flows to the Caribbean. On its drab and muddy eastern coast lies only the ramshackle port of Turbo. But the western stretch is spectacular, with steep, jungled, rocky cliffs coming down to a beach-dotted shoreline, and at the northernmost tip, up against the Panamanian border, lie two idyllic villages, Capurganá and Sapzurro.

Capurganá has been moderately developed—you can hire aqualungs and go diving for instance, but Sapzurro is still a shanty town with only one restaurant and only one simple hotel. Neither village is easy to get to—about about two days of hard travel from Cartagena. Both however, but both are worth the trouble and effort.

The best time to go is in the dry season, which runs from December to March. But please note: you must take care around Turbo, Sincelejo and Montería—guerrilla activity is common and much of the area is unstable.

Turbo

A booming banana town, Turbo has a frontier atmosphere that is added to by the hulks of the shallow-bottomed boats rotting in the port. Dusty, poxy and occasionally violent, Turbo is a door to other places—such as Capurganá or the Chocó—and little more.

TOURIST INFORMATION
Banks are closed on Mondays and Tuesdays and will only change cash. Make sure that you have enough when you arrive; travellers' cheques are effectively worthless. If you are heading for Panama, you will need to get an exit stamp from the DAS office on Carrera 19, between Calles 19 and 20.

GETTING THERE AND AROUND
By Plane
The airport, 4 km outside town, has three flights daily from Medellín (US$28).

By Boat
There are regular boats to and from Quibdo (see p. 295, under the 'Chocó' section, for more information about the 'Dirty River Express'), and occasional cargo boats from Cartagena.

By Bus
There are two ways of getting to Turbo, the first from Cartagena and the second from Medellín. From Cartagena, it is a day's hard travelling. First go inland, through Sincelejo, to Montería (6 hours and US$6, with **Expresso Brasilia**) and from Montería catch a rough-riding jeep to Turbo. This is an excruciating last-leg; the journey is long, hot and dusty, and the only relief is the tragi-comic thought that you might be participating in a forgotten leg of the Dakha rally (6 hours, US$7). There are many police and military checkpoints along the way so have your papers at the ready.

If you get stuck in Montería for the night, most of the hotels are on Carrera 2 between Calles 34 and 37. **Residencias Better** at Carrera 2 No. 36–26 costs US$4/6 for singles/doubles; **Hotel Sinu** on Carrera 3 and Calle 32 has air-conditioned rooms and a swimming pool for around US$20/30 a single/double.

From Medellín, there are also six daily buses to Turbo with **Gómez Hernández** and **Transportes de Urubá** (6 hours, US$7). If you are not going onto Capurganá, four hours further on from Turbo, also on Gómez Hernández, lies the quiet seaside town of **Arboletes**. The main attraction here is the bubbling mud pool: wallow for a while and then wash off in the sea. Rustic beachside accommodation can be had at **El Platanal**, US$2/5 for singles/doubles.)

WHERE TO STAY AND EAT
The following hotels both have restaurants. The **Castilla de Oro**, with air-conditioning, TV and hot water, is the best in town at US$18/30 for a single/double. Otherwise try the very friendly Residencia **Saussa**. The best pick of the residencias around the port area, the Saussa, has rooms with double beds and bathrooms for US$6.

Capurganá and Sapzurro

Capurganá is a small Caribbean village, exactly as one would imagine a small Caribbean village to be, with only a beach, a sandy main street, and a grassy main square. When you arrive you will feel as though you are miles from anywhere, which you are. It's a get away place where you can swim, sunbathe, walk through the hills, or bathe in waterfall-fed mountain rock pools. You can also hire horses.

There was nothing here, not even a shop, two years ago. But with the advent of the new aeroplane strip, moneyed holiday makers from Bogotá and Medellín have taken to coming, and those that came and liked it enough to stay have set up small restaurants along the beach and, even, back from the village, an unlikely and luxurious hotel.

Sapzurro, one hour's walk further north through the hills, is still only a small fishing village. There are no more than 40 houses in the village, which is set around a palm-fringed horseshoe bay with a crescent moon of white sand. The water is Caribbean blue, still and clear.

GETTING THERE
By Plane
There are four flights a week to and from Medellín ($40 each way).

By Boat
From Turbo there is a regular morning boat to Capurganá. The boat journey can be rough, and takes three to four hours depending on conditions (US$9).

WHERE TO STAY
Most people stay in Capurganá and only make day excursions to Sapzurro. There is one simple hotel in Sapzurro however, **Cabañas El Retiro**, US$6 per person.

Expensive
The **Hotel Calypso** is a 5-minute walk outside town and is less a hotel than a series of cabins set in leafy gardens. There is a tennis court and a restaurant. Cabins cost between US$30 and US$80, can hold two to five people, and are bookable at **Calypso Capurganá**, Carrera 43A No. 27A Sur 86, Medellín, tel 255 2279. The mailing address is PO Box 54211.

Moderate
The **Centro Nautico** is another series of cabins set just up from the beach. Diving gear and windsurfer hire is available and there is also a good restaurant. Cabins cost US$25/30 for a single/double and are bookable through most Bogotá tour agencies.

Inexpensive
The **Hotel Uvito** is a simple but clean two-storey pension at the edge of town, overlooking the beach. Family run and friendly, the best rooms are set around the flower-strewn balcony on the second floor; US$3 per person.

WHERE TO EAT
The best hotels, of course, have good restaurants, but there are a number of small eateries off the beach—**El Fogota** is the best of many. Try the delicious *arroz con cangrejo*—finely chopped crab mixed with rice.

ON TO PANAMA
From Sapzurro
Panama is only a half-hour walk from Sapzurro. There is a Panamanian consulate in Sapzurro, open Mon–Fri, mornings and afternoons, but your passport must have a

Colombian exit stamp from Turbo and you have to be well prepared for the immigration official across the border at Puerto Obaldia: be sure to have a visa, enough money and an onward ticket out of Panama. From Puerto Obaldia there are thrice-weekly flights on to Panama city.

From Turbo
There are some boats that ply the gulf north to Panama, but they are mostly uncomfortable and filled with contraband, so weigh the risks carefully before embarking.

Through the Darien Gap
This is a hard 7-day trek through marsh, jungle and Indian territory, and only for those stalwart enough to find adventure in hardship-that-is-fun-to-endure. The trip is easiest during the dry season, which runs from mid-December to mid-April, and should only be made with the minimum of baggage; only what you can carry. The *South American Handbook* has a long section on health for the journey, and Bradt's *Backpacking in Mexico and Central America* has special maps covering the whole route, with background information on the Cuna and Cholo Indians, the flora and the fauna. **Encounter Overland**, 267 Brompton Rd, London SW5, also offers organized three-week tours for 10 people, that begin in Cartagena and end in Panama City (US$1000).

Part V
THE SIERRA

A coffee worker in the Central Cordillera

It is a common caprice to imagine that travelling south is to travel downhill. But from the Caribbean, all the way south to Tierra del Fuego, the road only climbs and the way is all up.

They say that you don't judge a South American by his country, but by his altitude. And the Colombian Sierra—like the Colombian Caribbean, or the Colombian Pacific, or the Colombian Amazon—is a country within a country; another country. Mountain people are more stoical and wry than the *costeños*, less effusive. The climate is cool and dry; the light stark and bright—as dazzling at midday as theatre spotlights, but changing, by evening, to a deep and distant indigo. At mid-range altitudes, between one and three and a half thousand metres, the vegetation is temperate but lush, and the air as fresh and as sweet as honey. Over 4000 m, however, the mountains loom higher and higher, the sun frets their peaks, the peaks pile one on top of the other, and the wind whistles through the passes and highland plateaus with a dreadful howling. Colours fade from the landscape as you approach the snowline, and the only relief from the wintery highland paramo's dun-greys and greens are the small blue flowers that grow by the roadside; *pensamientos*, little thoughts.

The Sierra is Colombia's most populous region, predominantly rural, a leaf-shaped area, with three ranges of hills, or cordilleras, fanning out from a thick knot of land 200 km south of Bogotá, Colombia's highland capital. Distances between these cordilleras are measured in hours of rollercoaster travel, not kilometres. From Bogotá to Medellín, for instance, is no great distance, about 500 km, a mere pinch on the map, but in the Andes, where one is even less of a flying crow than usual, this means little.

228

For example, Bogotá stands at 2600 m above sea-level in the *Eastern* Cordillera; Medellín at 1490 m in the *Central* Cordillera—which means that the only way between them is to go down the side of one mountain and up the other.

Travel by bus between, or up into, the cordilleras is on spiralling roads and through hairpin bends marked by roadside shrines dedicated to unfortunates that went over the edge. You have to picture Grand Canyons covered with greenery (green gorges, green peaks, green ledges and green cliffs) to imagine these inter-cordillera valleys. At times the bus takes on views that you would more usually expect from aeroplanes, but swinging about inside them on those deep wallowing curves you more often feel as though you are on a boat. As you gain altitude the plants that grow on the roadside's telephone wires, with roots and blossoms dangling in the air like orchids, begin to thin out. The soft lowland scenery begins to harden. You pass through successive, startling and invisible climatic transitions, and finally the lowland's last fringe of trees, the 'eyebrow of the forest'. Ground vegetation thins and shortens as the temperature drops. Doggedly climbing, the bus dwindles to nothing amidst the scenery. And then, before dipping over the pass and back down into a valley, you pass through the highest areas, and here the road is lined by small Andean hamlets, each one cold, withdrawn and so precariously situated that it looks magnetized onto the cliff.

The Magdalena is the only river that penetrates the Sierra. From La Honda, the deep place, a hot river port halfway between Bogotá and Medellín, it flows 1600 km into the Caribbean. From high in the Sierra it looks like a silver streak, far away and unreachable. From the valley however, you discover that it is in fact a turgid, rolling lick of brown. The conquistador Jiménez de Quesada sailed up it in the 16th century, questing for El Dorado, but founded Bogotá instead. Riverboats used to navigate its tricky shallows and sandbanks in the 18th and 19th centuries, but the river has since proved too fickle and the boats are now all gone. In the early 20th century, the Medio Magdalena, the middle reach of the river, was one of the richest farming areas in the country, and it still is, but it is now more famous as a crucible of Colombian politics, and an unstable region for that.

Although the Sierra has borne the brunt of Colombia's violent history, it is mostly a quiet and tranquil place; airy, open, rural and, apart from the major cities and towns, little visited by foreigners. The colonial villages of Boyacá and Santander, such as Villa de Leyva and Barichara, are unspoilt. The Sierra Nevada del Cocuy in the Eastern Cordillera provides some of the best rock-climbing in the whole of South America. And San Agustín and Tierradentro, in the Southern Cordillera, are two of the American continent's most remarkable archaeological sites.

If you are travelling up into the Andes from the blanket heat of the lowlands, you will first experience a blessedly cool relief. But then can follow complaints of loss of appetite and sleeplessness, and a mysterious and undiagnosable ache rooted in the no-man's land between body and soul. This malaise (perhaps altitude sickness?) does not strike everyone, but within it lies the beginning, one suspects, of that famous and nostalgic Andean melancholy. Here's to it.

Bogotá

'A most sophisticated city that will never know joy.'
—from *Bogotá, 1982*, by María Mercedes Carranza

Founded by Gonzalo Jiménez de Quesada in 1538, Santa Fé de Bogotá lies at a lofty 2640 Andean metres above sea level. The Nicaraguan poet Rubén Darío described it at the beginning of the 20th century as 'The Athens of South America! A place long famous for its cultivation of intellectual disciplines, a city of Greek and Latin.' Many visitors are so surprised by the city's acceleration, size (over eight million inhabitants), and unscaleable class system when they first arrive, that they feel lost and stay only long enough to go to the famous Gold Museum, or to gawp at the baroque splendours of the capital's churches, the best examples of Spain's Golden Age in South America.

Bogotá is not the sunny South America of popular imagination. It's a surprise. It's a familar place that has turned up on the other side of the world, reminding you that you can no longer leave home confident of finding anything radically new. It is big, busy and cosmopolitan. The skies threaten drizzle in a perpetually mournful October. Some areas—amid the city's bran-tub of architectural styles—have been rebuilt in a mock-Tudor style. There is a tradition of taking afternoon tea. People dress in muted colours and walk the streets of the old town with furled umbrellas. In many respects it resembles a Latin London, and if you mention this similarity to the Bogotános they might be puzzled, but generally far from displeased.

Bogotá's cultural life is rich; the museums are full, the bookshops busy and the traditional Bogotáno (the *cachaco*) notoriously urbane, given to extemporizing poetry after long meals at the drop of a hat. The city might be solemn, but it is not sleepy—it sends up a vast, humming and chaotic energy into the chill mountain air. On a first impression, it is only this high-octane ambience which suggests that you might still, in fact, be somewhere in South America, not Europe. But stay longer, scratch the surface, look past those parts of the city that seem to have been born in Europe and educated in the USA, and you will find a city of *campesinos*: a donkey tethered to a skyscraper; a cow grazing on brilliant emerald grass on a roadside verge; a peasant with cracked feet resting on a park bench by his bundle.

Bogotá's high altitude can give you the staggers if you have just arrived from the lowlands, so take it easy on the first day. The lack of oxygen makes enthusiasms die quickly, and any objectives that at first seemed desirable, later seem not worth the effort. But the city has a number of excellent museums, a vibrant cultural life, a plethora of nightclubs and restaurants, all of them worth seeing. Any of the more remote Colombian trips—such as to the Isla Gorgona, or to the Serranía de la Macarena—also have to be organized from here.

Modern Bogotá radiates out from the small, original colonial town, La Candelaria, formerly known as the Barrio de los Principes because the Spanish nobility made their homes there. The plan of the city is long and thin, shaped roughly like Manhattan Island. East–west arteries are called *calles* (streets), and north–south thoroughfares are *carreras* (avenues). To the east of the city rises the abrupt wall of the cordillera; to the west, the industrial zone, and then beyond the factories a vast, flat grassland dotted with eucalyptus trees, the Bogotá Sabana. To the north lies comfortable shrubbed suburbs; and to the south, an uncharted slum bayou where millions of rural immigrants live in rudimentary houses along unpaved roads.

This makes for at least three cities within Bogotá, each one very different from the next. The colonial Candelaria, with its green-gabled, balconied houses that climb the skirts of the mountains, is quiet and sombre. The shrubbed northern residential sector, with its well-tended gardens and security guards, is always tranquil. Street life in the city centre, by contrast, is intense. The traffic hurtles and lurches (pedestrians beware! Taking the outside of the pavement is no longer an act of courtesy, but of courage). Every red traffic light announces a two-minute market as vendors move between the lines of cars. Street cries are amplified through little hand-held loudspeakers and anything and everything is for sale: washing machines, vacuum cleaners, crisp *obleas*—a delicious snack of huge communion-like wafers filled with *arequipe*, a kind of condensed milk, Márquez's latest novel, bubblegum, shoelaces, lottery tickets, or rare tropical fruits from the lowlands whoose tastes burst onto your tongue—some like fireworks, others like wads of rose petals. At six o'clock there is a commuter rush, but by nightfall the traffic has washed away. The streets fall quiet, and Bogotá's city centre comes to look like a composite stage set for some old Hollywood movie like *The Big Sleep*. Darkness presses down from the mountains. Brylcreemed men in three-piece suits move about the tango bars of the Candelaria. And a battered Pontiac taxi heads uptown, dodging the Septima's potholes, never stopping for any of the blinking red traffic lights that try to slow its way.

Bogotá is said to be dangerous. But then so is New York or any other modern metropolis. There are ways to avoid danger; like travelling by taxi at night. Taxis pick you up from where you were, and drop you off at where you want to be. Wheeling through the darkness, skirting trouble, the taxi stops outside the rectangle of light that leans out across the pavement from your destination. It's a club, a restaurant, a hotel, or a private address. The light welcomes you and out, onto it, you step. In Bogotá you pay a little more to avoid danger and, in return, this pays you; everybody knows that. It all becomes normal after a while. At first you only see the guards, rifles slung across their shoulders. Then you notice, propped-up inside their sentry-box, a guitar. You see a sinister cavalcade tearing through the city. But then you notice, through the bullet-proof windows, an elegant couple leaning back on cushions and, judging from their gestures, they are discussing some fine and subtle point. So their journey is not, after all, a security nightmare, but a reflective Sunday afternoon drive.

Bogotá has various districts, with varying degrees of safety, generally, moving south to north, from lawless to secure. But, wherever you are, do not, at night, carry valuables or large sums of money on you. That would be foolish; you might get mugged, so leave them instead in the hotel safe. Bogotá doesn't only look like a stage set for the 'Big Sleep'... Now, knowing that, you can relax.

History

Colombia's capital has always been aloof from South America and its own hinterland. While a traveller need now only book a plane ticket to travel from the coast up to the capital, in colonial times it was often easier to get to Europe than to anywhere else in the country. In Colombia, the very word *Bogotá* is still synonymous with distance, and in the

Amazon, the name for any area of removed and virgin jungle, miles from any settlement, is Bogotá. So even though Bogotá has always held the political reins of the country, it has been loosely, and at a long length. All of which perhaps goes some way towards explaining why the Colombian historian German Arciniegas once wrote, 'Bogotá has no history—only annals for the exclusive use of poets and, it may be, cynics'.

Conquest and Foundation: 1538

Bogotá, City of the Holy Faith, was founded with fitting solemnity, due legal forms and the blessing of God in the year of Grace 1538 by Don Gonzalo Jiménez de Quesada. Its full name was Santa Fé de Bogotá del Nuevo Reino de Granada de las Indias del Mar Océano, an overdone title considering that the city then consisted of only a church and twelve huts, each named after an apostle.

But there is a homesick feeling to this title. Quesada had described the Sabana, where he found himself and the city, as 'a wide and long plain, very flat and like that in which the city of Santafé is founded in New Grenada.' This far shelf of the Andes may not have been like home, but after a dreadful year of marching through the lowlands, it was near enough. It was not hot and savage like the lowlands, the air was as fresh as springtime in Castile and the 'great walled enclosures of the Lord of Bacatá and many other chiefs ... from afar had the appearance of sumptuous edifices of great majesty.' The people of that lofty valley, which Quesada called the Sabana, were the Chibchas, a highly civilized race. Bogotá was founded on top of their township, Bacatá. And it was their religious rites at Lake Guatavita that had lead to the myth of El Dorado. But just one generation after the Spanish arrival, the Chibchas were gone, felled by European diseases, and their religious sites replaced by churches.

'Bogotá, by now, had grown to have several hundred Spanish inhabitants, eight churches, a college of arts and grammar, a hospital and a pharmacy. No metropolis to be sure, but it would still be another half century before the Pilgrim Fathers were even to land at Plymouth.

The Colonial Years and Independence: 1600–1850

Colonial life in Santa Fé was as unvexed, even, elegant and serene as the circumscribed life of North America's own Royalist deep South.

Isolated in the interior of a far and little known continent the city was thrown onto its own resources for entertainment, which were considerable. There were routs and parties at the drop of a plumed hat; receptions for arriving and departing Viceroys; the investitures of Bishops; going-away parties, *despedidas*, for travellers (who 'ere they depart share a bounteous time'); birthdays, anniversaries, commemorations. And, not least, a calender of religious holidays and festivals that was strictly and enthusiastically observed. Of the Easter carnival, the Colombian diarist and historian Daniel Samper observed: 'obscurity, chicha and gallantry combined to provoke fights and fondness,' of which the net results were, 'two or three dead, a number wounded, and with time a notable increase in the population.' Some things never change ...

Colombian history seems to be exemplified by individuals, their lives acting like lenses through which an event or period can be seen and grasped all at one time. Quesada typifies the conquest, but the Viceroy de Solís is the prototype of the best and strangest of

Santa Fé's colonial times. Capable, worldly and scandalous in office, he was also, as a Franciscan friar, the apotheosis of the religious pre-occupation of the period.

Don José de Solís y Folch de Cardona, son of the Duke of Montellano, was descended from the Borgia family of Italian fame. He came to Santa Fé in 1756, and for six years ruled the colony with unusual ability and liberalism. Santafereaño society was delighted with his official conduct and scandalized by his private morals. He was a gay and brilliant lover of women, and his affair with María Lugarda de Ospina kept every salon in a state of pleasurable outrage. A portrait of the time shows a very gallant gentleman indeed; slim, handsome, with a fine clever face that manages to dominate his gorgeous clothes stiff with gold embroidery. But in 1762 an abrupt change occured and overnight the Viceroy became a friar, a follower in love and humility of the gentle Saint of Assisi. Instead of gossip, the alcoves now rang with tales of his piety and good deeds: the time he cared for his sick boatman; his gentleness with the needy; his order to sell his estate 'which is not mine but the poor's'; his gift of the splendid emerald known as the 'Orphan' to the Madonna of Chiquinquira; and his long and rainy pilgrimages, the last of which left him with pneumonia, eventually resulting in his death, on 27 April 1770, after he had received 'with great devotion the Holy Sacraments'.

But the Viceroy was only typical, for the number of sons and daughters of good family who renounced the world for the cloister in colonial times was astonishing. Most of the respected names of Santa Fé could be found in the rosters of the city's many convents. Those daughters of the colony who did not take the veil were educated in the strictest submission, though not, of course, in anything useful; sewing and flower arranging took up a large part of the curriculum. Then they married the men that their fathers selected, and lived the rest of their years in devoted and dependent security. Or at least many of them did; some were more spritely. After attending one of Bogotá's many balls, a writer of the time was prompted to remark: 'It is a perilous thing to have a beautiful wife, and very annoying to have an ugly one.'

Bogotá was still only a small city. The population was frequently ravaged by smallpox epidemics and earthquakes, and a census of the time records only 17,700 inhabitants. But this was soon to change. The revolution was coming, and with it a greater degree of political responsibility and devlopement. On the morning of 20 July 1810, the Spanish merchant José González Llorente insulted the criollo Francisco Morales over a trifling matter—the loan of a vase—so providing the spark that lit the revolutionary tinder. Independence was declared that afternoon.

The Modern Years: 1850–1950

After Independence, the Congress at Angostura changed Santa Fé's name to Bogotá and the city became the capital of Gran Colombia. The town developed gradually; by the middle of the 19th century, it had 30 churches; in 1884 the first tramway began to operate; at the beginning of the century the population had reached 150,000; by 1938, 400,000. This, of course, is nothing compared to the exponential growth rates that the city experienced in the 1960s and 1970s, when large segments of the rural population began to move to the capital.

It was at the turn of the century that Bogotá became famous for the refinement of its customs and culture, and for the discrimination of its taste. There was born a special breed, the *cachaco*, so called because of his dark frock coat and sombre apparel.

233

The *cachaco*, by definition, is born old. He is something of a dandified fogey: formal, reserved, elegantly dressed in the European manner, emotionally indirect, discreet, and renowned for his exquisite courtesy and social manner. He is also an intellectual, fluent in at least three languages, brilliant in his conversation—with that satisfactory Latin habit of light profundity—and frequently also in print. If the gift of language is a particularly Colombian characteristic, the Bogotáno has it to a remarkable degree; he is a poet. For this it is not necessary to be a professional; to be a gifted amateur will do. Kathleen Romoli, a North American who came to live in Bogotá in the 1940s, tells a story to illustrate the point:

> 'Where but in Bogotá would a day-labourer wreck the classic marble bust
> of a popular poet with a well-aimed rock, and then, transparently sincere,
> explain to the judge that it was because its well-tailored correctitude was
> an insult to the adored memory of the tousled, homely genius? (Case
> dismissed.)'

The *cachaco* is as fierce a regionalist as any Colombian, and on the subject of the Caribbean, he is less than circumscribed. 'Ohhh the *costeños* are a good people. But the climate! And Barranquilla? a disaster! Santa Marta is too lazy and Cartagena is nice for holidays, of course. But to live? Ohh no! Too florid.'

Although you may still hear small groups declaiming to each other on the streets of the Candelaria, or waving newspapers at each other in a café, the *cachaco* is a rare breed nowadays. Nevertheless, his exasperatingly elegant sense of irony still lives on.

The Present

Modern Bogotá is a cultural port—to the world and to its own country—and exhibitions of the latest from the New York and the Amazon nestle comfortably side by side. But although a premier cultural centre, with one of Latin America's largest publishing industries, Bogotá's place in recent world headlines has largely been due to cocaine and the Mafia drug lords. The drug problem has paralysed civic efforts towards reform and has put Bogotá at the forefront of South American cities trying to cope with the unpleasant contemporary realities of urban poverty and disrepair, crime, delinquency, drug terrorism and rural immigration. In the past 30 years, Bogotá's population has grown twentyfold, and estimates for the year 2000 suggest that it may reach 12 million. These are all seemingly intractable problems, light years away from the dilemmas that have confronted past generations.

GETTING THERE

By Air

Because of the rare altitude, the landing fields at **El Dorado** international airport, and at the secondary terminal **Puente Aereo**, are two of the longest in the world. Although they are only 1 km apart from each other, it is important to check which terminal your flight is leaving from. The airport is a 20-minute drive from the city centre; around US$4 in a taxi, or 50c in one of the buses that leave from Calle 19 and Carrera 20, marked 'Aeropuerto'.

There are daily shuttle flights all over the country: Medellín US$27; Cali US$30; Cartagena US$50; Barranquilla US$50; San Andrés US$74; Leticia US$59. All international departures are subject to a 15 per cent tax on tickets.

It is nearly always easiest to book flights through a tourist office, but below is a list of airline offices and their addresses in Bogotá should you want to book direct:

Avianca: Carrera 7 No. 16–36 (tel 241 5497)
ACES: Carrera 13 No. 26–53 (tel 281 7211)
Satena: Carrera 10 No. 27–13 (tel 234 9929)
SAM: Carrera 10 No. 27–91 (tel 282 1647)

By Bus

Bogotá's large and well-organized central bus terminal is outside the city centre, at Calle 33B No. 69–13, and has round-the-clock services for destinations throughout the country. Bus services to the terminal from the centre are poor, however, so catch a taxi instead; at around US$2.50 it can work out cheaper in the long run. Below is a list of costs and times to principal destinations throughout the country:

Cali: 12 hours, US$12
Medellín: 12 hours, US$13
Tunja: 2½ hours, US$3
Cúcuta: 18 hours, US$15
Popayán: 16 hours, US$15
Cartagena: 26 hours, US$25
Santa Marta:22 hours, US$22

For the Ecuadorean border, catch a direct bus to Ipiales, 24 hours, US$23.

By Train

The railway Station, **El Estación de la Sabana**, on Calle 13 and Carrera 18, has one train a week, the Tayrona Express, that leaves on Mon at 8.30 am, between Dec–Mar, for Santa Marta. There is only one class of ticket (US$20) and the journey takes a gruelling 28 hours.

GETTING AROUND

By Taxi

Getting around Bogotá by taxi is the quickest and easiest method during the day, and as the bus services stop at 9 pm, the only way to travel at night. All taxis have meters and should use them. A cross-town journey only costs about US$1, but the 'authorized' green and white tourist taxis that stand outside the Taquendema are about three times as expensive.

By Bus

Bogotá's bus system is as predatory, reckless and as crowded as a jungle. There are no bus stops, so flag down the bus that you think you want on any of the arterial Carreras (notably, the Septima, Decima or Caracas). Destinations are marked on small boards displayed in the front window. When you want to get off, tell the driver *por acá* (just here), shimmy through the turnstile, and jump off.

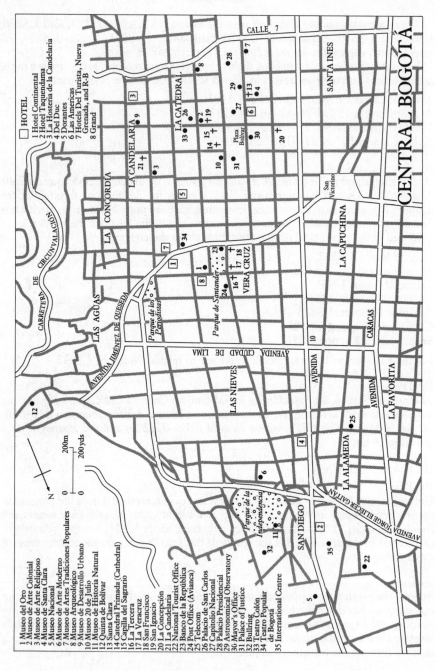

CENTRAL BOGOTÁ

HOTEL
1 Hotel Continental
2 Hotel Taquendama
3 La Hostería de la Candelaria
4 Del Duc
5 Las Américas
6 Dorantes
7 Hotels Del Turista, Nueva
  Grenada, and R-B
8 Grand

1 Museo del Oro
2 Museo de Arte Colonial
3 Museo de Arte Religioso
4 Museo de Santa Clara
5 Museo Nacional
6 Museo de Arte Moderno
7 Museo de Artes Tradiciones Populares
8 Museo Arqueológico
9 Museo de Desarrollo Urbano
10 Museo 20 de Julio
11 Museo de Historia Natural
12 Quinta de Bolívar
13 Santa Clara
14 Catedral Primada (Cathedral)
15 Capilla del Sagrario
16 La Tercera
17 La Veracruz
18 San Francisco
19 San Ignacio
20 La Concepción
21 La Candelaria
22 National Tourist Office
23 Banco de la República
24 Post Office (Avianca)
25 Telecom
26 Palacio de San Carlos
27 Capitolio Nacional
28 Palacio Presidencial
29 Astronomical Observatory
36 Mayor's Office
31 Palace of Justice
32 Bullring
33 Teatro Colón
34 Teatro Popular
  de Bogotá
35 International Centre

There is an Ejecutivo Bus that makes an express journey between the centre of town and the northern residential suburbs. The El Ejecutivo service does in fact have a bus stop, by the National Museum on Carrera 7 No. 25–66. To travel about a hundred blocks costs US$1.

TOURIST INFORMATION
The main branch of the **National Tourist Office** is on the ground floor of the building on Calle 28 No. 13A–15 and has a large selection of brochures and maps, and also a reference library should you want more detailed information on any aspect of Colombia. The office is open Mon–Fri, 8.30–12.30, and 2–5. There are also two other branches at the bus terminal and the airport, and both are very helpful on accommodation.

Inderena
Inderena represents Colombia's national parks and you will need to visit their office on Diagonal 34 No. 5–84 before visiting La Isla Gorgona, or the Lost City in the Sierra Nevada. Permits to the parks are free, are usually issued immediately, and it is not a bad idea to get as many as you think you might need at once to save back-tracking later on.

Money
The **Banco de La República** is at Carrera 7 No. 14–7. You can also change travellers' cheques at the **International Money Exchange** opposite the Hilton, at Carrera 7 No. 32–29. The **American Express** office is at the Tierra Mar Aire office, at Carrera 10 No. 27–91, in the Taquendema's Centro Internacional.

Security and Visas
If you lose your documents, go to the **Inspección Distral de Turismo** at Carrera 13 No. 26–62. **DAS**, the place to go to sort out any problems that you might have with your visa is at Carrera 27 No. 17–85.

Maps
The **Insituto Geográfico Agustín Codazzi** is at Carrera 30 No. 48–51, next to the Universidad Nacional, and is the best place to buy maps.

Tours
Apart from being useful for booking flights, many of Bogotá's tourist agencies will be able to organize trips for you to areas that would be difficult, or impossible, to visit alone. Most trips are organized for groups of at least five however, which makes it rather difficult for the solo traveller.

Tierra Mar Aire is Colombia's best known and probably most efficient tour operator, and their main office is at Carrera 10 No. 27–91, tel 286–111, in the Taquedama's Centro Internacional.

Aviatur, at Calle 19 No. 4–62, tel 282–7111, is the only company that organises helicopter trips to the Lost City.

For trickier trips, contact Colombia's most experienced tour operator, Earl Hanks, tel 242–7647.

Telecom
The main Telecom office is at Calle 23 No. 13–49, open Mon–Sat, 8–4.

WHAT TO SEE

There are two ways to get acquainted with Bogotá; from the ground, or from the air. And on top of the 3200 metre high mountain that stands behind the city like a drop curtain, stands Bogotá's best viewpoint, at the shrine of *Monserratte*. Easily reached by cablecar, the view from the top is as vertiginous and as exhilarating as the ride up. Your head presses against the clouds while Bogotá hums at your feet: there lie the skyscrapers of the international district, there the colonial quarter with its tiled roofs and cobbled streets. Beyond the city you can see the Sabana, and beyond the Sabana, in the far distance, the snow-clad mountains of Los Nevados, the volcanic range of the Cordillera Central. The shrine is dedicated to a statue of the Señor Caído, the fallen Christ, a particularly gaunt and pained image sculpted in the 17th century by Pedro Lugo de Albarracín. There is a windswept replica of a colonial village next to the church, and an array of shops selling religious mementoes. There are also two small cafés.

To get there, catch the cable car that leaves every quarter hour from the base of the mountain; 9–6 Mon–Sat; 6–6 Sun. The return fare is US$2. *But note*: during the weekends the traffic of other pilgrims is such that it is safe to walk to the cable-car station from the city centre, but, on weekdays, it is better to take a taxi—both there and back. The surrounding neighbourhood is dangerous and muggings are frequent, even during daylight hours.

The best place to start discovering Bogotá from the ground is in the **Plaza Bolívar**; the centrepiece of the city, usually an open and bare space, but also a square with a full and violent history. It was here in the Plaza that Quesada founded the City of Holy Faith in 1538; here, that Father Las Casas said the first mass; here, that Morillo set up gallows for the patriot rebels during the Wars of Independence; and here that Bolívar, galloping ahead of his troops after his victory at the Battle of Boyacá, was received with delirious acclaim. A statue of the Liberator now takes pride of place in the middle of the square. One of his hands holds the constitution, the other a sword, and his pose is that of a fencer. Gaunt featured, he faces the rubbled remains of the **Palace of Justice** that was taken over by guerrillas in 1985 and gutted by fire. The words that used to stand in gold embossed letters above the gates of the Palacio, were Santander's, 'Colombians, arms have given you independence, laws will give you freedom.' Bolívar (a *costeño*) and Santander (a *cachaco*) were fierce political opponents. The Palacio is yet to be re-built.

On the southern side of the square lies a massive stone building in a classical Greek style, the **Capitolio Nacional**, the seat of Congress. It was built in 1847 but due to numerous political uprisings was not finished until 1925, when the facade was designed by the English architect Thomas Reed. Just behind the Capitolio lies the **Palacio Presidencial**, also known as the Palacio de Narino, where you can see the changing of the guard daily at 5. The Palacio was built at the beginning of the century, but in 1948 it was sacked by a mob after the assassination of Jorge Gaitán, the same assassination that unleashed the hurricane of *La Violencia*.

The western side of the Plaza de Bolívar is flanked by the low-slung arches of the **Edificio Liévano**, today the Alcaldia, or Mayor's office. On the eastern side stands the church **La Capilla del Sagrario**, which is connected by an interior passage to the

238

neoclassical **Cathedral** next door. Built in the 1600s on top of a Chibcha temple, the Cathedral has a side alcove where rests the bones of the city's founder, Jiménez de Quesada.

These are the formal landmarks of the square, but the Plaza is also a node in the city's informal geography. Go five blocks west and on the corner of Avenidas Caracas and Jiménez, you will find the beginnings of Bogotá's netherworld of whores, transvestites and street dealing. On the other hand, walk up through the north-eastern corner of the square and you'll reach the shop and café-lined Septima, Bogotá's main commercial street. Carry on walking north and on the corner of the Septima and Avenida Jiménez, diagonally opposite the Banco de la República, you will find the wheeling and dealing of Bogotá's informal and open-air emerald stock-market. Watch for close groups of sombre-suited men, their hands closely chested as they pry open small white envelopes filled with uncut stones. (Bogotá's emerald dealers repair for lunch at El Mosaico, on Carrera 8 and Calle 14; go there if you want to see a continuation of what you saw on the street.)

Finally, to the east of the square, between Calles 7 and 13, and Carreras 1 to 8, lies the colonial centre of **La Candelaria**, a small area where old tiled homes nestle quietly around flowered patios in a Moorish style. Take your time wandering around this well preserved neighbourhood. There are a number of galleries, churches and museums to visit, but La Candelaria's true value lies in its atmosphere. As you enter, modern Bogotá falls away, you find yourself in a gentler city, still in touch with its past, and, looking up into the hills Santa Fé seems once again thousands of miles away from the rest of the world.

Churches and Colonial Art

The Spanish conquest was largely due to the devastating moral and physical power of its Church, and in the 17th and 18th centuries, all colonial art was religious art; not an experimental art in the modern sense, but a visual aid for spreading the faith and extending the Christian world. If this sounds very medieval and baroque, it was, and so was the aesthetic that reached the New World.

The sens-A-round of baroque colonial art was a very effective means of impressing the new Christian faith on the aboriginal population, and proved a remarkably efficent tool for overcoming language barriers. But it did not take long for the baroque—which had begun as an art movement in Europe—to end up as a way of life in the New World. For the newly arrived European, everything about the New World was already baroque: its rivers, never-ending; its trees, unheard-of; its sun, burning; and its tropical twilights, catastrophic. If the Spanish could have done so, they would probably have built fairy castles instead of churches. But the Colombian mountains did not provide the Spanish with marble for building ornate facades. So instead they made do with gold—mined in the Chocó and Antioquía—to gild the churches' heavily-carved wood interiors. Gold was also cheaper, easier to work and more effective than cutting stone. All of which explains the contrast between the tropical extravagance of the interiors of Bogotá's churches and the grey austerity of their exteriors. Surrounded by unknown forests, rivers, mountains and plains, and obsessed with their city's enduring isolation in a little known continent, the Santafereaños also saw in their churches' rich interiors a metaphor for their own rich interior life.

Five churches and two museums best illustrate the particularly Colombian themes outlined above. Just below the south-western corner of the Plaza Bolívar, on Calle 9 and Carrera 8, lies **La Iglesia Santa Clara**, perhaps the most representative of Bogotá's churches. Built between 1629 and 1674 as part of the convent order of St Clare, the church is of a simple single nave construction with an interior entirely covered with wall reliefs, frescoes, paintings, wooden images and altarpieces. The image of Santa Clara on the main altar is the oldest piece of woodwork in the church. As the Church is now open as a museum (Mon–Fri, 9–1), you can take your time and peer closer at the paintings; look out for canvases by Figueroa, a very influential painter in 17th-century New Granada. As the church was once a bastion of traditional Catholicism, the entrance is from the side, so that passers-by could not see the altar from the street. Entrance is free.

After Santa Clara, back-track to the Plaza Bolívar, head for its south-east corner, and a few yards up the hill, on Calle 10, opposite the Plazuela de San Carlos, stands the Jesuit **Iglesia de San Ignacio**. Begun in 1610, it was opened for worship in 1635 but not completed until 1767. Inside are magnificent baroque altar pieces—some of which are attributed to Juan de Cabrera, many remarkable wood sculptures by the great Pedro Laboria, and some fine paintings by Gregoria Vásquez Ceballos. If you are in town on the Saint's day, October 23, you will have a special opportunity to see an extraordinary gold chalice, so thickly encrusted with emeralds that it is called *La Lechuga*, the Head of Lettuce. The Church is open Mon–Fri, 9–11.30 and 3.30–5; Sat–Sun 9.30–11.30 only.

Next door to the church, just up the street, stands the **Museum of Colonial Art**. It is not Bogotá's most famous museum, but it is one of the city's best and most intimate. The old colonial house is typically simple, with an inner patio that in colonial times—like the miniature plaza of a miniature city—would have reflected the inner life of the house. The museum houses furniture carved and gilded with luxurious taste, and over 150 paintings and drawings by Vásquez Ceballos, the most important painter of the colonial era. Although the quality of Ceballos's work varies—the perennial problem of any commisioned artist—look out for his three-faced Christ, a depiction of the Holy Trinity so strange that it must be holy. The museum is open Tues–Sat, 10–1 and 2–5.30; Sun 11–5. Entrance is free.

Just down the street, on Calle 12 No. 4–31, lies the **Museum of Religious Art**. Although closed at time of writing for refurbishment, check to see if it has re-opened—it should be worthwhile.

Finally, on the corner of the Septima and Avenida Jiménez, opposite the Banco de la República and the Gold Museum, you will find a close cluster of three churches; San Francisco, Veracruz and La Tercera. Built in 1567, **San Francisco** is the most beautiful of the three. Its sombre interior is lit by countless candles, and by their light you can see some of the paintings and sculpted figures. The gilded wooden altar is a rococo masterpiece by Ignacio de Asccucha, and the carved ceiling is extremely beautiful. In one corner stands a coin-operated electric-candlelit altar, and in another a well-attended shrine to San Judas, the patron Saint of lost and desperate causes; also poets. The atmosphere is special, busy with the murmur of prayers, and the church is open daily 7 am–7 pm.

240

Museums

Many of Bogotá's museums are outstanding, and all those listed below are within walking distance of each other. But if you only have time in Bogotá for one visit, make a bee-line for the Gold Museum.

El Museo del Oro, the Gold Museum. Situated at Calle 16 No. 5–41, it is sanctuary to 30,000 gold artefacts—the largest such collection in the world, and a figure that lends some credibility to the myth of El Dorado. At the time of the conquest, Colombia's Indian artisans were already familiar with every gold-working technique then practised in Europe and the museum's well-labelled, glass-encased exhibitions reveal the rich traditions of the Muisca, Tayrona, Quimbaya, Sinu and Calima Indians. The marvel of all marvels is the last room, surrounded by bulletproof glass. When you enter all is in total darkness. The armoured door is closed. The light is gradually turned on, accompanied by a strange music. You then have five minutes to admire the incredible treasures, the most famous of which is the minutely detailed Muisca barge which represents the legend of El Dorado. There are two daily tours conducted in English—the first at 10 am, the second at 2 pm—and several daily films about Colombia's pre-conquest civilizations. The museum is open Tues–Sat, 9–4; Sun 9–12 noon. Admission is $1.50.

For information about the **Museum of Colonial Art**, see above, in the previous section.

The **Museo Nacional**, the National Museum, at Carrera 7 No. 28–66, was once the city's prison, but now houses exhibitions that range from pre-Colombian to contemporary art, distributed in several halls on three floors. The Department of Anthropology on the ground floor has facsimile Muisca and Tayrona artefacts made by present day Indians from around the country. The Department of History on the first floor holds colonial and post-independence works of art and other memorabilia, including a rogues' gallery of ex-presidents' portraits. And the Museum of Fine Arts on the top floor displays 19th- and 20th-century paintings. Its small collection of the country's best known contemporary painters—such as Fernando Botero, Enrique Grau, and Alejandro Obregón—is well worth climbing the stairs to see. The Museum is open Tues–Sat 10–6; Sun 12–5. Entrance is 50c.

El Museo del Arte Moderno, the Modern Art Museum, is at Calle 26 No. 6–05, with the entrance from Calle 24, and is a spacious modern building with a dynamic administration that frequently arranges travelling international shows, as well as having a permanent exhibition of modern Colombian painters. Contemporary Colombian painting is vigorous and dynamic and a dull show here is rare. There is a small theatre around the back, and the museum also has an excellent bookshop. Open Tues–Sat 10–7; Sun 12 noon–6, entrance 30c.

El Museo Arqueológico, the archaeological museum, lies just back from La Candelaria at Carrera 6 No. 7–43, in the Casa del Marquès San Jorge, one of the finest and most interesting of the stately colonial homes of Bogotá. The collection is one of the best in Latin America, and has beautifully presented exhibits from Mexico, Colombia, Ecuador and Peru set in the house's creaking, wooden-floored and whitewashed rooms. There is a good restaurant on site, and the museum is open Tues–Sat 9.30–5; Sun 9.30–1. Entrance is $1.

To get an idea of (or even to buy) some of the craftworks made around Colombia, go to **El Museo de Artes y Tradiciones Populares**, on Carrera 8 No. 7–21. Housed in an

241

old Augustinian cloister, the museum is open Tues–Sat 8.30–5.30. Cross over to the other side of the Plaza Bolívar and at Calle 10 No. 6–44, opposite the church of San Ignacio, is the **Museo del Trajes Regionales**, which displays regional dresses from different parts of Colombia. Open Mon–Fri 10–5; Sat 10–1, entrance 50c.

If you are interested in Bogotá's past, go to **El Museo de Desarrollo Urbano**, on Calle 10 No. 4–21. Inside this stunning colonial house you will find faded sepia prints and photographs of old Bogotáno life—good for a lazy browse. Open Mon–Fri 9–5; Sat–Sun 10–4, entrance 50c.

Finally, built in 1800 and donated to the Liberator for services rendered, **La Quinta de Bolívar** is the villa where Bolívar used to stay when in Bogotá. Set just outside the city centre at Calle 20 No. 3–23, at the foot of Monseratte, this simple and suprisingly rustic hacienda, surrounded by lush gardens, carries a permanent exhibition of Bolívar memorabilia. The Quinta is open Tues–Sun 10 am–023–5, entrance 50c.

FESTIVALS

Apart from Independence Day on 20 July, there are no festivals that consume Bogotá in the same way that they do other Colombian cities. There are, however, regular film, theatre, and poetry festivals, all of which are of high quality and well worth seeing if your visit to the capital coincides. Check *El Espectador* or *El Tiempo* for listings.

SHOPPING

Emeralds

Bogotá is a world emerald centre; see the 'Topic' on p. 162 for more information.

Arts and Crafts

Although there are *artesanía* shops throughout town, the best place to buy Colombian craftwork is at the shop in the **Museo de Artes y Tradiciones Populares** on Carrera 8 No. 7–21. The shop is open Mon–Sat 8.30–5.30 and has a representative selection of crafts from around the country.

For perfect gold-dip replicas of the work in the Gold Museum, go to **Galería Cano** at Carrera 13 No. 27–98 Torre B, tel 284–4801. The gallery also sells pre-Colombian pottery and clay figurines. There are also a number of souvenir, pre-Colombian pottery, gold and emerald shops in the Taquendema centre.

Errands

A traveller's survival bureaucracy—such as ticketing, visas, telephone calls, and post etc—can take up a lot of time, but you are most likely to find all of the offices that you will need for your errands in or near the Centro Internacional, by the Taquendema Hotel on Carrera 10 and Calle 26. For general shopping, Bogotá specializes in North American style shopping malls, 'with anything and everything under one roof'. Go to the snazzy and highly exclusive uptown **Unicentro** on Carrera 15 and Calle 123, or to the less glitzy **Chapinero** on Carrera 13 and Calle 48 for your general shopping needs.

Flea Market

El Mercado de San Alejo, the Sunday flea market on Carrera 3 between Calles 19 and 24, is good for a lazy afternoon browse.

242

Literature

When Christopher Isherwood visited Bogotá in the 1950s he wrote that he had never seen so many bookshops in one place in his life. Bogotá's publishing industry is large, and outlets are everywhere, but the **Librería Bucholz**, opposite the Taquendema at Carrera 7 No. 27–68 is one of the best.

For English language books, go to **Librería Aldina** at Carrera 7 No. 17–51. Aldina's is a Bogotá institution and has an excellent and lovingly collected range of paperbacks: from Penguin classics to cook books, and from Hammond Innes to André Malraux.

Finally, for a combination of the two above—plus a wide range of international magazines—go to **OMA** at Carrera 15 and Calle 89. There is a café attached to the bookshop where you can relax afterwards and peruse your buys.

SPORT

Bullfighting

The bullfighting season runs through December and February and there are fights in season every weekend at the **Plaza de Toros** on Carrera 5 and Calle 26. Entrance is US$1.

Cockfights

Wherever the Spanish went in the tropics, which includes the Philippines, they started cockfighting. Bogotá's principal cockfight ring, **El Club Gallístico San Miguel**, is at Calle 77 No. 19–65, and has cockfights on Friday and Saturday from 3 pm–3 am. Tickets are from US$1 to US$4.

BARS AND NIGHTLIFE

Bogotá's nightlife has been somewhat curtailed by the recent escalation of Mafia-sponsored disorder. But this disorder is not without its tragi-comic aspects. For instance, the punk band 'Los Sicarios', the Hit Men, who were in fact hit men, was quickly whittled away to just two members by the perils of their trade; bullets, knife wounds and overdoses. This is crazy, but true.

Nonetheless, Bogotá still has Colombia's most vibrant and expansive nightlife, and a fair number of nightclubs and bars. Salsa is the thing, and there are two main nodes of nightlife. The first lies around the bullring, on Carrera 5 and Calle 26, where you will find a number of *salsatecas* pumping out revelry on a weekend; try **La Teja Corrida**, entrance is US$3. The second can be found around the cluster of fashionable streets that lie between Carreras 12 and 15 and Calles 80 and 85. Stroll down the strip on Calle 81 and you will find a chic young crowd, well-travelled (just in from Milan, or Paris or India, or all three) and a double line of bars playing a medley of musics, from newest New York hip-hop, to salsa, hi-energy, and 70s disco.

For quieter drinks, head for **Bar Bohemio** on Calle 13 No. 3–95 for a naturally more bohemian atmosphere and intimate jazz. Or for sweet and nostalgic melancholy, go to the small bar at Carrera 5 No. 14–23 in La Candelaria and spend the night listening to scratched but unforgettable long-playing tango '78s.

Finally, on La Calera, the road that climbs through the hills above Bogotá, there is a string of plush nightclubs and restaurants, all with expansive nightime views of the city's blanket of twinkling lights. Occasionally they host specially imported shows, such as samba ensembles from Brazil. Check the newspapers for listings.

THE ARTS
Bogotá has a regular calendar of ballet, opera and theatre events, and a plethora of cinemas. *El Tiempo* and *El Espectador*, the country's two biggest newspapers, are your best sources of information and they both publish worthwhile weekend guides in their Friday and Saturday editions.

Theatre
Most of Bogotá's theatres are in La Candelaria. **El Teatro de la Candelaria**, on Calle 12 No. 2–59, regularly shows fringe events. The ornate and neo-classical **Teatro de Colón**, on the other hand, provides more orthodox entertainment—opera, ballet, and poetry recitals—and tickets are commensurately more expensive.

Fine Arts
Colombia has a burgeoning art scene and, apart from the regular museums, Bogotá has at least a hundred private galleries. Their range of quality is large, so check the glossy bi-monthly *Arte en Colombia*, available at the Museo de Arte Moderno, for full details.

WHERE TO STAY
Bogotá has accommodation aplenty throughout the city, but probably the most convenient place to stay, near all of the centres of interest, is in the city centre. Prices tend to rise as you head north from the Plaza Bolívar, and to fall as you head west. Anything west of Carrera 10 is uncertain, probably dangerous, and you are advised to avoid it. There is only cheap accommodation to be had in the colonial area, and conversely only expensive accommodation to be had in the mid-town's international centre.

Expensive
Two hotels with very different styles have shared Bogotá's hotel scene since the 1950s: the faded elegance of the Continental, in the heart of the business world and overlooking the colonial centre; and the Taquendema, which pioneered the international sector. Since 1986, their lead has been pipped however by the **Bogotá Royal**, at Avenida 100 No. 8A–01, tel 218–9911, an impressive steel and glass 80-room hotel north of the International centre. An ideal and quiet choice for business travellers, it has is a very good restaurant and an inviting bar that hosts a string quartet in the evenings. Rooms start at around US$65. The 700-roomed **Taquendema** at Calle 26 No. 10–18, tel 286–1111, was once *the* hotel in Bogotá and, surrounded by shops, it is very well situated in the core of the international centre. Rooms start at around US$60. Finally, the **Continental**, at Avenida Jiménez No. 4–16, tel 282–1100, is subdued, comfortable and old-fashioned, the architecture is art-deco and the bell-hops look as though they stepped out of a Dick Tracy comic strip. Time, at the Continental, stopped in the 1950s, and if you are not in a hurry, this is an excellent choice and good value with rooms beginning at around US$28.

For a splash-out, **Charleston** at Carrera 13 No. 85–46, tel 257–1100, offers spanking suites and discreet service in Bogotá's most fashionable district. Rooms begin at around US$80. Or treat yourself to some luxury at the sophisticated **Casa Medina**, Carrera 7 No. 69A–22, tel 212 6657.

Moderate

Perhaps the most beautiful hotel in Bogotá, but also one of the hardest in which to find a vacant room, is the restored colonial mansion, **La Hostería de La Candelaria**, at Calle 9 No. 3–11, tel 286 1479. All of the rooms are furnished with period antiques, and are excellent value at US$11/15 for a single/double. The **Dann Colonial** at Calle 14 No. 4–21, tel 241 1680, on the other hand, is a North American-slick hotel, even though it's in the heart of the colonial district. The rooms are light, clean and very good value at US$18/25 for a single/double. Finally, the **Del Duc** at Calle 23 No. 9–38, tel 234 0080, has spacious rooms, is modern and well-equipped, but small, so reservations are recommended.

Inexpensive

Old-time Bogotá life lives on at the **Hotel Dorantes**, on Calle 13 No. 5–07, tel 334 6640, in the Candelaria. The rooms are almost 1950s Parisian—with wooden floors and shuttered windows—but the atmosphere is too haunted and gaunt, the colour schemes too extraordinary, and the receptionist—a cipher—too poker-faced for you to pretend for long that you are in Europe. Popular with travelling businessmen, this colonial hotel is excellent value at US$5/7 for a single/double, but try to make a reservation first as rooms fill up quickly.

The colonial **Hotel Las Americas** on Carrera 8a No. 9–45, just off the Plaza Bolívar is included in this list because it is more of an oddity than a hotel. It has cold water, but no bathrooms, everything is set crooked, and it's hard to believe that the owner has even noticed the city growing around him during the last 100 years. Spartan but cheap at US$3/4 for a single/double.

For something a bit more comfortable than the eerie La Americas, try the **Del Turista** at Avenida Jiménez No. 4–95, tel 281 8110. It is a small family-run hotel, but the rooms are large, and cost US$6/8 for a single/double. If full, try the **Nueva Granada** or **Hotel R-B**, both are next door and have similar prices.

Finally, if you are down to your last pesos, the **Grand** at Calle 16 No. 5–58, opposite the Gold Museum, is the cheapest in the area at US$1.50 per person. It's basic, but has hot water.

WHERE TO EAT

Cafés

Like all of the best things in life, Colombian coffee doesn't so much push as lift. *The* Bogotá café, the one that not only serves the best coffee in town but is also a stomping ground for Bogotá's beautiful-young and distinguished-old is **OMA**, at Carrera 15 No. 82–60. Next door to OMA lies candle-lit **Pimms**, also good, and also with a small side menu of hamburgers, club sandwiches and salads. Closer to the centre, try the **Cafeteria Romana**; on the corner of Avenida Jiménez and Carrera 6a, diagonally opposite the Banco de La República, it is another classic Bogotáno café, wood-panelled, sombre looking and with a small, but good, side menu. Finally, for the traditional *chocolate santafereño*—hot chocolate with cheese and pan francés—go to the street café, **Pastelería Francés** at Carrera 7 No. 20–82.

Lunch

One of the nicest places to have lunch is at the **Café de Rosita,** a restored house in the Candelaria at Calle 9, No. 3–11. The fixed menu changes and improves daily; a modest US$4 a head.

For a full plate of spaghetti, go to one of the two small eateries just by the bullring on the downhill road that leads past the ring towards the city centre. Both have lively lunchtime (and early evening) crowds, and are very reasonably priced.

Dinner

'If you have an itch, Bogotá can scratch it', and Colombia's capital has a list of restaurants whose cuisines circle the globe. If you are pining for exotic home tastes, you can eat Arab, Japanese and Italian food. But if you are looking for traditional Bogotáno food, go to the cluttered colonial house, the **Casa Vieja,** at Avenida Jiménez No. 3–73. They say that *comida entra por los ojos* (food enters through the eyes) and everything here not only tastes good, but looks good too: the linen is immaculate, the plates earthenware, and the service informal but quiet. Begin with a fruit sorbet, *sorbete de curuba*. Then move onto an *ajiaco bogotáno*, a calming corn soup made with four varieties of potato, chicken, avocado and cream—absolutely delicious. To round off the meal, end with *nata de leche*, made from condensed milk skins, this is an unlikely treat that tastes of butterscotch. With a glass of wine, expect to pay about US$8 a head.

Unless noted, to dine at any of the restaurants below will cost between US$15–25 a head. Wine, of course, is extra.

For grilled meat, go to **Carbón de Palo** on Carrera 18 No. 90–57. The restaurant **Tramonti,** although touristic, has wonderful views over the city from high up on La Calera, the road that runs through the mountains east of Bogotá.

For Japanese food, Bogotá's best are **Nihonkan,** at Calle 90 No. 11A–31, and **Hatsuhana,** Transv. 21 No.100–43, tel 257 9409/610 3056. Or for a more creole approach to fish, try any of the restaurants in the **Fragata** chain. Consistently good, the two most convenient branches of La Fragata are at Calle 15 No. 9–30, and at Carrera 13 No. 27–98, on the second floor.

For a cozy atmosphere and delicious European food, go to **Refugio Alpino** on Calle 23 No. 7–49. Busy during the day with long and liquid business lunches, it is quiet and relaxed in the evenings. Or for Italian food, go to **The Piccolo Café** at Carrera 15 No. 96–55.

Finally, Bogotá's French restaurants are where the rich and powerful dine, entertain clients and clinch deals. They tend to be formal and very expensive. **Le Toit** for example, on the roof of the Hilton at Carrera 7 No. 32–16, is a restaurant organized in a grand style, and has a huge wine list and the most varied French menu in Bogotá. **Pajares y Salinas,** on Carrera 10a No. 96–08, is also excellent, currently 'in', and has delicious seafood. The only exception to the rule is the rustic, intimate, and much cheaper **La Bonne Table,** at Carrera 11 No. 64–31.

Excursions from Bogotá

Bogotá is a good base for excursions. Two of the best are to the Laguna de Guatavita, the birthplace of the legend of El Dorado, and to Villa de Leyva, one of the most perfect colonial towns in the Andes.

La Laguna de Guatavita

The Laguna de Guatavita, otherwise known as El Lago de Amor, is a lonely tarn in the Andes that shaped the history of Colombia—it was here that the myth of El Dorado was confirmed as fact. The Chibcha Indians had many sacred lakes scattered throughout Cundinamarca, but meteorite-formed Guatavita was the most important. As documented by the Spanish in the chronicles it was here that the Chibchas celebrated the coronation of new chieftains, or *caciques*. First the chieftain-to-be was stripped, sprayed with resin and dusted with gold. Then he was sent out into the middle of the lake, to the accompaniment of flutes and drums, whereupon he dived in, washing off the gold that was smeared on his body, while four other dignitaries threw in offerings of gold and emeralds. Why was this ceremony conducted? Perhaps for a sun god, or perhaps to satisfy the aeons-old longing of an unfaithful *caiqua* who, according to Chibcha lore, drowned herself and her love-child and who still haunts the lake's mirrored depths as a serpent.

There have been a number of attempts to recover the Chibcha treasure, none of them more than partially successful. The first was in 1545, by Jiménez de Quesada's brother, Hernán Pérez, who, by using a bucket and chain gang of Indian labourers, managed to lower the water by ten feet. He recovered 3000 pesos of gold, but rains re-filled the lagoon and he had to abandon the project. In 1585, Antonio de Sepulveda, a Bogotá merchant, carved a still visible notch into the rim of the lake. The water went down 60 feet, and apparently he recovered a fair amount of gold, but the walls of the cut collapsed, thousands of labourers were killed, and he too had to abandon the project. There were sundry other attempts throughout the centuries but the last came in 1899, following a spurious calculation that the lake still held over a billion dollars worth of gold, by a British-based comapany, Contractors Ltd. After drilling a plug hole, they drained the lake through a mercury filter. But the bed of the lake was metres thick in mud and goo, and the following day the sun baked it as hard as concrete. The lake has since filled up again with water, and is now protected as a National Park. Half a mile across and as round as a silver wheel, it still has a very special atmosphere.

GETTING THERE
Needless to say, although the lake is only 70 km from Bogotá, getting there is not easy, unless you hire a car or taxi for the day. A Flota Aguila bus runs from Carrera 15 No. 14–59 in Bogotá to Guativita Nueva, the nearest town to the lake. After turning off the main Bogotá/Tunja road, you pass through the small village of Sesquilé, and 6 km beyond the village (or 11 km before Guatavita Nueva), there is a sign by the side of the road directing you to the lake. Ask the driver to drop you off there—he will know when. From the road it is a 5-km walk up a dirt track to the lake.

247

WHERE TO STAY

You can camp, if you are discreet, by the lake. Otherwise ask around at the nearby farms, or head for substandard accommodation in Guatavita Nueva, or to a slightly better hotel in Sesquilé. Both places are cheap—around US$3 per person.

Villa de Leyva

A visit to the highlands of Colombia is not complete without a visit to Villa de Leyva, a few hours travelling outside Bogotá (see p. 250 for more information).

THE EASTERN CORDILLERA: BOYACÁ, SANTANDER AND NORTE DE SANTANDER

The three departments of Boyacá, Santander and Norte de Santander span the hilly 350-km gap between Bogotá and the Venezuelan border at Cúcuta. Topographically, they are in the fresh, hot and sweet subtropical *tierra templada*, the fortunate zone of the Andes that lies halfway between the bleaker highlands of the *tierra fria* and the humid swamps and jungles of the *tierra torrida*. Culturally, they are provincial corners—places where nothing is monumental or impressive, where nothing has yet been transferred to picture postcards. Yet every village here that is folded by hills, every nook, every nail-studded door and every adobe ranchito, speaks of a peculiar way of life and a charm that museum cities, with their over-photographed and over-admired stones, have lost. Rural, quiet, flowered by the scarlet ceiba or the brilliant yellow of the daffodil-like araguaney, and dotted with towns that more than slightly hint at the medieval, Boyacá and the Santanders represent, in many respects, the 'real' Colombia.

The region was one of the first to be settled by the Spaniards and throughout its hills they founded small, picturesque towns, such as Villa de Leyva and Barichara. During the Wars of Independence, both rebel and royalist armies marched through the region. Before the conquest, the area was the domain of the Chibcha Indians. But although the country people of the highlands are now often referred to as Indians, they are actually all *mestizos*, in whom the aboriginal strain merely runs strong. With a *runana* (a short poncho) slung over their shoulders and a squashed trilby hat perched uncertainly on their head, the most common Boyacanese types are slant-eyed, with high ruddy cheek-bones, wide mouths and flattish, rather oriental countenances. By reputation they are stolid, secretive and inclined to avoid contact with strangers. Yet more often they exhibit an exaggerated courtesy, and nearly everyone will address you as *su merced*, 'your grace' or 'your honour'.

All of the region's towns and main centres of interest lie on, or just off, the main Bogotá–Cúcuta road, and access to all of them is usually quick and easy. If you are looking for a quiet colonial village to pass a few days, visit Villa de Leyva, just outside Tunja, or Barichara, just outside Bucaramanga. If you want to go climbing, visit one of South America's least known and most spectacular mountain ranges, La Sierra Nevada de Cocuy. And if you are going onto Venezuela or the Caribbean coast from Bogotá, this region is also a good place to break your journey and spend the night.

Tunja

Most travellers that visit Boyacá usually pass straight through Tunja. At 1780 m it is higher than Bogotá and has an open, roof-of-the-world feeling. The air is as hard as diamond, and everything is sharply etched in the clear light; angular and definite. Spilling around the slopes of an open valley it has been variously described by an assortment of travellers as dirty (by Bingham), uninteresting (by Grubb) and dull, sad, cloudy and goitre-infested (by Mollien). To many the town is only notable as a marker for the turn-off to Villa de Leyva, and on a bad day, when Tunja is blurred in mist and flattened by cold and rain, the many seem right. On clear days, however, Tunja is a reminder that it was once a large Chibcha township, dedicated to worshipping the sun. A town that, in keeping with the pre-Colombian religious precedent, later became a city of imposing churches, built by the Spanish in the 16th century. These are worth seeing if you happen to stay over in town for the day.

GETTING THERE
The bus terminal is at the bottom of the hill, below the town. There are frequent buses to Bogotá (3 hours, US$3), Bucaramanga (6 hours, US$7) and every other hour to Villa de Leyva (1 hour, US$1). Outside Tunja, 15 km along the road to Bogotá, you will pass the Puente de Boyacá; an historical site that celebrates in bronze Bolívar's decisive victory against the Spanish on 7 August 1819. It is not worth getting down to see, but if travelling to Bogotá, look out for it on your left-hand side.

TOURIST INFORMATION
The **National Tourist Office** is in the Casa del Fundador, on the Plaza Bolívar. It is open Mon–Fri, 8–12 noon and 2–5. The **Banco de la República** is at Carrera 11 No. 18–12.

WHAT TO SEE
After the Wars of Independence, Tunja was almost nominated as the capital of Gran Colombia, and there is definitely something royal, powerful and medieval about its churches and historic homes. The **Casa del Fundador Suárez Rendón** was built in the 16th century by the founder of Tunja. It lies behind the tourist office and is open daily, 8–12 noon and 2–6. Look out for its ceiling frescoes that depict eclectic mythological scenes, with human figures, plants and animals. Some of Tunja's frescoes include pictures of elephants and, as South America has never been able to include elephants in its long list of naturally found fauna, it seems likely that—along with the other strange images—these were culled from the library of the scribe Juan de Vargas. His house, similar to that of the founder's and also now a museum, is on Calle 20 between Carreras 8 and 9 and is open Tues–Fri, 9–12 noon and 2–5. Entrance is 50c.

Churches
The simple, light-blue walls, delicately printed with a fleur-de-lys pattern, make the **Iglesia de Santa Bárbara** on Carrera 11 between Calles 19 and 20 the prettiest church in Tunja. The statues of the saints that line the main nave complete the church's sense of pageantry. By contrast, the **Iglesia Santo Domingo** on Carrera 11 between Calles 19 and 20, is one of Colombia's most heavily decorated churches. On the left, as you enter,

is the Rosario Chapel; constructed of wood, inlaid with silver and small mirrors, and finished in gold, it is a masterpiece of religious art. Finally, the **Iglesia y Convento de Santa Clara**, on Carrera 7 betwen Calles 19 and 20, was once the home of the mystic writer Sister Francisca Josefa, Colombia's equivalent of Saint Teresa. The convent is now maintained as a museum, and guided tours around the impressive 17th-century interior are available. Entrance to the convent is 50c; to the rest, free.

WHERE TO STAY
There is a problem with hot water in Tunja, and in many hotels it is only available in the mornings, if at all. Cheap hotels do not always provide you with enough blankets either.

If you are looking for luxury, go to the **Hunza** at Calle 21A No. 10–66; large, modern, comfortable and well-equipped, rooms are US$25/26 for a single/double. The **Hotel Don Carlos**, on Calle 11 No. 20–12, is clean, warm and friendly, and very good value at US$6/10 for a single/double—a good choice. **El Conquistadore**, a rambling colonial house just off the Plaza Bolívar at Calle 20 No. 8–92, is light and pleasant and charges US$4/6 for a single/double. Finally **Tayrona**, on Carrera 13 and Calle 19, is the cheapest in town, with rooms at US$1.50 per person.

WHERE TO EAT
There are a cluster of cafés around the town square, but for delicious food, in a restaurant that was once a colonial chapel, go to **El Bodegón de los Frailes** in the square's south-western corner.

Villa de Leyva

'*Suddenly a village emerged on a small round butte surrounded by swift streams. It seemed to me astoundingly Castilian in appearance despite its baroque church, and its slope of roofs around the plaza into which winding, narrow mule-paths debouched. The braying of an ass brought to my mind a picture of El Toboso...*'

—from *The Lost Steps*, by Alejo Carpentier

Founded in 1572 and recently declared a national monument, the mood and architecture of this small colonial town are almost completely intact. Water still dribbles out of the stone fountain and across the broken cobbles of the Plaza Mayor. Time seems to lose its importance amid the whitewashed homes draped with shrouds of orange and purple bougainvillea. Crooked wooden balconies lean out over the narrow streets. And in the high open hills around the town, red-tiled roofs pick out a counter-pattern to the fields' petit-point of greens. The only figure missing is the ghost of Don Quixote.

Villa de Leyva feels like a good place to write, and indeed it was here that Antonio Nariño first translated the *Rights of Man* in 1794. But Villa de Leyva is renowned for its supernatural atmosphere, and ever since its earliest days, the town has attracted politicians, clergymen and artists to live. Its status as an architectural gem, close to the capital, has now made it a fashionable weekend spot for Bogotános. So whilst deserted during the week, on Saturday the town hums with cars, day-trippers, and souvenir hunters. This weekend influx does not, however, detract from its special mood.

GETTING THERE
All buses stop at the terminal on the outskirts of town. There are eight buses daily to Tunja (1 hour, US$1) and four daily direct buses to Bogotá (4 hours, US$3). Collectivos assemble either in front of the bus terminal, or in the Plaza Mayor.

TOURIST INFORMATION
There is no official tourist office, but the **Café Rincón**, on the main square next to the church, sells a locally-written guide to the town. Occasionally they also stock an English version.

WHAT TO SEE
Villa de Leyva has a few sights. You could, for instance, go to the **Casa-Museo Luis Alberto Acuna**, on the main square, and see its hodge-podge displays of paintings and sculpture, executed by an artist under the influence of Chibcha mythology. Or you could visit the house of Antonio Nariño at Carrera 9 No. 10–39; or wander through the dusty corridors of the museum of religious art at the **Monasterio de las Carmelitas** on Calle 14 and Carrera 10: or, if it is a Saturday, go to the market held in the dusty plaza above town. But Villa de Leyva is not a place for flustered sightseeing, so wander instead across the immense town square, pause for a *tinto* in a café, strike up a conversation with a stranger, look in at the **Iglesia del Carmen** on the main square and listen out for the murmur of a prayer or the insistent dribble of someone's confession. And then continue your rambles through the backstreets, or up into the hills, looking out for humming birds as you stroll. The town is easily known—it only covers a small area—but it reveals itself best if you approach it gently.

FESTIVALS
There is a kite festival on 20 August.

WHERE TO STAY
All of the hotels in Villa de Leyva are converted colonial homes, but because Villa is tourist town, cheap places to stay are hard to come by.

The **Molina de Mesopotamia** is a higgledy-piggledy colonial mill set back a few hundred yards from the town. It is wonderful. All of the rooms are furnished with colonial four-poster beds, there is a very good restaurant, and up through the gardens lies a natural rock swimming-pool fed by spring water. One could go into raptures over the place and, if on a budget, it is worth splashing out on the US$14/20 charged each night for a single/double bedroom.

The **Hostería La Candelaria**, just beyond the Molina, is also good, and charges US$8 per person, including breakfast. Back in town, and just off the main square, the **Mesón de los Virreys** charges US$9/12 for a single/double.

La Roca, on the main square, is small, clean and friendly and charges US$6 for a room, whether for one or two people. The very cheapest is the basic **La Villa**, also on the main square, with beds available for US$2 per person.

WHERE TO EAT
There are a number of cafés around the main square and a good *Parilla*—for charcoal grilled meat—opposite the bus stations. But for excellent food and gracious service in colonial surroundings, go to the restaurant at the **Molina de Mesopotamia Hotel**.

AROUND VILLA DE LEYVA
Villa de Leyva is a perfect place for short excursions and/or long walks. Some can be covered on horseback—ask around the main square about the possibility of hiring a horse for the day.

El Fósil, El Infiernito and the Convento de Ecce Homo
Villa de Leyva stands on the raised floor of an ancient sea-bed. The mountains around the town abound with black ammonities and other fossils, and 5 km outside, on the road to Chiquinquíra, can be seen **El Fósil**, the complete fossil of a *Kronosaurus* dinosaur. To get there follow road signs, or ask any of the young children that sell fossils or rough emeralds along the way. Beyond El Fośil, 2 km along the same road, is the turning for the archaeological site known as **El Infiernito** (little hell), where you will find several huge stones, believed to be giant phalluses, and a solar calendar. The road continues through an eerie desert landscape, and if you were to kitty-corner for another 5 km you would eventually reach the **Convento de Ecce Homo**. Founded by the Dominican fathers in 1620, it is a large stone and adobe construction centred around a huge patio. Look out for the magnificent altar in the chapel. If you would rather ride out and then walk back, there is one early-morning bus each day to the Convent from Villa de Leyva; ask for the bus that goes to Santa Sofía.

Sanctuario de Iguaque
The Sanctuario de Iguaque is an extremely beautiful area of lake-dotted paramo, now a national park, 12 km north-east of Villa de Leyva on the road to Arcabuco. Standing at 3600 m the park has a visitors' site where you can camp, but you will need to bring your own food. The centrepiece of the park is the sacred **Laguna de Iguaque**, where, according to Chibcha belief, the creators of humanity, Bachué and her son disappeared into the waters after having turned themselves into snakes. The whole area exudes a peculiar, glowing beauty. The hike up to the lake from the visitors' centre takes one day each way, so take food, tent and warm clothing with you. To get to the park from Villa de Leyva, catch the 6 am bus to Arcabuco and get off when you see the park's sign by the roadside.

La Candelaria
Set in a desert landscape that looks as if it has been excerpted from a *sobrebarriaga* western, La Candelaria is a tiny hamlet 15 km south-west of Villa de Leyva. It is well

worth a visit if you want to feel miles away in place and time. The hamlet is famous for the **Monasterio de la Candelaria**, founded by the Augustinians in 1597 and now partly open to the public. The monastery has an incredible collection of paintings, all of which are rotting in the sun around the central courtyard, and a dusty, tome-filled library of illuminated manuscripts that conjure up prospects of medievalism and alchemy. Entry costs 50c and all visits are guided by a monk. Next door to the monastery is the lovely **Parador La Candelaria**, a more-than-tranquil colonial house where you can stay in clean and simple rooms around a flower-filled patio for US$5/8 (add another US$7 for full board). The Parador is so peaceful that loudest sound is the cough of the nun that sits by the front desk.

Unless you have the use of a car, getting to La Candelaria can be difficult. There is an irregular bus service from Villa de Leyva through the small town of Ráquira, which lies a few kilometres before the hamlet. Or you can trust to luck and try hitching. Your easist bet however is to hire a taxi or collectivo from Villa de Leyva.

The Sierra Nevada del Cocuy

If the Caribbean is a perpetual summer and Bogotá a perpetual autumn, the Sierra Nevada de Cocuy lives in a perpetual winter. This spectacular and compact range of mountains lies in the department of Boyacá, near Colombia's northern border with Venezuela. Its 15 peaks over 5000m attract mountaineers from all over Latin America, but are little known otherwise. The rock climbing is Colombia's best, but you must be experienced and well-prepared, with a full complement of mountain equipment, including crampons, if you want to do the full eight-day trek around the Sierra's peaks and high lakes (for an excellent description of the trek, see Hilary Bradt's *Backpacking in Colombia and Venezuela*). However, if you are just touring, the Sierra also provides the chance to do short one day walks up into the mountains, with accommodation in high cabins. It's a dramatically beautiful area and you will quickly expend your full mountain vocabulary walking through it: there are glaciers, glowering mists, craggy peaks, jagged horizons, snow, high passes, mountain paths walked by *campesinos* and mule trains, and clear, burnished mountain night skies.

Access to the Sierra is from two small towns—Guicán and El Cocuy, which are linked to each other by the Capitanejo road. Cocuy, at 2700 m, is a beautiful little town in its own right, but the mountains proper are a one- hour jeep ride further on. Guicán is a less picturesque village, but slightly higher at nearly 3000 m, with better access to the snowline. The best reason to go to Guicán, over El Cocuy, is that above the town there is food and accommodation to be had at Las Cabañas—a group of three cabins located at the foot of the Ritacuba peak, US$6 per person. From Las Cabañas it is a stiff three-hour walk up to the snowline—a recommended trip—or you can hire horses.

GETTING THERE
Guicán and El Cocuy share the same bus services, and there are four direct buses a day to Bogotá (12 hours, US$7). To get to the villages from Bucaramanga or Cúcuta, you must first change at Capitanejo, and from there it is a short ride to either of the villages.

WHERE TO STAY

In Guicán

There are two choices in town: the basic *hospedaje* with no name on Carrera 5 No. 3–11, that charges US$2 per person; or the better **Hotel Brisas**, nearby on Carrera 5 No. 4–57, that charges US$6 a double. Both have restaurants.

To get to **Las Cabañas**, leave Guicán by Calle 6 uphill and take the righ-hand fork at the outskirts of the village. After about an hour, you will join the road leading to Las Cabañas—follow it uphill. Las Cabañas lies about another two hours further on. If you do not want to walk, hitch, or inquire about jeeps in the town.

In El Cocuy

Cocuy's most pleasant hotel is the **Residencias Cocuy**, at Calle 7 No. 3–60, one block uphill from the town square. Clean and friendly, rooms are $3 for a double. If you are pining for hot water, however, go to the **Hotel Gutiérez** on Carrera 4 No. 7–30; rooms here are US$3.50 for a double. Both hotels have restaurants.

Bucaramanga

Bucamaranga, the capital of Santander, is a busy commercial centre of half a million inhabitants that lies on the junction of three main highways; the first from Venezuela, the second to Santa Marta, and the third south to Bogotá. Bucaramanga is a modern town that has grown at a fantastic rate and, except for a small section around the Parque García Rovira, there is almost no colonial architecture. The city has little of interest for the traveller—except perhaps for the local speciality; *hormiga culona*, a large-bottomed ant, fried and then eaten. Three hours outside town, however, lies the unspoilt colonial village of Barichara, a step back into the past (see below).

GETTING THERE

By Plane

Palonegro airport is just outside the city centre and has flights to all major cities: Bogotá (US$34), Medellín (US$30) and Cartagena (US$44).

By Bus

The Copetrán bus terminal, the place to go for all long distance journeys, is at Calle 55 No. 17B–57, and has regular daily departures to: Bogotá (10 hours, US$7), Santa Marta (US$11, 13 hours), and Cúcuta (US$5, 7 hours).

TOURIST INFORMATION

The tourist office is in the **Hotel Bucarica** on Carrera 19 and Calle 35. The **Banco de la República** is at Carrera 19 No. 34–93.

WHERE TO STAY

The **Bucarica**, on Carrera 19 and Calle 35, is very good value, and has a swimming pool, a good restaurant and spacious rooms for US$20/25 a single/double. The **Balmoral**, at

Carrera 21 and Calle 35, is clean and has rooms with private bath for US$6/8 a single/double. For a cheap night, try the **Tamana** at Carrera 18 No. 30–31; clean and friendly, rooms are US$3/4 for a single/double.

WHERE TO EAT
La Carreta, at Calle 27 No. 42–27, is excellent, famous for its meat dishes, set in beautiful surroundings, but not cheap. You can find the local speciality of fried ants at **El Maizal**, at Calle 31 No. 20–74.

Barichara

Founded in 1714, Barichara is a delightful colonial town at 1800 m, now designated as a national monument to preserve its character. The streets are paved with massive stone flags, and lined with balconied one-storey houses. There is little to see in town, although the peaceful atmosphere more than compensates. Two hours' walk north lies the picturesque hamlet of Guane. Ask to see the mummies in Guane's museum; the priest next door has the key.

GETTING THERE
The turn-off from the Cúcuta/Bogotá road is at San Gil, so change there for any one of the regular buses that go to Barichara (1hour, 50c).

WHERE TO STAY
Barichara has two simple hotels: the **Hotel Coratá**, which has spacious rooms with bath for US$3 per person, and the **Notoria**, which is clean and friendly, and run by an entertaining landlady renowned for her considerable conversational skills, also US$3 per person.

WHERE TO EAT
The **Coratá** has a restaurant, otherwise you can buy simple meals at the **Restaurante Bahí–Chala** for just over US$1.

Cúcuta

Cúcuta's wide streets and low houses are sure signs of earthquake country. Founded in 1733, the city was completely destroyed by an earthquake in 1875 and has since been rebuilt as a modern city. The climate is hot, with an average temperature of 30°C. Due to its proximity to the Venezuelan border, some of the city's 400,000 inhabitants deal in smuggling, so take care. Its location also made the city a crossroads during the Wars of Independence: after capturing Cúcuta in 1813, Bolívar set out from here to liberate Caracas and the city also entertained Colombia's first constituent congress, in 1821, which made it the visionary capital of a non-existent tropical republic as large as most of Europe.

Bolívar once said of Gran Colombia, 'Venezuela is a barracks, Colombia a university and Ecuador a convent'. The difference between Colombia and Venezuela is well outlined by local joke: A Venezuelan walking down the street drops his book without noticing. A Colombian, passing by, picks it up and hands it to him. The Venezuelan exclaims, 'My God! A Colombian that isn't a thief!'. The Colombian, ever quick, comes back with the sharp rejoinder, 'Well! It was only because I was so suprised to see a Venezuelan who might have read a book!'

Unless you are travelling to or from Venezuela, it makes little sense to come here as the city doesn't offer much to tourists. You might even prefer to make the quiet town of Pamplona, $2\frac{1}{2}$ hours away, your border-crossing base.

GETTING THERE
For information on how to cross the border, see below.

By Plane
The Camilo Daza airport 5 km outside town only serves internal destinations. There are several daily flights to Bogotá (US$39) and Cartagena (US$49). The **Avianca** office is on Avenida 5 and Calle 13.

By Bus
You must take care at the bus terminal on Avenida 7 and Calle 0—it's chaotic, badly organized and amok with crooks. Watch out for dubious money changers, ticket sellers, and security officers, and do not put your valuables into any bus company's 'security box'. There are regular buses to Bogotá (16 hours, US$13), Bucaramanga—change here for coastal buses (6 hours, US$5), and Pamplona (5 hours, US$4).

TOURIST INFORMATION
The **Tourist Office** is at Calle 10 No. 0–30. The **Banco de La República** is at Calle 11 No. 5–05.

Visas and Exit Stamps
The **Venezuelan Consulate** is on Calle 8 and Avenida 0, and is open Mon–Fri, 8–2. The **DAS** office is at Calle 17 No. 2–60 and is open 8–12 noon. pt weekends, you can get a DAS stamp (necessary for all entries and exits to and from Colombia) at the **Oficina de Imigración** at the airport, 5 km from the centre.

WHERE TO STAY
Cúcuta's best hotel is the **Tonchalá** on Calle 10 and Avenida B. It has a good restaurant, swimming pool and air-conditioning. Rooms begins at US$28/35 for a single/double. A good, inexpensive hotel with a swimming pool is the **Casa Blanca** on the main square; rooms cost US$12/20 for a single/double. The **Louis** on Calle 13 and Avenida 6 is small, but pleasant and friendly and has rooms for US$6/7 for a single/double. **La Bastilla**, at Avenida 3 No. 9–42, is the best of the cheapies, with simple rooms for US$3/4.

WHERE TO EAT
Bahí, just off the main square is good. Otherwise go to the Hotel restaurants; the restaurant at the **Hotel Cinera** on Avenida 4 No. 10–53 is reasonably priced.

256

On to Venezuela

From Cúcuta, take a taxi or a bus to San Antonio, the Venezuelan border town. Because the border itself has no immigration services, passports must first be stamped for exit at the DAS office in Cúcuta (see above). To enter Venezuela, you must also have a visa, obtainable from the consulate, also in Cúcuta. Upon entering Venezuela, passports are stamped at the immigration office in San Antonio, and from San Antonio Expresso Occidente buses leave twice daily for Caracas—a 14 hour journey.

This rigmarole can all be done in half a day if you hire a taxi. Cúcuta's taxi drivers are well experienced in shuttling around town between offices and borders, and paying one to do it all for you may in the long run save you money, and certainly time.

Pamplona

Two hours away from Cúcuta, Pamplona is a pretty, quiet, colonial highland town that you might prefer to make your border base over Cúcuta. Founded in 1549, the town is pleasantly set in the Valle del Espíritu Santo and is ringed by deeply banked hills. The town is famous for its university, and the population is mostly young and friendly. Most of the students come up from the coast because, as they say, the chill mountain air helps them to concentrate better, and besides, there is less *rhumba*.

GETTING THERE
There are several daily buses from the town square to Cúcuta (2 hours, $1.50) and Bucaramanga (5 hours, US$3). Faster collectivos are also available (US$3, 1 hour).

WHERE TO STAY
The best in town is the **Cariongo**, on Carrera 5 and Calle 9, with rooms at around US$14/18 for a single/double. The **Imperial**, on the main square, is a good choice and has clean rooms with private bath and hot water for only US$4/7. The **Orsua**, also on the main square, is simple and charges US$2 per person.

WHERE TO EAT
There are a number of inexpensive but pretty restaurants on the main square; **El Sifón** is one of the best, still cheap: a steak and chips will only set you back a couple of dollars.

THE CENTRAL CORDILLERA: MEDELLÍN, SANTA FÉ DE ANTIOQUÍA AND MANIZALES

There must be something energizing in the soil and the spring-like air between the Western and Central Cordilleras. Even the area's aboriginal Indians were brisk and warlike. The reliable chronicler Cieza de León wrote in the 16th century: 'Had the natives been more gentle, and of a good disposition, and not so bloody as to eat one

THE SIERRA :
CENTRAL AND
EASTERN CORDILLERAS

0   50   100 km   N

0   50 miles

NORTE DE
SANTANDER   Cúcuta
                    San
                    Antonio

VENEZUELA

Pamplona

Bucaramanga

Río Cauca

Río Magdalena

ANTIOQUIA

Santa Fé
de Antioquia

Medellín

Guane

SANTANDER   Barichara
                    San Gil

Capitanejo
              Guican

El Cocuy

Sierra Nevada
del Cocuy

BOYACA

Central Cordillera

Eastern Cordillera

CALDAS

Manizales

Nevada del Ruiz

Villa de Leyva

Túnja

CUNDINAMARCA

BOGOTÁ

another, and our Captains and Generals more compassionate so as not to consume them, the land therabout would have yielded much wealth.' De León was prescient; the land has yielded much wealth. Antioquía is the province that has supplied the world with the two great Colombian motifs of coffee and cocaine.

Flanked by the Atrato and Magdalena Rivers, and lying—culturally—between the exuberance of the Caribbean and the sadness of the Andes, the department of Antioquía retains something of a country-within-a-country atmosphere. It is not only the terrain that conspires to set it apart. The region was settled by *criollos* with a pioneer spirit comparable to the North American 'Conquest of the West'; neither Indians nor African slaves were used. And although it had little involvement with the country's fight for independence, Antioquía was among the first to set itself up as a sovereign state during the short-lived Granadine Confederation that followed, and was among the last to finally join the National Union in 1821.

It is Colombia's whitest department, with little of the creole or *mestizo* bloods so characteristic of the rest of the country. The local Spanish is distinct, en-un-ci-ated with an almost painful deliberation. And the attitude of the straw-hatted, white-shirted Antioqueñan *campesinos* (a particular type, called *paisas*), is almost northern in latitude. They are traditionally independent, shrewd and forward-looking businessmen. They are renowned for being loquacious, sociable, pushy, vigorous, and also bad drunks. They are proud of their differences, and willing to work hard to prove it. Their department's plantation-covered valleys and hills form steep green waves, coloured by the dark leaves of coffee bushes. In the first half of the 20th century it was Antioqueñan coffee wealth that provided the economic impetus for the diversification of Colombia's other industries. In short, the local—and recent—rise of the cocaine business is quite consistent with the *paisas'* long tradition of successful entrepreneurship.

Medellín

The climate is sunny and spring-like, with temperatures so well-adjusted that the atmosphere feels air-conditioned. But Medellín is no *zona rosa*. Colombia's second largest industrial city is a Lego town of red brick houses and cigarette-lighter skycrapers, set in a rolling Andean valley, 1500 m above sea-level. '*Hecho en Medellín*', Made in Medellín, is almost a Colombian by-word, and the city produces three quarters of the country's textiles; has steel mills, chemical plants, cement factories and machine shops; paint, food, cigarette and liquor factories, all grafted onto a deep-rooted coffee, cattle and land wealth. The city is brash and uncomplicated. By day its two million inhabitants move with a bright sense of purpose and industry through the narrow downtown streets around the city centre, El Parque Bolívar. And the city's origins—as a 17th-century settlement for refugee Spanish Jews—are now long lost among office blocks, modern churches, well-laid out parks, busy streets and brightly lit cafeterias.

Night time, however, is another story. It is only after 7 that you fully realize that whilst Medellín has always been a money centre, this no more true than now; as a laundromat for dirty narco-dollars. There is no curfew, but few venture out after dusk. The mood is palpably sombre, lanced by strong winces of paranoia. The highest cause of death among young males here is murder. And you come to understand that underneath its modern surface, Medellín has become, in many ways, a medieval city. The wealthy live in guarded fortresses and hire private armies for protection. The universities are cloisters; the slums are ruled by bands of assassins; citizens pay tribute to the drug lords who control the city like kings.

Medellín is home to the world's largest cocaine cartel, headed by Pablo Escobar, reckoned by Forbes Magazine to be the 14th richest man in the world. While living in El Poblado district with the other traffickers, Escobar was locally regarded by many of the poor as a latter-day Robin Hood; the much publicized Barrio Pablo Escobar, a development of 500 houses for Medellín's poor, stands testament to his charity. He has been a veritable one-man municipal economy: he employed legions of mechanics, drivers and bodyguards; hired lawyers to keep him out of jail, architects to build luxury homes, accountants to track his money, and financial advisors to invest it. According to one estimate, if the spin-offs from the cocaine industry were to leave Medellín, the unemployment rate would double—to 25 per cent. No wonder then that Escobar has enjoyed wide-ranging popular support in Medellín, a support engendered either through money or, more often, through fear.

Medellín, of course, is not a tourist stop. But while this may sound absurd, it is very unlikely that anything maladroit will happen to you—as long as you avoid the slums, and the pimping and whoring central district late at night. The city is not rich with reasons to linger, but you could use it as a jumping-off point for the remote Pacific coast. And 80 km outside the city lies the markedly quieter, less tense, and very picturesque village of Santa Fé de Antioquía (see p. 263).

GETTING THERE

By Air
The **José María Córdoba Airport** lies 30 km south-east of Medellín, a US$10 taxi drive away. Otherwise, catch a shuttle from Carrera 50A and Calle 53, or from the bus terminal (40 minutes, US$1).

Medellín is the best point for flying to the Pacific and there are several daily flights with Aces to Quibdó (US$17); three flights a week to Capurganá (US$34); and Bahía Solano (US$30). There are also regular flights to all other major destinations throughout Colombia: Bogotá (US$27); Cali (US$30); Cartagena (US$35); and San Andrés (US$65).

The **Avianca** office is at Carrera 52 No. 51A–01, and the **ACES** office is on the corner of Carrera 47 and Calle 57.

By Bus
All buses leave and depart from the modern bus terminal at Autopista Norte and Calle 78, a 15-minute drive from the city centre. There are regular buses to Bogotá (10 hours, US$9); Cartagena (16 hours, US$15); Cali (9 hours, US$10); Manizales (6 hours, US$5); Turbo (14 hours, US$7); Quibdó (10 hours, US$5); and Santa Fé de Antioquía (2 hours, US$2).

By Rail
To journey into the heart of the Medio Magdalena there is a daily train to Barrancabermeja from the railway station next to the bus terminal. The journey takes up to 14 hours and costs US$4.

TOURIST INFORMATION
La Oficina de Turismo y Fomento, at Calle 57 No. 45–129, is obliging, has lots of information, and good maps. Look out for *El Expresso*, a free monthly booklet with information about what is on in town. Four blocks away, at Carrera 48 No. 58–11, **Turantioquía** has good information on the region, and you should head here if you want to look around the department. Occasionally they organize trips to some of Antioquía's less accessible regions, such as Los Katios National Park. Both offices are open Mon–Fri, 9–11 and 3–5.30.

The **Banco de la República** is in the Parque Berrío.

WHAT TO SEE
Medellín looks best from above, when the details are blurred, and for a panoramic view of the city, take a taxi to **El Cerro Nutibarra**—a park that lies on top of one of the many

hills that break up through Medellín's mesh of streets. There is a very pretty reconstruction of a colonial village on top, a reasonably-priced balconied restaurant that looks over the valley, and the hill is also dotted with geometric sculptures, of mixed quality, used as kissing seats by view-struck Antioqueñan lovers.

Museums and Churches

Medellín has all the attractions of any major modern city: cinemas, zoos, parks and a representative collection of art galleries and museums. But only the churches retain any sense of the city's past. The rather dour **Basílica Metropolitana** in Parque Bolívar is a huge 19th-century Romanesque structure—allegedly the biggest in South America and the seventh largest in the world. In Parque Barrío, surrounded by office-blocks and downtown hotels, **La Basílica Candelaria** displays a gentler touch. But only the late 18th-century baroque interior of **La Ermita de Veracruz** on Calle 51 and Carrera 52 shows the full hallucinogenic force of colonial Catholicism.

Next door to La Ermita, **El Museo Nacional de Antioquía**—open Tues–Fri, 9.30–2 (entrance 50c)—has a good collection of paintings and sculptures by Colombia's most famous artist, Fernando Botero. His ironic volumes and whimsically bloated portraits have won him worldwide acclaim, and the pneumatic bronze torso outside El Banco de La República is another of his pieces. The museum also has a collection of 18th-century Republican oils, temporary exhibits of other Antioquean artists, and a small cinema club that shows off-beat films. The **Museo Etnográfico Miguel Angel Builes** at Carrera 81 No. 52B-120, is open Mon–Fri, 8–12 noon and 2–5, and has a large and worthwhile collection of ethnographic artefacts from around the country. Entrance is free.

Medellín does not quite live up to its reputation as the 'City of Flowers', but the **Jardín Botánico Joaquín Uribe** at Carrera 52 No. 73–298, has a large collection of orchids, in season from April to May, and is a pleasant place to spend the afternoon. Open from 9–5.30 daily, entrance is US$1.

SHOPPING

Shopping is easy in Medellín. Several of the downtown roads around the Parque Bolívar have been closed to traffic and converted into shopping malls, with shops and boutiques selling various goods of very high quality and price. The town also has a number of shopping centres—the largest being **Almacentro**. There is a huge daily market in the Plaza Minorista José María Villa, inaugurated in 1984 to remove hawking vendors from the city's streets. And at the popular flea-market held in El Parque Bolívar on the first Saturday of every month, you can buy *ruanas*, *carriels* (a distinctive, low-slung leather satchel worn by *antioqueños*), rare coins, Indian artefacts, Colombian bric-a-brac, and even exotic pets from the high Andes.

ENTERTAINMENT AND NIGHTLIFE

El Parque Bolívar is flanked by restaurants (both the good and the bad), west-end style cinemas (with a strictly 'Rambo' diet of films on offer), and louche bars. A busy meeting place in the day, it is deserted at night. Instead, most of Medellín's nightlife is concentrated in the rich district of El Poblado. Carrera 70, between Calles 44 and 40, used to be a pleasant place to stroll on Fridays, when amateur bands, open-air grills and up-market weekend revellers would convert the street into a colourful strip. There was once also a cluster of high-life discotheques perched above the city on the hill-road, Variente de las Palmas, but, owned by Mafiosi, they have all since been closed down. Medellín no longer has much of a nightlife as people now generally prefer to stay at home in the evenings. Otherwise, the daily regional newspapers, such as *El Colombiano* or *El Mundo*, carry listings of city events, theatres and cinemas.

FESTIVALS
The *Antioqueños* still haven't recovered from the death of the world's greatest tango singer, Carlos Gardel, who died in an aeroplane crash outside Medellín in 1935. Ever afraid of flying, he was persuaded by friends to make a musical tour of South America, by plane, *just this once*. The **Festival del Tango** in June commemorates his first and last flight, and everybody dances.

During the **Desfile de Silleteros** in August—Antioquía's largest annual event— hundreds of *campesinos* come down from the mountains bent double under the tremendous weight of their baskets filled with orchids, carnations, roses, golden rains and other flowers, and there are parades through the streets with floats, bands, singers and cavorting horsemen.

Unfortunately, the same caveats apply to Medellín's festivals as they do to Medellín's nightlife.

WHERE TO STAY
All of Medellín's hotels—the good, the bad and the indifferent—are in the noisy city centre, within a few blocks of each other, but conveniently located near to Medellín's banks, tourist agencies, post-offices, and airline offices.

Expensive
The only exception to the downtown rule is the **Intercontinental**, tel 266 0680, which stands high above the city, far from the centre, on Variente de las Palmas. Rooms are deluxe and cost a standard Intercontinental price—about US$40/60 for a single/double. Back in the city centre, the **Hotel Nutibara**, at Calle 52 No. 53–43, has a whole city block to itself and somehow manages to preserve an unlikely sense of repose despite the downtown bustle. Its 328 rooms have tiled bathrooms and antique furntiure, and there is a gym and turkish bath for the use of residents. Rooms cost US$25/35 for a single/double.

Moderate
The **Hotel Eupacla**, at Carrera 50 No. 53–16, and the **Hotel Normandie**, just around the corner at Calle 53 No. 49–96, are both clean, large and quite soulless, but good choices if you have just arrived in Medellín and are looking for a secure berth. Rooms are comfortable and cost US$13/21 for a single/double in both hotels. Slightly cheaper, the **Hotel Cannes**, at Carrera 50 No. 56–17, has small rooms, but the management is friendly and the hotel is quiet. Rooms cost US$12/15 for a single/double.

Inexpensive
Cheap hotels, at around US$4/8 a night for a single/double, include: the homey **Hotel Tropical**, at Calle 56 No. 49–105; the very good but usually fully-booked **Hostal**

Cumanday at Calle 54 No. 54–48, with silent rooms over looking a central atrium; and the **Hotel California**—the cheapest of the lot—at Carrera 54 No. 48–53.

WHERE TO EAT
Many of Medellín's good restaurants are around the city centre. **La Posada de la Montaña**, at Calle 53 No. 47–44, serves typicaly beefy Antioquenan food—designed to keep you going—for about US$8 a head. **Donizettis**, at Calle 54 No. 43–102, serves home-cooked Italian food, and **Chung Wah**, at Calle 54 No. 43–75, has a light Chinese menu at about the same price. Although miles from the sea, Medellín is also blessed with an excellent seafood restaurant, **Frutas del Mar**, at Carrera 43B No. 11–59; a meal here will cost you about US$10 per head.

Medellín's plushest restaurants are scattered along the Variente de las Palmas. You could head for the cavernous room at **Acuarius**, and try the rich starter of palm hearts and shrimps in cheese sauce. This can always be danced off in the deserted night-club next door that has walls lined with aquaria of piranha fish.

For cheap eats, try the fluorescent lit **Estancia** on Parque Bolívar. It's a self-service place, but grumpy waitresses clear the tin-topped tables and there is a constant buzz of exclamations and laughter from the local life gathered in wrinkled suits and sweat-rimmed hats around the crowded bar. A *corriente* of chicken, fish or meat costs 75c and you pay for what you get.

Santa Fé de Antioquía

Santa Fé de Antioquía lies 80 km north-west of Medellín. Founded in 1541 by Spanish gold miners, it was the capital of Antioquía province until 1826, when Medellín assumed the coveted position. The city's peaceful colonial atmosphere survives, along with its cobbled streets, balconied houses, and fine churches. Ringed by low hills, it is a noticably quieter place than Medellín. As the 9000 Santaferenos might say, 'Life here is *sano*'.

GETTING THERE
The road from Medellín to Santa Fé whirls, loops, and spirals through dramatic Antioqueñan countryside, providing splendid opportunities for characteristic Colombian driving, so very adept at tricky manoeuvres such as overtaking. There are ten buses a day to Medellín (2 hours, US$2).

WHAT TO SEE
The town is very small, so a short walk quickly familiarizes. The early 19th-century **Cathedral** faces onto the central town square, and its smooth and cool interior is so carefully inlaid with gold and light-blue tracery that it looks like Wedgwood china. The 18th-century Jesuit church of **Santa Bárbara**, one block away on Calle 11 and Carrera 8, is more dramatic, its interior a baroque accumulation of architectural arabesques. Two blocks down the street, on the corner of Calle 11 and Carrera 10, the **Museo Colonial Juan del Corral**, houses a hodge-podge of colonial souvenirs (such as the

table on which the independence of Antioquía was signed in 1813) and pre-Colombian artefacts. Open everyday, 10–5, entrance 10c.

WHERE TO STAY
The **Mariscal Robledo**, at Carrera 12 No. 9–70, is an old colonial house, now a comfortable hotel with swimming pool and good restaurant. Rooms are US$10/13 for a single/double. There is little in the way of mid-range accommodation in Santa Fé, but **Hospedaje Franco**, just off the main square on Carrera 10, is quiet and clean and has pleasant rooms, with private bath, for US$3 per person.

WHERE TO EAT
There are some small cafés on the main square, but your best bet for a filling and cheap corriente is at the mournfully named **La Última Lágrima**, The Last Tear, so-called because it is a last chance place, on the outskirts of town between the hospital and the graveyard. It serves good food for only US$2 per head and has no sign, but is easy to find: follow Carrera 3 out of town and it lies just past the hospital. Otherwise, the restaurant at the **Hotel Mariscal Robledo** is the best in town.

Manizales

Manizales's skyline is dominated by the snow-capped Nevado del Ruiz, the volcano that made world headlines in November 1985 when it erupted and buried the nearby town of Armero under a slurry of mud. Manizales was also damaged, although not as severely, and the volcano is still very much active.

Founded in 1848, this town of half a million people lies 250 km south of Medellín. It is the trading nub of the *Zona Cafetera*, the coffee-producing zone. As it is built along a knife-edged ridge, 2100 m high, the only way it can extend is in length, and it stretches for several miles, slipping off the backbone of the mountain a little on either side. Manizales is a modern, busy but pleasant town, usually covered in a pearly and bulbous haze of cloud; the perfect climate for growing coffee—cool but also very humid. The only reasons that you are likely to come here are for the international theatre festival in December, for the coffee carnival in January, or as a break in the journey south to Cali from Medellín.

GETTING THERE
By Plane
La Nubia airport is a few kilometres east of town and the airline ACES has good daily connections to Bogotá (US$22) and Medellín (US$18). The **ACES** office is at Calle 24 No. 21–34.

By Bus
The bus companies are all clustered between Carreras 18 and 20 and Calles 19 and 23. There are buses every two hours to Bogotá (8 hours, US$6); Medellín (8 hours, US$6); and Cali (6 hours, US$6).

TOURIST INFORMATION
The **Tourist Office** in the Plaza Bolívar, opposite the cathedral, is well-organized and open Mon–Fri, 8–12 noon and 2–6. The **Banco de la República** is at Carrera 23 No. 23–06.

WHAT TO SEE
Manizales is slim on sights, but it does have one or two museums. **The Gold Museum**, at the Banco de la República, has a small collection of Quimbaya goldwork, and is open Mon–Fri, 8–12 noon and 2–7. Entrance is free. The **Anthropology Museum**, which is only open in the afternoon, has an interesting collection of Quimbaya and Calima ceramics and an excellent view of the fuming Nevado de Ruiz. However Manizales's most famous museum must be the modern cinema-theatre auditorium, **El Teatro de los Fundadores**, which supposedly has the largest stage in the whole of Latin America.

WHERE TO STAY
The three star **Hotel Las Colinas** at Carrera 22 No. 20–20 has three bars, a good restaurant and comfortable rooms for US$20/25 for a single/double. The **Hotel Embajador**, on the Avenida Centenario, has good rooms for US$15/18 for a single/double. And the **Pensión Margarita No. 2**, at Calle 17 No. 22–14, is quiet and pleasant, and has clean rooms with private bath for US$5/7 for a single/double.

WHERE TO EAT
Vitani, on Calle 26 between Carreras 23 and 24, is quite smart, serves Italian food and has a good wine list; try the crab claws, *muellas de cangrejo*. **Los Sauces**, on the Avenida Centenario, overlooking the valley, is good and has an extensive fish menu for about US$7 per head. Otherwise there is a long strip of cafés, small restaurants and fast-food eateries along Carrera 23.

THE SOUTHERN CORDILLERA: SAN AGUSTÍN, TIERRADENTRO AND POPAYÁN

The Andes can be something of a mystery. Marching firmly thousands of kilometres north from Tierra del Fuego, it is the world's longest unbroken chain of mountains. In Ecuador it looks unflinching. But in Colombia it breaks into three cordilleras at a tight knot of land, some 200 km south of Bogotá, and its movements suddenly become more uncertain. Some valleys are wide and lush, others closed and parched; some mountains are covered in snow, while others, just as high, are green with pasture. The vagaries of the Andes in Colombia are mysterious, but should come as no surprise. Colombia, after all, tends to bend rather than obey rules, and it is usually easier to enjoy these variations than to ask for any explanations.

The terrain of Colombia's Southern Cordillera makes many areas isolated and

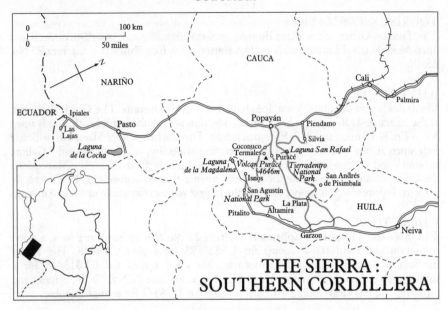

The Southern Cordillera

difficult to reach. In the past, this inaccessibility has been exploited by guerrilla fighters, specifically the M-19. Although the M-19 have since laid down their arms, the army are still deployed in great numbers here and road blocks and searches are common. Just be patient and obey the soldier's instructions. One trick that you should also be aware of is the *burundanga*-laced cigarette, cake, drink or sweet. *Burundanga* is a powerful, naturally-found barbiturate that has been used to knock-out and rob travellers, especially on long road journeys. One only ever hears stories, or stories of stories, but still, it pays to know the worst.

The largest group of Indians in this area are the Páez, who live around San Agustín. Numbering about 40,000, they are a member of the Chibcha linguistic family. A less acculturated group, the Guambianos, live a little further south, nearer Popayán. In fact, the further south that you travel, the more Indian the country becomes. Southern Colombia was settled by Pizarro's lieutenant Benalcázar as he quested north from Quito in search of Colombia's El Dorado, southern Colombia still, culturally, looks to Ecuador, rather than to Bogotá. Pasto, up against the Colombian border, also represents the most far-flung northern limit of the Inca empire, and although there are no Incan remains this is apparent in the people and their attitudes. Faces are more saturnine, less open; there is more Indian blood and less Spanish in the *mestizo* mix; and the *pastusos*—as the butt of national jokes—are perceived as kind, but rather dim.

The Southern Cordillera offers two of the most important archaeological finds in the Americas: the statues at San Agustín and the tombs at Tierradentro. Its other attractions include the Indian market at Silvia; hiking through high-altitude tropical forests in Puracé National Park; and 'La Joya Blanca', Colombia's white gem of colonial

266

architecture, at Popayán. Despite the above warnings the Southern Cordillera is also one of the most peaceful and tranquil areas in Colombia. And if you have just come north from Ecuador, this part of the country will confound any dreaded expectations that you may have once held of the country.

San Agustín

San Agustín is one of the most remarkable archaeological sites in the Americas; it's a place of magic that makes the idea of pixies seem possible.

First there is the the land, which is interior, hidden, and mountainous. Every road must ride, dodge or skirt its hills, high escarpments, precipitous gorges and cascading rivers. Then there are the Agustín statues. Comparable to the lonely and mysterious stone figures that look-out across the Pacific from Easter Island, they stand in this grand landscape, as if placed by nature rather than by design, their scattered forms as varied as those of the flowering trees, plants and shrubs that surround them. Somehow the tourism which the monuments attract have affected the local people very little, if at all, and even the police at the road checkpoints are ready to laugh. The weather is perfect—hot in the sun, cool in the shade. And you could easily spend a week touring the area, on horseback, or foot, or in a hired jeep. If you are rushing, however, three days would be enough.

History

Prehistory: 800 BC–AD 1600
The archaeological history of San Agustín is still virgin territory. Researchers know that people lived here for at least 2500 years—which pre-dates the ancient civilizations of Mexico and Peru—but at least twice during that time there were sudden and complete

Pre-Columbian grave, San Agustín

changes of population. There is no historical continuity in San Agustín and its history remains a blank.

The first change of population came around AD 50, when a new group drove out or subjugated the essentially primitive, hill-top dwellers who had previously been in the region. This first wave of invaders brought new systems of farming, of building villages, of road construction and also, probably, of religion. It is not known whether these people were the first San Agustín sculptors, but the general speculation is that the finest work was done during this time. Their tenure, however, was short. It seems that, for some reason, they left in the 5th century, and nobody else came to live in the region for at least 700 years. Around 1400, another large group, possibly the Andakí, travelled up from the Amazon basin, and re-settled the area. Again, these people could have been artists, but all trace of them had disappeared by about 1600.

Three different ecosystems meet at San Agustín—the Andean, the temperate and the tropical. That such a propitious region would have attracted early farmers and traders, is clear. It is known that the San Agustinians—whoever they may have been—cultivated corn, yucca and peanuts, that they gathered wild fruits and vegetables, and that they fished and hunted the surrounding rivers and hills. But any more details are scarce. Archaeologists can still only scratch their heads and scan the horizon, hoping for meaning. What did this land mean to its ancient inhabitants? And what were the origins of the statues whose stony faces stare out over the mountains, like so many guardians of a shrine? The story of how the site was discovered, only adds to the mystery.

Discovery: 1750–97

The Spanish chronicles of the 17th century talk about the area around the village of San Agustín in some detail. They speak of the settlement of the land, of the fertile soils and valuable minerals to be found, of building roads and a chapel, and of other administrative details. But, strangely enough, not one mention is made of the sculptures. What had happened to them? Had they been buried and hidden? Or did the Spaniards, with more important matters at hand, simply ignore them? Perhaps there are some as yet undiscovered sheets, yellowing in the archives of a Colombian convent, which hold the very first eyewitness account of San Agustín's sculptures. It seems possible: the earliest record of the site was found only recently, in the public library of Palma de Mallorca, in Spain. The strange story that the crisp but faded parchments told, runs as follows.

In 1758 a lone Franciscan priest, Friar Juan de Santa Gertrudis, whose Amazon mission was facing many difficulties, decided to cross the Eastern Cordillera and travel to Santa Fé in order to apppeal to the Spanish Viceroy for help. Accompanied by a few missionized Andakí Indians, the friar ascended the eastern flanks of the Andes and reached the headwaters of the Magdalena river at San Agustín, then only 'a village of no more than five miserable huts'. There were few people to welcome the traveller, but among them there happened to be another cleric from Popayán who had established a small mission at San Agustín. The reason for his mission was to become clear during the hearty meal that the cleric cheerfully offered to the tired Friar.

Over coffee, the cleric confided to Friar Juan that he was an inveterate treasure hunter, and that, with Indian help, he had been digging for buried gold amongst the ruins and monuments he had found scattered in the vicinity of the village. He continued to speak at length about the strange burial sites, and revealed that while his men had already dug out 19 tombs, they had so far only found one golden earring. His grave-robbing had not as yet proved very successful.

Friar Juan listened in amazement. And the next morning, while his Indian escorts were still asleep after a night of merrymaking, he set out to see for himself. He was troubled by what he saw:

> 'There are three bishops... all of stone... with their mitres. They are dressed in their rochets which are fringed with lace, well-worked and beautiful. Only one has arms, but one can see that the left held a bishop's crozier while with the right he was giving his blessing... From there I went to see another monument... They were five Franciscan Friars of the Observant Order shown from the knees up, carved of the same stone as the bishops. Two stand with hands folded and hidden in their sleeves... two others are shown as if preaching... the fifth wears a hood over his head and the hair in front is so finely worked that it looks quite real.'

There was no doubt in his mind that the statues represented Franciscan friars and mitred bishops in pontifical garb. This was immensely worrying. As the images were doubtlessly older than the Order of Saint Francis, Friar Juan reasoned that they could only have been made by the Devil. In his notebook he wrote, 'I believe that the Devil made these statues and said to the Indians: men like these, dressed in this manner, shall rule over this land.' The Devil had already done his work in God's new country, warning the infidels that Christ's ministers would soon be coming. Friar Juan—and others of his calling—was too late!

Subsequent Archaeological Research: 1797–Present

After Friar Juan came others, and with them the discovery that there were many types of stone images besides those described by the naive missionary. In 1797, Francisco José de Caldas (Colombia's scientist-martyr from the Wars of Independence) called public attention to the prehistoric monuments that he found around San Agustín. In the manner of a typical 18th century savant, he wrote:

> 'San Agustín is inhabited by few Indian families, and in its surroundings one finds traces of an artistic and industrious nation that has ceased to exist. Statues, columns, temples, altars and an outsized image of the Sun show us the character and strength of a great people who lived on the headwaters of the Magdalena River. But our historians have not transmitted to us the slightest notice of the works of art of this sedentary nation.'

Caldas closed with the recommendation, 'It would be very interesting to record and describe all the monuments found and scattered in the vicinity of San Agustín'. But the hidden valleys of San Agustín remained largely unexplored. All occasional travellers or explorers who visited the region in the 18th and 19th centuries spoke of the dense forest that covered the prehistoric monuments, of the torrential rainfalls that eroded the mountain trails, and of the difficulties they experienced crossing the rivers—there were no bridges, only wobbly poles. Penetrating into the forest at that time was an adventure that only a few treasure hunters or hardy naturalists were prepared to undertake, and so it was that San Agustín remained shrouded in legend. Even as late as 1911, the German archaeologist Pruess wrote, 'One feels lost here, as if on a dead-end street. Perhaps this is due to the oblivion in which the antiquities of the region have remained.'

Pruess did, however, bring about a rise of interest in San Agustín. The Spanish version of his scholarly and well-illustrated two-volume work, first published in 1929, prompted the local authorities into action, and in 1953 the Colombian government put the area under protection and established the first 'Archaeological Park'. Other researchers and scientists soon followed.

Until very recently, however, all archaeological work at San Agustín was dogged by a limiting bias: a fascination with statues and tombs. The task of archaeology in this Colombian massif was seen as one of pondering death instead of re-creating life. It was exclusively described as a necropolis, with the emphasis on stone carvings and burial practices obscuring all other aspects of the place. Even today little has been done to establish a timescale for the area's successive phases of development, and little is known about the aboriginal Indian's way of life and how it must have changed with each invasion. This work is still to be done. It has only recently begun, and the clues are slim; just faint signals beaming dimly from the past.

GETTING THERE
To get to the park, head for the small village of San Agustín. Tourist activities are all centered around the village (see p. 273).

WHAT TO SEE
The first thing to do is look at the landscape, especially just before sunset. During the day the hills and fields seem to follow each other in monotonous succession, but under the oblique rays of a setting sun, a play of shadows begins and the land begins to take another

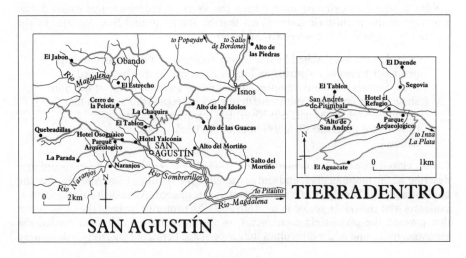

shape. Faint lines begins to cross the fields, distant shadows outline plots and patches, and here and there you can discern boundary lines, ridges, and sudden changes of colour. You suddenly realize that this is the ancient landscape coming to life. As the distinguished Colombian anthropologist and archaeologist Reichel-Dolmatoff once wrote:

> 'Our visual memory is sometimes overburdened, perhaps deformed, by
> the many illustrations of architectural features and monuments we have
> looked at so often... We often lose sight of the wider context of the land
> within which these objects were created, and it becomes necessary to
> look at the landscape afresh, as if for the first time, because the land, too,
> is a cultural object that has been moulded and transformed into what
> those ancient peoples called their home.'

Much of the land around San Agustín has only been cleared as recently as the 1950s, and vegetation still quickly reclaims any untended plots. The torn landscape still isolates and limits neighbours, as it must have done in pre-Colombian times. There are no plains or valley bottoms from which a growing village might have spread over the countryside, no centre from which a civilization could have confidently come to encompass surrounding groups. And the constant flux of stability and change in earlier centuries would have made, through time, one region more prominent over another, and one area more permanently occupied, or perhaps more easily abandoned.

All of this helps explain why San Agustín is so dispersed and mysterious. It is not a coherent archaeological site but, rather, a large cluster of many individual sites, each with its own characteristics and history. Over 40 sites have so far been found, scattered over an area of at least 500 sq km, and it takes at least a few days to see the most important of them. Local farmers, whilst tilling the soil or hunting, continue to find archaeological remains and they often know more about the whereabouts of sites than professional archaeologists.

Agustín Sculpture

It is impossible to find a consistent stylistic thread to Agustín sculpture. It is as if a thousand imaginations have been at work with no conventions to hamper them. Some of the sculptures are squat, others at least three metres high. Some have big, round eyes, others just narrow slits, or curved lids with heavy bags. Many have clenched teeth, with exaggerated eyeteeth like Dracula, but just as many others have open circles for mouths. Nearly all of the figures look straight ahead and have smooth backs with only the fronts carved, but there are always exceptions to any rule.

Religious significance can be attached to many of the sculptures. The eagle, for example, was a symbol of power and light, while the serpent was one of rain. Frogs, lizards and salamanders testify to long-gone water ceremonies, and one repeated theme is of a man with another on his back, like a male equivalent of an incubus. This might have represented a duality of character—with the lower figure man's ego, and the smaller carried figure man's spirit—or it may merely have been a representation of a person in a mask. Then there are figures of jaguars, a religious symbol important throughout the Americas. The presence of a jaguar cult in San Agustín reinforces the

271

idea that San Agustín is not in fact an isolated phenomenon, but instead a part of the wide substratum of Indian belief that stretches from Mexico to Bolivia. It may be that San Agustín's sculptures represent the work of several different civilizations, but it is perhaps just as profitable to think that they were the continuous product of a liberated people, free to do and imagine as they pleased.

Seeing the Sites

Attractions in the San Agustín area, such as the archaeological park, are best toured on foot. The sites cover a wide area and places further out are reached by jeep or on horseback. Don't let yourself be rushed; touring madly around the sites in just one day by jeep is like bumping around in a tin box. It is best to go slowly, taking in one site at a time. The tariff for jeep rentals is fixed, depending on where you want to go, and the price list can be obtained at the tourist office. The rate for hiring horses works out at about US$2 per hour; you must pay for the guide's horse and also tip him the equivalent of the cost of hiring a horse for the trip that you have made.

The Archaeological Park

The most important site is the Archaeological Park, where most of the graves and statues are found. Open daily from 8–6, it lies about 3 km outside town and a thorough visit takes about three hours. The park is threaded with well-signed paths. Entrance is 50c.

The park's archaeological finds are grouped in four *mesitas*, or tables, labelled A, B, C and D. These are mounds that the Agustíns raised over the graves of the most eminent members of the community, and on them stand sarcophagi and statues that once served as grave markers. **Mesita D** is just in front of the museum, by the park entrance. **Mesita B** has the park's largest tomb, surrounded by three mounds and several figures (look out for the 3-m high statue of a 'Bishop'). **Mesita A** has two mounds, each with a temple and a central figure flanked by warrior statues. And **Mesita C** has two statues, each with curved backs, a rare phenomenon amongst the park's statues.

Beyond Mesita C lies the large rocky area known as the **Fuente de Lavapatas**, a site probably used for ritual ablutions or for the worship of water-bound deities. In the bedrock of the stream a complex labyrinth of ducts and small terraces, with representations of serpents, lizards and human figures has been chiselled out. Shallow water flows over the whole relief and meandering channels distribute the water in such a way that it cascades into small basins. Further up the hill lies the Alto de Lavapatas, the park's oldest site. On top—overlooking a panorama of countryside that encompasses two mountain ranges, the entire archaeological park, and the town of San Agustín—you will see a couple of tombs, each guarded by statues.

Before leaving the park, visit the **Bosque de las Estatuas**, the Forest of Statues, one of the most beautiful parts of the park. Placed along a trail that threads its way through the undergrowth stand 35 statues, each transported from their natural setting, but repositioned through the forest like works of art.

Alto de Los Idolos

About 5 km from the town of San Agustín stands the second most important site in the area, the Alto de los Idolos, the Heights of the Idols, a large hill shaped like a horseshoe with the open end facing south. Open from 8–4, entrance is 50c. There are several burial mounds, each flanked by statues and, on the western end of the embankment, an enormous inclined statue, perhaps more than 4 m tall, that has been sunk into the ground. All of the statues face east into the rising sun.

Much of the Alto de los Idolos was used as a habitation site and excavations have revealed thick layers of potsherds and other occupational refuse that accumulated through the generations. Contrary to the idea that San Agustín is only a necropolis, modern archaeolgists regard the more ceremonial featues of the site as only secondary to such cultural remains.

Alto de Las Piedras
The next most worthwhile site is Alto de las Piedras, which lies 7 km beyond the small village of Isnos, and is best reached by jeep. Here, again, you will find several tombs flanked by statues. Two are worth looking out for; the famous 'Doble Yo', that shows a man with an alter-ego on his back, and another that shows a woman in an advanced state of pregnancy.

El Estrecho
El Estrecho is an impressive natural gorge 2.2 m wide (*just* that little bit too far to jump) through which the waters of the Río Magdalena flow. One of the best ways to get there is on horseback, a popular trip that takes 3 to 4 hours. On the way there, you could turn onto the path that leads to **El Tablon**, with its five statues of Moon Gods, and **La Chaquira**, where more statues crown the bluff that rises from the Magdalena canyon. On the way back, turn off the track to visit **La Pelota**, where you can see the only surviving painted statues in the region.

Longer Trips
One of the best longer trips to be made from San Agustín, is the two or three day horse trek to the source of the River Magdalena. The scenery is stupendous, and you stay at fincas along the way. Food and accommodation are simple, but then so is the life. Expect to pay about US$10 per day; the tourist office has details, or ask for the impish Pedro Jiménez at the **Hotel Central** who can also organize for you.

SAN AGUSTÍN: THE VILLAGE
Bent around the dimple of a hill, San Agustín is the small and friendly village that serves the region; all tourist services are located here. Renowned throughout Colombia as a relaxed place, the village was settled by hippies, both Colombian and foreign, during the 60s and 70s, and they form a population within, but apart from, that of the village.

GETTING THERE
There are two main ways of getting to San Agustín, both by bus. The first route is from the east, from Neiva (6 hours, US$4)—with some buses coming direct from Bogotá (12 hours, US$8). The second is from the west, from Popayán (10 hours, US$7) on an unmetalled road that passes through the high paramo of the **Puracé National Park**. The ride through Puracé is spectacular, and even if most of the journey is often through mist, it is impossible not to sense somehow that vast chasms lie beyond the fringe of tropical vegetation that edges the road.

All buses from San Agustín leave from in front of the **Residencias Familiar**, which is also the local source of bus timetable information. As there are only two buses daily to Popayán and Neiva, they are both always very crowded, so check times and buy tickets the day before you want to travel.

To get to Tierradentro, take one of the four daily buses to La Plata (5 hours, US$4), and change there for San Andrés de Pisimbalá.

TOURIST INFORMATION
The **Tourist Office**, at Calle 5 No. 14–45, is very friendly and helpful, and, unusually, monitors all tourist activites in the San Agustín area. It will organize tours and rent horses for you (and is in fact the best place to do such things); will change travellers cheques, although at a poor rate; and carries a plenitude of maps and leaflets on the area. It's open Mon–Fri, 8.30–12.30 and 1.30–5.30; Sat–Sun 9–noon and 1–5.

WHERE TO STAY
The choice is simple: you can stay in a converted colonial house in town, or in one of the more expensive converted colonial houses just outside.

The **Hotel Central**, well located on the main street, is very good and extremely friendly. Set on three floors, the rooms are clean and comfortable, most of them have hot water, and rooms are exceptional value at only US$2 per person. The hotel's bus-boy, the elfin Pedro Jiménez, recommends himself as a general fix-it man (which he can). Should the Central be full, walk a few yards down the street to the **Hotel Colonial**, prices are much the same.

Just outside town, on the road to the Archaeological Park, lies the **Hotel Yalconia**, which has a swimming pool, restaurant and rooms for US$15/20 for a single/double. 700 m further on, the even quieter **Osoguaico** has rooms for US$7/11—a very pleasant and tranquil place.

You can camp in the grounds of the Hotel Yalconia for US$2.50—enquire at reception.

WHERE TO EAT
There are a number of small cafés throughout the town, but good cheap meals can be had at **Pedro's** restaurant, next to the Hotel Central. The **Brahma**, next to the tourist office, has a vegetarian menu. San Agustín's best restaurant is at the **Yalconia**.

Tierradentro

Tierradentro is a smaller but equally remarkable archaeological site 100 km north of San Agustín as the crow flies. You could spend a couple of days here, walking through beautiful countryside, visiting the area's relics.

Tierradentro is a double-edged name with two possible translatable meanings. The first, the 'land within' is a reference to the inaccessibility of the area; the site is set in a valley high within the rough terrain of the Cordillera central. The second meaning, 'beneath the ground', is a reference to the mysterious tombs, or hypogeums, for which the area is famous. The hundred underground burial chambers so far found testify to an advanced civilization, or civilizations. But as at San Agustín, very little more is known about them. A number of statues similar to those at San Agustín have been found around the tombs, which suggests an Agustín influence, but there is no evidence to suggest that the tombs and the statues are related, either in time or by ceremony. And whilst the few recovered clay and gold handicrafts are fairly advanced, any further evidence has also long since disappeared, either robbed by Spaniards during the conquest, or by subsequent grave-robbers. Tierradentro is, if possible, an even more engimatic site than San Agustín.

The tombs, however, are fascinating. Hewn out of soft rock by hard flint, spiral stairs lead down into the burial caves whose roofs are supported by pillars. The dead were cremated, and inside the chambers you will see niches where the ashes were stored. All of the interiors are covered with paintings and geometrical shapes, the most common being a rhombus, coloured red and black against a white background. The depth of the tombs varies from 3 to 9 m and nothing like them has yet been found in the Americas.

GETTING THERE

Getting to Tierradentro is tricky. Services to and from the central village of San Andrés de Pisimblá are irregular at best, and buses do not actually stop at the village but at the crossroads, Cruce de Pisimbalá, a 2 km or 20-minute walk outside.

From Popayán, take one of the two Sotracauca buses to Cruce de Pisimbalá (5 hours, US$3). From San Agustín, take the earliest morning bus to La Plata (5 hours, US$4), and from La Plata take a connection onto Cruce de Pisimbalá. If there are no connections to be had that day, and you do not want to spend the night in La Plata, you can hire a jeep for US$15, or try hitching or walking the 20-odd kilometres to Tierradentro. If you do spend the night in La Plata, try the **Hotel Berlin** on the main plaza; its restaurant is servicable and rooms cost US$3/4 for a single/double.

TOURIST INFORMATION

Brochures and tourist information can be found at the museum and administrative offices, 1 km out of the village. Horses can be hired in the village; ask around the main square, at your hotel, or at the museum.

WHAT TO SEE

The archaeological park has several sites worth visiting and, with only one exception, they are all a short walk from the administrative centre. Take a torch to fully apppreciate the tombs, which are gloomy and dark. The main sites and the museum are open from 8–5. The countryside is magnificent.

Go first to see the pottery exhibits at the museum and then walk 15 minutes uphill to the park's most important site at **Segovia**. Here over 20 burial caves of various sizes have been discovered and the decorations on most of them survive. Ten minutes further on, past the small chipped-paint houses of the local Páez Indians, you will come to four more caves, at the site known as **El Duende**.

Circling back to the village you will pass through **El Tablón** where ten stone sculptures, similar to those at San Agustín, are thrown together under a roof in a fenced-in field. Head down through the village and then up again, to the brow of the the hill that rises to the south. Here, lies **Alto de San Andrés**, a scattered site of several tombs, two of which are still in excellent condition. Make sure to see them.

One of the most dramatic sites, however, is at **El Aguacate**, a remote mountain ridge two hours' walk up from the village, beyond the Alto de San Andrés. There are several ornate burial caves here, and also a grand view, with the landscape of Tierradentro spreading out around you in a sea of steep green waves.

WHERE TO STAY
Accommodation in Tierradentro is simple, but good, with most of the hotels to be found on the road between the village and the museum. **Residencias Lucerna**, just by the museum, is quiet, very friendly and highly recommended; rooms cost US$2 per person. Nearer to town, **El Viajero** is also good, with rooms similarly priced, and it also has a cheap but wholesome restaurant. If you are looking for a place with a swimming pool, go to the state owned **El Albergue de San Andrés**. It has a fair restaurant and rooms are US$7/11 for a single/double.

WHERE TO EAT
You can arrange to eat at private homes, or go to the restaurants at the hotels **El Viajero**, which works out at about US$1.50 a head, or **El Albergue**, which is more expensive and only nominally better.

Neiva

The only reason to come to Neiva is to stop over while travelling from Bogotá to San Agustín or Tierradentro; it's a hot and unremarkable town of 200,000 people.

GETTING THERE
By Plane
There are daily flights with Satena and ACES to Bogotá (US$30). **Satena's** office is at the airport, the **ACES** office is at Carrera 5 No. 12–77.

By Bus
All buses leave and arrive from the square at Carrera 2 and Calle 4.
There are several daily buses to Bogotá (6 hours, US$5); three buses daily to San Agustín (6 hours, US$4); and occasional buses to Popayán (US$6, 8 hours) via La Plata, where you can make a connection for Tierradentro.

TOURIST INFORMATION
The **Tourist Office** is in the Edificio de la Gobernación, on the main square. The **Banco de La Republica** is at Carrera 5 No. 5–73.

WHERE TO STAY
There is a Bambuco festival at the end of June when hotel prices rocket and rooms are very hard to find.

The two-star **Hotel Chicala**, at Calle 6 No. 2–57, is Neiva's best, is quiet, has a swimming pool, and is good value at US$20/25 for a single/double. The **Hotel Plaza**, on the main square, also has a swimming pool, and has a wide range of rooms that cost from US$10/13 upto US$20/25 for a single/double. The **Gran Hotel** at Carrera 7a No. 3–25 is simple, but clean, and has rooms with private bath for US$4/6 for a single/double. Perhaps the best cheapie in town is the **Gaitana**, at Calle 7 No. 3–29, which has rooms for US$2.50 per person.

WHERE TO EAT
The **Hotel Chicala** has an excellent and very reasonably priced menu; a three course meal with one drink will cost you about US$7. Otherwise, the **Hong Sing**, at Carrera 6 No. 7–66, is good for Chinese food; and **El Caima**, on Carrera 8 and Calle 6, has a wide range of dishes. Both are inexpensive for what you get.

Popayán

Popayán, La Joya Blanca, Colombia's 'White Jewel', was founded 450 years ago. In 1983 it was destroyed in 18 seconds by an earthquake. It was a beautiful colonial town, and after seven years of rebuilding it is so once again. You could spend a very calm two days here taking uncharted walks through the colonial streets. It's a quiet place that has an hypnotic effect on jangled nerves. And, like a graceful old matriarch, both classical and a little weary, the city shows no sign of its turbulent history. As the verse goes, Popayán is:

> Lovely and still, sitting apart
> Remembering the splendid years.

Its mountain air is rinsed; its cobbled streets vacuum-clean; its inhabitants modest but friendly; and its weather hovers pleasantly around the 20°C mark all year round.

The city is justly famous for its Easter celebrations. And if you want to go trekking in the mountains of the Cordillera Central, the Puracé National Park is only 60 km away.

History

Two hundred years ago, Popayán was more worldly and cultivated than New York. As a local capital—adminstratively dependent on Quito when Ecuador, Colombia and Venezuela formed one Spanish territory—it was an obligatory stop-over on the gold route between Cartagena and Lima. Great wealth passed through the city. Maps of the time marked its location with drawings of turreted castles to show the city's importance. It was once considered as the possible capital of Colombia. The geographers of the 18th century described it as a 'great, rich and proud town'. And wealthy criollo families from Colombia's southern sugar estates who settled in Popayán established it as an aristocratic cultural centre. Locals proudly boast that over twelve Colombian presidents have come from the city.

Popayán today has the patrician air of a university town and, indeed, there is a university, named after Francisco de Caldas, the Colombian savant who discovered the relation of altitude to the boiling point of water. He was born and killed in Popayán, executed in the town square, when only 45, for his writings in the cause of Independence. A statue now marks where the gallows once stood.

But that was years ago. Nowadays the city is a backwater and all that remains of the city's past glories are the architecture, and the dearly-held, but half-mocking, epithet, 'All the world is Popayán.'

GETTING THERE

By Air

Just behind the bus terminal, a 20-minute walk from the city centre, Popayán's **Machangara Airport** has two flights daily to Bogotá (US$40) with Intercontinetal de Aviación.

By Bus

All buses leave from the central terminal, a 20-minute walk due north through town. There are buses every half hour to Cali (3 hours, US$3); 10 buses daily to Bogotá (15 hours, US$10); and several buses a day to Pasto (6 hours, US$6) and Ipiales (7 hours, US$7).

To get to Tierradentro, take one of the three Sotracauca morning buses to Belalcázar and get off half-way at El Cruce de San Andrés. To get to San Agustín take either the 8 am or midday Transtambo bus (6 hours, US$6).

TOURIST INFORMATION

The **Tourist Office** is at Carrera 6 No. 3–65 and is extremely helpful and well-informed. The office is open Mon–Sat, mornings and afternoons, Sun mornings only. The **Banco de La República** is at Carrera 6 No. 2–78

WHAT TO SEE

One of the best introductions to Popayán is to climb the knoll just outside town. On top, a statue of Benalcázar rides in bronze. And from the white stone base of the monument you get a bird's eye view of the Payanese inheritance; from the conquistador above you, to the colonial centre in the northern part of town below.

Prelates shaped much of Popayán's history: the powerful families that settled in the area donated a good deal of their wealth to 'good works'. Popayán's bishopric dates from 1546; and, as if in compensation for the distance that separated Nueva Granada from the dominion of Rome, a long succession of wearers of the purple made the city into a religious centre, a city of churches. It is a real pleasure to stroll through Popayán's streets, but you will soon notice that the city's ecclesiastical architecture is almost neo-classical in its sobriety. If there is any baroque, it is without the baroque's characteristic boldness and imagination. And any rare flourish you might see above the city's portals are not for decoration, but are indicators of social and political rank instead. The Payanese took the burden of their importance seriously, and the resultant art—like so much that is reactionary and conservative—was restrained, almost severe, but also very, very expensive. 'Good works' got you to heaven, and the amount of gold that was caked onto some of Popayán's altars as part of a God-bound ticket is still staggering.

Unfortunately, many of Popayán's churches were irreparably destroyed by the earth-quake in 1983. The tourist office can give you up-to-date information, but the **Church of San Francisco** on Carrera 9 and Calle 4 is still, for instance, being reconstructed. San Francisco was the church that held the 'Voice of Popayán', a 2½-ton bell whose resonant tone was the result of 50 lb of gold added to the bronze during casting. The church was once the pride of Popayán; its interior was filled with masterpieces of baroque woodcarving, but all of them have since crumbled. Go instead to visit the church of **La Ermita**, on Calle 5 and Carrera 2, the only church to have survived all of Popayán's many earthquakes. Its white silhouette can be seen at the top of Calle 5, a narrow stone-paved street lined with modest houses, and it is open for mass daily at 5 pm. Inside lookout for the statue of the Señor de la Cana, the Lord of the Sugar Cane, who holds a sceptre in his right hand. The churches of **Santo Domingo**, on Calle 4 and Carrera 5, and of **San Agustín**, on Carrera 6 and Calle 7, have both been repaired and are also worth visiting.

Museums
Popayán also has a number of minor museums, all open Tues–Sat, mornings and afternoons, with entrance fees set at a nominal 50c or so.

The **Casa Museo Negret** at Calle 5 No. 10–23 is a beautiful old house with a collection of the contemporary artist's geometrical, painted steel sculptures. The **Casa Valencia** at Carrera 6 No. 2–69, is a colonial mansion built around a vast patio paved with irregular slabs, and it gives you a good idea of what the pattern of colonial life might have been in Popayán 200 years ago. The **Casa Mosquera**, at Calle 3 No. 5–14, was once the residence of El Gran General Tomás Cipriano Mosquera (four times President of Colombia) but is now home to a museum of religious paintings. Mosquera's Casa also has on exhibit a strange letter from Charlotte Napoleon, dated 7 April 1882, in which she thanks the Mosquera family for sending her a lock of Bolívar's hair and, as a returned sign of admiration and gratitude, encloses a lock cut from the Emperor Napoleon's head when he was in exile on St Helena.

FESTIVALS
Popayán's Easter celebrations are the most famous and ornate in Colombia, and they are renowned for a piety and sombre pomp that rivals those of Spain. Thousands of the faithful flock from both Ecuador and Colombia to see the elaborate processions that begin on the Tuesday of Holy Week and end on the Friday, and Popayán's full cast of Saints are paraded through the streets. The Festival of Religious Music is also held at the same time. If you are near Popayán at this time it is a good idea to arrive a few days early, book a hotel bedroom, make a side trip, and then return for the festival—it is definitely worth seeing.

WHERE TO STAY
You get good value for your money in Popayán, and there is a wide choice of hotels, nearly all of which are converted colonial buildings with balconies, inner courtyards and tiled floors.

El Monasterio at Calle 4 and Carrera 10, as the name suggests, was once a monastery, and is Popayán's best hotel. Its cloisters and tranquil gardens still maintain a semblance of quiet reverence and rooms cost US$20/27 for a single/double. **Los Balcones**, at Calle 3 No. 6–80, is a friendly, intimate, comfortable and well-located hotel with airey rooms for only US$8/10—a good choice. **La Casona del Virrey** is just off the main square and has rooms centred around a quiet central patio costing US$4/6 for a single/double. **El Viajero**, at Calle 8 No. 4–45, has clean rooms with private bath and hot water for US$3/4. **The Panama**, on Carrera 5 and Calle 7, is the best of the cheapies.

WHERE TO EAT

Although slightly out of the centre, the **Mey Chow**, at Carrera 10A No. 10–81, serves lightly cooked Chinese food (a relief perhaps after so much tough beef) for about US$8 a head. There are number of cafés in the streets around the main square and the **Taberna La Tolda**, at Calle 3 and Carrera 6 is a friendly student-type place. **El Danubio**, at Carrera 8 No. 5–33 is inexpensive, has a good menu, and is also open to midnight.

SHORT EXCURSIONS

Silvia

For centuries, the Cordillera Central was the home of various Indian tribes—such as the Páez around San Agustín—but the only group to have fully preserved their traditions, language and dress are the Guambianos. These farmers live in a communal society based around co-operation in work and production. The men wear long blue skirts; the women wrap themselves in a sari-like dress of the same material, and wear an impressive amount of jewellery around their necks in a fashion similiar to that of the Indians of northern Ecuador.

Although the Guambianos are dispersed throughout a number of villages in the region, their centre is the town of Silvia. On Tuesdays they come here to sell fruit, vegetables and handicrafts. The market begins at dawn and continues until the early afternoon. The handicrafts for sale are very similar to those of the Ecuador's Otavaleños. After the market is over, follow the road out of the village as it meanders through captivating scenery.

Getting There
It is best to get there as early as possible, so catch a dawn bus to Pindamó on the Cali road (half an hour, US$1), and from there take a collectivo on to Silvia.

Where to Stay
Silvia is best visited as a day trip, but if you want to spend the night, stay at the **Hotel Cali** on the main square; rooms are clean and cost around US$2 per person.

Puracé National Park

This park, about 60 km east of Popayán, contains one of the most spectacular mountain regions in Colombia. With peaks ranging between the altitudes of 2500 m and almost

5000 m, the park offers a wide variety of landscapes: several volcanoes, more than 20 lakes, the source of three main Colombian rivers (the Magdalena, the Cauca and the Caquetá), sulphur springs, waterfalls and lush vegetation. The region is perfect for trekking, but you must be well prepared: a tent, good shoes, warm clothes, food and a sleeping bag are all necessary. If you do not want to go through the exertions of trekking, the park still has much to offer. At the northern end, around the visitor's centre, you can visit the **Cascada de San Nicolás**, the **sulphur pools (termales) at San Juan**, and make the five-hour climb to the top of the **Puracé Volcano**. All of these are easily reached from the park's centre at Pisimbalá. The driest months are January and February, but for more information—such as maps—contact the Tourist Office in Popayán.

Getting There
From Popayán, take the Neiva bus that passes through La Plata, and get off at the park Centre at Pisimbalá (2 hours, US$2).

Where to Stay
The only accommodation to be had the in park is at **Pisimbalá** in one of Inderena's three very pleasant cabins (US$4 per person). Although the cabins have open fireplaces, nights can be cold, so take warm clothes and/or a sleeping bag. As the cabins often fill up on weekends, it is a good idea to book first through the Tourist Office in Popayán. The Centre also has a restaurant.

Pasto

Pasto lies 50 km south of Popayán at 2534 m above sea level, has a population of about 350,000, and is the last major Colombian city before Ecuador. Although it is situated almost on the equator, the climate is chilly, about 15°C. This is the best place to stop for the night if en route to the border, and one hour west of town lies the picturesque Laguna de la Cocha where you could spend a quiet day or two.

Pasto was one of the first Spanish settlements in Colombia, and although the general impression is still one of small houses drawing together for comfort from the stern majesty of the surrounding mountains, the town has lost nearly all of its colonial character. This has largely been due to earthquakes. Towering west of the city, at a height of 4276 m, stands the fuming Galeras Volcano; a ride to the top in a taxi for a fantastic view of the city and the surrounding countryside will cost you about US$3.

On January 5 and 6, following on from the New Year's Eve celebrations, Pasto hosts the famous 'Blancos y Negros' festival. The Fiesta dates back to colonial times when slave masters would paint their faces with black grease and, in turn the next day, slaves would dust their faces with white talc. Wear your roughest clothes as you will doubtlessly be painted both colours several times—the merriment has a certain velocity.

History
During the Wars of Independence, and even after, Pasto was a thorn in the flesh of the patriots. Royalist to the marrow, the *Pastusos* resisted liberation to the last gasp and

281

beyond. During the course of the revolution, the city was taken and re-taken by contending forces at least 15 times. It was here that the Colombian patriot Antonio Nariño was captured, clapped in irons, and shipped to Spain to rot in a dungeon for six years. And it was here, in 1830, that a bloody struggle ensued when Ecuador seceded from the confederation of Gran Colombia, and Pasto wanted to go with it. Determined to save the Pastusos in spite of themselves, Colombian troops persuaded them otherwise. Pasto still, however, feels more Ecuadorean, more Andean-Indian, than any other town in Colombia.

TOURIST INFORMATION
The **Tourist Office** is at Calle 18 No. 25–25, just off the main square. The **Banco de la República** is at Calle 18 No. 21–20.

VISAS
Although all immigration formalities are conducted at the border, the **Ecuadorean Consulate**, should you need it, is at Calle 17 No. 26–55 and is open Mon–Fri 8.30–12.30 and 2.30–6.30. And the **DAS** office, for Colombian entry stamps, is at Carrera 37 No. 18–77 and is open Mon–Fri 9–12 noon and 2–6.

WHAT TO SEE
Pasto is rather unexciting, but you could visit the **Church of San Juan** on Calle 18 and Carrera 25. The church dates from the town's foundation in 1537, was partially destroyed in 1969, but has since been restored; the interior decoration is rich. There is also a **Gold Museum** in the Banco de la República building on Calle 19 No. 21–27, with a good collection of gold and pottery from the Nariño area. The museum is open Mon–Fri, mornings and afternoons, Sat morning only. Entrance is free.

SHOPPING
For centuries Pasto has been famous for its lacquer bowls—an esoteric kind of fame, but true. These bore designs in rustic floral patterns, in reds, golds, greens and light blues. The lacquer was made to an Indian recipe, by masticating the gum of mopa-mopa bushes, and the result was supposed to be indestructible. Most of the bowls now look like horrible Japanese replicas, but you can see and buy the real McCoy at the **Casa del Barniz**, on the corner of Carrera 25 and Calle 13.

WHERE TO STAY
Pasto's hotels largely cater for border traffic. The **Hotel Agualongo**, just off the main square, on Carrera 25 and Calle 18, is the best in town, and has rooms for US$25/30. The **Hotel Sindagua**, at Calle 20 No. 21B–16, has rooms for US$9/12 for singles/doubles, with breakfast included. The **Hotel San Francisco**, at Calle 16 No. 25–17, has a very pretty inner atrium worked with art-deco iron railings and tiles, and has rooms costing US$5/6 for a single/double. In the same price range, try the **Hotel Zorocán** at Calle 18 No. 23–29; all of the rooms come with private bath and hot water. Just outside Pasto's red-light district on Calle 19, the **Hotel Manhatten** at Calle 18 No. 21B–14, is pleasant, clean and old-fashioned. Rooms rooms cost US$2.50 per person.

WHERE TO EAT

The best restaurants are in the northern part of town. **El Chalet Suizo**, at Calle 20 No. 41–80, has expensive, but very good food. Closer to the centre, **La Esquina de Brasil**, at Calle 19 No. 28–12 is also very good. Otherwise your choice is limited to eating at hotels, such as the **Agualongo**, or at fast food chicken places, such as **Mister Pollo**, at Calle 17 and Carrera 26.

SHORT EXCURSIONS

One hour east of Pasto lies the placid **La Laguna de la Coche**, the largest lake in southern Colombia, as misty and glowering as any Scottish loch. The area is good for walking, or you can tour the lake in a putt-putt visiting the island in the middle, which has been set aside as a nature reserve. Excellent food and accomodation can be had by the lake's shore at the Swiss-style **Hotel Sibundoy** for US$18/22 for a single/double, or, more humbly, at the **Hotel Quechua**. Rooms at the latter are simple, clean and cost US$3 per person. To get to the lake, take a bus bound for the Putumayo, get off at Pueblo El Encano, and then walk 3 km down to the shore. Alternatively, a taxi from Pasto will cost about US$6.

Two hours beyond La Laguna, lies **Sibundoy** and the Sibundoy valley, home of the once-famous yage *brujos*, or witchdoctors. Yage is the dream-liana, the plant that makes men clairvoyant, and Indians have used it for generations to break the walls of space and time. In or around the village you might meet some Indians claiming to be *brujos* and willing to offer you the yage experience, but take care. Simple accommodation can be had just outside the village at the **Residencias Turista**, which has rooms with private bath and hot water for US$3 per person, or you can camp in the hills. There are three buses a day to and from Pasto (3 hours, US$2).

Down the mountains and far away, nine hours beyond Sibundoy, lies a particularly volatile area of the Amazon where guerrillas and narco-traffickers are an everyday part of life, so it's best to back-track to Pasto.

Ipiales and on to Ecuador

The usual crossing to Ecuador is through the uninspiring border town of Ipiales. The road from Pasto takes two hours, is paved, comfortable and, skirting huge wide canyons, passes through beautiful scenery. The actual border—open 6–12 noon and 2–8—lies 2 km beyond Ipiales and all customs and formalities are done there. Connections between Ipiales and the border are easy and fast; a taxi will only cost you US$1.50. Money is easily changed at the border. For what happens on the other side, see under Tulcán in the Ecuadorean section of this book (p. 68).

If you have some spare time at Ipiales it is worth taking a US$5 taxi to visit **Las Lajas**, an ornate Gothic church that has been built atop a bridge spanning a canyon, just outside town. Second only to Lourdes as a pilgrimage site, a local poet once described the church as 'a miracle of faith over gravity', and if you go there you will see why.

WHERE TO STAY
It is more comfortable to set off for Ecuador from Pasto. But if you get stuck in Ipiales for the night the **Rumichaca** has good rooms for US$5/7 for a single/double, the **Zaracay** has single/double rooms for US$4/6, and for budget accommodation go to the quiet and clean **Belmonte**, which has rooms for US$2 per person.

WHERE TO EAT
Your choice is very limited, but the **Rumichaca** has a good and inexpensive restaurant. Otherwise, the **Greenhouse**, at Carrera 6 No. 16–73, is good value.

Part VI
THE PACIFIC

A pirogue laden with produce

The Pacific coast is separated from the heartlands of Colombia by the mountains of the Western Cordillera. Most of its history is natural history. And with the exception of Cali—the country's third biggest city—most Colombians consider the Pacific as little more than 800-odd kilometres of jungle, mangrove swamps, pioneer littoral, malaria, rain and poverty.

Huge armies of clouds from across the ocean crash and break against the Andes, and it rains heavily for much of the year. Beaches are black-sanded, and do not recall the gentle coves of the Caribbean. The sea is often marled by river water. The vegetation is wild and savage; the sun, vehement. And apart from a few residual Indian tribes—such as the Waunana, the Katios, and the Noanama—the inhabitants of the Pacific are mostly black, descendents of the slaves shipped south from Cartagena to work the gold mines of the Chocó and the sugar plantations around Cali. Their shining black faces, the clear whites of the eyes of their children, the sight of their rocking chairs leant against the jambs of open doorways, and of big women with hefty breasts and large bottoms crammed into gaily patterned dresses, are glimpses of North America's Blues; at times it feels as though you might be travelling through some remote corner of the Mississippi delta.

But the poverty, and the tall, half-clad men who punt their shallow dug-outs through the web of rivers that feed into the sea, are stronger reminders of the muddy Congo. The area is in fact often compared to Africa, which is the worst kind of reputation to gain, for, like Africa, the Pacific has a tendency of sliding from the Colombian consciousness. As a result, most of the area remains underdeveloped, unknown, and little visited.

But there are exceptions to the rule. Although modern Cali lies in the lush Cauca Valley, 100 km across the cordillera from the sea, its mood is flavoured by the Pacific.

You are likely to stop there if travelling north to Bogotá from Popayán. La Isla Gorgona, 70 km west of Cali's port Buenaventura, is a Pacific paradise. And Bahía Solano, on the northern stretches of the coast, is a wildly placed beach resort, preserved by its inaccessibility, and unusually for the west coast, has white sand.

CALI

Standing at 1030 m above sea level, Cali combines the sensuality and extravagance of the *zona torrida* with the temperate determination and high-altitude vigour of the cool sierra. The city is renowned for its beautiful women (with statistically more winners of national beauty contests than any other city), its salsa (the city has a disproportionate number of official orchestras—35—for its population of one and a half million), and its *medio ambiente*, or halfway mood (which is something to do with the altitude, neither up nor down, but halfway up the stairs). It is a modern, gay, and buoyant place; nonchalant but clean; well-planned and airy; summery, but without the indolence of dog-day summer heat.

The city is divided into east and west by the Río Cali and the park-lined Avenida Colombia that skirts its banks. But the real division of the city is between south and north. The southern part is large, contains the commercial centre, but dwindles into unattractive barrios of low buildings the further south that you go. By contrast to the north, beyond the palm-lined Plaza de Caycedo, lies the old colonial section; a small area abutted by gleaming hotels and expensive-looking apartment buildings.

Cali's formal sights, however, are few, and the city's real appeal lies in those unweighable attractions of atmosphere and people. This is most noticeable in the evenings, when a cool breeze whips up and blows away the heat of the day, and the Avenida Sexta—the city's pulse—becomes a bustle of pavement cafés, salsa grilles and svelt, strolling couples.

Note: There are cartels, and then there are cartels. The Medellín cartel is the only one to have directly confronted the government, but Cali has its cartel too, just as big and powerful as Medellín's, only more discreet. The difference between the two is perhaps best illustrated by the fact that the Medellín Mafioso Gacha, nicknamed 'the Mexican' is now dead, whilst a Caleño Mafioso, nicknamed 'the Canadian', is still alive. Cali *is* quieter than either Bogotá or Medellín, but bombs and deaths are not uncommon here, and after 10 you must take care. Watch out for thieves and prostitutes of all sexes; the male, the female, and the inbetween.

History

Founded in 1536 by Sebastián Benalcázar as he quested north from Quito to Bogotá, Cali led a leisurely colonial life for its first 300 years. In those halcyon days, 'morals were severe, crimes rare and years passed without a homicide or theft.' The hidalgos walked the unpaved calles in coats of scarlet broadcloth, embroidered and buttoned with gold, wore satin breeches buckled at the knee, capes of velvet edged with silver, waistcoats of flowered silk and ruffled shirts of the finest batiste. The ladies were as equally gorgeous, and their elaborate, many-petticoated dresses were made of bright fabrics adorned with gold and silver, or gold-flowered brocade, or gleaming *lampassé*. Both men and women wore the same high-crowned beaver hats on their powdered hair. And when the streets were muddy, they changed their gold-buckled shoes for heavy wooden clogs. The less wealthy wore as rich clothes as they could, and the peasants dressed in homespun cotton or wool, in colours as brilliant as those affected by their betters.

Being cosseted by a life as comfortable as cotton wool did not, however, dampen the Caleño spirit, and during the Wars of Independence the criollos of the valley threw themselves enthusiastically into the fight. When one Royalist entered the city, 'he did not find one able-bodied man... all of them had gone to war'. He did, however, find a remarkably stubborn militia of women. And when news came through of Bolívar's victory at Boyacá, it was 'a guerrilla force largely composed of women determined to give no quarter' that waylaid the Spanish governor as he marched from Popayán, killing him and routing his escort.

Cali returned to its ease after the revolution, and did not begin to boom until the beginning of this century when the sugar industry began to take off. The sugar cane, which still stands three metres tall throughout the valley, has the highest sugar content in the world. Milled, extracted and refined at huge plantations—such as Piedinche and El Paraíso, now preserved just outside town—it provided the impetus for the development of Cali's other industries. Since the 1950s the city has quadrupled in size, experiencing a higher rate of growth in 40 years than during its previous 400.

If Cali is sugar, so is Cuba; and if Cuba is music, so conversely is Cali. Salsa arrived in Cali in the 1930s and 40s when boats from the Caribbean—carrying the first songs by such Cuban bands as La Sonora Mantancera and the Trio Matamoros—passed through Panama and docked at Buenaventura. Folklore—but especially musical folklore—does not always respect national boundaries (especially when the conditions are right) and Cali's black sugar-plantation workers quickly picked up on the music of their Cuban counterparts. Salsa boomed in Cali, and by the 70s the city had formed its own distinctively slinky version of that famous 1–2–3/1–2 wood-clack clave beat—salsa *romantica*. Cali, Salsa and Caleña nightlife became inseparable, and at its highpoint, during the 70s inferno, the city's underground life spawned such classic books as Andrés Caicedo's dark-humoured *Que Viva La Musica!*, and Umberto Valleverde's more rum-bunctious *La Reina Rhumba*. Caleña dancing is also remarkable and distinctive, known for its fleeting and rapid fancy-footwork, and can be seen in the black *barrios populares*, such as Juanchito.

TOURIST INFORMATION
Cali has two tourist offices, only five minutes away from each other, and both are worth visiting. The **National Tourist Office** is at Calle 12N No. 3N–28. The regional tourist office, **Cortuvalle**, is at Calle 16N No. 4N–83, and arranges tours of the city and the outlying haciendas. Both are open Mon–Fri, mornings and afternoons. The **Banco de la República** is at Calle 11 No. 4–14

GETTING THERE
Palmaseca Airport is 20 km outside town, and there are regular flights to all major Colombian destinations: Bogotá (US$32), Cartagena (US$60), San Andrés (US$75),

and Leticia (US$57). To get to the airport, take a shuttle from the bus terminal ($\frac{1}{2}$ hour, US$1); altrnatively a taxi from the centre will cost about US$6. In town, the **Avianca** office is at Carrera 4A No. 13–52), the **ACES** office at Calle 10 No. 3–32.

WHAT TO SEE
Cali is short on sights. But strolling gently north from the Plaza Caicedo along—or a few blocks back from—the park-lined river makes for a strainless and pleasant tour.

Begin by heading two blocks north of the Plaza Caicedo to the **Iglesia de San Francisco**, on the corner of Calle 10 and Carrera 6. Built in the 18th century, the church's interior was renovated at the turn of this century. Its large marble and wood altar, which was made in Spain and delivered to Colombia at Buenaventura, had to be carried by mule over the Western Cordillera. Next to the church stands the curiously skewed brick bell-tower **El Torre de Mudéjar**, one of the best examples of Mudéjar art in the Americas. Heading north again, at the corner of Calle 7 and Carrera 4, stands the oldest church in the city, **La Iglesia de la Merced**. It was built in 1680, on the spot where Cali's founding mass was celebrated in 1536. The adjoining convent houses two museums, both of which offer cool and quiet respite from the daytime city's hot pavements and streets. **El Museo Arqueológico**, which holds a scant collection of pre-Colombian pottery, and **El Museo de Arte Religioso**, which has a small collection of colonial paintings executed in the elaborate Quiteño style, are both open Tues–Sat, 9–12.30 and 2–6 admission 50c.

As you step out of La Merced, the hill of San Antonio rises above you to the north-west. The walk up to the small 18th-century church perched on top shades through Cali's old, small, and very quiet colonial quarter. The hill affords a wonderful view of the city, and at your feet burbles or slithers (depending on the season, wet or dry) the Rio Cali. Back down by the river, and a little further north again, at Avenida Colombia No. 5 Oeste-105, stands Cali's excellent modern art museum, **El Museo de la Tertulia**. The museum houses a good and well laid-out collection of modern Latin American artists, hosts travelling shows and has a *repertory cinema*. Finally, five minutes walking uphill from La Tertulia, the **Natural Sciences Museum** at Carrera 2 Oeste No. 7–18, has a selection of Colombian fauna and is open Mon–Fri, 9–5.

SHORT EXCURSIONS

Haciendas
There are a number of famous colonial haciendas in the flat green country near Cali. One is **El Paraíso**, home of María, the protagonist of Jorge Isaac's classic romantic novel, beloved by every Colombian but doubly so by the people of the valley (*'Come! Let's rove about in the woods where the fairies tune their lutes. They just told me that you dream of me and that they will make me immortal if you love me!'*).

Next door to El Paraíso stands the larger hacienda of **Piedchinche**, which houses in its fine grounds the **Sugar Museum**. Both haciendas are open Tues–Sat, 9–4, entrance free. They are both a short walk from Amaime on the Cali/Buga road, half an hour outside Cali.

Closer to the city, just beyond the Universidad del Valle south-west of the city centre, lies Cañasgordas. A lovely old hacienda, Cañasgordas was once the refuge of the rebel

288

bishop of Quito and Cuenca, Don José de Cuero y Cayzedo. Don José 'hid' for eight years in and about Cali—known by every Caleño but betrayed by none—until the day when his brother-in-law galloped to the hacienda and shouted: 'Open Cuñado, the Royal Decree acquits you!' Don José replied, 'So it had to be. God does not permit injustice,' came out, and was promptly arrested. The easiest way to get to Cañasgordas is in a taxi (about 15 minutes, US$4.)

NIGHTLIFE AND ENTERTAINMENT
The **Avenida Sexta** is the main strip, lined with pavement cafés and salsa grills. For a a bohemian atmosphere, head for the dive at Calle 17 No. 6–52. **Juanchito** is notoriously the most famous weekend place for dancing and for watching dancing, but the area can be rough and the atmosphere hot, so go, at least, with a friend, and take care.

WHERE TO STAY
For deluxe accommodation, there is the **Hilton** in the quiet northern area, or the **Hotel Don Jaime**, at Carrera 6A No. 15N–25, on Cali's main strip, the Sexta. Rooms at the Don Jaime cost US$25/34 for a single/double.

More moderately priced in the town centre, the large **Hotel Aristi** has a roof-top pool and rooms for US$18/25 for single/double. The **Merced**, just around the corner from the colonial section at Calle 7a No. 1–65, also has a swimming pool and the rooms are slightly cheaper, at US$12/17 for a single/double.

The **María Victoria**, at Calle 18 No. 3–38, is a good choice. This rickety colonial building is clean and friendly, and has large simple rooms with private bathroom for US$6/8 for a single/double. The unsafe area framed by Calles 15 and 17 and Carreras 2 and 6, is filled with tarts; the best cheapie, **Bremen**, lies slightly away from here, at Calle 6 No. 12–61. Rooms here cost US$4/5 for a single/double.

WHERE TO EAT
Cali Viejo lies a ten-minute taxi drive north of the city centre, and is reminiscent of Cali's colonial days. You are served *comida típica*, 'typical' food (try the *tamales*—a tasty chicken mush wrapped in banana leaves, or a *platos estillos*—a mound of beans and beef scratchings piled over rice). The black waitresses are turbaned and dressed in homespun white cotton, and you eat on wood and leather tables on the shady patio of an old hacienda. A meal will cost about US$10 a head.

Los Girasoles, on the corner of Carrera 6N and Calle 35, is a chic restaurant with suited waiters, good for lunch. The menu is mostly fish, and the atmosphere is informal but elegant. For a quiet, perhaps even intimate, dinner, head to **El Callejón de la Capilla**, in the colonial section at Carrera 5 No. 1–35. Both of the above are quite expensive—you can expect to pay between US$10–15 for a meal.

China, at Avenida 6A No. 24N–52, is Cali's best Chinese restaurant. **El Restaurante Vegeteriano** makes 'your diet your medicine' and is at Calle 18N No. 6–25, but is only open for lunch. **Rick's Café Americano**, at Calle 21N No. 53B–28, is neon-glitzy, white-tiled and open-plan, and has a North American menu of broiled hamburgers and ribs, or fresh salads. Finally **Beckers**, at Calle 8N No. 17–09, is a mixture of nightspot-bar and restaurant.

BUENAVENTURA

'Buen ojo, buen aventura', she said, a cryptic remark which meant both 'A
sharp eye brings good fortune' and 'Watch out in Buenaventura'.
—from the *The Fruit Palace*, by Charles Nicholl

Over the mountains of the Western Cordillera, 100 km from Cali, lies Buenaventura,
Colombia's biggest port on the Pacific coast. It is a rain-stained and unattractive town,
but there are some beaches an hour's boat ride away, and it is also the starting point for
any excursion to La Isla Gorgona.

TOURIST INFORMATION
The **Tourist Office** is at Calle 1 No. 2–34, and is open Mon–Fri, mornings and
afternoons. **Inderena** is at Calle 3 No. 2–50 and is open from Mon–Fri, mornings and
afternoons, but it is very unlikely that they will give you a permit for La Isla Gorgona;
permits are usually only obtainable from the Bogotá office. The **Banco de la República**
is at Calle 1 No. 3–73.

GETTING THERE
By Plane
Satena flies small, light aircraft from the airport 15 km outside Buenaventura to Cali
three times a week (US$15), twice weekly to Guapí (US$18), and once weekly to Quibdó
(US$19).

By Bus
The best way to travel the spectacular road between Buenaventura and Cali is to pay a
little more than the bus fare and go on one of the collectivos that leave from in front of
Buenaventura's pier (2 hours, US$4). Otherwise there are frequent buses (3 hours,
US$2)

By Boat
Occasional cargo boats ply the Pacific seaboard to places like Guapí in the south, and
Bahía Solano in the north. Enquire at the building of **Combustibles Mónaco Ltda**, at
Calle 6 No. 22–10.

WHERE TO STAY
El Estación is the best hotel in town; a restored colonial mansion that looks as white and
as fresh as a wedding cake. Balconies run the full circumference on each floor, and
rooms cost US$35/45 for a single/double.

    El Gran Hotel, on the beachfront at Calle 1 No. 2A-71, has large rooms with good
views for US$6/8 for a single/double. The best of the cheapies is the **Cordillera**, at
Calle 6 No. 3–35, which has rooms with private bathroom for US$3/5 for a single/
double.

WHERE TO EAT
Las Balcones, at Calle 2 No. 3–94, has good seafood in a wood-panelled second floor
restaurant for around US$4 a head. **El Fuente de Soda de Venus**, on the corner of

Carrera 4 and Calle 3, is a classic dimly-lit and low-life terraced bar, with bell-hop suited waitresses and an intimate view of Buenaventura's street life.

Excursions from Buenaventura

Juanchaco and Ladrillos

Buenaventura's best beaches lie a rough 3-hour boat trip away, at the one-time fishing villages of Juanchaco and Ladrillos. Both villages have rinky-dink cabins and hotels set up from the beach, and both are marked by a scrabbling and collective disorder which suggests that no-one is really in charge. Although unexpected developments are the rule rather than the norm—which can make visiting a tetchy and improvised business—the black sand beach at Ladrillos stretches for empty miles, rocky cliffs come down to the shoreline, pelicans fly in ragged chevrons over the water, and when it rains everything is reduced to a cacophany of light, water and noise. The mood is dramatic, somehow prehistoric.

GETTING THERE
There are three boats a day from the pier in Buenaventura (US$10 return, three hours); ask at the office for specific times. When you arrive at Juanchaco, head straight through the village on a 15-minute walk to Ladrillos, where better and quieter accommodation and beaches are to be found.

WHERE TO STAY
The **Hotel Oasis** is a down-homey place, friendly, with plant-filled verandahs slung with hammocks. Rooms are small, but come with mosquito nets and cost about US$5 per person. **El Morro**, a five-minute walk further on, is the last hotel in Ladrillos. Although simple, it has a beautiful and commanding position on a bluff overlooking the sea. Again, rooms cost about US$5 per person.

La Isla Gorgona

La Isla Gorgona lies 70 km west of the Colombian mainland; is 9 km long and 2½ km wide; is the mountainous remains of a prehistoric cordillera that once extended from Panama to Ecuador; is covered with jungle, ringed with white-sand beaches, and would make for a perfect tropical paradise if only it wasn't so hard to reach.

History
The island was once populated by Cuna Indians from Darien, but it was Pizarro who put it onto the European map in 1527 when he stopped at the island on his way south from Panama to Peru. Because some of his men died of snake-bite, Pizarro—remembering the woman of Greek myth whose hair was a wreath of snakes—called the island Gorgona. For the next two centuries the island was used as a base for British pirates. And then in 1959, during the cruel and bloody period of La Violencia, it was converted into a prison. Escape was impossible as the sea was full of sharks, and some of the convicts were allowed to roam free over the island; some have even stayed on. In 1985, Inderena

managed to legislate for Gorgona to be turned into a national park, and La Isla is now, once again, a magical and remote place.

GETTING THERE
Ah! the hard part. First you will need a permit, only obtainable from the **Inderena** office in Bogotá. Then, if you can afford US$200 for a week's visit, any good tourist agency—such as **TMA**—can arrange the trip for you. Otherwise you will have to catch as can do. First head for the small Pacific port of Guapí—which is connected to Cali by daily flights with **ACES** (US$19)—and then from Guapí hitch a ride on one of the irregular Inderena launches to the island.

WHERE TO STAY AND EAT
Board and lodging is with the friendly Inderena rangers, and costs only a nominal US$2 per night per person.

EL CHOCÓ

El Chocó is the northernmost department of the Colombian Pacific. In contrast to its prosperous eastern neighbour, Antioquía, the Chocó is Colombia's darkest province, and whatever is true of the Pacific littoral—poverty, underdevelopment, malaria and rain—is doubly true here. The area's only redeeming feature is the presense of platinum and gold in the river gravels, but little comes out now.

The Chocó is mainly inhabited by Blacks and Indians. Although the history of the two populations followed similar lines—slavery, escape and then refuge freedom—they were traditionally kept apart by the fears of their Spanish slave masters of a joint, racial insurrection. The division persists today, and in the Chocó Indians and Blacks generally disdain each other. The black population keeps its African heritage of music and matriarchy alive while expanding its plantations through the Chocó's muddy river deltas and coastal lowlands. The Chocó's nomadic Indians, meanwhile, shrink back into the jungle from the encroaching planters and it is only in the most inaccessible areas—such as Alto Baudo, Bojaya and Cocoordo—that they still live untouched by Colombus's arrival and the world that followed.

The Noanama are the Chocó's largest Indian group, and like the many other tribes of the area, their origins are uncertain. Their language is very similar to that of the tribes living on the Western coasts of Panama and Ecuador; legend connects them with the pre-conquest civilization of San Agustín; their characteristic stirrup-pottery suggests links with pre-Inca Peru; whilst other considerations have lead researchers to believe that their earlier home might have lain in the Amazon basin and that they later moved west, across the Andes and up to the Pacific. And yet their whole outlook, water-borne way of life, and appearance, with flowers in their hair, suggests far-away Polynesia.

When the English traveller Cochrane first saw them in 1825, he found them using Leche de Caucho, rubber tree sap, as a caulker. Rained upon and damp enough to be singularly impressed by such an eminently practical innovation, he remarked, 'I have no doubt that this milk will one day be in great repute.' He was right.

Dispersed and displaced, you might have the good fortune to see a stray Indian family wander into Quibdó—the department's capital. High-stepping and half-smiling, they can look as if they're floating an inch or two above the ground, a look of 'other' on their lean, pudding-bowl framed faces, their eyes disturbingly sighted at a focal point that extends through people into an invisible distance.

The Pacific coast has been preserved by its inaccessibility, and the only tourist spot is at Bahía Solano. Otherwise travel through the thickly wooded and mountaineous Chocoan interior is rough and possibly dangerous, but rewarding. There are vague plans for a Pacific–Atlantic river link, to rival the Panama canal, and for an extension of the Pan-American highway through the Darien gap, but until these distant times arrive the Chocó remains virgin.

Quibdó is the main base for explorations. From there, you can either go north, along the Río Atrato and into the Gulf of Uruba; or south, from nearby Istimina, along the San Juan River and out into the sea, looping back through the Pacific to Buenaventura.

Quibdó

Quibdó is the wettest place in the world. The buildings are rainstained. The town's cindered streets are hopscotched by people trying to keep their feet dry. Bicyclists must learn how to cycle whilst carrying an open umbrella. And small green-gold fish swim in the roadside's semi-permanent puddles. Poor, hot and dirty, even laundry is a problem for Quibdó never really dries.

There is little to see in this river port, but the heat is an occupation in itself. Follow the local advice and do nothing in the morning, rest in the afternoon and regather your strength in the evening. Down by the river front, ebony-skinned men unload tropical hardwoods from ramshackle river steamers and old black women wander by with tin bowls of fruit balanced on their heads. Try the red-skinned marranon,the fruit of the cashew nut, which has a deliciously tart mixture of apple and pear tastes; or the fruit of the Chontaduro palm, which looks like a conical plum or a small mango, but has a savoury, almost cheesy meat inside; or the Borojo (see 'Fruit Topic' on p. 161).

People rarely stay in Quibdó (Mosquito city) longer than they have to and use it only as a stepping-off point to other places. But the town does have all of the centrifugal eccentricities of remote and peripheral places. And during the 1989 'Drugs War' the Quibdóans asked visiting Bogotáno journalists, 'So, what are you going to do about the problems in *your* country?'

GETTING THERE

By Bus and Plane
There are daily buses from Medellín and Cali, with prices ranging from US$7–10, but in each case the journey takes at least 12 hours, and the likelihood of reaching your destination is always limited by the possibility of derrumbes, landslides. Flying to the Chocó—in a light, twin-engined aircraft—is not much more expensive, takes one twentieth of the time, and helps to recall a more Golden Age of travel. The Rolls Royce engine hum, staggered layers of clouds pass below,your ears pop and re-pop in an

imperfectly pressurized cabin, and the jungle floats easily below as an innocent sea of broccoli.

There are daily flights with **Satena** and **ACES** from Medellín (US$17), Bogotá (US$30) and Cali (US$25), but book ahead as seats are often full.

By Boat

To Turbo, there are daily river trips, down the Rio Atrato, on the '**Dirty River Express**' (8 hours, US$25). These high-powered, fibreglass speedboats leave early every morning from the dock in front of the Flota Occidental Office on the river front, but book the night before to be assured a seat.

The trip is exciting but uncomfortable. The boat dodges floating tree trunks at high speed, skids around sudden bends, and the jungle whips by in its full and mad verdant glory. Rain is frequent, and no matter how hot you were in Quibdó, the high breeze is cold, so take a jacket.

The slowest but most adventurous way down the Rio Atrato is on one of the cargo boats that leave for Turbo, and occasionally Cartagena, from March onwards when the river is up. The boats are simple, smell of hot wood, fruit and engine oil, and you will need to take your own supplies and a hammock. Bargain with the captain, but expect to pay about US$20. The journey takes around 5 days, depending on the number of ports of call.

To head south to Buenaventura, you must first catch one of Quibdó's several daily buses to Istimina, a small village of two wooden streets and assorted alleys set on a bluff overlooking the San Juan River. The journey takes 4 hours and costs US$2. Boats only leave from Istimina for Buenaventura when full (US$25 for the trip), so if you need to spend the night, try the simple **Residencias Orsan** (US$3 per person).

WHERE TO STAY

The family-run **Residencias Oriental**, at Carrera 3 No. 24–08, is an extremely friendly place and the *dueño* could not be a more hospitable and helpful man. There is no sign outside, but it is across the street from the ACES office in the centre of town. The rooms are small but clean, and even though bathrooms are shared, this is the nicest place in town (US$6 per person). The **Residencias Citara** at Carrera 1 No. 30–63 is also recommended, but more expensive at US$10/12 for a singles/double with bath.

WHERE TO EAT

The air-conditioned restaurant **Ricuras**, at Calle 24 No. 3–30, serves excellent breakfasts, but suppers are more pricey, at US$8 per head. The **Restaurant Portilloi** at Carrera 4 No. 23–46 is also good, but prehaps the best value in town is to had at the open fronted **Restaurant El Paisa**; everyone eats there and can tell you where it is.

Bahía Solano

The rip-tide surf and dark-sanded beaches at Bahía Solano evoke no memories of the Caribbean; this is the pioneering Pacific.

Although the largest settlement on the Pacific coast, daily re-discovered by Bogotános as a holiday spot, the area around Bahía Solano is poor and services are still quite basic, although improving. The best swimming is at El Valle, south of Solano, and at La Playa Blanca (white sand beach), on the island at the mouth of the river. From here you can organize excursions into the Chocó—the dugout trip from Valle is popular (US$20)—and there is also good diving and fishing along the coast.

GETTING THERE
There are no roads, and therefore no buses; the only way in is by air. There are regular flights with **ACES** and **Satena** from Medellín (US$32), Bogotá (US$52), Quibdó (US$12) and Cali (US$37).

WHERE TO STAY
Locals offer accommodation, but the best hotels are the **Hotel Bahía** (good at US$5 per person) and the **Hotel Balboa**. **Cabanas El Almejal** in El Valle costs US$8 for a double cabin and is bookable through the airline ACES.

Part VII
LOS LLANOS

Llanero horseman

Sobre el llano, la palma;
Sobre la palma, el cielo;
Sobre mi caballo, yo;
Y sobre mí, mi sombrero

Above the plain, the palm;
Above the palm, the sky;
Above my horse, I;
And above me—my hat.

—says the llanero, and believes it. The plainsmen of these vast inter-Andean pampas that stretch for over 250,000 sq km from Colombia's Eastern Cordillera up to and beyond the Venezuelan border, are as tough as rawhide, as untamed as their horses, and as proud as the devil himself. Their creed is *hombría*, which can only be feebly translated as manhood. Bolívar had *hombría*. As did the horsemen that he recruited from the ranks of the llanero bandit, 'the murdering tiger', General Páez. And so did the army of mainly llanero horsemen that Bolívar lead to victory at the decisive Battle of Boyacá in 1819, so winning independence for New Granada.

Colombia's Llanos are over 80 per cent savannah. The English novelist Lisa St Aubin de Terain described them as 'flatlands, whose name stretches over the plains with a resigned echo of their flatness and that only.' Sparsely populated by *mestizos*, in whom the Guahíbo blood runs strong, the Llanos are an area of the Colombian map scribbled by lost and indecisive rivers that flood in the wet season. For most of the year, the Llanos is soggy marsh and travel is impossible. However, between December and March, the rivers recede to mere trickles and these dry months mark a period of activity for locals, when they can transport goods—such as rice and beef—into the highlands.

Los Llanos could become Colombia's breadbasket. But as the Colombian president Betancur once wrote, in oblique reference to the lawlessness of the area: 'As a politician I realize that there are not many votes, but a lot of country; and as a governor that there is a lot of country and not much government'. The jungled plains south of Villavicencio are particularly unstable, rife with guerrillas and narco-cultivators.

Los Llanos is a place to enjoy and suffer, and it's hard to gauge what it holds for the traveller or tourist. Very few go, and of those that do, usually only because they know a local rancher. For the rest, there is a sense of adventure perhaps to be had in the details of local llanero life. And then there are the sunsets of course, which are unparalleled and inspire mental travel—that's to say further travel; an exploration of the geography of the imagination.

The gateway to the Llanos is the city of Villavicencio, three hours by bus from Bogotá. East of Villavicencio lies Puerto Carreño, and beyond Puerto Carreño, on the Orinoco River by the Venezuelan border, is Puerto López. Both of these small towns are destinations of sorts, which is shorthand for places that are worth travelling through but not rich with reasons to linger. South of Villavicencio lies La Serranía de la Macarena, a remarkable (and remarkably dangerous) national park rarely visited by travellers. And then south-east of La Macarena, at the edge of the Amazon jungle, lies San José de Guaviare, a microcosm of the political life of the Llanos.

For more information about Los Llanos, consult the book *Llanos de Colombia* published by Lithografía Arco, and visit the office of the Gobernación del Departamento de Meta, Calle 34 and Carrera 14, in Bogotá.

Villavicencio

As you come spiralling down by bus or car from Bogotá, the first view of the Lllanos is from Bella Vista, a small kink in the road. In front, 1000 m below, the mountains sink into a mottled plain, and huddled against the last hills is Villavicencio, capital of the Intendecia del Meta, and jumping-off place for the Llanos.

Villavo, as it known among locals, is a busy, sprawling and modern town of 200,000 inhabitants. The days are hot, about 25°C, but the temperature drops pleasantly in the evenings. Villavo is the main cattle and agricultural centre of the region, and Bogotá's main groceries supplier; there is little here for the tourist. The **Instituto de Roberto Franco** at Carrera 3 No. 33–76 (open Mon–Fri, mornings and the afternoons), houses a modest collection of llanero fauna; and the **Centro Folklorico El Botalón**, at Carrera 33 No. 33B–13, hosts daily shows of llanero music after 8. *La musica llanera*, with its direct flamenco roots, is known by the general term, *joropo*. Culturally, the music looks across the plains to Venezuela, from where the distinctive llanero harps of the early 20th century came. As with vallenato, llanero music in turn imbibes and feeds back into, local folklore. But whereas vallenatos are nearly always about love, joropos are nearly always about the countryside, with women compared to its beauty rather than the other way round. The singer Manuel J. Laroche is one of the most highly regarded exponents of the genre.

TOURIST INFORMATION
The **Tourist Office** is at Carrera 33 No. 33–45, on the main square, and is open Mon–Fri, 8–12 noon and 2–6. The tour agency **Umabari** can also advise you; their office is at Calle 39 No. 31–42. The **Banco de La República** is at Calle 38 No. 32–09, also on the main square. And the **Inderena** office is at Calle 41A No. 26–34.

GETTING THERE
By Plane
Vanguardia airport is just outside town. **Satena**, whose office is at Carrera 31 No. 39–33, has flights to Puerto Carreño. The local carrier, which has an office at Calle 40 No. 31–15, has flights to San José de Guaviare.

By Bus
All of the bus offices are at Carrera 29 and Calle 38. There are frequent buses to Bogotá (3 hours, US$3); buses every hour to Puerto López (2 hours, US$2); one bus a week, on Tuesdays at 4 pm, in the dry season, to Puerto Carreño (40 hours, with an overnight stop, US$25); and one bus daily to San José de Guaviare (14 hours, US$10).

WHERE TO STAY
The two star **Hotel Don Lolo**, on Carrera 41 and Calle 21, is the best in town, and has a swimming pool, restaurant and rooms for US$20/25. The **Hotel Inambu**, at Calle 37A No. 29–49, is centrally located, is the next best in town, and has good rooms for US$10/13 for a single/double. The **Residencias Don Juan**, at Carrera 28 No. 37–21 is an attractive family house, clean and safe, that comes with a sauna and has rooms for around US$8/12 for a single/double—a good choice. The **Medellín**, at Calle 39 No.

Traditional llanero musicians

33A–81, has clean rooms with bath for US$5/7 for a single/double. **La Embajada de Llanera**, at Calle 39 No. 33A–56, is simple but OK, with rooms for US$2/4 for a single/double.

WHERE TO EAT
Apart from at hotels, Villavo's best bet is at **La Brasa**, on the main square on Carrera 33 and Calle 38.

Puerto López

Two hours north-east of Villavo, on the banks of the Meta River, Puerto López is a port of call for large river boats. The road east of López carries on for another 150 km through Puerto Gaitán. East of Gaitán, the road forks and 50 km further down the northern fork the road stops at El Porvenir. Across the river from Porvenir, there is meant to be a cheap tourist centre, with a swimming pool, at Orocue.

GETTING THERE
By Bus
There are buses every hour to Villavicencio (2 hours, US$2)

WHERE TO STAY
In Puerto López, there is the **Hotel Tío Pepe**, which has a swimming pool, and the cheap but friendly **Residencias Popular**. The owner of the Popular might be able to arrange tours for you, or a trip to Puerto Carreño.

Puerto Carreño

Puerto Carreño is a town of 5000 people that lies in the far eastern corner of Colombia, on the Orinoco River, by the Venezuelan border. The DAS office and Venezuelan consulate are on the Plaza Bolívar.

GETTING THERE
By Plane
There are three flights weekly to Bogotá and Villavicencio with **Satena**.

By Bus
In the dry season, from December to March, there is one bus weekly to Puerto López (40 hours, US$25).

By Boat
You will have to be extremely patient; there are boats—going both ways, into Venezuela, and back to Colombia's Puerto López—but no regular service. Ask down by the river front.

WHERE TO STAY
The **Residencias Vorágine** and **Mami** are your best bets; both have rooms with fans for about US$4/6 for a single/double.

La Serranía de la Macarena

La Macarena existed before dinosaurs walked the earth, before the Andes rose, before South America separated from Africa, and before the Amazon sea dwindled to a river. It is the oldest geological place in the Americas, and its 131,000 ha conserve 1800 million years of evolutionary history, from protozoa to man, with the catalogued diligence of a library. As a highland it was a refuge of many species from earthquakes, glaciers and eruptions, and as cataclysm followed cataclysm, it became a kind of Noah's ark.

One hundred and fifty kilometres south of Villavicencio, and occupying 13 per cent of the Department of Meta, the Macarena is the meeting point of Colombia's three most important ecosystems; the mountain, the savannah, and the jungle. Its rare geology manifests itself in a contrasting landscape of jagged rock, jungle, rivers, canyons and 300-m high waterfalls. Its flora and fauna includes: nearly 4600 species of plants— including the surreal Flor de Guaviare, with long fibrous strands splaying out from a central node and ending with white pom-poms, making it look like a 1970s space-toy sculpture; the 12-m long guayabero crocodile; monkeys, wolves, deer, anteaters, tapirs, bats and turtles; and over a third of all tropical species of birds... La Macarena is the climax of Colombia's biological diversity. Its biological systems are the most perfectly complicated and closed in the world.

But 'So what, and what for?' ask the 24,000 invading *colonos*, *campesinos* who cultivate coca in the Macarena for a living. They have been arriving in the Macarena for the past 20 years: fleeing violence, looking for cheap or free land, or actually sent there by agrarian reform officials who found it easier to invade a defenceless patch of nature than risk expropriating a few hundred hectares from wealthy local landowners. With transportation out of the Macarena to the mountain agricultural markets virtually non-existent, the only crop that the *colonos* can grow for any kind of return, is coca. With the *colonos* have come their ideological vanguard, guerrillas, and so the Macarena is also the domain of the country's largest guerrilla organization; the Colombian Revolutionary Armed forces, or FARC. The few scientists who enter the area have to deal with them. And yet the *guerilleros* also realise that defending the environment is good public relations. The local FARC leader has often interceded on the behalf of biologists who want to visit this repository of genetic history. All of which makes the politics of La Serranía as every bit complicated as its biology. *Eso es Colombia.*

GETTING THERE
It is hard to visit the Macarena, and usually only foolhardy adventurers, diligent biologists or intrepid journalists are prepared to negotiate its hurdles of guerrillas, *colonos* and army posts. However, the village of Vistahermosa, two hours drive south of Villavicencio, is the usual jumping-off point; beyond Vistahermosa, you are on your own.

San José de Guaviare

The village of San José de Guaviare lies on the banks of the Guaviare river, about 400 km south-east of Bogotá as the crow flies, and is a parable for the region. In 1987, surrounded by a sea of coca growers, adventurers and guerrillas, each acting under their own authority, the village was an inferno. 'Welcome to the 7th Front of FARC' said a limp banner hung between two trees. Cocaine buyers used to speed up and down the deep, coffee-coloured Guaviare river, in fast launches bristling with arms. There was no other state here but the FARC's, and FARC members passed freely through the streets of local villages in broad daylight, in military gear, like members of a victorious army.

They held the area in tight control, took their customary 20 per cent commission from the growers of coca, controlled the lives of the *colonos*, started indoctrination programmes and recruited young men—apparently at the point of a gun.

San José had all of the hallmarks of a town riding high on the drug boom. Only cocaine was grown—no food. A plantain cost nearly US$1, a stick of yucca the same, and a hen US$40. The intimidated *colonos* obeyed the guerrillas' whims. And the guerrillas rigged the local elections so that eight of the nine elected councillors were members of the UP—the national, legitimate Communist party.

Then the *sicarios* arrived, lured by money and the prospect of cleaning up undesirable left-wing elements. The *sicarios* were assassins, trained in the Eastern Cordillera, in the emerald regions of Boyacá. They killed not only UP members, but also *campesinos* who came from, or went into, the guerrilla zones.

San José was ruled by terror. The *colonos* stayed locked inside their houses after 6. The cafés and cantinas were full of assassins, prostitutes and adventurers. Eight, nine, ten corpses was the usual daily tally. On one occasion, when 80 *sicarios* arrived to establish their rule, they entered a café, took out their revolvers with glacial calm, shot one of the men sitting around the table, and left to do the same in another establishment a few paces further on. Any bullets left-over in the revolver, were dispatched into a dog. In the café *Los Amigos*, there is one dog that survived two bullets; he is called, with grim humour, 'sicario'.

The *campesinos* were caught between the cliff and the sea, between two opposed groups, each as violent and implacable as the other. The state was impotent; in truth, non-existent.

But all of this has since changed and San José is no longer an adventurer's nightmare. The 5000 hectares previously devoted to coca now grow food. The consumption of *aguardiente* has fallen from 200,000 bottles annually to just 20,000. A plantain is now worth 5c and a hen US$5. There are bingo parties, the streets are paved and everything breathes tranquillity. San José is now a model Colombian village, a parable of what could be.

The pendulum of the story swung in December 1987 when a huge, sweeping helicopter offensive, lead by the 7th Army Group, forced the guerrillas back into the southern jungles. At first the *campesinos* viewed the army with fear. Most of the villagers earned their livelihood from growing coca; the guerrillas had described the army as being in league with the *sicarios* (which in some parts of the country they are); and so many fled to the mountains. It was a small, hermetic, frightened and silent village population that the army found. But the army helicopters brought in more than troops. They also

301

brought advisors, who suggested substitute crops, dispensed loans to buy seed, and arranged transport to get the produce to market. Government solutions for poor people are usually as equally poor. But the Guaviare advisors provided what had been missing for so long in the area—a simple word so often abused and misunderstood in the West; development.

GETTING THERE
There is an irregular local plane service from Villavicencio. Tickets are bookable there from the office at Calle 40 No. 31–15.

Part VIII

THE AMAZON

Amazonian Yagua Indian

'Don't bungle the jungle!'
—Washington DC catchphrase, 1990

Though most of the mighty Amazon is in Brazil, it also extends into the neighbouring Andean countries, including Colombia. All of south-eastern Colombia is one vast green plain, little explored and settled by white men. Populations are sparse, with only handfuls of isolated Indian or *mestizo* communities scattered along the river banks. There are no roads, and the only means of transport are boat or plane. The climate is, of course, extremely hot; breezes are only billowy, never cooling, with wind speeds rarely exceeding one metre per second. Rainfall is high, about four metres a year.

There is a completely overwhelming sense of nature in the Amazon. It's a rampant sea of flora, and sea is the appropriate, even if over-used, metaphor. Being surrounded by a thousand million billion trees, plants, shrubs, animals, mushrooms—*plants everywhere!*—can lead to over-heated tropical reveries. For instance, whilst looking at the jungle, your attention might be caught by just one leaf, a single leaf, falling, a brown dot spiralling against the trees' muddy greens; just one, on its way down to the ground, where it will decompose and be reabsorbed into the trees above, its complicated sugars and minerals carried to the branches by saps, where another leaf will form, which in turn will fall, just one pico-element in the Amazon's cycle of nutrients that is a whirling and extravagant dance of energy through matter. As the French anthropologist Claude Lévi-Strauss once wrote, 'Nature is good for thinking about, not just eating'. For more information on Amazonian ecology please turn to the Amazon section in the Ecuadorean half of this book (see p. 130).

Colombia might have over 400,000 sq km of jungle, but it only has access to 160 km of the Amazon's 6000-km length, at the river port of Leticia. Leticia is the best starting point in Colombia for excursions into the jungle. From here you can visit the biologists' station in the heart of the jungle at Amacayacu National Park, or catch a river boat down through Brazil to the Atlantic Ocean. Alternatively Mitú, a small village further north on the Brazilian border, is a centre of anthropological research, but tourist services here are non-existent.

When travelling in the Amazon, you must be patient—regular transport is rare. An adventurous spirit also helps. And if you want to explore further afield, away from Leticia in areas such as around Mitú, you will need a full index of explorer's equipment, which includes, at least; a hammock, mosquito netting, machete, your own water and food supplies, medical kit, a boat even, and some alternative money—such as rifle ammunition, knives, clothes or cigarettes.

History

The Colombian Amazon lies outside Colombia's formal history of firm dates, viceroys, battlefields and Wars of Independence. Much of it still lies outside the range of state control. Nevertheless, it does have a memorable history of its own.

The Amazon was first—inadvertently—explored by Francisco Orellana, the conquistador who floated away from Pizarro's Quito-based expedition down the great river and out into the Atlantic Ocean by mistake. Missionaries followed on his heels, and the 17th, 18th and 19th centuries saw the foundation of scattered Jesuit, Franciscan and Capuchin missions throughout the jungle. The missionaries were relatively benign, but at the end of the 19th century rubber fever, in the commercial guise of the London-financed, but Peru-based company, *La Casa Arana*, took its toll. Slavery was reintroduced, and in the heart of Colombia's rubber-producing area, La Chorrera, the toll on the aboriginal Witoto Indians was horrendous. Between 1900 and 1910, the population shrank from 50,000 to about 10,000. The British consul Roger Casement described in his 'Blue Book' how the Indians were left to starve to death in the 'cepo', a wooden board with holes in it, much like stocks, in which the feet were clamped. 'More than once ... dead and putrefying bodies lie beside living prisoners ... Levine has said there were days in 1906 and 1907 when "you could not eat your food on account of the bodies lying unburied about the place".'

Following a parliamentary debate at the House of Commons in 1912, and an official denouncement by Pope Pius X in the same year, the company was officially closed. But with the outbreak of the First World War in 1914, demand for rubber increased and the company's activites continued. Memories of the *Casa Arana* among the Witoto Indians have since been hard to erase.

In the 1930s colonists from the highlands threatened the Indians. In the 1980s the *colonos* were followed by *narco-traficantes*, who set up huge cocaine processing laboratories in the jungle. The most famous of these, Tranquilandia, was raided in 1984. At the plant, police found nearly 14 tons of processed cocaine; plus cars, tractors, chemicals, helicopters, light aircraft; and all the conveniences of modern life, such as washing machines, televisions, air-conditioners and microwave ovens.

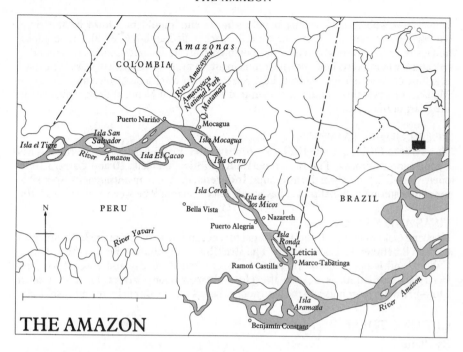

THE AMAZON

But despite the various attempts to use or open up the Amazon, the jungle remains largely invincible. Its central part, inhabited by different Indian tribes, is almost untouched. And the area as a whole remains a near-virgin linguistic and cultural mosaic of at least 30 different Indian groups.

Leticia

Leticia lies in a foot of land, stretched out on tip-toes, in the extreme south-east of the country, deep into the Amazon jungle. On the map it looks like an afterthought. But the town, and the Amazon River navigation rights that it confers, were heavily fought for. Founded as San Antonio in 1867, as part of the Viceroyalty of Peru, it was transferred to Colombia in 1934 after border warfare, and its name changed to Leticia.

The town is a busy centre of commerce with Brazil and Peru—not all of it legal. In the 1970s its prime three-border location made it a drugs trading centre, scarred by all the violent hallmarks of the boom. But the bonanaza has since moved on, and Leticia is now a quiet, gentler place; Colombia's tourist centre in the Amazon.

Leticia is always hot and humid, with the temperature hovering year in and year out at around the 30°C mark. Butterflies the size of plates flutter through the streets, red insects the size of pin-heads congregate around any patch of damp, trails of green ants stream through your hotel garden, and puckish leoncito monkeys—no bigger than hamsters—climb around willing people's heads and shoulders. Down by the river, wobbly-looking canoes, low on the waterline, are pulled up onto the thick mud banks, and yams, or fruit, or huge prehistoric-looking fish are hefted out. Leticia is surrounded by nature, which exerts itelf upon the municipality in the most freakish of ways. The town is of little interest in itself, but from here you can either catch a boat down the Amazon to Manaus, or travel three hours upstream to the Acamayacu National Park, which lies in the heart of the jungle.

TOURIST INFORMATION
The **Tourist Office** at Calle 10 No. 9–86, open Mon–Fri, mornings and afternoons, has a good supply of maps. The **Banco de La República**, on Calle 10 and Carrera 10, is open Mon–Fri, but only in the mornings. **Inderena**, the government agency responsible for administering national parks, has an office on Carrera 9 between Calles 9 and 10.

VISAS AND STAMPS
If leaving Colombia from Leticia you must first get an exit stamp from the **DAS** office on Carrera 8 between Calles 9 and 10. The **Brazilian Consulate** is next to the DAS, on Calle 9, and is open Mon–Fri, 10–4. Visas are issued quickly and cost US$4. The **Peruvian Consulate** is next to the Hotel Anaconda on Carrera 11, and is open Mon–Fri in the mornings and the afternoons. Visas take one day to issue and cost US$6.

GETTING THERE
By Plane
Flying into Leticia with a commercial Avianca flight from Bogotá is the cheapest way to arrive (US$59); a boat from Puerto Assi down the Putamayo, for instance, costs twice as much. Leticia's airport is a 15-minute walk or US$2 taxi drive out of town, and there are four flights a week to and from Bogotá. The **Avianca** office is at Carrera 11 No. 7–82.

The Brazilian airline **Cruziero** has three weekly return flights along the route Manaus–Tabatinga–Iquitos. A flight to Manaus costs US$90; a flight to Iquitos (US$75).

By Boat
Travel by boat on the Amazon *is* cinematic, not least because you travel at a uniform and given speed (slow) towards a fixed point (your destination). This revolutionized the Hollywood director D. W. Griffith's camera direction technique, but makes boat journeys on the Amazon rather montonous. The boat chugs along dragging a sheet of foam behind it. The banks are distant (just green smudges on the horizon). Time passes, the heat grows, hours slip away into nothing, you swing in your hammock and days somehow come to seem strangely insubstantial.

Boats down the Amazon for Manaus leave from the Brazilian town of Benjamín Constant on Wednesdays and Saturday nights. The journey takes 4 days and costs around US$40, with food included. To get to Benjamín Constant catch a collectivo (40c) or taxi (US$5) from Leticia across the Brazilian border to Tabatinga, from where there are two ferries a day, at 11 am and 4, across the river to Benjamín Constant (1½ hours, US$2).

Boats upstream to Iquitos and Peru leave from the Brazilian town of Ramón Castilla. There are two or three boats a week (3 days, US$15), and from Iquitos you can catch a plane to Lima. To get to Ramón Castilla, follow the directions for Benjamín Constant described above.

Before leaving Colombia, make sure to get an exit stamp from the DAS office in Leticia. Brazilian entry stamps are provided at Tabatinga, and Peruvian entry stamps at Puerto Alegría.

WHERE TO STAY

The **Hotel Parador Ticuna**, on the edge of town, has cabins with verandahs set in lush green gardens, for US$20/27 for a single/double. The hotel has a swimming pool, and the management is also responsible for the lodge on Monkey Island. In town, on Carrera 11, the modern **Hotel Anaconda** has air-conditioned rooms for the same price.

The **Marina**, on Carrera 9 between Calle 9 and 10, is fine, and has rooms with air conditioning and private bathroom, for US$6/10 for a single/double. The **Fernanado**, on Carrera 9 and Calle 8 is also good, clean and friendly and has rooms for US$7/9 for a single/double.

The best budget hotel is the **Residencias Leticia**, down by the waterfront near the market area, with rooms for US$3/4 for a single/double.

WHERE TO EAT

Food in Leticia, although relatively expensive, is delicious, with river fish—such as the mouth-watering *gamitana*—served with plantains, fried yucca and fresh vegetables. Go and eat on the latticed verandah of the restaurant **Maiporé** on Calle 11 and Carrera 8; here, a huge meal of *gamitana* will cost you only US$4. The cafes along Carrera 11, the main strip, serve fruit juices and snacks. And the **Colibrí**, set back from the town on Calle 11 and Carrera 5, serves hamburgers and other western dishes for around US$4 a head.

TOURS AND SHORT EXCURSIONS

Because Leticia is a tourist centre, a number of travel agencies have sprung up, and these arrange group tours. The best is **Turamazonas** on the Plaza Orellana, but also good, and slightly cheaper, is **Amazonia Tours**, near the Hotel Anaconda. All of the tours however, from whichever agency, are quite expensive, and their routes well-trodden. They are also arranged for groups of at least five people, so while there can be a number of tours in the high season (around Christmas), single travellers may have to wait several days in the low. If you want to stay in the jungle proper and see wildlife, the Acamayacu National Park (see below) is far and away your best bet.

Some of the nearby Yagua and Tikuna Indian villages are the scene of tragi-comic Indian theatre. Picturesque stuff, put on for tourists by the agencies, they are all 'musts' on tour itineraries, and rather sad too.

Amacayacu National Park

Amacayacu National Park provides a singular chance to see virgin jungle, quite cheaply, and from a comfortable base—all of which are important considerations when visiting the Amazon.

The park lies about three hours journeying upstream from Leticia. It covers some 1700 sq km and takes in a large area of varied jungle vegetation. To the north of the park, at San Martín, there lives a traditional community of Ticuna Indians; to the west is the *colono* settlement of Puerto Nariño. Transport through the park is mostly on narrow streams in small dug-out canoes, which are easily hired, but there are also two signposted walks. The Inderena visitors' centre—where you can sleep and eat—is comfortably arranged and is used by international biologists to study Amazonian flora and fauna. At a recent counting, an English team of ornithologists identified over 470 species of birds in the park alone.

When visiting the jungle it is worth remembering that nothing reveals itself suddenly; it all takes time. Sit still, and then when everything has fallen quiet around you, animals—birds, monkeys, and maybe even a tapir—might begin to appear.

GETTING THERE
There are three ways of getting to Amacayacu from Leticia. The first is to rent a boat, which can take up to 12 people and will cost you about US$60. The second is to catch one of the twice weekly chugging, smoke-stacked river bus boats to Puerto Narino (7 hours, US$2), and get off at the Park just before Puerto Narino. The third is to catch a lift with Inderena if they happen to have a boat going that week. Whichever way, the journey takes at least 4 hours.

WHERE TO STAY
Accommodation is in hammocks or simple bunks at the station. The Inderena management are extremely friendly, and will make sure that you know what you are doing and what is available—there is a strong mood of bonhomie. The centre is built on stilts, 3 m above the ground. There is a raised walk through part of the jungle; trails through the rest; and, just outside the camp, a 30 metre-high ceiba tree with a rope ladder dangling

Amazonian Molacca

308

from the high canopy. Entrance to the park is US$2, accommodation is US$2.50 per night, and food is US$7 daily for three large and very delicious meals.

Puerto Nariño

Puerto Nariño lies a few kilometres upstream from the park and is the second largest village of the region. The village is so prosperous and orderly that it looks as if the streets were laid first and then the houses placed in and around them afterwards. The population is half *mestizo* and half Ticuna, but this is no wild west town; the river banks are mown, the verges strimmed, and there is not a trace of litter. A gentle place.

WHERE TO STAY
The **Brisas del Amazonas** is quiet and pleasant and has an excellent restaurant. Rooms are US$8/12 for a single/double, and the management can arrange tours. On the river front, the un-named *Residencias* next to the disco has rooms at US$4 per person.

LANGUAGE

Members of Latin America's conversational upper-classes usually command three languages; Spanish, French and English. Invariably El Pueblo, however, does not. So whilst you would easily be able to travel around Colombia and Ecuador speaking only English, having even just a smattering of Spanish will make all the difference to your trip. It will save you money, ease your way, provide access, entertainment and, not least, save you from the embarassment of having a deaf-man's face each time that you gather with Spanish-speaking friends.

Learning Spanish

Take heart, Spanish is easy to learn; you just have open your mouth a bit more. And if you were to embark on a three-month trip with only the rudiments—a few conjugations, a vocabulary of one hundred words, and some simple constructions—by the end you would at least *feel* like a native speaker.

Begin a month or two before you set-off. Cassettes are a boring but relatively painless method of learning. Better, however, are classes. Every large western city abounds with Latin American or Spanish students willing to earn a few extra pounds by teaching in an evening college. In London, the Spanish Institute at 102 Eaton Square, tel (071) 235 1484, provides a wide-range of inexpensive classes organised around the academic calendar. If you have a choice, choose a Latin American teacher over a Spaniard; Latin American Castilian is softer, and Spanish Castilian is after all the language of the conquistadors. Speak and practice *sin verguenza*, without shame, and your efforts will be rewarded. Note: if you already speak Spanish the familiar 'tu' form of address is increasingly used over the formal 'usted', especially on the coasts.

Pronunciation is phonetic, with the stress on the penultimate syllable if the word ends in a vowel, and on the last syllable if the word ends in a consonant. Exceptions are indicated by accents. For example:

Bogotá: *Bog-o-TA*
Medellín: *Med-a-YEEN*
Barranquilla: *Ba-ran-KEY-ya*
Cali: *Kali*
Villa de Leyva: *Beeya de LAY-va*

Quito: *Key-toe*
Guayaquil: *Guay-a-KEEL*
Cuenca: *KWAYN-kah*
Vilcabamba: *Bill-car-BAM-ba*
Jipijapa: *HEE-pee-HA-pa*

Useful Words and Phrases

yes	*sí*
no	*no*
I don't know	*No sé*
I don't understand	*No comprendo*
Does someone here speak English?	*¿Hay alguien aqui que hablé inglés?*
Speak slowly	*Hable despacio*

310

Can you help me?	*¿Puedes ayudarme?*
Please	*por favor*
Thank you (very much)	*(muchas) gracias*
You're welcome	*de nada*
It doesn't matter	*no importa*
All right	*está bien*
Excuse me	*perdóneme*
Be careful!	*¡Cuidado!*
Maybe	*quizas*
Nothing	*nada*
How do you do?	*¿Cómo está usted?*
Well, and you?	*¿Bien, y usted?*
What is your name?	*¿Comó se llama?*
Hello	*Hola*
Goodbye	*Adios, hasta luego*
Good morning	*Buenos dias*
Good afternoon	*Buenas tardes*
Good evening	*Buenas noches*
What is that?	*¿Qué es esto?*
What	*qué*
Who	*quién*
Where	*dónde*
When	*cuando*
Why	*por qué*
How	*cómo*
How much?	*¿cuánto?*
How many?	*¿cuántas?*
I am lost	*Me he perdido*
I am hungry	*Tengo hambre*
I am thirsty	*Tengo sed*
I am sorry	*Lo siento*
I am tired	*Estoy cansado*
I am sleepy	*Tengo sueño*
I am ill	*No siento bien*
Leave me alone	*Déjeme en paz*
Good	*buena/bueno*
Bad	*mal/malo*
It's all the same	*es igual*
Slow	*despacio*
Fast	*rápido*
Big	*grande*
Small	*pequeño*
Hot	*caliente*
Cold	*frío*
Up	*arriba*
Down	*abajo*

311

The following words and phrases are slangy—you might not want to use them with a policeman. But peppering your conversation with a few ribald expletives is always good for jocular taxi-drivers, and the like.

Fine/cool	*chévere*
Great, fantastic	*vacano*
How pretty!	*qué lindo*
Son-of-a-bitch	*hijo puta*
Thief	*ladrón*
Grave robber	*guaquero*
What a problem!	*¡Que vaina! (literally, what a thing)*
Damn!	*¡Carajo!*
Why not?	*¿Como no?*
Basuko	*crack (cocaine derivative)*
Marijhuana	*bareta (literally, a staff)*
Prostitute	*puta*
Lay-about druggie	*marijuanero*
Street kid	*gamín*
I have a hangover	*Tengo guayaba*
To get rid of a hangover	*Desguayabarme*
Hey!	*¡oyé!*
Calm down	*calma te*
To play the fool	*hacerse el gringo*
To party	*rhumbear*
A party-goer, party-maker, musician	*rhumbero*
Intense, wild, strong	*tenaz*
Charming and lively, but indomitable	*vivo (esp. of costeños)*

Shopping, Service, Sightseeing

I would like...	*Quisiera...*
Where is/are?	*¿Dónde está/están?*
How much?	*¿Cuánto vale eso?*
Open	*Abierto*
Closed	*Cerrado*
Cheap/expensive	*barato/caro*
Bank	*banco*
Beach	*playa*
Bed	*cama*
Church	*iglesia*
Hospital	*hospital*
Money	*dinero*
Museum	*museo*
Pharmacy	*farmacia*
Post office	*correos*
Sea	*mar*
Shop	*tienda*

Time

What time is it?	*¿Qué hora es?*
Month	*mes*
Week	*semana*
Day	*día*
Morning	*mañana*
Afternoon	*tarde*
Evening	*noche*
Today	*hoy*
Yesterday	*ayer*
Soon	*pronto*
Tomorrow	*mañana*
Now	*ahora*
Later	*despues*
Early	*temprano*
Late	*tarde*

Days

Monday	*lunes*
Tuesady	*martes*
Wednesday	*miércoles*
Thursday	*jueves*
Friday	*viernes*
Saturday	*sábado*
Sunday	*domingo*

Numbers

one	*uno/una*
two	*dos*
three	*tres*
four	*quatro*
five	*cinco*
six	*seis*
seven	*siete*
eight	*ocho*
nine	*nueve*
ten	*diez*
eleven	*once*
twelve	*doce*
thirteen	*trece*
fourteen	*catorce*
fifteen	*quince*
sixteen	*dieciséis*
seventeen	*diecisiete*
eighteen	*dieciocho*

313

nineteen	*diecinueve*
twenty	*veinte*
twenty-one	*veintiuno*
thirty	*treinta*
forty	*cuarenta*
fifty	*cincuenta*
sixty	*sesenta*
seventy	*setenta*
eighty	*ochenta*
ninety	*noventa*
one hundred	*cien*
hundred and one	*ciento-uno*
five hundred	*quinientos*
thousand	*mil*

Transport

Airport	*aeropuerto*
Bus stop	*parada*
Bus/coach	*autobús/bús*
Train	*tren*
Railway station	*estación del tren*
Boat	*barco*
Port	*puerto*
Ticket	*billete*
Customs	*aduana*
Seat	*asiento*

Travel Directions

I want to go to...	*Quiero ir a...*
How can I get to...	*Como puedo llegar a...*
Do you stop at...	*Para en...*
Where is...	*Dondé está...*
When is the next...	*Cuándo es el proximo...*
Where does it leave from...	*De dondé sale?*
How long does the trip take?	*Cuánto tiempo dura el viaje?*
How much is the fare?	*Cuánto vale el billete?*
Good trip!	*Buen viaje!*
here	*aquí, aca*
there	*alla*
close	*cerca*
far	*lejos*
full	*lleno*
left	*izquierda*
right	*derecha*
forward	*adelante*
backward	*atrasada*

north	*norte*
south	*sur*
east	*este/oriente*
west	*oeste/occidental*
corner	*esquina*
square	*plaza*

Driving

rent	*aquilar*
car	*coche/car*
motorbike	*scooter*
petrol	*gasolina*
garage	*garaje*
map	*mapa*
This doesn't work	*Esta no funciona*
Where is the road to...?	*¿Dondé está el camino a...?*
Is the road good?	*¿Es buena la carretera?*
breakdown	*avería*
Driver's licence	*carnet de conducir*
driver	*conductor*
speed	*velocidad*
exit	*salida*
entrance	*entrada*
danger	*peligro*
narrow	*estrecha*

Restaurant and Menu Vocabulary

DRINKS (*bebidas*)

Water	*agua*
Fizzy drinks	*colas*
Beer	*cerveza*
Wine (red/white)	*vino (tinto/blanco)*
Black coffee	*tinto*
White coffee	*café con leche*
Instant coffee	*café (No-Es-Café)*
Fruit juice	*jugo*
Tea	*té (con limón)*

MEATS (*carnes*)

Chicken	*pollo*
Hen	*gallina*
Rabbit	*conejo*
Lamb	*cordero*
Pork	*cerdo*
Guinea Pig	*cui*
Chop	*chuleta*

Roast	*asada*
Grilled	*parillada*
Beefsteak	*bistek*
Liver	*hígado*
Sausage	*chorizo/salchicha*

FISH (*pescado*)

Catch of the day	*mojarra*
Cod	*bacalao*
Sea Bass	*pargo*
Trout	*trucha*
Tuna	*atún*

SHELLFISH (*mariscos*)

Shrimps	*langostinos*
Prawns	*gambas*
Lobster	*langosta*
Squid	*calamare*
Crab	*cangrejo*

VEGETABLES (*legumbres*)

Garlic	*ajo*
Rice	*arroz*
Potatoes	*papas*
Onions	*ceballos*
Carrots	*zanahoria*
Mushrooms	*champiñones*
Beans	*frijoles*
Peppers	*pimientos*
Lettuce	*lechuga*
Tomato	*tomate*
Salad	*ensalada*

OTHER

Butter	*mantequilla*
Ice	*hielo*
Salt	*sal*
eggs	*huevos*
Vinegar	*vinegre*
Sauce	*salsa*
Bread	*pan*
Soup	*sopa*
Honey	*miel*

SELECTED BIBLIOGRAPHY

There are four wonderful and illuminating books that collectively span Ecuador and Colombia, and each one is a classic in its own way. Read them if no others:

Conrad, Joseph, *Nostromo*. Perhaps Conrad's greatest novel, Nostromo recreates the political, economic and military history of an imaginary Latin American country (in fact, a thinly-veiled Colombia).

García Márquez, Gabriel, *One Hundred Years of Solitude*. Set in the semi-mythical Colombian village of Macondo, Márquez's seminal work draws much of its so-called magical realism from the resonant oral histories of Colombia. A key, along with Márquez's other works, to understanding the country.

Nicholl, Charles, *The Fruit Palace*, Pan, 1985. Lyrical and compelling account of an English journalist commissioned to investigate the 'Great Cocaine Story'. A good pre-travel primer.

Miller, Tom, *The Panama Hat Trail*, Abacus, 1986. Witty Ecuadorean travelogue pegged around the Panama hat.

GENERAL

History

The history of this book owes much to Malcolm Deas, the historian of Gran Colombia. Two of his excellent, erudite and always entertaining essays can be found in the *Cambridge History of Latin America* edited by Leslie Bethell, and a third in the *London Review of Books* (22 March 1990).

Selected Writings of Bolívar, edited by Lecuna and Bierck, Banco de Venezuela, 1951.

Galeano, Eduardo, *Open Veins of Latin America*, Monthly Review Press, New York and London, 1973. Rewarding polemic devoted to the continent's social, cultural and political struggles.

Pendle, George, *A History of Latin America*, Pelican 1968. A good general introduction.

Natural History

Andrews, Michael, *Flight of the Condor*, Collins, 1982. Highly recommended.

Hecht, Susanna and Cockburn, Alexander, *The Fate of the Forest*, Verso, 1990. Incisive political and natural history of the Amazon.

Morrison, Toni, *Land Above the Clouds*, Deutsch, 1974.

Travel and Fiction

Carpentier, Alejo, *The Lost Steps*, Gollancz, 1956. North American musicologist travels through Gran Colombia on a quest for his mystical self in the jungle hungly-mungly. A classic of South American fiction.

Crewe, Quentin, *In the Realms of Gold*, Michael Joseph, 1989. Highly recommended South American travelogue with honest and perceptive chapters on both Colombia and Ecuador.

317

Brooks, John (ed), *The South American Handbook*, Trade and Travel Publications, 1990. Annually updated and very thorough.

Hatt, John *The Tropical Traveller*, Pan Books, 1983. Wise and witty advice from an inveterate globe trotter.

Lévi-Strauss, Claude, *Triste Tropiques*, Peregrine, 1978. Complex, original and always eccentric, Lévi-Strauss's glorious and inspiring Amazonian travelogue is one of the finest travel books ever written.

Waterton, Charles, *Wanderings in South America*, Century re-print, 1983. Victorian travelogue by the father of taxonomy.

ECUADOR

History

Gartelman, Karl Dieter, *Digging up Prehistory: the Archaeology of Ecuador*, Ediciones Libri Mundi, 1989

Hemming, John, *The Conquest of the Incas*, Penguin, 1983. Authoritative and readable history.

Medina, José (ed), *The Discovery of the Amazon*, Dover 1988. Exonerates Orellana from the charge of treason levied against him by Pizarro after he floated down the Amazon. A fascinating work of detective scholarship.

Von Hagen, Victor, *The Four Seasons of Manuela*, Plata Press, 1952. Lusty biography of Bolívar's mistress.

Von Hagen, Victor, *Ecuador*, Plata Publishing, 1978. Gossipy history of the country, region by region.

Ecuador: A Fragile Democracy, LAB books, 1983.

General

Bemelmans, Ludwig, *The Donkey Inside*, 1941. Classic travelogue.

Cuvi, Pablo, *Through the Eyes of My People*, Ediciones Libri Mundi, 1989. Enjoyable, hip inside view of the country by prominent Ecuadorean journalist with accompanying coffee-table photographs.

El Ecuador visto por Los Extranjeros, Viajeros de los Siglos XVIII y XIX, Biblioteca Ecuatoriana Minima, 1960.

Michaux, Henri, *Ecuador—a Travel Journal*, Peter Owen, 1970. Impish, irreverant, surreal and very charming short travelogue by the late 19th-century Belgian mystic, poet and painter. Hugely enjoyable.

Rachowiecki, Rob, *Ecuador and the Galápagos Islands: a travel survival kit*, Lonely Planet, 1989. Backpacker's guide.

Rachowiecki, Rob, *Climbing and Hiking in Ecuador*, Bradt Publications, 1984. The best climbing guide available. Good maps.

Thomsen, Moritz, *Living Poor*, Eland Books, 1989. Moving journal kept by a Peace Corps worker of his years spent in a small village north of Esmeraldas.

Whymper, Edward, *Travels Amongst the Great Andes of the Equator*, Peregrine Books reprint, 1990. Worth getting hold of, even if you are not a keen climber.

COLOMBIA

History

Castro Caicedo, Germán, *Mi Alma se la Dejo al Diablo*. Gripping investigation of strange goings-on in the Amazon when a North American entrepreneur sets up a business using Indian labour.

Dix, Robert H., *The Politics of Colombia*, Praeger, 1980. Thorough analyis.

Hemming, John, *The Search for El Dorado*. Very readable narrative history.

Molano, Alfredo, *Siguiendo El Corte*, El Áncora Editores, 1989. Gripping series of interviews with participants in La Violencia.

Pearce, Jenny, *Colombia: Inside the Labyrinth*, LAB Books, 1990. Although written from an orthodox (and perhaps out-dated) left-wing perspective, persevering readers of this committed piece of reportage will be rewarded with detailed accounts of La Violencia.

Reichel Dolmatoff, *Colombia*, 1965. Pre-history by Colombia's most eminent anthropologist.

Romoli, Kathleen, *Colombia: Gateway to South America*, 1941. Warm and very useful general description of the country.

General

de Friedemann, Nina S., *Ma Ngombe* Carlos Valencia Editores, 1979. Very good anthropological investigation/travelogue amongst the palenquero villages of the Caribbean coast.

Dydyński, Krzystof, *Colombia: A Travel Survival Kit*, Lonely Planet, 1988. Backpacker's Guide.

Ocampo López, Javier, *Las Fiestas y el Folclor en Colombia*, Editores Ancora, 1984.

Minta, Stephen, *García Márquez: Writer of Colombia*, Jonathan Cape, 1987. Puts the writer in his Colombian context. Very good.

Rouillard, Patrick a series of coffee-table books with photographs of the country, Editorial Colina.

Samper Pizano, Daniel, *Collected journalism*, Paza and Janes Editores Colombia, 1983. Humorous.

Articles

Colombia received its fair share of distorting media attention during the Drugs War of late 1989. Three articles stood out among the welter of paper:

Garfitt, Roger, *Granta No. 29* (New World issue).

Massing, Michall, *New York Review of Books*, 22 December 1988.

Financial Times Survey, July 1989.

319

ECUADOR INDEX

Note: *Italic* numbers indicate maps. **Bold** numbers indicate main reference

accommodation 7
 see also section at end of each town or region
Achupallas 83
addresses: finding 5
air travel:
 to Ecuador 3
 to Quito 49–50
Alausi 83
Alcedo Volcano 126
Alfaro, Eloy 38–9, 87
Almagro, Diego de 83
altitude: effects of 44
Alvarado, Pedro de 45
Amazon 130–9
 discovery of 54
 wildlife 131–2
Amazon Indians 133–4
Ambato 70, **74–6**
Anaconda Island 136
Andean Indians 70–1, 75–6, 83
Apuela 63
Atacames 100, **113**, 114
Atahualpa 33, 45, 86

Bahía de Caraquez 110–11
Baltra 119–20
banks 6
Baños 43, 69, **77–9**
bars 56
Bartolomé 126
baths, thermal 43, 78, 92
Bats, Henry 25
Beagle, voyage of 25, 117
Bemelmans, Ludwig 52, 61
Benalcázar, Sebastián 45–7, 86, 101
best of Ecuador *16*, 17
Biblían 91
birds 25–6
 books on 6–7
 of Galápagos 115, 122–3
Black Turtle Cove 121, 126
Bolívar, Simón 26–9, 36–7, 48, 81, 102
 statues 102, 104
border formalities 68, 97
bribes 11–12
budgeting 2
bullfighting 56

buses 19

Cajabamba 82
Calderón, Abdon 88
camping 7
Cañar 84
Cañari 84, 85–6
car hire 19
Carachi valley 60
Caras 44–5
Cascadas de Peguche 63
Caspicaro 53
Cayambe 60
Cervantes, Miguel de 35
Cevallos, Rodrigo Borja 40
Charles Darwin Research Station 127
Chimborazo 69, **81**
Chordeleg 91–2
Chorrerans 107
Chugchilan 73
climate 1–2, 44
 of Galápagos 116
climbing 56
coast 100–14
 northern 111–14
Coca 137–8
cockfights 80
Coco Solo 111
Cojimies 111
Colorados 98
Colta, Lake 82–3
Colta Indians 83
Columbian border 67–8
Condamine, Charles Marie de, *see* La Condamine
consulates 20
Costeños: compared to Sierraños 100–1
Cotacachi 60, 63
Cotopaxi, Mt 69, 72–3
Cotopaxi National Park 25, 69, 72–3
crops 29–30
Cuenca 69, **84–92**
 Cathedral 88
 El Sagraria 88
 history 85–7
 museums 89
 Parque Calderón 88
 Ruinas de Todos Santos 88

320

COLOMBIA INDEX

Note: *Italic* numbers indicate maps. **Bold** numbers indicate main reference

Other Cadogan Guides available from your local bookshop or from UK or USA direct:

From the UK: Cadogan Books, Mercury House, 195 Knightsbridge, London SW7 1RE.
From the US: The Globe Pequot Press, 138 West Main Street, Chester, Connecticut 06412.

Title

Australia .... ☐
Bali .... ☐
Berlin .... ☐
The Caribbean... ☐
Greek Islands (2nd Edition) .... ☐
India (2nd Edition) .... ☐
Ireland (2nd Edition) .... ☐
Italian Islands (2nd Edition) .... ☐
Italy .... ☐
Mexico .... ☐
Morocco .... ☐
New York .... ☐
Northeast Italy .... ☐
Northwest Italy .... ☐
Portugal .... ☐
Prague .... ☐
Rome .... ☐
Scotland .... ☐
South of France: Provence, Côte d'Azur, Languedoc-Roussillon...... ☐
South Italy .... ☐
Southern Spain: Andalucía & Gibraltar .... ☐
Spain (3rd Edition) .... ☐
Thailand .... ☐
Tunisia .... ☐
Turkey (2nd Edition) .... ☐
Tuscany, Umbria & The Marches (2nd Edition)... ☐
Venice .... ☐

Name ....

Address ....

.... Post Code ....

Date .... Order Number ....

Special Instructions ....

....

Please use these forms to tell us about the hotels or restaurants you consider to be special and worthy of inclusion in our next edition, as well as to give any general comments on existing entries.

Hotels

Name ....

Address ....

Tel.. Price of double room ....

Description/Comments ....

....

....

Name ....

Address ....

Tel.. Price of double room ....

Description/Comments ....

....

....

Name ....

Address ....

Tel.. Price of double room ....

Description/Comments ....

....

....

Name ....

Address ....

Tel.. Price of double room ....

Description/Comments ....

....

....

Restaurants

Name ....

Address ....

Tel... Price per person ....

Description/Comments ....

....

....

Name ....

Address ....

Tel... Price per person ....

Description/Comments ....

....

....

Name ....

Address ....

Tel... Price per person ....

Description/Comments ....

....

....

Name ....

Address ....

Tel... Price per person ....

Description/Comments ....

....

....

Restaurants

Name ....

Address ....

Tel... Price per person ....

Description/Comments ....

....

....

Name ....

Address ....

Tel... Price per person ....

Description/Comments ....

....

....

Name ....

Address ....

Tel... Price per person ....

Description/Comments ....

....

....

Name ....

Address ....

Tel... Price per person ....

Description/Comments ....

....

....

General Comments

General Comments